D1467825

THE HISTORY OF PUBLIC WELFARE
IN NEW YORK STATE
1609–1866

PATTERSON SMITH REPRINT SERIES IN
CRIMINOLOGY, LAW ENFORCEMENT, AND SOCIAL PROBLEMS

1. Lewis: *The Development of American Prisons and Prison Customs, 1776-1845*
2. Carpenter: *Reformatory Prison Discipline*
3. Brace: *The Dangerous Classes of New York*
4. Dix: *Remarks on Prisons and Prison Discipline in the United States*
5. Bruce *et al: The Workings of the Indeterminate-Sentence Law and the Parole System in Illinois*
6. Wickersham Commission: *Complete Reports, Including the Mooney-Billings Report.* 14 Vols.
7. Livingston: *Complete Works on Criminal Jurisprudence.* 2 Vols.
8. Cleveland Foundation: *Criminal Justice in Cleveland*
9. Illinois Association for Criminal Justice: *The Illinois Crime Survey*
10. Missouri Association for Criminal Justice: *The Missouri Crime Survey*
11. Aschaffenburg: *Crime and Its Repression*
12. Garofalo: *Criminology*
13. Gross: *Criminal Psychology*
14. Lombroso: *Crime, Its Causes and Remedies*
15. Saleilles: *The Individualization of Punishment*
16. Tarde: *Penal Philosophy*
17. McKelvey: *American Prisons*
18. Sanders: *Negro Child Welfare in North Carolina*
19. Pike: *A History of Crime in England.* 2 Vols.
20. Herring: *Welfare Work in Mill Villages*
21. Barnes: *The Evolution of Penology in Pennsylvania*
22. Puckett: *Folk Beliefs of the Southern Negro*
23. Fernald *et al: A Study of Women Delinquents in New York State*
24. Wines: *The State of the Prisons and of Child-Saving Institutions*
25. Raper: *The Tragedy of Lynching*
26. Thomas: *The Unadjusted Girl*
27. Jorns: *The Quakers as Pioneers in Social Work*
28. Owings: *Women Police*
29. Woolston: *Prostitution in the United States*
30. Flexner: *Prostitution in Europe*
31. Kelso: *The History of Public Poor Relief in Massachusetts: 1820-1920*
32. Spivak: *Georgia Nigger*
33. Earle: *Curious Punishments of Bygone Days*
34. Bonger: *Race and Crime*
35. Fishman: *Crucibles of Crime*
36. Brearley: *Homicide in the United States*
37. Graper: *American Police Administration*
38. Hichborn: *"The System"*
39. Steiner & Brown: *The North Carolina Chain Gang*
40. Cherrington: *The Evolution of Prohibition in the United States of America*
41. Colquhoun: *A Treatise on the Commerce and Police of the River Thames*
42. Colquhoun: *A Treatise on the Police of the Metropolis*
43. Abrahamsen: *Crime and the Human Mind*
44. Schneider: *The History of Public Welfare in New York State: 1609-1866*
45. Schneider & Deutsch: *The History of Public Welfare in New York State: 1867-1940*
46. Crapsey: *The Nether Side of New York*
47. Young: *Social Treatment in Probation and Delinquency*
48. Quinn: *Gambling and Gambling Devices*
49. McCord & McCord: *Origins of Crime*
50. Worthington & Topping: *Specialized Courts Dealing with Sex Delinquency*

The Eight Degrees of Charity

As set down by

Maimonides

Theologian, Philosopher, and Physician, 1135–1204

There Are Eight Degrees or Steps
in the Duty of Charity

❡ The first and lowest degree is to give, but with reluctance or regret. This is the gift of the hand, but not of the heart.

❡ The second is, to give cheerfully, but not proportionately to the distress of the sufferer.

❡ The third is, to give cheerfully, and proportionately, but not until solicited.

❡ The fourth is, to give cheerfully, proportionately, and even unsolicited, but to put it in the poor man's hand, thereby exciting in him the painful emotion of shame.

❡ The fifth is, to give to charity in such a way that the distressed may receive the bounty, and know their benefactor, without their being known to him. Such was the conduct of some of our ancestors, who used to tie up money in the corners of their cloaks, so that the poor might take it unperceived.

❡ The sixth, which rises still higher, is to know the objects of our bounty, but remain unknown to them. Such was the conduct of those of our ancestors who used to convey their charitable gifts into poor people's dwellings, taking care that their own persons and names should remain unknown.

❡ The seventh is still more meritorious, namely, to bestow charity in such a way that the benefactor may not know the relieved persons, nor they the names of their benefactors, as was done by our charitable forefathers during the existence of the temple. For there was in that holy building a place called the Chamber of the Silent, wherein the good deposited secretly whatever their generous hearts suggested, and from which the poor were maintained with equal secrecy.

❡ Lastly, the eighth, and the most meritorious of all, is to anticipate charity by preventing poverty: namely, to assist the reduced fellow-man, either by a considerable gift, or a sum of money, or by teaching him a trade, or by putting him in the way of business, so that he may earn an honest livelihood, and not be forced to the dreadful alternative of holding out his hand for charity—This is the highest step and the summit of charity's golden ladder.

PUBLICATION NO. 44: PATTERSON SMITH REPRINT SERIES IN
CRIMINOLOGY, LAW ENFORCEMENT, AND SOCIAL PROBLEMS

THE HISTORY
OF PUBLIC WELFARE IN
NEW YORK STATE
1609–1866

BY

DAVID M. SCHNEIDER, PH.D.

Director, Bureau of Research and Statistics
New York State Department of Social Welfare

65655

Montclair, New Jersey

PATTERSON SMITH

1969

SBN 87585-044-8

Library of Congress Catalog Card Number: 69-14944

TO
GOVERNOR HERBERT H. LEHMAN
IN APPRECIATION OF HIS SERVICE
TO THE ADVANCEMENT OF SOCIAL WELFARE
IN THE STATE OF NEW YORK

FOREWORD

There is an old saying that "history makes men wise." As we seek guides for planning and action in this sorely troubled world, eyes turn toward the past in search of long-neglected lessons of experience. Those of us engaged in public welfare have long noted and keenly felt the scarcity of historical works in the literature of our field. In recent years the University of Chicago School of Social Service Administration has been active in supplying the lack with its excellent series of monographs, of which this work is a part. The New York State Department of Social Welfare takes pride in sponsoring this important contribution.

History, if well studied and applied, can help in solving many of the perplexing questions that confront us. Which of our problems are recurrent or chronic, temporary or permanent? How did our forerunners meet them, and with what results? What were the errors that we should avoid, and what the wise measures that we should continue or revive? In providing clues to these and related questions, history becomes not merely a branch of knowledge but a tool that can be used effectively in meeting our present problems and charting the future.

In reading this history of public welfare in New York State, one is struck by the many evidences of "cultural lag" operating in this field as in other aspects of social life. There is an inertia in the historic process that results in the survival of institutions, customs, and ideas of one stage of development, long after a new stage requiring fresh approaches and new practices has come into being. Instance the chaotic state arising from the lack of uniformity in the settlement laws throughout the nation—many of which correspond to a stage of society that disappeared a long time ago and are now utterly inapplicable to a closely knit, highly mobile population in an industrial order.

An old truth is strikingly illustrated in these pages, namely, that there is no straight line of progress in our public welfare history. Fluctuations between progress and retrogression, sometimes very violent, sometimes hardly perceptible, are discernible throughout. A practice or an institution that constitutes a progressive step at the time of its establishment becomes a barrier to further progress in a later generation. Experiments are continually introduced. Some succeed and are retained, others fail and are swept into the discard, perhaps to reappear on a permanent basis in a subsequent period when changing conditions have made them practicable or even necessary. The law of 1824, which introduced the principle of county responsibility for all institutionalized dependents, gradually broke down, and many years passed before the principle it embodied again won general acceptance. These pages also bring to light some interesting historical cycles. For example, poor relief in colonial times was predominantly outdoor in character; in a later period it became mainly indoor or institutional; in our own time the pendulum has been steadily swinging back toward outdoor relief—though on a different and higher plane than that known to our forefathers.

Dr. Schneider's work reveals the heartbreaking persistence of the same old blunders and half-baked experiments in economic crises, repeated in spite of the plain evidences of past experience—a round of soup kitchens and bread lines, hastily organized private citizens' committees, and finally the reluctant entrance of public emergency relief mechanisms on the scene. Let us hope that this oft-repeated relief cycle is at last broken forever, and that some solution may be found ere long to the phenomenon of the economic crisis itself.

In spite of cycles and fluctuations, there has been a gradual progression upward through the centuries. Slowly but steadily the stigma of pauperism has been removed from successive groups of needy persons, and services which used to come under the head of "poor relief" or "charity" are now granted to all as a matter of course. Free medical aid is no longer considered primarily as a function of poor relief. In colonial times provision for free education was a charitable enterprise, and the children of the poor had to attend "charity schools" conducted by private organizations, or else attended "public" schools only by special sufferance. Today free public education is not only available to every child in New York State but is compulsory, and is universally recognized as one of the firmest pillars of a democratic society. Services to deaf-mutes and

other groups of physically handicapped persons have passed out of
the hands of poor-law officials. State care for all the mentally ill has
been an established principle in New York for nearly half a century,
and patients no longer have to be certified as paupers before gaining
admission to our state hospitals.

Lest we indulge ourselves with an unwarranted feeling of superi-
ority over past generations, however, let us keep in mind the dis-
turbing but stubborn fact that many of our public welfare practices
are but the disguised survivals of the blunt, harsh methods of the
old overseers of the poor. It is easy to be shocked by the seeming
barbarities of the past as they are revealed in this work; it is far
more useful to save our indignation for the outworn practices of the
present.

One should retain a realization of the time factor in approaching
the historical study of public welfare—that is, to view particular
events within their proper frame of reference—lest our values and
interpretations be distorted. When, for example, we speak dis-
paragingly of the Elizabethan poor law of 1601, which served as the
basis for our colonial poor-law legislation, we too often forget the
progressive features of that famous statute. Seen in the light of its
time, it marked a tremendous step forward. We are likely to over-
look its embodiment of the progressive principle that the "impotent poor"—including the aged, the young, the halt, and the
blind—were entitled to public assistance, and that work should be
found for the able-bodied unemployed. Our stress is usually placed
on the principle of local responsibility incorporated in the same law.
But this was a perfectly logical and natural development for that
age and is reactionary only when applied to our own. The fault,
be it emphasized, lies not in the Elizabethans who introduced the
principle when it served a practical purpose, but in ourselves who
perpetuate it in a world that has moved far beyond the conditions
of Elizabethan England and Colonial America.

Public welfare concepts are gradually getting away from the old
idea that a grudging grant of material relief sufficient to keep the
human body alive is all that the needy individual has a right to
expect of society. In former times, as this book amply illustrates, a
minimum of material relief was accompanied by a maximum amount

of moral degradation, and the dependent person was made to feel
the full weight of community censure. Often the mere status of dependency was all the evidence required as proof that such censure
was merited. The old poor-law officials doled out just enough to
meet the minimum needs of the recipient's body, and no more. Then
came the moral reformers who cast disapproving eyes on material
relief and insisted that uplifting the character of the poor should be
the major, if not the only, concern in granting aid to the needy.
The poor-law men failed to heed the precept that man does not live
by bread alone; the reformers failed to realize that man must have
bread to live at all. Today we are less likely to pass hasty judgment
on our needy neighbors and to think more in terms of minimum
physical and cultural requirements commensurate with standards of
human dignity in an advanced society. Public welfare alone cannot
cope with this larger problem. Our vast economic resources must
be called into play to find a solution to the problem of a growing
population in an era of reduced opportunities. Our economy must
find means of providing our citizenry with the opportunities leading
to a decent, independent, self-supporting existence. For example,
the immediate problem arising out of the great depression is easily
posed, if not easily solved: employment is the simple and all-embracing solution to unemployment. Public welfare, or "poor relief,"
as it was known in former years when it occupied a much narrower
area of action than it does today, has successively been used as a repressive, palliative, therapeutic, and preventive instrument. The
last-mentioned stage, of course, is still in its infancy. A new concept
is now arising that views public welfare as a major medium for re-
distributing the national income on a more equitable basis.

One of the great tasks of our expanding democracy is to fix minimum standards of physical and cultural existence beneath which
no person shall be allowed to fall—barring disasters beyond human
control. That goal still lies far ahead and can be but dimly per-
ceived at present. But it is a goal toward which our democracy must
strive if it is to fully realize itself. Bentham wisely classified the
"disposition to look ahead" among the distinctive marks of civilization. Looking ahead, we must stand on the firm foundations laid
down by past experiences. We cannot fully comprehend direction

without knowing whence we have come. In presenting us with this sound, skilfully prepared history of public welfare in New York State, Dr. Schneider shows us the road traveled down the centuries to our own day. He has placed in his debt not only those directly involved in the social welfare field but students of American history and laymen interested in the evolution of our society.

DAVID C. ADIE

COMMISSIONER OF SOCIAL WELFARE
STATE OF NEW YORK

PREFACE

Public welfare, as used in the following pages, includes all fields of social work financed or controlled by public agencies, whether federal, state, or local. Since the course of public welfare in New York was profoundly influenced by developments in the field of private social work, it has been necessary to discuss phases of the latter from time to time as they affected the sphere of our interest. Certain services, such as medical aid and free education, were included in our survey at particular stages of their evolution when they were regarded and administered as "charities" and before they passed into the areas now comprehended by "public health" and "public education." Occasional use has been made of such obsolescent terms as "pauper," "charity," and "lunatic" in instances where they best express contemporary attitudes.

The reader of this volume may feel that an inordinate amount of space is devoted to New York City in relation to the rest of the state. There are several reasons for this seeming disparity: (1) the metropolis had many important welfare problems peculiar to itself; (2) nearly all types of public welfare institutions within the state had their origin here; (3) significant changes in the public welfare structure of New York City occurred at comparatively frequent intervals, while the pattern in the rest of the state remained more or less uniform over long periods of time; (4) beginning with the post-Revolutionary period, the poor-relief burden in New York City, in terms of expenditures and the number of persons receiving assistance, was about equal to that of the rest of the state put together; (5) the extant historical records relating to public welfare are more complete for New York City than for the other parts of the state.

All attempts to divide history into epochs are more or less arbitrary. The chronological arrangement which marks the sections of this work is no exception to this rule, but each section does begin or end with some important step in the evolution of public welfare. This volume brings the historical record up to the point preceding the establishment of the Board of State Commissioners of Public

Charities (now the Department of Social Welfare) in 1867, which ushered in the period of state supervision. The second volume, which should be completed toward the end of 1939, will bring the story of public welfare up to 1938.

In acknowledging the generous aid accorded to me from many sources during the preparation of this book, I must first pay tribute to my colleague, Albert Deutsch, research associate in the State Department of Social Welfare. I owe him an immeasurable debt for his unsparing editorial aid, based on his own extensive researches in American social-welfare history. Mr. Deutsch contributed considerably to the organization and style of this work. I am grateful to Commissioner David C. Adie for his kindness in writing the Foreword and for his active co-operation and constant encouragement. For the able assistance of Mr. Norbert M. Goodwin during the early phase of this work, I wish to express my heartfelt thanks. Acknowledgment is made to the following individuals who have read parts of my manuscript and given me the benefit of their comments thereon: Dr. Alexander C. Flick, New York state historian; Dr. Dixon Ryan Fox, president of Union College; Dr. Victor H. Paltsits, chief of the American History Division and keeper of manuscripts of the New York Public Library; Professors Evarts B. Greene and Samuel McKee, Jr., of Columbia University; Professor Frank Monaghan of Yale University; Professor W. F. Galpin of Syracuse University; Professor Richard J. Purcell of the Catholic University of America; Dr. Philip Klein, of the New York School of Social Work; Miss Elsie M. Bond, of the New York State Charities Aid Association; Dr. Nels Anderson, of the Works Progress Administration; Dr. E. Wilder Spaulding, of the United States Department of State; Dr. Edward T. Devine, of New York City; Dr. A. Everett Peterson, of the New York City Art Commission; Dr. Henry W. Thurston, of Montclair, New Jersey; and Dr. Augustus H. Shearer, librarian of the Grosvenor Library at Buffalo. None of the afore-mentioned persons is responsible for errors in this book. Final responsibility for all statements of fact and expressions of opinion is entirely my own. At various times during the progress of the work, valued research assistance was made available by the Gibson Committee of New York City, the Civil Works Administration, the New York State Temporary Emergency Relief Administration, and the Works Progress Administration. The aid of the two last-mentioned organizations was especially helpful.

The research work of Miss Clara M. Paquet, Department editorial assistant, in old manuscripts and town records has been of special value. Grateful mention is made of her preparation of the Index, jointly with Miss Mildred Guffin, Department librarian, who also arranged the bibliographical notes.

Appreciation is extended to Messrs. John C. Guffin, Frank E. Morse, Leonard F. Requa, Jr., J. H. Berkowitz, Mrs. Anne M. Keegan, Mrs. Lucille R. Greenbaum, Mrs. Florence B. Redden, and Misses Marjorie F. Chase and Tulla C. Odencrantz, of the Department staff, for varying types of assistance.

I also wish to acknowledge the research assistance received at different times from Messrs. F. N. Furness, Andrew H. Marchbin, Daniel C. Sharol, and Francis Hart.

Splendid co-operation on the part of the staffs of various libraries greatly facilitated the necessary research work. Mr. Charles F. McCombs, of the New York Public Library, and Miss Bertha F. Hulseman, of the Russell Sage Foundation Library, were particularly helpful. I also wish to express my appreciation of the co-operation afforded by Dean Edith Abbott and the University of Chicago Press.

D. M. S.

TABLE OF CONTENTS

PART I

THE CONGREGATIONAL SYSTEM IN NEW
NETHERLAND, 1609–64

CHAPTER I

POOR RELIEF UNDER THE DUTCH

THE SOCIAL BACKGROUNDS

In the fall of the year 1609, Captain Henry Hudson steered his sturdy "Half Moon" ("Halve Maen") up the river that now bears his name. The English navigator, in the pay of the Dutch East India Company, had originally set out to find a northeast passage to the Indies but had been forced to change his course westward when his mutinous crew refused to proceed on the journey through the bitterly cold, unknown Arctic. Reaching the coast of America he had sailed into the splendid lower bay that Verrazzano had explored nearly a century earlier and into the river that the Florentine navigator had missed.

The captain and his crew were enchanted by the luxuriant beauty of the valley which spread out before them. One of Hudson's officers, Robert Juet, wrote in his journal: "This is a very good Land to fall [in] with and a pleasant Land to see." He also noted that the Dutch sailors who went ashore found the land "pleasant with Grasse and Flowers and goodly Trees, as ever they had seene, and very sweet smells came from them."[1] However, after learning that the newly-found river did not lead to India or China, as he had hoped, Hudson turned back toward Europe to report his failure to his employers.

The Dutch East India Company paid little attention to the glowing description of the harbor and the land along the river that Hudson had explored or to intimations of the rich fur trade that might be carried on with the native Indians. Huge profits were being reaped in the East Indies trade, and the Company was concentrating its efforts on reaping still greater profits in the same part of the world. There were ambitious burghers, however, who were ready to seize the opportunity rejected by the East India Company. These groups began to send trading expeditions to the land explored by Hudson to obtain cargoes of furs in exchange for a few tools and baubles.

3

In 1621 their High Mightinesses, the Lords States-General of the United Netherlands, granted a charter to the Dutch West India Company, giving the Company a monopoly of Dutch trade in an area including the whole American coast. Among other privileges the Company received the right to plant colonies and to govern them under very limited supervision of the States-General.

In 1623 the province of New Netherland was formally organized, and in the following year the first settlement was made at Fort Orange (now Albany) by a few families of Walloons. Manhattan Island was purchased from the Indians in 1626 for the equivalent of twenty-four dollars, giving the Company some legal title to its *de facto* occupation. Fort Amsterdam was erected on this site and became the seat of government with Peter Minuit serving as the first officially designated director-general of the province.

At first the Company showed little interest in colonizing New Netherland on a large scale. To squeeze profits from its venture as quickly as possible was the Company's sole aim, and it felt that this end could best be achieved by confining itself to the fur trade with the Indians. But it soon learned that the venture could not safely be conducted without introducing a systematic scheme of colonization. The area under exploitation contained rich resources which might be seized in a series of military raids. Its boundaries were disputed. It lay in a critical position between New England and Virginia. The land had to be peopled with farmers and workers who would not only strengthen its defense but would eventually increase the Company's revenues. But these settlers needed incentive and opportunity to better their lot if the colony were to become prosperous, loyal, and a fruitful source of trade. Nevertheless, the West India Company, ruled by its desire for immediate returns with the least possible effort, made only late and reluctant efforts in this direction, even when the open rivalry of England stood forth as a constant threat to its domain. Only after pressure from several of its more far-sighted directors did it actually adopt a policy of colonization.* This policy was embodied in a "Charter of Freedoms and Exemptions" ratified by the States-General in 1629.

* This policy fell short of successful realization. Up to 1653 there were no more than 2,000 colonists in New Netherland, although the population increased to 10,000 by 1664.

The Company's first attempt to extend settlement beyond Manhattan took the form of assigning great tracts of coastal and riverfront land to a few privileged individuals called patroons, and of authorizing the beneficiaries to settle colonists upon these grants. Restrictions not far removed from feudalism were imposed on such colonists. They were bound to the service of a patroon and might be returned to the Netherlands at the expiration of their contract term should they refuse to continue their service. They could not secure title to any land within the patroonship on which they served, nor were they permitted to buy land from the Indians. They were obliged to have their corn ground at the patroon's mill and were subject to the jurisdiction of the patroon's court. Their crops were liable to pre-emption by the patroon, who also levied ground rent. Any discoveries they might make of mineral deposits or fisheries were by the terms of the charter the property of the patroon; and he was obliged to reward them in such cases with only the sum specified in the contract under which they entered his service. The patroon had first purchase rights. All "private and poor people" (unvermögend Personen) were expressly excluded from the "Exemptions, Privileges and Freedoms" showered upon the patroons. As an added incentive to the latter, the States-General in Holland gave its pledge that it would exert itself to provide the patroons with "vagabonds and outcasts, who live on alms and in idleness and crime" to be bound to their service "for board and clothing only."[2] Very few persons of this description were sent over, however.

Like the settlers within the patroonships, the "free" inhabitants were forbidden to traffic in furs or to manufacture cloth; and between them and the enjoyment of liberty stood the Company, avaricious and arrogant, making its will the law, levying quit-rents and excises, monopolizing transport, collecting freight charges, and seizing upon a fixed percentage of the value of outgoing produce and incoming goods. Not until 1650, twenty-four years after the organization of a regular administrative staff in the colony and only after a vigorous plea by delegates sent to The Hague, was New Netherland permitted to import free of duty even a cargo of purely agricultural supplies.[3] Moreover, on several occasions whole cargoes of goods were confiscated without reason other than the Company's desire to persecute colonists who had protested against its high-handed methods. The owners could seek redress only through an appeal to the States-General.* Theoretically the colonists on a patroonship enjoyed freedom from all imposts, but actually they were shut off from both civil and economic freedom. "The colonists under the patroons," says Brodhead, "were subjected to the double pressure of feudal exaction and mercantile monopoly."⁴ The provisions of the Charter of 1629 were somewhat liberalized in 1638 and 1640, but no essential changes were effected.

Immigrants who were able to finance their own settlement could secure land under freehold or leasehold in Manhattan, Fort Orange (Albany), or other areas reserved to the Company or not included in the grants to the patroons. Yet it may be questioned whether their lot was very much better than that of their fellow-colonists under the patroons.

The government of New Netherland was based roughly on the model of a Dutch municipality in the Old World. At the head stood the director-general and his Council consisting of five members. The councilors were also invested with judicial powers, sitting as a court of justice in all but capital cases, which had to be tried in the mother-country. The chief law officer of the province was the schout-fiscal in whom was vested the combined duties of a sheriff and an attorney-general. The town government consisted chiefly of burgomasters, schepens, and schouts who exercised legislative and judicial functions. Throughout the Dutch period, with but little modification, the chief officers in the province remained appointive, in spite of the reiterated demands of the colonists for some measure of democracy. Several times the colonists residing in New Amsterdam and its vicinity chose men

* The original "Charter of Freedoms and Exemptions" specified sixteen miles on one side of a navigable river or eight miles on both sides as the maximum limit of a patroonship, and as deep into the interior as the proprietor could make his authority extend; or sixteen miles of coastal land, with the same provision respecting the interior (Nicholaes van Wassenaer, "Historisch Verhael," in *Narratives of New Netherland*, ed. J. Franklin Jameson [New York, 1909], pp. 90 ff.). Later the dimensions of a patroonship were reduced to one Dutch mile along water front and two Dutch miles into the interior; patroon status was made dependent upon performance of the requisite function named in the original charter—settling fifty colonists over fifteen years of age within a given number of years (Samuel G. Nissenson, *The Patroon's Domain* [New York, 1937], *passim*).

from among themselves to represent them before the director-general and the Council. In 1641, upon the director's invitation, they selected twelve men to co-operate with the executive in measures against the Indians. Attempts to gain a permanent status for the "Twelve Men" as representatives of the commonalty in general matters were frustrated by the director, who abolished the body in February, 1643. In September of that year the commonalty of New Amsterdam chose a board of "Eight Men" to consider certain propositions submitted by the director and Council, but their efforts to assume quasi-legislative functions met with failure. A third body, called the "Nine Men," was selected in 1647 to advise the executive on matters of defense and fiscal needs. This board, which functioned for several years, was very active in petitioning the home government in behalf of the colonists for redress against the high-handed policies of the director and Council.[5]

From the beginning the colony suffered from gross misgovernment. The records show unceasing strife between all the social elements in the colony: the traders continually opposing the patroons, the patroons at odds with the Company, both patroons and traders pitted against the directors-general, and the Company at war with all. Dominated by a short-sighted policy, thinking only in terms of immediate profits for itself, lacking in vision, the Company in the end defeated its own purposes. When its final accounts were cast up after the loss of the colony to the English, little or nothing remained to console it for the forty years of work in New Netherland.

The Company ruled the colonists with an iron hand and stubbornly resisted all efforts of the settlers to secure for themselves a voice in the government. It exhibited a gift for choosing colonial administrators (directors-general) who at best were wasteful and incompetent, while at worst they were dictatorial and deceitful. Minuit, who had been appointed director-general in 1626, was recalled to the Netherlands on charges that he had shown too great favoritism toward the patroons and had been too diligent in fattening his own purse. His successor, Bastiaen Jansz Krol, served less than a year in a temporary capacity, being replaced in 1633 by Wouter van Twiller. The latter appears to have been a man of loose character and gross incompetence with an aptitude for antagonizing both the colonists and the Company, and in 1637 he in turn was re-called, being superseded by Willem Kieft. The public record of Kieft is notable chiefly for the unsavory deeds with which it is replete. This aspiring Company servant first lent color to his career in New Netherland by demanding, without logic or reason, tribute from the Indians in the vicinity of Manhattan. The success of this venture proving small, Kieft seized upon the first available pretext to massacre scores of unsuspecting aborigines with whom the Dutch settlers had hitherto enjoyed peaceful and friendly relations. The Indians retaliated quickly and effectively, and within a short time all the whites who remained alive in the south part of the colony were penned up either in Fort Amsterdam or at Gravesend on Long Island. From Westchester to the Lower Bay the farms of the colonists lay in ashes.

In 1647 the Company replaced Kieft with Petrus Stuyvesant, a man of much intelligence and vigor, but with a fatal penchant for dictatorial rule. Stuyvesant added to the burden of taxation under which the New Netherlanders labored, resisted all appeals, and persecuted relentlessly all representatives of the popular will. In 1649 the colonists drew up a "Remonstrance" addressed to the government in Holland and relating their grievances against the Company and its officials. In this historic document they informed the States-General:

Trade is by their [the Company's] acts so decayed, that it amounts to nothing. It is more suited for slaves than freemen, in consequence of the restrictions upon it and annoyances which accompany the exercise of the right of inspection. The Recognition [export duty] runs high, and of inspection and confiscation there is no lack; hence legitimate trade is entirely diverted, except a little, which exists *pro forma*, as a cloak for carrying on illicit trading. In the meantime the Christians are treated almost like Indians, in the purchase of the necessaries with which they cannot dispense. This causes great complaint, distress and poverty.[6]

The "Remonstrance" of the inhabitants of New Netherland, complaining of their tribulations under the tyrant, Stuyvesant, must be taken with some qualification. The good burghers had a faculty for magnifying petty grievances into monstrous proportions. Notwithstanding his extreme harshness and dictatorial attitude, Stuyvesant did manage to introduce many improvements into the province, particularly during the last decade of his administration.

That some poverty existed among the commonalty there is no doubt. A letter dated 1658, quoted by the historian, O'Callaghan, declares that when New Netherlanders with large families died, they left "not a stiver behind," and that the expense of burial, payment of debts, and care of dependents had to be assumed by their neighbors.[7] And when a tax was assessed in 1657 to pay for the services of a clergyman, Domine Polhemus, the magistrates of Brouchkelen (Brooklyn) protested that the community was too poor to meet it: "Many there are among them [the congregation of the Dutch Reformed church] who cannot [pay the tax] and who rather need that others should come to their aid."[8]

POOR RELIEF IN NEW NETHERLAND

The duty of relieving dependency was intrusted almost exclusively to the clergy, following the common practice at the time, although the secular authorities participated in this function to a limited extent. Throughout the entire Colonial period, Dutch and English, outdoor relief formed the dominant pattern of social service.

In the seventeenth century the cities and towns of Holland, whence the first settlers came, apparently had a highly organized system of institutional relief—in fact, the Dutch poor-relief system was probably the most advanced in Europe. Temple states that common beggars in that province were sent to the workhouse if able to labor, and to the hospital if not. He also remarks that charity was practiced everywhere in Holland with excellent provisions for all sorts of dependent persons "that can want or ought to be kept, in a Government."[9] The many hospitals, he says, were objects of admiration to travelers from other parts of Europe, and among them he particularly praises the home for aged seamen at Enckhuyzen. It appears from contemporary accounts that every Dutch town had its almshouse where the aged could find shelter; orphan asylums were established in several of the large cities.

An imitation of this pattern was hardly possible in the colony of New Netherland, made up as it was of thinly scattered pioneer settlements. For the amelioration of poverty the colonists had to depend mainly on the neighborly sympathy of those who suffered under the common pioneering difficulties. Under the conditions of life in the colony, the church defined itself as the center of social activity and the congregation as the most "natural" social group outside the family. Throughout the history of New Netherland, therefore, relief tended to become systematized as a congregational function, and the clergy and deaconry became its logical administrators. Dependents were generally cared for as familiarly (and with little of the stigma attaching to charity in later times) as though collectively they belonged to the family next door. Contemporary data on the workings of congregational relief are somewhat meager, but the strength of the pattern is proved by its persistence in the older communities at a time when Dutch sovereignty was many years in the past.

SIECKENTROOSTERS: THE FIRST SOCIAL WORKERS

In the United Netherlands visitation of the sick was part of the duty of the Dutch Reformed ministry. But where a community was too scattered or too poor to warrant the fulfilment of this function by the regularly ordained clergy, it was intrusted to authorized agents of inferior ecclesiastical standing known as *krankenbesoeckers* (visitors of the sick) or *sieckentroosters* (comforters of the sick). Such workers, after passing an examination prescribed by the church authorities, were appointed to visit ill persons at their homes and to offer them counsel designed to further their spiritual welfare. For their guidance the church had prepared an elaborate form composed mainly of consolatory texts from the Scriptures.[10]

So important was the function of *sieckentrooster* considered, that the first Charter of Freedoms and Exemptions, granted in 1629, ordered the immediate employment of such a functionary: "The Patroons and colonists shall in particular, and in the speediest manner, endeavor to find out ways and means whereby they may support a Minister and Schoolmaster . . . . and they shall, for the first, procure a Comforter of the sick there."[11]

But even before the Charter, there were by 1626 two *sieckentroosters* active in New Amsterdam. One of them, Bastiaen Jansz Krol, a native of Friesland sent to New Netherland in 1624 by the Dutch Reformed church as the colony's first comforter of the sick, later earned the distinction of serving as director-general for a short period (1632–33). The other, Jan Huygen, or Huych, was a nephew of the first official director-general, Peter Minuit. The two comforters of the sick seem to have pursued their common calling uneventfully on Manhattan Island for several years. Record is lacking of their labors in the homes of the sick, but notes from several sources attest that on Sundays they shared the duty of reading "some texts out of the Scriptures, together with the Creeds" to pious gatherings.

THE FIRST ALMSHOUSES

Most of the relief granted to dependent persons under the Dutch was administered in the homes of the recipients. The almshouse, or "deacons' house," maintained for the most part by collections taken up in the churches, was not a catchall institution for all types of dependents and misdemeanants as it was to become in later days. Rather was it a congregational home where impoverished old people might be cared for by their neighbors and pass their final years in peace.

The first deacons' house in New Netherland probably was that established in Rensselaerswyck at some date not definitely known, but certainly before 1652. The people in the main settlement of that patroonship were fortunate in two ways: They were far enough from New Amsterdam to escape the ruinous consequences of Kieft's attacks on the Indians; and at least until 1652 they were able, through licenses by which the patroon delegated his fur-trading privilege, to turn an honest guilder in peltries. In 1652, when Stuyvesant asserted the sovereignty of the Company over the main settlement and erected the village of Beverwyck from a portion of Rensselaerswyck, he conveyed to the deaconry a site south of a stream called the Fuyck Kill, for an almshouse and a farm on which produce could be raised for the inmates.[12] Probably this represented the first provision for a poor farm, in the later sense of the term, in the area now comprising New York State. A revealing light is cast on the general attitude toward the almshouse in a letter written in 1657 by the first Lutheran pastor at Rensselaerswyck:

Neither is there any house for the preacher here. All the houses are occupied, so that there are none to rent . . . . and the congregation is not willing to build me a house. But a Poor-house has been established here, and, God be praised, as there are yet very few poor people here, I have made arrangements with the deacons and lived therein until now.[13]

Even one occupying the social eminence of a clergyman looked upon the deacons' house as a very good and welcome sort of lodging with no stigma attached.

A deacons' house was erected at New Amsterdam in 1653, on a site now designated as 21–3 Beaver Street. Some years later it was replaced by another, where 34 Broad Street now stands; this in turn was supplanted in 1701 by a third deacons' house at 37 Wall Street under the English regime.[14] From the locations of these congregational homes it seems unlikely that any of the three could have been supported by an adjacent farm, but it is probable that they obtained food from a poor farm or *Arme Bouwerie*, which had been presented to the Dutch Reformed church of New Amsterdam by one Deacon Frawley about 1650. This tract was located near Newtown on the present site of Steinway, Long Island.[15] It appears to have been a common practice to arrange for the cultivation of such farms on various terms and to use the produce in assisting the poor. "A certain bouwery situated on the other side of Hellgate," bought "for the behalf and best [behest?] of the poor," is mentioned in a complaint voiced before the Colonial Council by Domine Megapolensis and Johannes de Peyster, schepen and deacon, in 1655. The gist of the complaint was that Abraham Rycken, not content with receiving from Stuyvesant a grant of land near the said bouwery, which had been previously assigned by the director for the use of the poor, had proceeded to fence in a public road and thus greatly hinder access to the poor farm. A colonial remonstrance of 1653 contains an item regarding a tract in Gravesend which had been granted to several persons, reserving a certain part for the poor, and which Stuyvesant, five years after his accession, had granted in its entirety to Cornelis van Werkhoven.[16]

RELIEF AND RELIGION

An indirect effect of the congregational character of relief in New Netherland was its stimulation of what might appear as religious intolerance. The proscription of other creeds would hardly be expected to find a champion in Domine Megapolensis, who had befriended the Jesuit, Father Jogues, and had played a leading part in obtaining that missionary's release from the Mohawks. Yet it was Domine Megapolensis, who in 1657, with Domine Drisius, petitioned the bourgomasters and schepens of New Amsterdam not to grant freedom of worship to the Lutherans, on the ground that the burden of supporting the Lutheran poor would rest upon the Dutch Reformed congregation. From the wording of the petition it is evident that the congregational system had acquired a *de facto* public character, while the congregational treasury remained almost entirely dependent upon congregational funds. This was attributable to the nominally established status of the Dutch Reformed church and to the fact that the deaconry had accepted the duty of relieving the needy in general. The petition reminds the burgomaster and schepens: "It is known to your Hon. Body that there is no other means provided for the support of the poor, save what is collected in the church. This is given to widows, orphans and to all who make suitable application whatever may be their religious persuasion."[17]

With the relief function of the Dutch Reformed congregations recognized in practice as involving a public duty, formal approval of the Lutherans as a religious body would permit them to organize, proselyte, win members from the established body, and raise moneys for the construction of churches and other denominational purposes, though continuing to rely on the funds of the Dutch Reformed congregations for the support of their poor. At any rate, this was the possible sequel to toleration which was feared by the petitioners, and under the circumstances it is only just to allow that there was more logic than bigotry in their position. In fact their fears were partly realized by certain incidents which occurred after the English accession.

METHODS OF RAISING RELIEF FUNDS

The church was considered the proper agency for the dispensation of poor relief. The clergy were given control over poor relief, and occasional attempts by civil officers to wrest this control from them were frustrated. When such an attempt was made by the magistrates of Wildwyck in 1657, they received a sharp reproof from Director-General Stuyvesant, who wrote them:

We have been informed that . . . . you have arrogated the disposal of what is collected in the community either for the Church or for the poor. If it is so, then it is our opinion and we command, that the disposal and distribution of it shall concern only the Consistory and remain until further order in its hands.[18]

Collections for the poor were regularly taken up at every Sunday service and the proceeds handed over to the deacons. These sums were occasionally supplemented by individual bequests or donations. Funds for the poor were also collected at weddings, it being the custom to put up a poor box into which the wedding guests dropped their offerings which were later gathered up by the deacons. Once when hard pressed for money, Director-General Kieft had a poor box placed in his own home, where all the fines and forfeitures intended for the poor were deposited. When the deposits had accumulated to a considerable sum, Kieft emptied the box and borrowed the money, promising to pay interest on it. One of the complaints contained in the "Remonstrance" of 1649 was that neither the interest nor the principal of this loan—and others made to the city officials—had ever been paid back to the poor fund.

In 1648 the deacons of the New Amsterdam church petitioned the Council "to make them a present of 500 guilders for the poor."[19] We have been unable to ascertain the fate of this petition; it appears probable that it was rejected.

Fines and forfeitures imposed for infractions of the law afforded a principal source of income for the poor fund. Many ordinances contained provisions allotting parts of fines to the poor. For example, an ordinance of 1641, establishing a fixed value on wampum as a means of halting the debasement of colonial currency, imposed a fine of ten guilders on violators, the whole amount to go to the poor.[20] In the famous "mutiny" trial of Jochem Kuyter and Cornelis Melyn in 1647, a third of the fines imposed was allotted to the poor fund. In this case the "rebels" appealed to The Hague and had their fines remitted. Director-General Stuyvesant and the Colonial Council decreed, in 1655, that one-third of all fines levied for discharging guns on New Year's Day, planting Maypoles, beating drums, or selling wine, beer, or brandy without paying excise, should be added to the poor fund.[21] In the same year the lottery was introduced at New Amsterdam as a means of increasing the poor fund. The prizes in this instance consisted of a "certain quantity of Bibles, Testaments and other books according to catalogue." The public authorities ordered the books valued at 100 per cent above their invoice, of which total the poor were to receive a third. Gysbert van Imbroeck, the promoter, was allotted the remainder.[22]

It is impossible to estimate the proportion of indigents in the population of New Netherland. It appears, however, that such persons were relatively few and that the actual expenditures for poor relief were inconsiderable. The deacons' houses or almshouses established in several of the settlements generally had but few inmates, and the need for home relief never reached sizable proportions. The deacons intrusted with the poor funds were accustomed to loan out surplus money at interest. In 1647 the poor fund at Rensselaerswyck was so large that the deacons loaned a part of it to the patroon himself.[23]

The Dutch West India Company, concentrating its efforts on getting dividends, contributed very little to the amelioration of poverty. Indeed, if the charges of the colonists may be believed, it actually obstructed relief of the poor. In their "Remonstrance" of 1649, the colonists alleged that the Company had misappropriated relief funds raised by the people themselves:

The Poor, who, however, are best provided for, have nothing except what is collected in the church, in addition to a few fines and voluntary offerings from the inhabitants; but a considerable portion of the money is in the hands of the Company, who took it, from time to time, and retained it. They have long promised to pay interest, but notwithstanding all that is done in the matter neither principal nor interest can be obtained from them.

The colonists also charged that the Company had failed to establish needed charitable institutions:

There is, occasionally, a flying report of an hospital and of asylums for orphans and for old men, &c., but as yet not a sign of an attempt, order or regulation has been made about them. From all these, then, it is sufficiently apparent, that scarcely any proper care or diligence has been used by the Company, or its officers, for any ecclesiastical property. . . . .

The Company replied to these and other accusations in two documents, one drawn up in its own name and the other signed by its secretary for New Netherland, Cornelis van Tienhoven. In the first answer it was declared categorically: "The Company's circumstances admitted of the building neither of an hospital nor orphan

asylum, which are not very necessary there as yet." In van Tienhoven's answer it was charged that the failure to build these charitable institutions was principally due to the colonists' unwillingness
to contribute their just share to such projects. Van Tienhoven wrote:

'Tis also denied and cannot be proved that any of the inhabitants of New
Netherland have, either voluntarily or when requested, contributed or given
anything for the building of an Asylum for orphans, or for the aged. . . . . If
the people require institutions as above stated, they must contribute toward
them as is the custom in this country; and were there Asylums for orphans and
the aged there, revenues would be necessary, not only to keep the houses in
repair, but to support the orphans and the aged people.

As for the charges of misappropriation of poor funds, the Company
evaded the issue by shifting responsibility to the deacons:

As regards the deacons' or Poor-fund, the deacons are accountable for that,
and are the persons of whom inquiry should be made as to where the money is
invested which they have, from time to time, placed at interest; and as the
Director never had charge of it, such not being usual, the deacons, and not the
Director, are responsible for it.[24]

An examination of all the documents in the case leaves no room for
doubt, however, that the charges of the colonists against the Company's administration were substantially justified.

THE ORPHANMASTERS

Identified after a fashion with the public welfare scheme in New
Netherland were the orphanmasters. In keeping with Dutch custom, orphanmasters were proposed for New Amsterdam in 1653 and
were later appointed there and at Beverwyck and Wildwyck. It
might be inferred, from their title, that these officials were charged
with the particular duty of looking after the welfare of dependent
widows and orphans; but in reality they confined their efforts almost
exclusively to widows and orphans *with property*.

In 1653, when the appointment of orphanmasters was first proposed at New Amsterdam, the director-general and Council decided
the city was not as yet in a position to employ such officials. It was
suggested instead that the deaconry "keep their eyes open and look
as Orphanmasters after widows and orphans" and report to the city
or colonial authorities in cases where special curators might be
needed to safeguard estates. Negligent curators were to be called to

account by the burgomasters and schepens. The records show that
in 1655 the burgomasters themselves rather than the deacons were
designated as orphanmasters in the case of the six orphan children of
Pieter Cecer, deceased:

Therefore their Worships, the Burgomasters, as Orphan masters, have
deemed it necessary, that tutors and guardians for said children be appointed
and they have selected as such and herewith appoint Pieter van Linde as being
the stepfather of the mother, and Isaac Kip as witness for the youngest child.
They are hereby authorized to sell or employ the goods and property, left by
deceased, for the benefit of the children, to hire out or bind out the children
to honest and suitable people and to do everything, that time and circumstances point out as proper. They shall be held, when called upon, to render
account, produce vouchers, etc. to the Orphan masters[25]

About three weeks earlier, the burgomasters had informed the
director-general and Council that there were widows and orphans
whose welfare demanded special attention and had suggested that
they commission certain persons to serve solely as orphanmasters.
In response, no doubt, to this and to further appeals, the director-
general and Council "elected and confirmed" Paulus Leenderts van
die Grift and Pieter Wolfertsen van Couwenhoven as orphanmasters
of the city, under date of February 25, 1656.[26] Meanwhile, on January 20, the burgomasters took account of several complaints by the
guardians of the Cecer children, to the effect that search had
disclosed neither goods nor estate for the discharge of debts or
the support of the orphans: "Therefore the Orphanmasters herewith order said guardians to take the estate, as far as it is known to
them, to the stewards of the dead and of the Indian sufferers, or to
the Deaconry, who are to clear the estate and take care of the children."[27]

In short, once it was certain that the children were without inheritance, the orphanmasters transferred their charges to the regularly constituted poor-relief functionaries. On the other hand, the
Wildwyck court records reveal that a widow with children by two
former husbands had been compelled to give bond for the education,
training, and support of all her offspring before she could secure permission to embark on her third venture in matrimony.[28]

The orphanmasters occasionally bound out children under their
jurisdiction. In 1660 they bound out Hendrick de Graaff to a

burgher, Nicelaas Boot, for three years. Boot was to furnish board and clothing and at the end of the term give the boy 150 florins should he wish to go to Holland, or "two ordinary hogsheads of tobacco . . . ." should he remain in the colony.[29]

OTHER ASPECTS OF CHILD WELFARE

Perhaps no particular notice would have been given to orphans without property if a shift in Company policy and the ready co-operation of the city fathers of Old Amsterdam had not resulted in an interesting experiment in immigration. The sparse population of New Netherland (then less than 2,000) was one of the points scored against the Company in the "Remonstrance" of 1649. As a means for correcting this condition without undue expense to itself, the Company proposed the transportation to America of several hundred dependent children, who were plentiful in Holland as a consequence of wars and marine disasters. Mainly because the English wars interfered with transportation, the plan lagged until 1654. On May 4 of that year, however, the Amsterdam directors of the Company informed Stuyvesant that they were sending some boys and girls from the city's orphan asylum to increase the population and promote agriculture in New Netherland. An extant letter of July 9, addressed to Stuyvesant and sent by the burgomaster of Amsterdam, heralded the first consignment:

HONORABLE, WISE, PRUDENT, RIGHT, DISCREET SIR:

Being informed by the governors of the alms-house of the vast number of poor people wherewith they are burdened and charged, we have concluded to relieve them and so do the Company a service, by sending some of them to New Netherland.

We have, therefore, sent over in the ship belonging to the bearer hereof, 7 @ 25 boys and girls, requesting you, in a friendly manner, to extend to them your kind advice and assistance, and to advance them if possible; so that they according to their fitness, may earn their board. If you consider that the population of that country could be advanced by sending over such persons, we shall, on being informed, lose no time to have some more forwarded.[30]

The first group arrived in the autumn of 1654. On November 9 the director-general and Council resolved "to hire the house of Mr. [Isaac] Allerton and lodge there the children sent over by the poor-masters [of Amsterdam], and to direct Peter Lefevre, who has hired the same house, not to move into it for this and other weighty reasons."[31] This was the first public home for orphans in New Netherland.

It was the practice to bind out these imported orphans as apprentices and servants for from two to four years. The girls who married with the consent of the director-general before their time of service had expired were entitled to immediate release. Children who served out their time might renew their service by mutual agreement with their former masters or might choose to remain free, in which event they were allotted twenty-five morgens (about fifty acres) of land each or as much thereof as they could cultivate.

Dependent children were also transported from Holland to the Dutch colony on the South (Delaware) River, which was included in New Netherland. In a letter dated October 10, 1658, Vice-Director Alrichs of that settlement informed the municipal authorities of old Amsterdam that a shipment of children had arrived safely and had been bound out under agreements stipulating from forty to eighty guilders as cash payments at the conclusion of their terms of service. Further consignments were requested, "but, if possible, none ought to come less than 15 years of age and somewhat strong, as little profit is to be expected here without labor."[32]

EDUCATION IN NEW NETHERLAND

The Dutch hold a pioneer position in the history of public education. Common schools, rare in other countries, were made available to a large part of the population in seventeenth-century Holland. Education was then mainly an adjunct to religion. In keeping with the precepts of the Dutch Reformed church, the state religion of Holland, which emphasized individual salvation and the necessity for each person to read the Bible for himself, the Dutch were forward in establishing common schools. In many parts of the country free education was afforded to the poor in schools supported by public funds.

It could not be expected, of course, that common-school education in the colony of New Netherland would follow the broad liberal pattern of Holland. None the less, it does appear from the records that such education was established earlier in this colony than in any other part of America. The first common school was founded at New

Amsterdam in 1638, with Adam Roelantsen serving as the first schoolmaster. Schools were established thereafter in other settlements of New Netherland, but these were usually temporary in nature, set up by wandering schoolmasters as they went from place to place. Schools were usually supported jointly by contributions of the inhabitants and public funds. Pupils were required to pay for their tuition, but children of the poor were taught free. In a list of instructions to a new schoolmaster at New Amsterdam, it was specified that besides his annual salary he should receive a certain stipend from each pupil who could afford it, but that "the poor and the needy, who ask to be taught for God's sake, he shall teach for nothing."[33]

Until the later years of the Dutch period, there were no separate schoolhouses in the colony. Classes were usually held in unused rooms of public buildings, in churches, or in rented quarters. The failure of the Company to build a permanent school served as the basis of one of the complaints of the colonists in the "Remonstrance" of 1649:

The plate has been a long time passed around for a Common school which has been built with words; for, as yet, the first stone is not laid; some materials have only been provided. However, the money given for the purpose hath all disappeared and is mostly spent, so that it falls somewhat short; and nothing permanent has as yet been effected.[34]

Pointing out that "now, the school is kept very irregularly, by this one or that, according to his fancy, as long as he thinks proper," the colonists urged the speedy establishment of a permanent "public school, with at least two good teachers."

In its answer to the "Remonstrance," the Company again disclaimed responsibility for the delay in building a schoolhouse, shifting the blame to the churchwardens, who were supposed to have charge of the funds collected for the erection of a suitable building. A site had been selected for the school, and meanwhile "other teachers keep school in hired houses, so that the youth are not in want of schools to the extent to the circumstances of the country."[35] In 1652 one of the rooms of the city tavern (later the *Stadt Huis*) was used for a school, but repeated efforts to force the Company to build a separate schoolhouse failed, and there was none in New Amsterdam when it was captured by the English in 1664. Nevertheless, by the time of the surrender, nearly every town and village had its schoolmaster, who usually taught part-time while filling some minor ecclesiastical post. Sometimes the other duties of the schoolmaster were quite varied, as in the case of Carel De Beauvois, appointed teacher in Breuckelen in 1661, who was also chorister, grave-digger, and court messenger.[36] Throughout the colony poor pupils were invariably accepted free of charge, while the others paid prescribed fees. Children of wealthy families were usually taught by private tutors. The Dutch system of common schools survived for some years after the English conquest, but gradually broke down as the English influence became dominant in the colony.

MEDICAL AID

The first hospital was established at New Amsterdam about 1658. The institution, a Company project, was available only to sick soldiers and Negroes. The cost of food and heat had to be paid by the patient unless he were a Negro slave and hence received no wages. Need for a hospital was first reported to Stuyvesant and the Council by Company Surgeon Jacob Hendricksen Varrevanger, who stated on December 12, 1658, that he had found the recovery of sick Negroes and soldiers seriously jeopardized by the unsanitary conditions prevailing in such houses as would receive them. He requested that a building be provided where these employees could be given medical care under proper conditions, and that a dependable caretaker, cook, and servant be placed in charge. Soldiers were to pay for food and fire from their wages and rations, and the colored men were to be cared for at the expense of the Company. The director and Council responded favorably, and in December, one Hilletje Wilbruch (or Wilbuick) was appointed matron at one hundred florins per year. The exact date of opening is unknown, but the hospital is listed as in operation in July, 1660, and it continued in use until 1680, sixteen years after the first Dutch surrender.[37]

One provision for public welfare which can certainly be credited to the Company is the appointment of a salaried midwife at New Amsterdam. Record exists of one Lysbet Dircksen officiating in this capacity in 1638. A house was built for her at public expense

under Director-General van Twiller. She appears to have had a
regular line of successors in office. Hellegond Joris was appointed
midwife in 1655, and in 1660 the Council voted her a salary of one
hundred guilders a year for attending the poor.[38]

THE FIRST WORK-RELIEF PROGRAM

The introduction of the first known instance of work relief occurred in the South River colony in the settlement called New
Amstel, during the years 1658–59, following the transfer of the
rights of exploitation in that area to the municipality of old Amsterdam. The growing season was characterized by heavy rains which,
in this low-lying country, resulted in crop failures and caused an
epidemic of fever, ague, and dysentery. In the period of scarcity
which followed, a large part of the population of six hundred found
itself without bread and "as poor as worms." To meet this emergency the authorities decided to undertake, at the expense of the
colony's treasury, much work which the settlers, under more favorable conditions, would have performed themselves. To provide employment and income for the distressed, barns and fences were built,
the church was enlarged, and a public granary and other buildings
were erected.[39]

The New Netherland authorities provided two interesting theories
of the causes of poverty and pauperism in the colony. In December,
1656, the deaconry of New Amsterdam complained to the burgomasters and schepens that tapsters (saloonkeepers) were enticing
their patrons to place their goods in pawn for drink, resulting in the
impoverishment of their families.[40] This was one of the earliest instances in which the saloon was advanced as a cause of poverty in
the New World.

Another reason was advanced when, on September 4, 1659,
Stuyvesant reported to the Amsterdam chamber of the Company
that most of the immigrants sent over were "traders and hence persons unaccustomed to labor," who quickly became a charge on the
deaconry.[41] In 1660 he told the same body:

We hope . . . . that when you send over some farmers and later some lads
of 15 or 16 years . . . . you will inquire as much as possible for industrious persons, used to work, and not take up and engage whomever chance may throw

Washington Irving's "History of New York" (London, John Murray, 1823), p. 23

in your way, so that the money you advance be not spent without advantage; this has been the case with . . . . most of the children from the Orphan Asylum, accustomed and more inclined to carry a beggar's gripsack than to labor.[42]

SETTLEMENT PROBLEMS: THE FIRST GENERAL POOR LAW

The earliest settlement problems in New Netherland revolved in large part about the transient poor from New England and Virginia. Among the English colonists in the seventeenth century were many bond servants who had come to America under contracts which bound them to serve colonial masters for certain terms of years, usually in return for their passage. Some had been transported to America as a punishment for law-breaking, to work as bond servants with no return but board and lodging. These and others were far from delighted at the prospect of laboring for little or nothing in a land where freedom could be gained in a night's walk. Numbers of them became fugitives long before their terms of service were up and sought safety in the Dutch colony rather than in the wilderness to the west. In 1642 the authorities on Manhattan Island had their attention drawn by complaining residents to these footloose individuals, "who too often carry their passports with them under the soles of their shoes." Director-General Kieft thereupon issued a proclamation forbidding any householder to harbor a stranger or to give him more than one meal or a night's lodging without notifying him (the director-general) of the fact, together with the name of the guest.[43] This marked the introduction in this area of a method for detecting vagrants and other undesirables that was to be a constant feature of the poor-law system for the next two centuries.

In his highly imaginative *History of New York*, Washington Irving gives us an amusing description—probably apocryphal, since no basis for it has been found in the records consulted—of an ingenious device, said to have been introduced by Director Kieft, for the punishment of vagrants and beggars:

This was nothing more nor less than a gibbet, of a very strange, uncouth, and unmatchable construction, far more efficacious, as he [Kieft] boasted, than the stocks, for the punishment of poverty. It was for altitude not a whit inferior to that of Haman, so renowned in Bible history; but the marvel of the contrivance was, that the culprit, instead of being suspended by the neck, according to venerable custom, was hoisted by the waistband, and kept dangling and sprawling between heaven and earth for an hour or two at a time—to the infinite entertainment and edification of the respectable citizens who usually attended exhibitions of the kind. . . . .[44]

The first colony-wide poor law in New Netherland, passed October 22, 1661, developed mainly out of the necessity for finding means to protect the city of New Amsterdam from a steady influx of itinerant poor. The immediate occasion for this ordinance was the complaint of the city's deaconry respecting "the many applications and great trouble which they daily experience" from the poor of outlying villages, "with whose characters and wants they [the deacons] are utterly unacquainted." As a result, the deacons averred, "their treasury is . . . . greatly diminished, and they would, by that means, be unable to assist the Poor and Needy of this City." In response to this complaint, Stuyvesant and the Colonial Council promulgated an ordinance "to the end that the Lazy and the Vagabond may as much as possible be rebuked, and the really Poor the more assisted and cared for," declaring:

That from this time forward, no assistance shall be given by the Deacons of this City New Amsterdam, to any persons residing outside the jurisdiction of this City, unless they bring with them from the Deacons or Overseers of the Poor at the place of their residence a certificate of their character and poverty in manner as follows:

N.N. residing under the jurisdiction of N.N. hath applied to us for some assistance and support, and, as his character and poverty are well known to us, we would willingly have provided him therewith, but the low state of our Treasury hath not allowed us to do so. We have, therefore, to request, on his behalf, the Deacons of the City of *Amsterdam* in *New Netherland* to lend him a helping hand according to their usual discretion.[45]

The ordinance contained the assurance that all poor persons carrying such certificates would "be provided for, and assisted here as circumstances permit." It would appear from the prescribed wording of the certificate that outlying villages unable to maintain their own poor could send the latter to New Amsterdam where they would be cared for. But that the authorities of New Amsterdam did not so construe the law is indicated by an order issued by the burgomasters to the local deaconry in January, 1662, ordering them "not to give assistance to anybody, except to the poor of the city."[46] Generous treatment was to be accorded to the latter, however; the deacons were directed "to provide these poor with clothing, food and a little money," and to "make note of to whom assistance is given." The latter specification marks an interesting step in the development of record-keeping in our poor-relief administration.

Having disposed of the particular poor-relief problem affecting New Amsterdam, the ordinance of 1661 proceeded to lay down a uniform method of maintaining a poor fund in each locality: "But in order that each Village or Settlement may be better able to assist and support its own Poor, it is further Resolved and decided that, from this time forward, in all Villages and Settlements, collections shall be made and something laid up for the poor and Needy." In all localities where there was a settled ministry, the deacons were responsible for establishing and maintaining a poor fund. But in all villages lacking ministry—"where there is no Preaching"—the magistrates were directed to "nominate and qualify two proper persons, who shall go around every Sunday with a little bag among the congregation and collect the Alms for the support of the Poor of that place." It may be inferred that the magistrates were the overseers of the poor mentioned in the first part of the ordinance. Local magistrates were warned that disciplinary measures would follow their neglect to carry out the terms of the act.

The ordinance of 1661 was the first and last colony-wide poor law during the Dutch period. Three years later New Netherland fell into the hands of the English.

SUMMARY

To the last, poor relief in New Netherland continued to be preponderantly neighborly and congregational. Poor-relief functions were vested in ecclesiastical officials of the Dutch Reformed church, although churches of other denominations were directed to take care of their own poor. In localities where there was no religious organization, responsibility for relief was placed in the hands of civil authorities (magistrates and two collectors appointed by them). Poor funds were raised mainly through weekly collections and were supplemented by the proceeds of court fines allocated in whole or in part to the poor and by individual donations and bequests. The West India Company showed little concern for the welfare of needy persons in the colony. It was bitterly assailed on several occasions by representatives of the colonists for its failure to establish welfare institutions such as existed in Holland, including hospitals for the sick, asylums for the aged and for orphan children. The Company, contending that it should not be asked to bear the burden of poor relief, countered with the charge that the colonists were not sufficiently interested in such institutions to pay for their erection and support out of their own pockets. However, several deacons' houses or almshouses were established in New Amsterdam, Rensselaerswyck, and other settlements. There is record of a temporary orphan asylum being established in New Amsterdam in 1654 to accommodate children sent there from the almshouse in old Amsterdam. *Sieckentroosters*, or comforters of the sick, who might be called the first social workers, appeared on the scene at the very beginning of the colony's history. By the end of the Dutch period, nearly every locality had its common school, and in most settlements children of the poor were taught free of charge. In 1656 "orphanmasters" were introduced into New Netherland, but the duties of these functionaries were related to the estates of propertied orphans rather than to the care of dependent orphans. Poor relief remained a local responsibility throughout this period, although the poor law of 1661 seems to have permitted localities with inadequate poor funds to send indigent residents to New Amsterdam for assistance. The ordinance of 1661 represented the only colony-wide poor law passed during the days of Dutch sovereignty.

BIBLIOGRAPHICAL REFERENCES

1. "The Third Voyage of Master Henry Hudson," in *Narratives of New Netherland*, ed. J. Franklin Jameson (New York, 1909), pp. 17, 19.
2. *Documents Relative to the Colonial History of the State of New York*, ed. E. B. O'Callaghan (New York, 1853–87), I, 99, 100. Hereinafter referred to as *Docs. Rel. Col. Hist.*
3. A. Everett Peterson, "Population and Industry," in *History of the State of New York*, ed. Alexander C. Flick (New York, 1932–35), Vol. I, chap. x, *passim*.
4. John R. Brodhead, *History of the State of New York, 1609–1691* (New York, 1853–71), I, 198.
5. Herbert L. Osgood, *The American Colonies in the Seventeenth Century* (New York, 1904–7), II, 144–50.

6. "The Representation of New Netherland," in *Narratives of New Netherland*, p. 322.
7. *Ibid.*, II, 52.
8. Henry R. Stiles, *A History of the City of Brooklyn* (Albany, 1869–70), I, 132.
9. Sir William Temple, *Observations upon the United Provinces of the Netherlands* (Cambridge, 1932), pp. 104 ff.
10. New York State Historian, *Ecclesiastical Records, State of New York* (New York, 1901–16), I, 46. Hereinafter referred to as *Eccles. Recs. N.Y.*
11. *Docs. Rel. Col. Hist.*, II, 557.
12. Cuyler Reynolds (comp.), *Albany Chronicles* (Albany, 1906), p. 47.
13. *Eccles. Recs. N.Y.*, I, 385.
14. I. N. P. Stokes, *Iconography of Manhattan Island, 1498–1909* (New York, 1915–28), II, 242; IV, 428. Hereinafter referred to as Stokes, *Iconography*.
15. *Eccles. Recs. N.Y.*, VII, 292.
16. *Docs. Rel. Col. Hist.*, I, 555; XIV, 326.
17. *Eccles. Recs. N.Y.*, I, 387.
18. *Ibid.*, p. 536.
19. New York State Secretary of State, *Calendar of Historical Manuscripts in the Office of the Secretary of State, Albany, N.Y.*, ed. E. B. O'Callaghan (Albany, 1865–66), I, 120.
20. New Netherland, *Laws and Ordinances*, ed. and trans. E. B. O'Callaghan (Albany, 1868), p. 26.
21. *Ibid.*, 205.
22. New York City Burgomasters and Schepens, *Records of New Amsterdam from 1653 to 1674 Anno Domini*, ed. Berthold Fernow (New York, 1897), I, 188, 191. Hereinafter referred to as *Records of New Amsterdam*.
23. Joel Munsell, *Annals of Albany* (Albany, 1850–59), I, 92.
24. *Docs. Rel. Col. Hist.*, I, 300, 340, 423, 424.
25. New York City Orphanmasters, *Minutes of the Orphanmasters of New Amsterdam, 1655 to 1663* (New York, 1902–7), I, 4. Hereinafter referred to as *Minutes of the Orphanmasters*.
26. *Records of New Amsterdam* II, 45.
27. *Minutes of the Orphanmasters*, I, 13.
28. "Orphan Masters in Old Ulster," *Olde Ulster*, II (1906), 14–15.
29. *Minutes of the Orphanmasters*, I, 154–55.
30. *Docs. Rel. Col. Hist.*, I, 556.
31. *Ibid.*, XIV, 296.
32. *Ibid.*, II, 52.
33. William H. Kilpatrick, *Dutch Schools of New Netherland and Colonial New York* (U.S. Bureau of Education Bull. No. 12 [1912], Whole No. 483), p. 68.
34. *Docs. Rel. Col. Hist.*, I, 300, 317.
35. *Ibid.*, pp. 423–24.

36. Mrs. Schuyler Van Rensselaer, *History of the City of New York in the Seventeenth Century* (New York, 1909), I, 442.
37. F. H. Bosworth, *The Doctor in Old New York*, "Half-Moon Series" (New York, 1898), II, No. 8, 296–97.
38. *Ibid.*, p. 285.
39. O'Callaghan, *History of New Netherland*, II, 375.
40. *Records of New Amsterdam*, I, 33–34.
41. Stokes, *Iconography*, IV, 198.
42. Alexander C. Flick (ed.), *History of the State of New York*, I, 330. Hereinafter referred to as *History of the State of New York*.
43. Brodhead, *op. cit.*, I, 335.
44. Washington Irving, *A History of New York, from the Beginning of the World to the End of the Dutch Dynasty* (rev. ed.; New York, 1867), p. 227.
45. New Netherland, *Laws and Ordinances*, pp. 411–12.
46. *Minutes of the Orphanmasters*, II, 124–35.

PART II

NEW YORK AS AN ENGLISH COLONY, 1664–1776

CHAPTER II

ENGLISH INFLUENCES AND DUTCH SURVIVALS

In September, 1664, Director-General Peter Stuyvesant surrendered New Netherland without a struggle to the English military forces under Colonel Richard Nicolls. Resistance would have been futile; the bankrupt West India Company had been unable to send armed assistance to Stuyvesant, and the latter's autocratic rule had alienated the support of a large number of the Dutch colonists themselves. The territory became the proprietary province of New York, owned by the king's brother, the Duke of York, and named after him.

The English, however, had long since gained a foothold in the province through early settlements in towns situated on Long Island. For years they had enjoyed an autonomous existence under the nominal sovereignty of the Dutch. One year before the surrender the towns of Hempstead, Flushing, Gravesend, Jamaica, Newtown, and Oyster Bay threw off even this nominal allegiance; they formed a federation and proclaimed Charles II as their sovereign.

With the passing of the colony from Dutch to English rule, New Amsterdam, Fort Orange, and Esopus became respectively, New York, Albany, and Kingston, and other changes in place names occurred.

The new English province was administered by a governor and council acting for the Duke of York, who later became James II. Although autocratic and arbitrary in form, the government was conciliatory in practice, as indeed it had to be in view of the independent spirit of the settlers and the fact that the Dutch in the early years outnumbered the English at least three to one. In spite of the unceasing demands of the colonists for popular representation, however, two decades passed before they forced the establishment of a general assembly. This body, set up in 1683, was dissolved by James II three years later and was not re-established until 1691 under William and Mary.

In local government, the Dutch system was changed to conform more closely to the prevailing British administrative pattern. Beginning in 1665 the burgomasters, schepens, and schout were superseded by a mayor, aldermen, and sheriff, although it was not until 1683 that the English county was introduced into New York as an administrative unit. In pursuance of the shrewd policy of conciliating the defeated colonists, the transition from Dutch to English institutions and customs was effected gradually. In the Articles of Capitulation signed by the Dutch and English on August 27, 1664, it was provided that "the Dutch here shall enjoy their own customs concerning their inheritances," the same concession being extended to certain other customs and practices. In many localities, as we shall see, old Dutch methods continued for years after the introduction of English rule. Article 12 of the Capitulation declared: "All publique writings and records which concern the inheritances of any people, or the reglement of the church, or poor, or orphans, shall be carefully kept by those in whose hands now they are."[1]

The first provincial governor, Richard Nicolls, proved himself a man of prudence, tact, and some ability. He guaranteed to the inhabitants security of property, liberty of conscience, maintenance of existing customs in the inheritance of property, and equal rights to Dutch and English colonists. As governor he made little attempt to coerce the non-English population. Early in his administration, however, he initiated a policy of wholesale parceling-out of the best lands of the province, making grants of tremendous tracts, apparently on a basis of rank favoritism. The colonial government originally intended to establish through these manorial grants loyalist strongholds at strategic points in the province. But this practice, inaugurated by Nicolls, was continued by his successors long after the ostensible need for manorial "strongholds" had passed, despite all attempts at reform. The effect of this lavish policy was to create, on the one hand, a relatively small number of powerful landed families, and, on the other hand, to bring poverty and the status of tenantry to hundreds of settlers whose chief ambition had been to earn free title to as much land as they could occupy by actual use. In a vast expanse of fertile uncultivated territory, these settlers found themselves facing the alternative of tilling the virgin soil as tenants or of taking up land on the frontier. But the frontier settlers were remote from a market where they might trade the fruits of their industry for common comforts and necessary supplies and were exposed to the attacks of hostile Indians and whites. Through the parceling-out of landed privilege to a favored few, the provincial authorities aroused in the small farmers a spirit of dissatisfaction and even rebellion, which manifested itself long before the outbreak of the Revolution.*

Early in 1665 Governor Nicolls summoned delegates from English towns on Long Island to meet with him at Hempstead to ratify a code of laws already drawn up by him. This code, known as the Duke's Laws, was based on statutes governing the New England colonies, with modifications in conformity with the needs of a proprietary government, and was formally promulgated on March 1, 1665. The English portion of the province—the territory now comprising roughly Kings, Queens, Nassau, Richmond, Suffolk, and Westchester counties—was constituted as a shire named Yorkshire, which, in turn, was divided into three districts or ridings. A high sheriff was appointed for the shire and a deputy for each riding.

Local government was based largely on that prevailing in England. The Duke's Laws provided for division of the shire into parishes, each to have its own church, and authorized the freeholders of each parish to elect a constable and eight overseers. Among other duties the overseers were authorized to raise and apportion levies and assessments for "provision for the poor" and "maintenance for the Minister." The overseers were further empowered to choose from among themselves two churchwardens.[2] Thus, in the first provincial code adopted in New York, civil and ecclesiastical functions were vested in the same local officials.

It is significant that the Duke's Laws placed no dependence on voluntary contributions as had the Dutch regional ordinance of 1661, but provided for raising poor-relief moneys directly from the tax fund, following the English practice. In conformity with the English poor-law system also, the parish was designated as the poor-

---

* In 1750 the tenants of Livingston Manor rebelled and were followed by tenants in Cortlandt Manor and Rensselaerswyck. The disorders culminated in forcible evictions, crop- and home-burning, timber destruction, bloodshed, and loss of lives.

relief administrative unit. However, an amendment to the Duke's code passed in October, 1665, authorized the riding to act as the relief unit in the care of the insane. The amendment stated:

That in regard the Conditions of distracted Persons, who may be both very chargeable and troublesome and so will prove too greate a Burthen for one Towne alone to beare, each Towne in the Rideing where such person or persons shall happen to bee, are to Contribute towards the Charge which may arise upon such occasions.[3]

This was the first application of the "district union" plan in the poor-relief administration of New York.

Another notable exception to this system of local responsibility for the poor was provided in Dutchess County, where the administration of relief remained in the hands of county officials for several decades. This anomaly was due to the small number of inhabitants in Dutchess County during most of the colonial period, rendering it imperative for the county to assume many of the functions fulfilled by local officials in more densely populated areas. Although organized in 1683 as one of the original twelve counties, Dutchess had so few inhabitants that it was attached provisionally to Ulster County until 1713. Even at this time its inhabitants totaled less than 500. In 1723 its population was barely more than 1,000; in 1731 it was 1,727.

The supervisors of Dutchess County were charged not only with raising the poor fund but with the task of disbursing it as well. The county supervisors' record-book for 1726 contains an interesting example of poor-relief procedure during this period: "To Collnell Leonard Lewis for ye Disbursements and Sarvice Done to ye County in procureing a place for John Williams in New York Who was Blind and Was Like to have fallen upon ye County, allowed 1£, 10s."[4]

In 1732 the supervisors gave five shillings to the sick wife and children of Samuel Taylor, Jr., "for a charitable Suply to Maintain them in distemper called the Small Pox." In 1741 they voted eight pounds to John Cook "for maintaining a poor Child."[5] The previous year (1740) witnessed the passage of an act "for the better Relief of the Poor in Dutchess County," in which the responsibility for poor relief was formally vested in the supervisors. The latter were charged with providing for inhabitants "in real need of relief" upon the certification of the justices of the peace.[6] The same act directed the county supervisors to defray the funeral expenses of all persons meeting accidental death within the county and lacking estate or effects sufficient to cover the funeral costs. When the authorities of Dutchess County refused to accept this responsibility on the ground that it conflicted with previous statutes, placing responsibility for all poor relief on the localities, the Colonial Assembly passed another statute in 1743 specifying that the funeral expenses of poor persons who met accidental deaths must be borne by the whole county, but that the relief of the living poor should be charged to the town or precinct. The formula worked out in this law was a rather curious one: dead paupers were a charge upon the county, the living upon the locality.[7] The trend of poor relief from this point moved steadily toward the crystallization of the narrow local systems prevailing in England and New England.

To return to 1665, the Duke's Laws contained two additional provisions relating to the field of public welfare. One assigned to the poor all fines levied for violation of the laws against trading with or accepting goods from members of the servant class; the other ordered trustees of the property of orphan children to render an account of their stewardship on pain of fines or removal. Poor relief during the ensuing years was evidently not a burdensome problem in the new province. In a description of New York in 1678 Governor Edmund Andros dismissed the subject in a laconic sentence: "Noe Beggars but all poore cared for."[8]

The year 1683 saw some profound changes in the administrative setup of the province. The first general assembly met that year and drew up a "Charter of Libertyes and priviledges" which struck at the autocratic rule vested in the governor and transferred a large degree of power to the people's representatives in the legislature. In that year too the county as a political unit was introduced into the province with the erection of the twelve original counties. The sections of the Duke's Laws referring to poor relief were superseded in 1683 by "An Act for the Defraying of the publique & necessary Charge of each respective City, towne and County throughout this Province & for maintaining the poore, & preventing vagabonds."

The act provided for the annual election of commissioners and a treasurer in each town, city, and county, these officials to have charge of raising and disbursing public funds in their respective administrative units. The principle of local responsibility for poor relief was explicitly stated, together with its derivation from the mother-country:

.... Whereas itt is the Custome & practice of his Majestys Realm of England, and all the adjacent Colonys in America that every respective County Citty towne parish & precinct doth take care and provide for the poor who do inhabit in their respective precincts aforesaid.

Therefore itt is Enacted by the authority aforesaid thatt for the time to come the respective Commissioners of every County, Citty, Towne, parish Precinct, aforesaid shall make provission for the maintenance support of their poor respectively.[9]

The act of 1683 is notable chiefly for two reasons: (1) It was the first law of its kind to apply to the entire province, the Duke's Laws of 1665 having been limited in application to the English part of the province constituted as Yorkshire; (2) it was entirely secular in character, putting an end to the previous division of poor-relief responsibility between civil and ecclesiastical authorities.* It was seriously lacking in several respects, however; it provided no agent for the collection of the tax which the commissioners were authorized to levy, nor did it provide any penalty for failure to pay the rate. An effort was made in 1691 to remedy these defects, but the result was a vaguely worded statute which left obscure the vital matter of whether the poor rate was to be included in the general levy or was to be levied and disbursed separately.[10]

The ambiguity of the act of 1691 occasioned such sharp dispute that it was repealed ten years later. Another law was substituted, the preamble of which represented the preceding act as "very Inconvenient and burthensome to the Inhabitants of this Province, and hath occasioned many heats, animosities, Strifes and Debates, and other differences." The law of 1701 shows an intention to vest in the counties far more supervisory power in the financing of local relief than they had previously enjoyed. It directed the county justices of the peace to examine annually and allow the public charges of the

---

* The provisions in the statute relating to "the prevention of vagabonds" will be discussed in the following chapter.

several towns in the county and to issue to each town a warrant for electing two assessors and a collector who should fix a rate and secure the prescribed taxes. The justices at the same time were to make provision for support of the poor in the several localities and also to appoint a county treasurer to receive and disburse the moneys collected. However, provision for the poor was mentioned separately from "the publick and necessary Charge," leaving it still in doubt whether the poor fund was to be included in the moneys turned over to the county treasurer or retained by the town authorities.[11] The cities of New York and Albany were expressly excluded from the provisions of the act because "by their several charters [they] differ in the wayes and means for the defraying their public Charge, and maintaining their poor from the Severall Counties of this Province."

For some reason confirmation of the act of 1701 by the royal authority was delayed until 1708. In the interim the provincial assembly deemed it necessary to pass another act "for the better Explaining and more Effectual putting in Execucion" of the troublesome law of 1691. The new law, enacted in 1703, provided for the election of county supervisors, to meet annually at the county seat to decide on budgets and rates for their respective localities. It established the board of supervisors as the governing body in the county. Unfortunately, however, it repeated the vague phrasing of its predecessors and did little to clarify the question of poor-relief financing and administration. Out of its vast and involved clutter of phrases—the sentences run to more than four hundred words in length—the counties remained unable to deduce sufficient authorization or a definite formula for relieving the poor.[12]

SURVIVALS OF CONGREGATIONAL RELIEF

The Dutch constituted a major part of the population for many years after the surrender of New Netherland. The English governors displayed much tact in refraining from forcibly imposing English administrative forms and customs upon the conquered settlers, wisely depending upon time and inevitable population shifts to accomplish this end. The result was that the old manners and customs survived among the Dutch inhabitants long after the colony passed into the hands of the British.

Kings County offers an interesting illustration of the persistence and extension of Dutch culture following the surrender of 1664. The Dutch school at Flatbush was taught until 1758 by masters who spoke only the language of the Netherlands. At Flatlands the Dutch school records begin in 1675—a year after the second surrender—and continue almost unbroken until after the Revolution.[13] In 1675 Governor Andros, requesting aid for a "house-raising" in behalf of a certain victim of misfortune in the area, addressed his communication "to the Constables and Overseers of Bruyckline" who in all probability were none other than the Dutch Reformed deaconry and the schouts under a new nomenclature.[14]

Upstate, along the Hudson Valley, the Dutch occupied most of the settlements, and here, as on the western end of Long Island, Dutch culture persisted and expanded in spite of English rule. On the east, in the lower valley, there were solidly English settlements accustomed to govern themselves in the New England fashion. French Huguenots had settled and now dominated the towns of New Rochelle and New Paltz, but, in the main, the valley was Dutch, as many place names from Westchester northward attest today. Attempts to introduce the Duke's Laws were made at certain points in this area, such as Esopus, which was renamed Kingston under the English regime; yet it is recorded that for many years after the surrender Dutch magistrates decided cases according to Dutch law. The Dutch school at Albany, started in 1650, had two hundred scholars in 1744, and Poughkeepsie established a Dutch school in 1730, more than fifty years after the second surrender. As for the Dutch Reformed church it prospered and grew throughout the provincial period, making converts among Huguenots and Lutherans. In 1776 New York had eighty-one churches belonging to this denomination, in comparison with sixty-one Presbyterian and thirty Episcopal churches.[15]

One of the articles of the resurrender of 1674 had provided that "each congregation whether Lutherans or others may support their own poor." The implication of this provision is clear. The congregational system of poor relief actually survived as a going institution over a large part of provincial New York and in many areas functioned as the only relief agency. Though the cities of New York and Albany evolved fairly complete plans for public poor relief before the Revolution, the Dutch Reformed churches in these communities continued to exercise their traditional functions in that field, maintaining homes for the aged, giving support and educational aid to dependent children, supplying medical care, and contributing to the relief of imprisoned debtors and other unfortunate groups. As late as 1773 an act establishing a system of local relief in the county of Albany expressly exempted the Reformed churches from any change which the act might bring: *"Provided always* That Nothing in the said Act shall be construed to abridge or diminish the Rights and Privileges of the Corporations of the Reformed Protestant Dutch Churches in the City of Albany and the Township of Schenectady."[16]

An entry in the deacons' account-book for July, 1666, shows that the Albany almshouse was supplied with regular medical service. At this time Dr. Cornelius van Dyck was caring for the inmates at a salary of one hundred guilders a year.[17] Bequests of land and money to the deaconry for the use of the poor were not unusual. Sometimes property was transferred for this purpose during the life of the owner, on condition that the latter should be cared for by the church until his death.

The homely, neighborly, and comprehensive character of Dutch congregational poor relief is well illustrated in such items as appear in the deacons' account-book at Albany for 1665:

To small beer for the use of Uncle Peter I g. 13 s. Jangen de Brouster, for wetnursing Aaron Isack's child 35 g. Antony Jansen for 6 small measures of brandy which was used when the old captain was laid out, 4 g. 4 s. To William Brouwer in money 8 g. for which he pawned 1 pair of white stockings until he could return the money.[18]

The functions accepted by the deacons included comforting the aged, caring for the young, granting provident loans to the temporarily needy, and making proper provision for funeral services. Referring to funerals, the Albany book contains an extraordinary entry for the year 1700. It concerns the expenditures for the funeral of Gerrit Swart's widow, last of the old line of congregational poor, and among the details are listed:

Making the coffin, 24 g. [guilders]; cartage, 10 s.; A half vat and an anker of good beer, 27 g.; 1 gall. rum, 21 g.; 6 gall. Madeira for women and men, 84 g.; Sugar and *cruyery*, 5 g.; 150 sugar cakes, 15 g.; tobacco and pipes, 4s. 10 d.; Hendrick Roseboom, *doodgraver* [gravedigger], 30 g.

The total charge was two hundred and thirty-two guilders, and on auditing it the deacons found that in the case of one item the claim was extortionate. It seems that Roseboom, the *doodgraver*, asked twelve guilders for sending out invitations. The deacons paid the money under protest, warning Roseboom that they would never allow such a charge again.[19]

A year prior to this occurrence (1699) the Albany congregational almshouse was so thinly populated that the deacons had rented part of it as a private residence. The rental was one hundred and eight guilders per annum, or something less than half enough to pay for the obsequies of the widow Swart.[20]

An interesting incident connected with congregational poor relief is found in the Albany records for 1686, relating how a Negro slave named Hercules was brought before the court "to answer ye follonius takeing out of his Masters hause a small chest wherein some baggs of wampum was contained belonging to ye Poor of ye Lutheran Church."[21] The culprit confessed stealing the wampum set aside for the poor. A severe sentence was meted out to him; the court ordered, as an example to others, "ye sd neger Hercules to be whipt throw ye towne att ye cart tale by ye hands of ye hangman."

The Reformed church authorities in New York decided to erect a new church in 1692, and in 1701 they disposed of the congregational almshouse on Broad Street and purchased a new property on Wall Street for the same purpose.[22] The Albany church authorities in 1720 applied for a charter in terms which bear witness to the prosperity of their institution and their adherence to the established system of congregational poor relief:

The Humble Petition . . . . Most Humbly Sheweth That the said Minister, Elders and Deacons and the other members in Communion of the said Reformed Protestant Dutch Church have at their own charge built and erected a church within the City of Albany . . . . and have allso purchased Certain two Tenements and Lotts of ground for a poor or alms house and for a Minister's dwelling house; and sundry other small Tracts of Land within the said City and the Rents and incomes whereof are by them . . . . employed for the relief of the Poor and other Persons and charitable uses. . . . .[23]

Concern for the welfare of children was evinced by the deacons of the New York church at a meeting in 1724, when they denied the applications of a husband and wife for relief because of their evil lives, but expressed their willingness to look after the children of the couple. The condition specified was indenture before a magistrate, and the purpose "a Christian education" for the children. Other entries in church records show that the New York church maintained a free school for poor children until the eve of the Revolution.[24]

In 1713 the Dutch Reformed Consistory at Albany notified the Schenectady church of the arrival of corn, pork, and bread from the Consistory of New York, destined for distribution to a distressed colony of Palatines at Schoharie.[25] The Schenectady authorities were asked to send wagons to transport the supplies.

In an earlier connection it has been mentioned that the Dutch Reformed clergy fought toleration of the Lutherans through fear of having to care for the Lutheran poor. It has been noted also that the duty of each congregation to care for its poor was made a part of the resurrender agreement of 1674. Three years earlier there occurred an incident which touches on this particular question. On October 24, 1671, the Mayor's Court of New York City received a petition from one John Folshave, who desired "some support and relief in his sicknesse." The petition was referred to the deacons of the Dutch Reformed church. After inquiry, the Dutch deacons decided that the said "John Fossacre" was a member of the Lutheran church and that the latter body should properly be charged with his support. The final disposition of the case is contained in the minutes of the Mayor's Court: "Uppon complaint of the deakons of the Lutheran Church, It is ordered that they shal give no more allowance to John Fossiker, til further ordered."[26] The case of Folshave or Fossacre or Fossiker, as he was variously called, caused the Dutch Reformed deacons to complain that they were being charged with the care of some of the Lutheran poor, though collections for the poor were regularly taken up in the Lutheran church. They asserted further, that the Lutheran deacons gave no account in public meeting of the funds thus collected. In response the court ordered that each congregation thereafter should maintain its own poor and that the Lutheran deacons should annually account for their poor fund in public meeting, as did the Dutch Reformed church.

The congregational method of relief received a strong stimulus from another quarter in 1693, when a serious attempt was made to establish the Anglican church system in the southeastern part of the province. In that year a law was passed "for Settling a Ministry and Raising a Maintenance for them in the City of New York, County of Richmond, Westchester and Queens County."[27] The act provided for the induction of a "good sufficient Protestant Minister" in New York and in Richmond, and ministers for Westchester, and two for Queens. It directed that the freeholders of each city, county, and precinct covered by the act should meet annually "for the chusing of ten Vistry men and two Church Wardens," who, together with the justices of the peace, were to decide and levy the rate "for the maintenance of the Minister and Poor of there respective places."

In 1695 the assembly balked at the established church implications of the act of 1693 and tried to amend the law so that the provisions might clearly extend to the dissenting clergy.* At this juncture, however, their path was barred by Governor Fletcher who declared unequivocally that only the Anglican clergy were to be endowed with the privileges described. The system of clerical support and poor relief became firmly established in some parts of the four counties and continued in effect for many years. A typical entry in the town records of Hempstead for this period reads:

Hemsted Jenewary the 30 day 1707–8

Att a meeting of the Justisses Churchwordin and westry the asesars are heare by ordered to ases every free holder and sogerner in hemsted and the bounds theare of for to raies the sum of fourty seven pounds five shillings in mony Forty pounds for the minister and five pounds for the Pore and two pounds five shillings for the Collectters salerry.[28]

SUMMARY

In surveying the administrative pattern of poor relief in provincial New York, we find no such uniformity as existed in the New England states, where local responsibility under secular auspices was almost universal, or in Virginia, where the Anglican church was

---

* As Osgood points out, an anomalous situation arose in New York City, where the majority of freeholders entitled to vote were dissenters. For some time dissenters controlled, or at least greatly influenced, church affairs in the city. This situation was remedied in 1704 when Trinity parish was granted a charter permitting it to have its own vestry and churchwardens with power to act independently of the city vestry. Thus New York City for some years had both a civil and an ecclesiastical vestry, and on several occasions bitter disputes arose as to the proper functions of each (Herbert L. Osgood, *American Colonies in the Eighteenth Century* [New York, 1904–7], II, 16–18).

established as the state church for most of the colonial period and where poor relief was administered mainly by men who served in dual capacities as ecclesiastical and civil officers. In large measure, the differences of public poor relief in the various areas of New York are attributable to the peculiar circumstances that characterized the necessity of grafting English forms and customs on a predominantly Dutch population, together with the steady infiltration of immigrants from various parts of Europe bringing with them their native traditions and manners. In some parts of the province public poor relief was administered on the congregational plan with the Dutch Reformed, the Anglican, the Lutheran, or some other church exercising official or quasi-official authority; in others, the relief system was wholly secular in form. In some areas there was complete local responsibility; in others the county exerted varying degrees of control.

BIBLOGRAPHICAL REFERENCES

1. *Docs. Rel. Col. Hist.*, II, 251.
2. New York State, *Colonial Laws of New York from the Year 1664 to the Revolution* (Albany, 1894), I, 24. Hereinafter referred to as *C.L.N.Y.*
3. *Ibid.*, p. 79.
4. Dutchess Co., N.Y., Board of Supervisors, *Old Miscellaneous Records of Dutchess County (the Second Book of the Supervisors and Assessors)* (Poughkeepsie, 1909), pp. 34, 196.
5. *Ibid.* (*Third Book of the Supervisors and Assessors*) (Poughkeepsie, 1911), pp. 38, 233.
6. *C.L.N.Y.*, III, 126.
7. *Ibid.*, p. 333.
8. *Documentary History of the State of New York*, ed. E. B. O'Callaghan (Albany, 1850), I, 62.
9. *C. L. N. Y.*, I, 132.
10. *Ibid.*, p. 237.
11. *Ibid.*, p. 456.
12. *Ibid.*, III, 126.
13. *History of the State of New York*, III, 72.
14. Stiles, *History of the City of Brooklyn*, I, 198.
15. *History of the State of New York*, III, 69, 71–72.
16. *C.L.N.Y.*, V, 585.
17. Joel Munsell (ed.), *Collections on the History of Albany, from Its Discovery to the Present Time* (Albany, 1865–71), I, 26.
18. *Ibid.*, pp. 5, 6, 7, 17.
19. *Ibid.*, p. 53.

20. *Ibid.*, p. 52.
21. Albany Common Council, *Minutes* (MS), III, 3-4.
22. *Eccles. Recs. N.Y.*, III, 1461-62.
23. *Ibid.*, III, 2148.
24. *Ibid.*, p. 2235; IV, 2337.
25. *Ibid.*, III, 2002-3.
26. *Records of New Amsterdam*, VI, 340, 348, 353.
27. *C.L.N.Y.*, I, 328-31.
28. North Hempstead, N.Y., *Records of the Towns of North and South Hempstead, Long Island, N.Y.* (Jamaica, 1896-1904), II, 310. Hereinafter referred to as *Records of North and South Hempstead.*

CHAPTER III

SETTLEMENT AND REMOVAL IN
COLONIAL NEW YORK

Settlement regulations during the English colonial period were largely modeled upon practices in the mother-country, although they did reflect in some measure problems indigenous to New York. The repressive settlement laws of England at the time of the capture of New Netherland dated back to the "Black Death" of 1349, which reduced the country's population by about one-third and resulted in great scarcity of labor. The famous "Statute of Labourers" enacted in 1350 was aimed at forcing laborers to stay in their own towns and work at wages arbitrarily fixed, thus preventing them from seeking wage increases justified by the existing labor scarcity. Severe penalties were imposed upon violators of the statute. An act of 1388, during the reign of Richard II, decreed that "beggars impotent to serve" must remain in the localities where they happened to be at the time of proclamation, provided they could be maintained there; otherwise they were to be returned to the villages of their birth. Against "sturdy vagabonds" and "valiant beggars" extraordinarily severe penalties were invoked, and through this act and succeeding ones a scale of graduated punishments was built up: public whipping for the first offense, loss of ears for the second, and hanging for the third. The branding of vagabonds was prescribed by an act of Henry VIII. With the progress of inclosure—the conversion of common fields into sheep pastures—large numbers of peasants were driven from the land and crowded the highways of England in search of new ways of life. Although these expropriated peasants were in no way responsible for the chaos which ensued, the repressive laws against vagrants were applied with increasing severity. The important Settlement Act of 1662, in the reign of Charles II, made it lawful for any parish to remove within forty days any newcomer occupying a tenement of less than ten pounds yearly rental value, on suspicion of being a potential parish charge.

It also provided for certification of laborers leaving their own parishes in search of employment.

In time provisions similar to those of the English Settlement Act of 1662 were embodied in the laws of New York. But years before the capture of New Netherland, the English towns on Long Island were forced by purely local circumstances to come to grips with problems of settlement. Apparently this region, separated by the Sound from New England proper, offered a convenient refuge for fleeing lawbreakers and a place of banishment for malefactors from the mainland towns. These individuals, in their search for sustenance, appear to have caused considerable trouble for the settled inhabitants of the area. The Long Island settlers received little aid from either the New England colonies or the New Netherland government in ridding their localities of these wanderers. Describing conditions in Suffolk County about 1650, Richard M. Bayles tells us: "In some towns, the people took the matter into their own hands and organized military companies to protect their villages against the approach of these marauding vagabonds."[1] But even such extraordinary measures did not succeed in solving the problem of keeping out undesirable strangers, and the towns of eastern Long Island, enjoying autonomous rule under the Dutch, were early constrained to adopt stringent settlement regulations as barriers against suspected delinquent and dependent newcomers. Inhabitants entertaining strangers were often required by the town to give security against the possibility of the newcomers' becoming public charges; sometimes they were forbidden to entertain any stranger whatever, with or without security. Until formally admitted as an inhabitant of a town, a newcomer might at any time be warned to depart by the authorities. This practice of "warning out" was one evidently adopted from the New England colonies with which it is especially identified. An early example of a qualified application of "warning out" is found in the records of the General Court of East Hampton, Long Island, for October 7, 1651: "Itt is ordered that Daniel Turner shall within the space of ffortnite eythe sojurne in some ffamily or bee a servant to some man or else Depart the towne."[2]

Four years later a stranger evidently suspected of mischievous propensities was given warning by the East Hampton authorities that he could remain in that town only if some inhabitant posted security for him: "It is Ordered that when Daniell ffairefelds time is Expired in May next with Goody Mulford that whosoever shall afterwards Entertaine him shal be bound in a bond of £20 for his good behavior & the sd Daniell after to be subject to ye Law."[3]

On June 13, 1678, the constable and overseers of the same town ordered "yt noe person in or belonging to this towne shall receive or Entertaine any person yt is alreadie come hither or yt shall hereafter come above one week unlesse they have license or libertie from the authority of this towne for ye same & yt uppone ye penaltie of paying five shillings a weeke for every weeke yt any house keper Doth entertain any such person or persons Contrarie to this order. . . . . "[4] A subsequent regulation voted by the town authorities in 1698 specified that the penalty should be levied only after the stranger had disregarded an order to depart, and that the fines collected should be devoted to the relief of the poor.[5]

The first province-wide provision of the English period relating to settlement was enacted in 1683 as a section of the first general poor law in New York. This section of the act was expressly designed "for the prevention and discourageing of Vagabonds and Idle persons to come into this province from other parts, and also from one part of the Province to another." It provided that any newcomer intending to settle within the province who had no visible estate or a "manuall craft or occupacon" must give sufficient security against his becoming a charge upon the desired place of settlement. This security must be posted for a period of two years before he could be admitted as an inhabitant. The act also declared that "if any Vagabonds, beggars or others, remove from one county to another and cannot give security as aforesaid itt shall be lawful for the constable to returne such persons to the county from whence they came." On the other hand, strangers having "manuall crafts or occupacon" could easily gain settlement. Such persons could "at all times come and inhabitt in any part within this Province & bee always admitted," the only requirement being that they must apply to the proper authorities for settlement within eight days after their arrival.[6]

Thus while the settlement of skilled workers and persons of means was encouraged, the poor unskilled laborer was looked upon with extreme suspicion, and every obstacle was placed in the way of his gaining a legal settlement. In every essential this act followed a pattern already in effect in the New England colonies. The section of the act of 1683 pertaining to settlement and removal was repeated in substance in 1691, and several times thereafter.

The problem of runaway bond servants must have been particularly troublesome at this time, for in 1685 the governor of the province, Thomas Dongan, found it expedient to issue an order against harboring strangers even more stringent than that issued by William Kieft during the Dutch period. Governor Dongan's order read:

Forasmuch as many Loos &nd Ydle persons do dayly run Away or Absent themselves from their service to ye Great prejudice both of this And the neighbouring Collonists to prevent the same, it is hereby ordered that no Inhabitant within this Government do Att any time Entertain or Lodge Any vagabond suspected persons or any whatsoeuer who cannot Give An account of themselves from where they came And whither they are Going or produce A certificate or pass from the Gouvernour or Magistrates of the place they came from.[7]

During this period various localities supplemented the provincial laws with settlement regulations of their own. These local regulations usually were modeled on laws already in effect in the mothercountry or in New England; some were later written into the New York provincial statutes. In March, 1683, the Common Council of New York City passed an ordinance requiring the constable of each ward and division within the city to carry on periodically a "Strict Search and Enquirey" within his district "after All Strangers that Shall Come Reside or Inhabitt" therein. Lists containing all the names of such strangers and other information concerning them were to be submitted to the mayor or, in his absence, to the eldest alderman, so that potential public charges could be removed before gaining settlement. Should a stranger be unreported for forty days after his arrival and then become a public charge upon the city, the cost of his relief was to be charged to the ward or division wherein he resided, and the constable was to pay a forfeit of twenty shillings for his failure to report the stranger.[8] The same ordinance, repeated almost word for word, was embodied in the by-laws of the city of Albany in 1686.[9]

The English-settled towns on Long Island, which were strongly influenced by New England attitudes and practices, displayed excessive suspicion toward strangers seeking residence in the community. The town of Southampton early enforced a regulation requiring newcomers to give to the town trustees or overseers of the poor written notice of their desire to gain settlement within forty days after their arrival. In 1705 a warrant was issued to the town constable charging that one Ebenezer Taylor had been "indeavoring to settle himselfe as an Inhabitant" without having given notice within forty days as required. The constable was directed to warn Taylor either to depart or to post security against his becoming chargeable to the town and to arrest him if he failed to comply.[10]

In 1721 an important addition was made to the provincial settlement laws with the enactment of a statute "to prevent Vagrant and Idle Persons from being a Charge and Expense to any the Counties, Towns, Mannors or Precincts within this Province."[11] The act made it mandatory for any householder entertaining a stranger for a period of three days to notify the mayor or a justice of the peace, giving the name, quality, condition and circumstances of the stranger. When the latter's character or economic standing was in doubt, the mayor or two justices of the peace were authorized to examine him. If he were found to be without sufficient means and likely to become a public charge, the local authorities were directed to order the constable to "Send the Said Stranger to the place from whence he or She last Came." The constable in turn was directed to

Deliver Such Stranger or Vagrant Person together with his Warrant, to Some Constable of the City, Town, Mannor or precinct of the place from whence he or She last Came; and so to be Carried from Constable to Constable, until the Said Stranger Shall be Carryed to Some place in which he or She has remained During the time of Forty Days, or untill Such person is Transported to the place of his or her Nativity, if within this Province, or into the Neighboring Colonies of Jersey, Connecticut, or Massachusetts bay, if from thence he or She Came.

Should the stranger have sojourned in a locality within the colony for forty days or more, the person or persons who had "entertained" him there were required to give security that he would not become a public charge. In case of failure to post such bond, the process of passing on the stranger from constable to constable was to be continued "till Transported to the place where he or she were born or out of the Province." The cost of transportation was to be charged to the county where the stranger had dwelt for forty days or more.

It is easy to see that the "passing-on" system, which was the common method of removing the nonresident poor in this country until well into the nineteenth century, entailed much hardship and humiliation for the victim. The law of 1721 contained a clause that would be hard to match for legal brutality even in that early day, except in the treatment of slaves. It provided that if any person removed from a locality because of the possibility of his becoming a public charge were to return to the place whence he had been removed, he was to be apprehended and retransported in accordance with the passing-on system, "and Shall by every Constable into whose charge the said Vagrant Shall come be Stripp't from the wast upwards & receive, if a man not exceeding Thirty one lashes, if a woman not exceeding Twenty five lashes on the bare back and so as often as he or She Shall return after Such Transportation."

From this time on, removal of persons actually or potentially destitute in provincial New York seems to have been of frequent occurrence. Local records of the period reveal many instances of the manner in which these removals were carried out. Several examples may be cited. In 1736 the supervisors of Orange County allowed "to Adrian Strought for whipping a man and conveying him away, £2," and "to Adolph Lent for conveying a Negro Wench out of the County by order of the Justices, 7 shillings." In 1741 George Coleman was paid one pound and nineteen shillings "for transporting of a vagabond man and watching him one night, and making a coat for said man by order of ye justices," and "also for transporting a vagabond woman and six other vagabonds, 7 shillings." James Fleet was allowed two shillings "for warning out two vagabonds by order of ye Justices."

Corporal punishment was inflicted upon the return of nonresident poor in connection with removal. This development probably reflected the fact that settlement problems were growing increasingly complex and irksome with the passage of years. Besides the whipping post, the stocks became a favorite form of punishing indigent wanderers. In 1755 Orangetown added stocks to its penal equipment, to be used in the punishment of vagrants and disorderly persons.[12] Forty shillings and two pence were assessed against the town of Yonkers for the construction of a whipping post and stocks in 1772; at the same time charges were allowed for transporting two women with three children each from the county. The constable of Cortlandt Manor had removed one of these families no less than three times—evidence perhaps that the itinerant poor were growing hardened to their lot.[13] The constable of another Westchester town, Rye, was allowed charges "for transporting of one Deborough Con sundry times, and her child."[14]

While nonresident persons likely to become public charges were customarily removed by means of the passing-on system through the colonies, the peculiar situation of New York City did not always permit such easy solution. Immigrants who had entered the country through New York, bound for some other part of the province, were often returned as paupers to the port of entry which was thus faced with the dilemma of maintaining them as public charges or sending them back to their native lands.* The port city was also a favorite "dumping-ground" for vagrants driven out of neighboring towns. It often proved more convenient and less expensive for the city to pay the transportation expenses of nonresident poor to their places of settlement, in the colonies or abroad, than to maintain them indefinitely as paupers. Numerous entries in the records of New York City attest to the frequency with which this expedient was adopted. The Common Council, on April 26, 1720, ordered "that in case James Lowry an Ancient Man do Transport himself to Bristol in the Eagle Brigantine now bound thither that this Corporation will pay to the Owners thereof towards his passage the sum of forty shillings he being A poor man and an Object of Charity."[15]

In the same year the churchwardens of the city were ordered to give to one-armed John Wilke six shillings "towards bearing his Charges to his Travell from this City towards Philadelphia" and

---

* As the tide of immigration rose and New York became the chief landing-place for immigrants in the United States, this problem of maintaining the foreign-born poor became so acute that, finally, in the nineteenth century the state and then the federal government were forced to intervene and to assume a major share of the responsibility so unjustly thrust upon the city.

eight shillings and six pence toward the transportation expenses of Ann Thorp and her three children to Woodbridge, New Jersey, where her husband lived. In 1721 forty shillings were granted to a poor widow, Sarah Meals, "to Enable her to Remove herself into the County of Albany where she designs to dwell in the future." In 1723 the churchwardens were authorized to grant Christian Tobias fifty shillings, providing "the said Christian Tobias & his wife & children transport themselves out of this Province in Vanhornes Vessell to Antegua without Delay that they be no longer a charge to the Parish."[16]

On September 18, 1730, the Mayor's Court ordered the churchwardens to supply one Daniel Richardson with "a pair of New Shoes, and Six Shillings in money to Enable him to travel to Bucks County in pensilvania to his two Sons and who Dwell there, he being old infirm not able to Labour for his Livelihood and an object of Charity." The money and the shoes were to be transmitted to Richardson through a constable who was directed to make certain that the old man left the city. The following entry in the *Minutes of the Mayor's Court* for December 2, 1735, shows how a blind dependent's passage to Great Britain was arranged for:

John Yorston, a blind Man, who hath been supported in the poor House of this City, upwards of four years, having made application to the Court, to pay for his passage to England, in order to return to his Relatives in Scotland, if he had wherewith to pay his passage: It is therefore Ordered that for the Ease and Relief of this Parish, that the Church Wardens do agree with Capt. Bryant or Capt. Smith for the Passage of the said John Yorston to England on the easiest Terms; and that they supply the said John Yorston, with necessary Cloathing and Bedding for his passage.[17]

The most comprehensive provincial law of settlement was enacted in 1773, on the very eve of the Revolution. This statute was evidently based on the English Settlement Law of 1662 to which we have alluded; some of its passages are word-for-word repetitions of this act. Indeed, the New York law of 1773 may well have been intended to protect New York City from the large number of indigent persons descending upon it from other parts of the province as well as from other provinces, just as the English Act of 1662 was intended in part to protect the city of London from vagrants.

A preamble to the act of 1773 explained that "the Laws of this Colony relating to the settlement and support of the poor, are very deficient and ineffectual for that purpose." The main provision of the act authorized local churchwardens or overseers of the poor to make complaint before two justices of the peace against a newcomer living in "any Tenement under the Yearly Value of five Pounds," and likely to become a public charge. Complaint had to be registered "within forty days after such Person or Persons shall come to settle in such Parish, Town Precinct or District." If the two justices (of whom one constituted a quorum) decided that the complaint was justified, they were authorized to issue a warrant "to remove and convey such person or persons to such Parish, Town Precinct or District where he or she or they were last legally settled either as a Native, Householder sojourner Apprentice or Servant for the space of forty Days at the least," unless sufficient security were posted against becoming a public charge in the locality. The stranger was given the right to appeal the decision of the justices of the peace.[18]

To preclude the possibility that newcomers might conceal themselves until the "probationary" period had passed and then emerge to claim settlement, the act directed that the forty days required for settlement should be counted only from the date on which a written notice of intent to settle, delivered by the newcomer to a churchwarden or overseer of the poor, should be entered "in the Book kept for the Poor Accounts." On their part, the overseers or churchwardens were bound to register such notices within forty-eight hours after receiving them. Proof of their neglect in this duty was punishable by a fine of forty shillings "for the use of the party grieved," or, in default of this, a jail sentence of twenty days.

Under no circumstance could a soldier or other common employee in the service of the Crown gain legal settlement until his discharge. A resident of any local area could gain legal settlement without complying with the written-notice provision if he performed the duties of some local public office for one year or if he paid his share of the local public taxes for two years. Single persons who were lawfully hired and who worked for one year in the same service were considered to have a settlement without necessity for written notice. Exemption from written notice was also allowed in the case of apprenticed persons, whether bound by indenture or by other written document. Churchwardens and overseers of the poor were required to receive persons who had been removed to their localities in accordance with the terms of the act, or to forfeit ten pounds to the poor fund of the area from which the removal was made.

Newcomers might secure undisturbed residence by delivering to the churchwardens or overseers a certificate signed by the corresponding officials in the place of their settlement attesting to the legality of such settlement. A certificated person, however, could not gain settlement by simple residence and was subject to removal whenever he might appeal for relief or become a public charge, unless in the meantime he had rented a tenement of five pounds minimum yearly rental value or had administered some public office for one year. Nor could the apprentice or hired servant of a certificated person gain settlement by virtue of his apprenticeship or service. The advantage of certification was that it provided the authorities of a town with an address to which, if removal appeared expedient, a newcomer might be sent without fear of subsequent litigation and legal costs.

Reasonable charges to cover costs of removal were to be paid by the locality to which removal was made. No appeal from an order of removal might be taken unless the churchwardens or overseers of the poor involved were given reasonable notice, and the justices of the peace were to determine whether notice in a given case was reasonable or not. Other provisions made it the duty of the justices at their General or Quarter Sessions to impose fines on the agents of "vexatious Removals and frivolous Appeals."

The importance of the settlement act of 1773 lay mainly in the fact that it laid down a comprehensive rule for gaining legal settlement. Previous settlement laws were in effect really laws of removal. The provisions embodied in that act were destined to govern the New York area not only for the two remaining years of the provincial period but, at least in substance, for more than twoscore years of statehood.

PROBLEMS OF THE IMMIGRANT POOR

The earliest attempt to regulate immigration in the province may be traced back to 1676, when the Common Council of New York City issued an order directing every master of a vessel entering the port to give an account of each passenger landing there. Masters violating this order were to be fined a "Merchandable Bever" for each passenger not accounted for.[19] This order probably was originally aimed at the detection of vagrants, criminals, and other suspicious characters, rather than at the exclusion of persons of small means who in other respects might be desirable colonists. The poor law of 1683 offered freedom of settlement to "all those that have manuall crafts or occupacon" on the mere condition that such persons apply for settlement within eight days after arriving in a given locality.

The same law contained a provision directing the captain of every vessel bringing passengers into the province to present within twenty-four hours after arrival a "list of all such passengers hee brings into this Province with their Qualityes & Condicons unto the Chiefe Magistrate of each respective Citty, County, Towne, aforesaid, under the penalty tenne pounds current money of this Province."[20] Should any passenger prove undesirable or unable to give security for his "well demeanor," the master of the vessel was obliged to transport him to the place whence he came, "or att least out of this Province and dependencies."*

Towns easily accessible to immigrants sometimes enacted local ordinances to regulate their entry and settlement. In 1688, for example, the town of Kingston on the Hudson issued the following ordinance, probably directed against undesirable immigration by way of New York City:

It is further enacted and ordered, that no manner of vessels shall be admitted to bring strangers from any other town or county, but shall give notice thereof to a constable where they are, and put in security for their maintenance; for want thereof such man shall be bound to take care for himself of his maintenance.[21]

---

* Massachusetts passed a similar law in 1700. It is interesting to note that in 1722, that province enacted another law imposing a fine of one hundred pounds upon masters failing to present lists of their passengers within twenty-four hours of casting anchor; the proceeds of such fines were assigned to the poor fund of the port.

New York City on November 18, 1731, adopted an ordinance entitled "A Law to Prevent Strangers from Being a Charge to This Corporation," which stated:

That if the Master of any Vessell or Boat shall Import any Strangers or Passengers into this City and do not in the Space of twenty-four hours After His Arrival give an Account of their Names to the Mayor for the time being, such Master shall forfeit forty Shillings for the said default.[22]

Long before New York entered statehood, immigration had brought in its wake a long train of hardships and injustices. A large proportion of immigrants entered this province and country as bond servants, bound out to masters for a prescribed number of years. Bond servants who had served out their terms usually received a tract of land and were supplied with essential equipment for pioneering. Neither by this class nor by any other, however, was the province of New York settled at a satisfactory rate at the beginning of the eighteenth century. To remedy the situation, Governor Lord Lovelace, and after him Governor Hunter, entered into a scheme to import, under what was virtually a mass bond-service contract, a body of peasants from the Palatinate, one of the German regions ravaged by French military invasion. The first consignment of these people arrived in 1709, and soon afterward Lord Lovelace was writing to England:

I have not yet been able to divide the lands among the poor German Protestants, the snow being upon the ground and no distinction can yet be made between profitable and unprofitable land. I have been forced to support them by my credit here, though I have not any directions about that matter from your Lordships, nor the Lords Commissioners of Trade, yet I hope your Lordships will please to order the payment of such bills.[23]

The British government ultimately granted £10,000 to be expended for further transportation, and consequently in 1711 between 3,000 and 4,000 Palatines were shipped into the province. Of these, 2,227 were sent about a hundred miles up the Hudson, while 357 remained in New York City. A third influx of Palatines occurred in 1722. In all, the mass emigrations from the Palatinate added nearly 10 per cent to the total population of the province.

The Palatines consigned to the borders of the Hudson in 1711 were settled in five villages—three on the east side of the river, on land belonging to the great Livingston grant, and two on the west bank, which was the property of the Crown. Governor Hunter contracted with the manorial proprietor to supply the new colonists with bread and beer.

Soon it was charged that Livingston was scrimping on the settlers' rations, that the land assigned to the Palatines was barren, and that certain sums of money promised the immigrants had not been paid. In retaliation, the Palatines refused *en masse* to perform any further labor on the ground assigned them. Governor Hunter, in an attempt to break what was probably the first strike of agricultural workers in the New York provincial area, went to the length of sending in troops to intimidate the settlers. The latter, who had had experience of military coercion in the land of their birth, remained unmoved. In July, 1712, Hunter stopped the bread and beer rations of all who refused to work, but in September he capitulated and revoked the contract binding the Palatines to service and notified them to shift for themselves. The loss to the promoters was £20,000.

The health problem constituted one important phase of immigration not yet touched upon. The wretched conditions of immigrant ships were most conducive to the development and spread of cholera, smallpox, and other diseases. The shipmasters of the time generally aimed to land their passengers as quickly and cheaply as possible, whether or not contagious or infectious disease was rife among them. It therefore became necessary for port authorities to protect the colonial population from the results of this unprincipled negligence. The process of protection evolved very slowly, however.

The Hudson Valley communities, perhaps because their viewpoint was less confused by the exigencies of commerce, seem to have recognized the need for protection sooner than New York City. As early as 1702, the city and county authorities of Albany issued a proclamation referring to the "great sickness and sudden death" then being visited upon New York City (which was in the throes of a serious epidemic), and prohibited persons to depart from Albany by "Sloop, Boat, Canoe, or other Vessell . . . . except it be an Expresse." The proclamation likewise forbade persons hailing from

New York to approach any closer to Albany than "ye Island called Bearen Island, twelve miles to ye south of this Citty, and there to remain till further order from us."[24]

A petition to the Common Council of New York City in 1710 declared that contagious diseases were present among arriving emigrants from the Palatinate and pleaded that the newcomers be prevented from landing within the borders of the city during the hot season. Apparently no notable quarantine provision was established by the port city, however, until 1738, when the Common Council took action against a threatened invasion of disease from the South Atlantic region:

> June 27, 1738, This Board having this day Received Informations that the small Pox was pritty Rife at south Carolina and that a purple or Spotted Feaver began to Spread there, It is Therefore Ordered that one of the Pilots for this Port be Constantly in waiting at or near sandy hook, and go on board all Vessels bound hether, and Acquaint all Masters Coming from Barbados, Antigua or south Carolina; that it is the Order of this Board, that before they Come into this Harbour, they first Anchor as near as may be to Bedlows Island, and there wait till they be Visited by some of the Physicians of this City, and not put on shoar any of the Goods or Persons on board, nor suffer any to Come on Board of them, but such as shall be sent by the Mayor to Visit them, untill Report be made to the Mayor of the Condition and State of health of the People on board, and untill he has leave to way Anchor and Come into the harbour and unload, And for the more Effectual prevention of the Small Pox or any other Infectious or Contagious distempers Spreading in or through any parts of this Province. . . . .
>
> Whereupon it is Ordered by this Court of Common Council that Dr. Roeliff Kersted be, and is hereby Appointed the Doctor and Physician to go on board such Vessels as shall Come into this Port Harbour or Bay to Visit the same, and to put the said Order of Council in Effectual Execution.[25]

Thus, a lower quarantine zone was established at a point not far from its present location, while Bedloe Island, where the Statue of Liberty now stands, was designated as Upper Quarantine. Later, in 1758, the city purchased Bedloe Island and began the erection of a hospital there for victims of contagious diseases.[26] Meantime, patients of this class had to be cared for in Manhattan. In 1760 the Bedloe Island structure was completed and all sick persons were removed to that place. There is extant a letter from Governor Colden to General Amherst, under date of May 26, 1762, in which the new facilities are mentioned: "The Mayor tells me that the Corporation have a house on Bedlow's Island of four rooms each of twenty feet square for the reception of the sick, and another House on the said Island where the Physicians & Surgeons may be accomodated."[27] The inspection of ships at Quarantine continued to be a function of New York City until 1755, at which time the province assumed exclusive charge of the procedure.

As has been stated, an adequate system of quarantine protection was slow in developing; and the next century, with its rising tides of immigration, was to bring recurrent calamities, disputes, and changes in responsibilities and technique.

SUMMARY

This chapter has traced the development of laws of settlement and removal patterned on English models as well as conditions of early immigration. The latter subject was to become increasingly associated with the problems of poverty, dependency, and public welfare with the passage of years. It is possible to adopt a more tolerant attitude toward the crude settlement laws and removal practices of our provincial forerunners when it is considered that these methods, instead of being mitigated and eliminated by their successors, were still in vogue hardly more than a century ago. The basic problems of settlement and removal even in our own day remain unsolved, often entailing a great deal of avoidable misery. As for immigration in its relation to poverty, dependency, and disease, the nineteenth century witnessed far more cruelty and misery in these respects than could have been dreamed of during the provincial period.

We now turn to other aspects of public welfare in provincial New York.

BIBLIOGRAPHICAL REFERENCES

1. Richard M. Bayles, *Historical and Descriptive Sketches of Suffolk County* (Port Jefferson, L.I., 1874), p. 21.
2. East Hampton, N.Y., *Records of the Town of East Hampton, Long Island* (Sag Harbor, N.Y., 1887), I, 15.
3. *Ibid.*, p. 93.
4. *Ibid.*, p. 421.
5. *Ibid.*, II, 412.

6. *C.L.N.Y.*, I, 132–33.

7. Quoted in *Olde Ulster* (a periodical), II (1908), 237, from the *Book of Deeds* in the Ulster County Clerk's Office, I, 19.

8. New York City Common Council, *Minutes of the Common Council of the City of New York, 1675 to 1776* (New York, 1905), I, 135. Hereinafter referred to as *N.Y.C., M.C.C., 1675–1776*.

9. Munsell, *Annals of Albany*, VII, 171.

10. Southampton, N.Y., *Records of the Town of Southampton* (Sag Harbor, N.Y., 1910), V, 93. Hereinafter referred to as *Records of the Town of Southampton*.

11. *C.L.N.Y.*, I, 56–61.

12. Frank B. Green, *History of Rockland County* (New York, 1886), pp. 47–48.

13. Stephen D. Horton, *Sixteen Nine to Eighteen Seventy: Early History of the Town of Courtland and the Village of Peekskill* (Peekskill, 1912), p. 23.

14. Charles W. Baird, *History of Rye: Chronicle of a Border Town, 1660–1870* (New York, 1871), p. 184.

15. *N.Y.C., M.C.C., 1675–1776*, III, 225.

16. New York City Mayor's Court, *Minutes*, February 7, 1720; January 18, 1720; May 9, 1721; April 2, 1723 (MS, in office of New York County Commissioner of Records). Hereinafter referred to as *N.Y.C., M.M.C.*

17. *Ibid.*, December 2, 1735.

18. *C.L.N.Y.*, V, 513–22.

19. *N.Y.C., M.C.C., 1675–1776*, I, 10.

20. *C.L.N.Y.*, I, 132.

21. Marius Schoonmaker, *History of Kingston, New York* (New York, 1888), p. 185.

22. *N.Y.C., M.C.C., 1675–1776*, IV, 80.

23. *Eccles. Recs. N.Y.*, III, 1720.

24. Munsell, *Annals of Albany*, IV, 149.

25. *N.Y.C., M.C.C., 1675–1776*, IV, 429–30.

26. *Ibid.*, VI, 124.

27. "The Colden Letter Books," in New York Historical Society, *Collections for the year 1676*, "Publication Fund Series" (New York, 1877), IX, 210.

CHAPTER IV

THE PATCHWORK OF PROVINCIAL RELIEF

The provincial laws relating to the poor were largely "preventive" in character, concerned mainly with keeping indigent or potentially indigent persons from gaining settlement, rather than with the actual relief of dependency. Poor-law administration in the province was lacking in uniformity, and in clarity, for that matter. It is significant that the laws invariably were drawn up for particular cities or counties and were studded with exemptions; general poor laws were rare. The administration of poor relief differed in many parts of the province in accordance with the varied backgrounds and needs of the inhabitants. Statutes attempting to regulate certain aspects of public welfare were frequently disregarded by localities where circumstances made it more convenient to adopt a contrary system.* In many districts where the population was sparse and widely scattered, it was not necessary to adopt any definite poor-relief system, since occasions for relieving dependency were so few. Each case requiring public relief was dealt with independently as it arose, in a more or less haphazard manner.

Reports sent by various provincial governors to the mother-country, particularly in the last quarter of the seventeenth century, give the impression that the poor-relief problem in New York was negligible indeed. Governor Andros in 1678 informed the Lords of Trade in London that there were no beggars and that all the poor in the province were cared for. Eight years later Governor Dongan reported to the same body: "Every Town & County are obliged to maintain their own poor, which makes them bee soe careful that noe Vagabonds, Beggars, nor Idle Persons are suffered to live here."[1] Replying to a suggestion made by the Board of Trade and Plantations that a workhouse be erected in New York City, Governor

---

* For example, the explicit directions in the Duke's Laws of 1665 ordering each locality to elect eight overseers and two churchwardens were ignored by a number of towns within the area covered by the ducal code.

Bellomont in 1699 expressed amusement at the idea, assuring the Board that "there is no such thing as a beggar in this town or country." We must take these statements with a grain of salt, of course, since they were written by men defending their administration and trying to paint the condition of the province in as rosy a hue as possible. Nevertheless, we may safely assume that poor-relief problems really did not reach any large proportions during the early colonial years. As the population increased and the social life grew more varied, these problems became more complex and the need for a permanent, carefully regulated poor-relief policy became more acute. When the Dutch surrendered the colony in 1664, the population was estimated at less than 12,000. In 1720 the estimate was 31,000; in 1731 it was 50,289; in 1771, 168,007. At the end of the Revolution it was given as 233,896.[2]

In spite of the harsh attitude manifested toward strangers, the relief of dependent persons actually settled in a locality was often characterized by generosity and neighborly warmth. Largely because of the rigid restrictions on settlement, persons dependent on the freeholders for support were few in the early days, and the cases that could be considered "unworthy" were fewer still. We are told that the town of East Hampton had for many years but one pauper, a woman friendless and alone. This single dependent was well cared for by the town, and when she subsequently fell sick the townspeople, who had no physician in the community, obtained medical attention for her from New York City and near-by towns, continuing their humane aid over a long period and at great expense.[3]

The English settlements on Long Island, as has been noted, enjoyed autonomous government for some years prior to the first surrender of New Netherland in 1664. Their methods of relieving the poor were simple and direct, as exemplified by an entry in the "First Book of Purposes" of the town records of Oyster Bay in 1661:

All we whose names are heare under writen doe hereby Ingage our sellves that we will give frely towards the maintenans of the widdow croker so much Indian Corne for a yeare beginning at the first Day of February 1661 and to end the first of February 1662 previded we may be no more troubled with her more then the rent of the hous and that there be a person appointed to receiv it and to look to it and her that it may not be wasted. . . . .[4]

Fifteen freeholders of the town pledged to contribute from one to three bushels of corn each toward the widow Croker's relief. A year later, it appears, a tax was levied on all freeholders, "according as they have lots and rights in the Towne," for the maintenance of the poor widow.

Relief in kind was commonly practiced in many other parts of the province in those days, even in the city of New York. The accounts of Southampton for 1696 reveal how the town's first dependent, John Earl, was relieved in kind:[5]

> March ye 19th 1696. Account.
> Abraham Howell 12 loads of wood for Earl... 1 lb. 10s.
> To half a bushel of wheat.................. 3s.
> To 1½ bushels of corn...................... 7s.
> To a barrel of pork for Earl.............. 3 lbs.
> Ellis Cook for a Steer for Earl............. 4 " 3s.

The practice of boarding out paupers was also frequently resorted to in provincial New York. Thus, the town records of Huntington in the mid-eighteenth century contain such items as: "paid to ye widow Esther Titus for Sarah Chichester, 2 pounds, 6s., 8d."; and "to Nath Wickes for keeping Mary Gunnery, 4 pounds."[6] In 1771, the south precinct of Dutchess County (now Putnam County) paid a lump sum of 23 pounds to John Ryder for caring for the three-year-old orphans, Abigail and Levina Discomb, until they should "arrive to the age of eighteen years." In return for this payment, Ryder promised "to save the Precinct harmless from any further charge that may happen by said children" in the interim.[7] Before the poor law of 1773 made it mandatory for persons within certain degrees of consanguinity to provide for dependent relatives, paupers were often boarded out at public expense with their own parents, sisters, brothers, etc. In 1753, for instance, a blind dependent of Oyster Bay is recorded as being maintained by her father at the town's expense.[8]

Sometimes, when there were no permanent poorhouses, houses were hired temporarily to shelter the town's paupers. The practice of hiring a house for the poor was established in Southampton in 1724 and was continued for some years until the town secured an almshouse of its own.[9] The same custom, as will be shown, was followed in New York City for many years.

While certain aspects of provincial poor relief reflect a kindly and neighborly spirit, the prevailing attitude toward dependency was stern, cold, and strait-laced. In some parts of the province, a peculiarly harsh custom was adopted for branding the recipient of public relief with an unmistakable stigma. We refer to the practice of forcing the dependent to wear a badge of pauperism conspicuously upon his person, a custom derived from the mother-country. In 1696 a statute was enacted in England directing that each person receiving relief must wear on the shoulder of his right sleeve a badge or mark with a large letter "P," signifying "pauper," together with the initial of his parish. If the said pauper were a married man, his wife and children were also required to wear this pauper badge, to be cut in red or blue cloth. The same act authorized any justice of the peace to punish a poor person refusing to wear such badge by ordering his relief allowance reduced, suspended, or withdrawn altogether, or else to commit him to the house of correction, there to be whipped and kept at hard labor for a term not exceeding twenty-one days.[10]

A decade after the passage of this English statute, the city of New York adopted a similar method for deterring dependency. The Common Council, in 1707, decreed that "The Church Wardens of this City put A Badge upon the Cloths of such poor as are Clothed by this City with this Mark N:Y in blew or Red Cloath att their discretion."[11] That this practice survived late in the provincial period is indicated by the action taken at a town meeting at Oyster Bay held on April 1, 1755, when James Sands was "Chosen to Inspect Into the Poor and to See the Letter P: Sett on there garment as a Token of there Being Supported by ye Town."[12]

POOR-RELIEF DEVELOPMENTS IN NEW YORK CITY

The unsteady, trial-and-error character of the development of colonial poor relief was nowhere so evident as in New York City, especially during the first quarter-century of English government.

Under Dutch rule, relief had been administered mainly through the congregational plan, with very little supervision by the civil authorities. In the score of years following the Dutch surrender, relief was dispensed in a haphazard manner, while authority for raising and disbursing poor funds remained vague and ill-defined. The provisions of the poor law of 1683, attempting to establish a uniform, secularized administrative pattern for the province, do not appear to have had any noticeable effect on the relief policy, or rather on the lack of such policy, in New York City. In November, 1683, the municipal authorities sent a petition to Governor Dongan explaining the government of the city and recommending certain changes. They suggested, among other things, that overseers of the poor be elected, besides aldermen, in each of the six wards into which the city was divided. Governor Dongan approved of their plan, but the inhabitants do not appear to have carried it out. Consequently, Dongan found it necessary in 1685 to address a letter to the Common Council recommending that it take measures for the relief of the local poor.[13]

The Common Council responded in October of that year by directing the city aldermen to certify to the mayor the names of persons in their respective wards who "are poore and Wanting almse for their Susteanance," so that the operation of relief might be expedited. But the situation remained in an unsatisfactory, indefinite state, for in February, 1688, the Common Council again urged the aldermen to make inquiries in their several wards concerning persons in need of relief and to present lists of such persons to the mayor. It was also ordered that the latter "Doe Releve the poore as hee hath don fformerly Vntill ffurther Ordor."[14] This arrangement seems to have placed an intolerable burden on the mayor, for two weeks later, on February 26, the Common Council made an important change in the administration of relief. It directed that thereafter the aldermen and the assistant aldermen were to "provide for theire poore in their Owne Ward & Bee paid out of ye Publick Tresury for what they disburst uppon ye Said accompt."[15] This practice of making the ward the relief unit in the city and charging the alderman with the double duty of certifying and relieving dependents in his own ward was to be revived from time to time during the succeeding centuries, with political consequences that may easily be imagined.

The raising of adequate relief funds through a central authority
proved so difficult that in January, 1690, the Common Council, noting the absence of sufficient funds to meet the current relief needs,
ordered the constables to collect voluntary offerings for poor relief
from the residents of their respective wards.[16]

An attempt was made to establish some semblance of order in the
municipal administration of relief in December, 1691, when two
aldermen, Johannes Kip and Teunis de Kay, were appointed as overseers of the poor who were empowered to act jointly in disbursing
relief to all persons deemed "objects of charity."[17] It appears, however, that the other aldermen continued to administer relief to the
poor in their several wards from their own purses until reimbursed
from the municipal treasury. Relief at this time was customarily
given in the home in cash. A typical relief item from the city records
dated September 17, 1691, reads:

Ordered that the Two Woemen and two Children without the gate in the
House of John de La Vall the one called Topknott Betty the other one Stillwells
wife with the Children be prouided for as Objects of Charity & that four
Shillings a weeke bee allowed them for one months time.[18]

On the same day, the Common Council directed that three
shillings per week be paid to Mrs. Arthur Strangwich for the maintenance of her husband who was "an object of charity." An identical
weekly sum was ordered to be paid to a landlady for maintaining
"the Widow Barbery," also an object of charity.

In 1693 the city came under the Act for Settling a Ministry. This
statute provided for raising a maintenance for a Protestant ministry
in the southern part of the province (with the Anglican church im-
plicitly favored) and also for a poor rate. Poor relief was to be administered by ten vestrymen and two churchwardens to be elected
by the freeholders. It does not appear that the terms of the act
were carried out in New York City at the time. In 1695 the city
experienced a critical emergency, and a temporary measure was enacted by the provincial assembly entitled "An Act to Enable the
City of New York to Relieve the Poor and defray their necessary
and Publick charge." The preamble referred to the great distress of
the poor together with the fact that the city's public buildings were
in a sad state of repair and "the highways streets and Lanes so

Mirey and foul that they are Noysome to the Inhabitants of the said City as well as of his Majesties Liege Subjects resideing and travelling to and from the same," principally because no annual fund was being raised for these matters.[19] The statute provided for the annual appointment by the Common Council of "five good and Sufficient Citizens . . . . who shall be called overseers of the Poor and Public works and buildings." The overseers were empowered to raise an annual public tax for the public charges and for "the necessary reliefs of the Same impotent, old blind and such others being Poor and not able to work &c." We might infer from the dual responsibilities of the overseers and the fact that poor relief and public works are mentioned together, that a public work-relief program was intended by this statute, although this intention is never made explicit in the wording of the law.

The Common Council named five overseers, as specified. Only four responded, however, and for some unexplained reason the Council failed to fill the existing vacancy. Directed to take a census of public dependents in the city and to estimate the poor rate needed for the following year, the overseers reported a rate of £100 for poor relief. But attempts to raise this sum through taxes proved unsuccessful, and during the year the overseers were forced to draw upon other city funds and to accept an advance of £10 from one of the aldermen, Jacobus van Cortlandt, in order to meet relief needs.*

In 1702, the first year of Queen Anne's reign, a great epidemic of yellow fever broke out in New York City, causing the death of about five hundred inhabitants out of a total population of approximately forty-four hundred. This precipitated an emergency situation in poor relief. The city found itself bound by the provincial statutes limiting the annual poor rate to about £150, which had to be fixed on a certain day in the year. The fixed maximum was grossly inadequate to meet the crisis resulting from the epidemic, and the city fathers appealed to the legislature for aid. The assembly thereupon passed an "Act for the better Support and Maintenance of the

---

* A scarcity of flour and a rise in bread prices in 1696 caused the poor of the city to petition the authorities for aid. It was at this point that the municipality was forced to seek a loan of ten pounds from one of its richest citizens, Alderman van Cortlandt, to relieve the poor "in their Present Necessity" (*Minutes of the Common Council, 1675-1776*, I, 426, 429).

Poore in the City of New York for the future," stating in the preamble that

the Mayor, Aldermen and Common Council of the City of New York, have represented unto the General Assembly of this province, that in the late Calamitous Distemper, which it please Almighty God to afflict the Inhabitants of the said City, the number and necessitys of the Poor were much increased; and the Sum of Money raised for the mainteinance of the Poor in the said City, was farr short of giving them a necessary Support in this Emergency.[20]

The act empowered the city authorities to raise special tax levies for relief purposes at any time in the year, should an emergency arise, instead of fixing the poor rate at a given time of the year, as previously required. The maximum poor rate permitted to New York City, which formerly had been restricted to a part of £300 allowed for all public charges, was raised to £300, with the proviso that the act was to be enforced for a limited period not exceeding two years.*

About this time a vigorous movement was in progress to give the Church of England a favored footing as the established church in New York City and elsewhere in the province. The city had previously resisted attempts to supersede the civil poor-relief authorities with vestrymen and churchwardens as had been ordered in the law of 1693 for settling a ministry. Now, however, the overseers of the poor disappeared from the picture. In the early 1700's it was the Common Council (and later the Mayor's Court) which, with the Anglican churchwardens and vestrymen, formed the administrative body in the municipal relief system.† The Dutch Reformed and Lutheran deaconry, as already indicated, continued to be responsible for their respective congregational poor. The vestrymen were mainly responsible for levying the poor rate and supervising its collection. The churchwardens were charged with the actual distribution of the poor funds, usually upon specific orders from the Mayor's Court. Appeals for aid were made to the Mayor's Court, and if applicants were considered deserving, the wardens were given specific

---

* The poor rate rose steadily during the colonial period, reaching several thousand pounds in the later years.

† At first ten vestrymen were elected, but after 1745 there were fourteen, two being chosen from each ward.

instructions as to their relief. The Mayor's Court, an institution set up under Governor Nicolls in the cities of New York and Albany, consisted simply of the mayor and aldermen sitting as a court rather than as a legislative body.

In November, 1713, the justices and vestrymen of New York City informed the Common Council "that the poor of the said City are perishing for want of Cloths and Provisions and that there is an Absolute Necessity for their Speedy relief." This emergency was met through the flotation of a loan of £100 for a period of six months, in anticipation of taxes. Early in the same year a list of the city's poor had been entered in the minutes of the Mayor's Court.[21] It comprised less than a score of names and probably represented only those dependents who were considered permanent cases, since other entries at this time show many unlisted persons as recipients of relief for temporary periods.

A minor crisis in municipal poor relief occurred in November, 1720, when the churchwardens informed the Mayor's Court that funds were lacking to pay the minister's salary "or to Supply the dayly Occasions of the Poor," and that they—the churchwardens— had "disburst and Expended upwards of fifteen pounds of their own Moneys to preserve several Poor People from Perishing." In this instance the Court ordered that the churchwardens continue to disburse their own funds until a tax could be levied, and that they be repaid with interest from the receipts.[22]

Other crises more or less severe came in 1741, 1753, and during and after the French and Indian War which ended in 1763. The difficulties of 1741 seem to have been occasioned largely by a particularly severe winter,* and gave rise to a notable venture in voluntary relief. Notices published in the *New-York Weekly Journal* during the month of January, 1741, indicate that a fund of £500 was raised for the poor and placed for disbursement in the hands of Abraham Lefferts and Abraham van Wycke, who probably constituted the

---

* "The winter of 1740–41 was remembered for many years as the 'Hard Winter.' The intense cold continued from the middle of November to the close of March. The snow was six feet on a level, the Hudson was frozen at New York, and great suffering was felt among the poor" (Mary L. Booth, *History of the City of New York* [New York, 1867] I, 353–54).

first citizens' emergency relief committee in the city. These gentlemen proposed to make their headquarters at the house of Nicholas
Roy, "opposite to the late Black Horse Tavern," three mornings
each week, and there receive the applications and attend to the
needs of the poor. The utmost discretion was promised respecting
the relief of "any Credible Families [who] are in real Want, and
scruple to make it known."

The hardships of 1753 were caused by the efforts of the city
merchants to check the import of English half-pennies; they refused
to accept such coins save at a reduced value. As a result, the poor,
who probably had few enough half-pennies of any kind to start with,
found their ability to buy essential goods seriously impaired. Clubs
and staves were flourished with much abandon in a protest demonstration which followed; the threat of violence was serious enough
to warrant a grand jury investigation.[23]

Poverty must have increased markedly in the city during the
French and Indian War. In January, 1759, the *New York Gazette*
carried news of "a very considerable Collection" having been made
for the poor, "all the necessaries of life at this time being at a much
higher price than was ever known in this City." In January, 1765,
it was necessary to borrow £200 from the general tax fund to carry
on poor relief, the money raised for this purpose having been completely expended. During the same month the *New York Gazette or
Weekly Post-Boy* noted the existence of a severe post-war depression:

The declining state of business in the city together with the high rents and
prices of the necessaries of life, having reduced very many families and poor
people generally to great distress especially since the late severe weather, contributions for their relief have been made by several humane gentlemen.

An order of the Common Council dated May 6, 1767, shows that
the distress of the past year had made it necessary to hire at least
two extra dwelling-houses for the care of the poor.[24]

RISE OF INSTITUTIONAL RELIEF IN PROVINCIAL NEW YORK

The English poor law of 1601 (43 Elizabeth, c. 2), which served
as the foundation for the general poor-relief policy in Great Britain
and the American colonies, made a distinction between three classes
of dependents: those who cannot work, those who have no employ-

ment though they are willing and able to work, and those who will not work. Out of this distinction there developed a threefold system of institutional provision for dependents: (1) the poorhouse, for the "impotent" poor; (2) the workhouse, for the able-bodied poor who were "worthy"; and (3) the house of correction, for the able-bodied poor who were "unworthy," that is, the types then known as valiant rogues and sturdy beggars.*

While these three institutional types were clearly defined in theory, no marked distinction was maintained in practice. In most instances it was highly impractical for a town to construct three separate institutions, or even two. A workhouse might be used as a place of punishment for vagrants and other "unworthy" able-bodied poor and as a place for setting the "worthy" able-bodied poor to work. Sometimes it housed the latter and the impotent poor; occasionally it included all three types of dependents under its roof. It was this combination workhouse, poorhouse, and house of correction that was finally adopted in New York City.

Under Dutch rule there had been several poorhouses in the colony maintained by the Dutch Reformed church for its indigent members. There was apparently no stigma attached to inmates of these institutions, who were regarded as worthy poor. These congregational almshouses continued to function for many years after the colony came under British hegemony. In 1701 the consistory of the Dutch church in New York City auctioned off its old poorhouse in Broad Street, which had become dilapidated, and built a new one at the present site of 37 Wall Street.[25] In a petition requesting the incorporation of the Dutch church of Albany, presented to the provincial authorities in 1720, it is stated that the congregation had "purchased Certain two Tenements and Lotts of ground for a poor or alms house, and for a Minister's dwelling house."[26] However, it was not until 1735 that the first poorhouse under civil auspices was built in the province. Quite naturally, it was located in the most populous town, New York City. The erection of this institution was the culmination of a development dating back many years.

Institutional provision for the able-bodied poor had been recom-

* It should be noted that workhouses and houses of correction (or bridewells) existed in England prior to the enactment of the Elizabethan poor law.

mended in instructions couched in identical language, sent by the Crown to Governor Benjamin Fletcher in 1692 and to Governor Richard Bellomont in 1697: "You are to endeavour with the assistance of the Councill to provide for the raising and building of Publick Work houses in convenient Places for the employing of Poor and Indigent People."[27]

But on April 27, 1699, Lord Bellomont reported to the Lords of Trade:

A Bill to enforce the building of publick workhouses (which is another instruction from his Majesty) to imploy the poor and also vagabonds I offered to the Assembly, but they smiled at it, because indeed there is no such thing as a beggar in this town or country; and I believe there is not a richer populace any where in the King's dominions than is in this Town.[28]

In 1714, however, the Common Council appointed a committee "to Consult with the Mayor about the building of a poorhouse and house of Correction in this City" and to "Consider of A Convenient place to Erect the same, of the Demensions and Materialls and of ways & Means for Raising a fund for the compleating thereof."[29]

No record of the committee's report has been found; perhaps it was never made. Certain it is that the idea of constructing a permanent institution for paupers and vagrants was dropped for the time being. Instead, the city adopted the policy of sending indigent persons to a private dwelling-house, the mistress or keeper of which was paid for receiving and maintaining the poor. Thus, though the city as yet had no municipal poorhouse, a congregate method of housing public dependents was introduced. In August, 1714, one Samuel Garratt, being "very Sick and weak,"was ordered into "the poorhouse" by the Mayor, and the Mayor's Court directed that he be supported "untill he be able to work for his living," and that the churchwardens pay the "woman of the poor house for his Support hitherto."[30]

It appears that the first "poor house woman" was one Elizabeth Burger. On July 5, 1715, the churchwardens were ordered to pay "to Elizabeth Burger Keeper of the poor house Six pounds New York Money for Supplying her with necessaries for the use of the poor and for her Care and trouble about them for one year."[31] The greater part of the poor continued to be maintained by relief in their own homes as before. It seems likely, from the records, that the population of the poorhouse at this time consisted almost exclusively of the friendless and helpless for whom the incidental care available in ordinary private dwellings would not be adequate.

The need for municipal institutions for the dependent and misdemeanant classes was more keenly felt as time went on and the population continued to increase. The charter of 1730 recognized this need by empowering the city to construct an almshouse and one or more houses of correction and workhouses.[32] Four years later the Common Council voted favorably on a resolution authorizing the erection of a building to serve all three purposes "on the unimproved Lands of this Corporation on the North Side of the lands of Coll. Dongan, Commonly Called the Vineyard," which lay near the site of the present City Hall.[33]

THE FIRST POOR HOUSE OPENED IN 1736

In March, 1736, the institution was completed and was given the all-embracing name of "House of Correction, Workhouse and Poor House." It was a two-story structure, 65 feet by 24, built of stone. In the same month plans for its operation were drawn up, and a committee of the Common Council was appointed "to enquire upon what terms this corporation may hire an able and sufficient person to be keeper of the House of Correction and overseer of the workhouse and poorhouse."

In order to set "such poor to work as are able to labour and to prevent their being a Charge and Burthen to the Publick by sloth and Idleness and for Carrying on Trades, Occupation and Manufactures," the committee, in its report, recommended:

That the said house of correction Workhouse and poorhouse be furnished with all convenient speed with the following Tools and Utensils (to witt) four spinning wheels one or two large wheels for making of shoes, two pairs of wollen cards, some knitting Needles, twelve pounds of Flax, 500 pounds of old Junck, twelve pounds of wool, twelve pounds of Cotton, two or three Hatchells, and such other Tools, Utensils and Furniture as for the future shall be found needful and necessary from time to time. . . . .[34]

John Sebring was selected as the first superintendent. His salary was fixed at £30 annually, with board for himself and his family. He was responsible to the city churchwardens who were in turn responsible to the vestrymen and justices of the peace. His duties, as defined by the Common Council, were to

sett on Work all such poor as shall be sent or committed thither and able to labour; and also all disorderly persons, parents of Bastard Children, Beggars, Servants running away or otherwise misbehaving themselves, Trespassers, Rogues, Vagabonds, poor persons refusing to work, and on their refusal to work and labour to correct them by moderate Whipping, and to yield a true Account to Every General Quarter Sessions of the peace to be held for this City and County of all persons committed to his custody, and of the offences for which they were committed.[35]

Slaveholders might send slaves to the institution to be whipped; the lashing was administered at a fee of one shilling and sixpence. Fetters, gyves, shackles, and facilities for applying the lash were suggested as necessary equipment for the house of correction. Elementary education and industrial training in preparation for apprenticeship in some useful trade were recommended for such destitute children as might be sent to the almshouse for maintenance. In this respect the committee's attitude appears far more enlightened than that manifested in the average almshouse of a later time. And if "the westermost division of the Cellar" was chosen for the confinement of the unruly, the committee did not hesitate to say that "the upper Room at the west End of the said House should be suitably furnished for an Infirmary and for no other Use whatsoever." This infirmary gradually developed into a separate hospital, later becoming the great city institution known as Bellevue Hospital. On the basis of these modest beginnings, some historians claim for Bellevue the distinction of being the oldest public hospital in this country. The first physician appointed for the almshouse was Dr. John van Buren who held office for thirty years at a salary of £100 yearly, out of which he paid for all needed medicines.[36]

In 1739 a separate structure was erected in order to shelter destitute victims of contagious diseases. Other additions to the combination poorhouse–workhouse–house of correction were subsequently made during the provincial period.

Following the erection of the poorhouse in New York City, similar institutions were built in other parts of the province. A provincial statute enacted in 1747, applying only to Dutchess County, authorized local overseers of the poor in that county to hire or erect dwellings for setting the able-bodied poor to work, and to purchase materials for that purpose. The legislature passed acts of a like nature for other counties. It is notable that all these statutes provided for the establishment of workhouses and poorhouses by individual towns and precincts. The English system of town or district unions for the maintenance of mutually controlled institutions was introduced at a relatively late date in the colonies. Massachusetts authorized town unions for the support of workhouses in 1743. With but one exception, relating to the care of the insane during colonial times, the system was not introduced in New York until the nineteenth century.

CHILD WELFARE

The system of apprenticeship formed the cornerstone of child welfare in provincial times. As a part of the poor-relief policy in New York, it may be traced back to both the English poor law of 1601 and the Dutch practice which has been described in chapter i. The records of Southampton for 1694 contain the following item illustrating the practice of binding out children in groups:

At a meeting of ye Trustees ye 14 of June did then order that according to ye directions of ye Justices to take care of the poore and orphans within our parish, and the children of Thomas Reeves and Ben Davis deceased being both fatherless and motherless, that Isaac William and Aaron Burnatt do bond out said orphans, According on ye 15th day were five of the said orphans bound out. . . . .[37]

In the event of misfortune which temporarily prevented the support of children by their parents, the authorities might relieve the family in its home or they might place the children in other hands until the parents were again able to care for them. In the case of a prisoner (probably a debtor) who petitioned for relief for his family, the Common Council of New York ordered, under date of February 27, 1694, "that the Overseers of the Poor doe put out the Children of the Said Petitioner in Some Good Reputable Families for their Subsistance dureing his Imprisonment."[38] In January, 1719, the Mayor's Court directed that: "The Church Wardens Inspect in what Condition the Widow & Children of Thomas Grisson are in at The Bowry and if they find Their Children Objects of Charity that they Relieve them at Their Discretions or putt them out Apprentice for a Term of Years."[39]

Throughout the provincial period, dependent and neglected children were commonly disposed of by apprenticeship or indentured servitude. When a boy was bound out, it was specified as a rule that his master should teach him to read, write, and cipher. Thus when Justus Whitfield was apprenticed by order of the New York Common Council on May 24, 1720, "to Learn the Art of a Marriner," his prospective master, one Jasper Busk, was "to Provide him with Meat Drink & Apparell to learn him to Read Write and Cypher & to give him two good New Suites of Apparell at the Expiration of the Term."[40] Justus was to have thirteen years in which to learn his art, since he was apprenticed at the age of eight years. From the records of Amenia in Dutchess County we learn that boy apprentices in that town commonly received at the end of their service a beaver hat, "two good new suits," a new Bible, and "twenty Pounds York money in neat cattle or sheep to be appraised by Indifferent men." Girl apprentices were supplied with two suits of clothes, a new cloak and bonnet, a Bible, and "30 Pounds of good live Geese feathers."[41]

Children might be indentured at any age up to twenty-one. A New York order for apprenticeship in 1726 names George Williams, aged four years, and an order of a year earlier designated apprentice-

This Indenture Made the Sixteenth day of July Anno Domini one thousand Seven Hundred Sixty Eight Witnesseth that Conrad Winneger and Sim Wright two of the Overseers of the Poor of Amenia Precinct in Dutchess County and Province of New York by and with the Consent of Daniel Castle and Roswell Hopkins Esq two of his majestys Justices of the Peace for Said County by Virtue of a Law of this Colony in that Case made Provided hath placed and Bound Isaac Osborn Son of John Osborn Late of Amenia Precinct aforesaid Deceased Apprentice unto Colbe Chamberlain of Said Precinct farmer with him to Dwell Continue and Serve from the Date hereof until he Shall Attain the full and Compleat age of Twenty One years During all which Term the Said Apprentice his Said Master well and faithfully Shall Serve his Secrets keep his Lawful Commands gladly Do and Obey Harm to his Said Master he Shall not Do nor willfully Suffer to be Done by others the goods of his Said Master he Shall not Imbezil or waste nor them lend without his Consent to any at Cards Dice or any other unlawful Games he shall not play Taverns he Shall not frequent fornication he shall not Committ Mattrimony he Shall not Contract from the Service of his Said Master he Shall not Depart at any time

From the "Amenia (Dutchess Co.) Precinct Book for the Poor, A.D. 1760–1820" (MS)

A COLONIAL INDENTURE FORM, 1768

Service of his Said Master he Shall not Depart at any time or absent himself without his Said Masters Leave but in all things as a good and faithfull Apprentice Shall & will Demean and behave Himself towards his Said Master and all his During Said Term And the Said Master Doth hereby Covenant agree and Promise to find and allow unto his Said Apprentice Sufficient Meat Drink washing and Lodging and all other Necessaries fit and Convenient for Such an apprentice During Said Term and Shall and will Learn and Instruct Said Apprentice to Read write and Cypher So as to be able to keep Book and at the End and Expiration of Said Term Shall and will find Provide and Allow and Deliver unto his Said Apprentice two Suits of apparel good and new the one Suit fit for the Holy Days and the other Suit fit for the working Days and twenty Pounds york money in Cattle to be appraised by Indifferent men and a new Bible In witness whereof the Parties these Presents have hereunto Set their hands and Seals the Day and year first above written

Sealed and Delivered
    In the Presence of

Ichabod Rogers
Mich: Hopkins

Cornelius Dürreyer
Simeon Wright

Dutchess County ſſ July 16: 1768 we the
Subscribers two of his majestys Justices of the
Peace for Said County Do hereby Consent to the
Binding the above named poor Child apprentice
witness our Hands

Alec Chaam_____
Jemial Castle

Richard   his

ship as an alternative for Joseph Byng, "an Infant Aged Eighteen Months or thereabouts," the son of a felt-maker confined in the common jail.[42] Occasionally, as has been observed, a group of dependent children were offered for apprenticeship at one time. On June 11, 1750, the *New York Gazette or Weekly Post-Boy* printed a notice to the effect that several children of age ten or less, available for apprenticeship, were at the almshouse.

While the indenture system offered by far the best means of disposing of dependent and neglected children, the lot of apprentices was generally a hard one, and the rights given them by law were frequently disregarded in the absence of public supervision. The records reveal, however, that the authorities occasionally put their foot down in instances of flagrant violations of such rights. On August 21, 1716, the Mayor's Court of New York ordered Peter Ament, a cooper, to appear for his examination regarding the charge that he failed to supply his apprentice with sufficient clothing. The complaint had been made by Henry Colie, father of the apprentice in question, who petitioned the Court either to cause the lad to be properly clothed or to have him released from his apprenticeship.[43]

There is some indication that the authorities kept track, in a hit-and-miss fashion, of the municipality's minor wards. A Mayor's Court order of 1735 directs the churchwardens to "remove Mary Lewoll, a Parish Child at Nurse with Elizabeth Lowns, from the said Elizabeth Lowns, she being negligent in her Duty to the said Infant, and that they place the said Infant with Mrs. Laurier, the Wife of Michael Laurier, till further order."[44]

An interesting instance wherein preventive measures were urged against possible delinquency occurred in 1716, when Jonathan Haight of Rye informed the Westchester Court of Sessions that "one Thomas Wright, an orphan in that town, hath no certain Place of Abode there, but lives like a Vagabond and at a loose end, and will undoubtedly come to Ruine unless this Court take some speedy and effectual care for ye prevention thereof."[45]

EDUCATIONAL PROVISION FOR POOR CHILDREN

A free public-school system did not come into being in New York until late in the nineteenth century. During the provincial period free public schools were relatively few, and these were open mainly to the children of taxpayers. The majority of the poor children of the province were excluded from the benefits of school education. The first proposal for popular education in New York province was made in 1691 when a bill was introduced in the assembly providing for the appointment of "a schoolmaster for the educating and instructing of youth, to read and write English, in every town in the province." This bill, evidently intended to accelerate the replacement of the prevailing Dutch culture by English, failed to pass. In October, 1702, Governor Cornbury urged "the erecting of Public Schools in proper places," and the following month the assembly responded by passing "An Act for Encouragement of a Grammar Free School in the City of New York," authorizing the city to levy fifty pounds annually for the maintenance of the school and a schoolmaster. The institution was opened in 1704 and closed five years later.[46] Not until 1732 did the provincial government renew its interest in education, when it enacted a statute to "encourage a Public School in the City of New York for teaching Latin, Greek and Mathematicks." Provision was made in this measure for free tuition to twenty students allotted among several counties. The school was abandoned after operating for six years. Here the interest of the provincial authorities in encouraging primary and secondary education at public expense came to an end. The authorities, as representatives of the Crown, regarded the common school mainly as an effective medium of propaganda for the Church of England and for royalty. The majority of provincial New Yorkers were unwilling to subject their children to such influences. This factor appears to have been largely responsible for the failure to establish and maintain province-encouraged common schools in New York.

Meanwhile, several "charity schools" were established by the Society for the Propagation of the Gospel in Foreign Parts. Significantly enough, this was an Anglican organization—and the Anglican church was definitely a royalist institution with the king at its head, positively and without secrecy bound to carry on propaganda for the Crown as well as the faith. The Society established schools at several points in the southeastern counties. Each of these schools apparently offered primary education to the very poor with-

out charge.[47] In 1704 it opened a school in New York City for
Negro and Indian slaves, and it is claimed that through this institution "many were raised from their miserable condition and became
steadfast Christians." Early in 1710 the Society founded a charity
school in New York City for white children, with forty poor boys in
attendance. It was later taken over by Trinity Church and operated
under its auspices thereafter. The custom of preaching "charity sermons" to obtain clothing and other necessities for the poor pupils
was begun in 1754 and continued for many years.[48]

The authorities of New York City in 1714 made an unsuccessful
attempt to raise funds to maintain "a public schoolmaster for teaching the poor to Read & write."[49] A later effort to encourage primary
education among such poor pupils as could not be accommodated
by the charity school is evidenced by the order of the Common
Council on October 14, 1731, to pay eight pounds out of public funds
to the widow Sarah Huddleston

. . . . as a Gratification for the trouble and Care she and her late Son Thomas
Huddleston deceased have taken in teaching several Poor Children of this Corporation to Read and Write and Instructing them in the Principles of Religion
over and above the Number allowed by the Venerable society for propogation
of the Gospel in forreign parts.[50]

Among the communities in which town schools were established
by people of English descent or birth were Eastchester, Rye, and
White Plains. At New Rochelle the French clergy conducted a school
until the mid-eighteenth century. It is unlikely that any of these
schools offered tuition entirely free. The community of Johnstown
established a free school in 1769.[51] At times dependent children were
relieved in kind, as shown in an action of the Mayor's Court of New
York City, November 1, 1726, ordering the churchwardens to "supply Phillip Cordus a sickly Boy at the House of Anantie Delamontagne with a pair of Schoes A pair of Stockings A Blankett and
some Course Linnen to make a Straw Bed, he being poor and an
Object of Charity."

Children born out of wedlock who became public charges were
ordinarily disposed of like other groups of dependent children. The
drain on local treasuries from this source must have proved burdensome, for in 1774, the provincial assembly enacted a law for "the

Relief of Parishes and other Places from such Charges as may arise from Bastard Children born within the same." This act was derived almost word for word from an English statute of 1733 (6 Geo. II. c. 31), which in turn was based on an act passed in the eighteenth year of Queen Elizabeth's reign. Explaining in its preamble that "the laws now in being are not sufficient to provide for the securing and indemnifying Parishes and other Places, from the Great Charges frequently arising from Children begotten and born out of lawful Matrimony," the act of 1774 authorized justices of the peace in any locality to apprehend and confine in the common jail or house of correction any man charged by a single woman, under oath, with being the father of a bastard child chargeable or likely to become chargeable to the locality, upon application of the overseers of the poor or any substantial householding resident. The putative father was to be held unless he gave security to indemnify the parish or other local unit, or to appear at the next general or quarter sessions and to abide by the orders made there.[52]

Protection was afforded to the alleged father through the right of appeal against unjust detention. In cases where "the putative Fathers and lewd Mothers of Bastard Children run away out of the Parish or Place and sometimes out of the County, and leave the said Bastard Children upon the Charge of the Parish or Place where they are born," the churchwardens or overseers of the poor of the said locality were authorized to seize the property of the absconding parents against the cost of maintaining the child as a public charge.

SPECIAL RELIEF FOR THE MENTALLY AND PHYSICALLY HANDICAPPED

As a rule, public relief for the physically handicapped in New York province did not differ essentially from the forms of relief meted out to other classes of dependents. They were ordinarily supported in their own homes, boarded out with private families, or placed in the poorhouse when such an institution was available. At times a type of vocational relief was afforded them, with the aim of rehabilitating them to a position of self-support. An instance of a more indirect method of relieving the physically disabled is contained in the minutes of the Mayor's Court in New York City for February 11, 1718, in relation to a dependent blind man:

Thomas Clifton who has lately lost his eye sight by hard Labour and sickness and Thereby rendered uncapable of getting a livelyhood for himself and his wife it is Therefore Order'd that the Church Wardens do provide for the wife of the said Thomas Clifton a Flax wheel and a pair of Wool Cards in Order for their better support they being Objects of Charity.

This practice of providing occupational tools to applicants as a means of public relief also extended to the able-bodied poor. For example, in 1733 the churchwardens of New York City were ordered to provide one Vincent Delamontagne, "with a Bundle of twine for the making of a fishing Net towards his Support he being an Object of Charity."

The treatment of the insane poor constituted one of the most perplexing problems in public poor relief. In all ages, the care and treatment of the mentally ill naturally has reflected current attitudes toward insanity, its nature, and causes. During a large part of the provincial period mental disease was frequently regarded as a manifestation of demoniacal possession and treated accordingly. Even when insanity was recognized as something other than demoniacal possession, the treatment of the mentally sick was often characterized by cold brutality or else complete indifference and neglect. Consideration was seldom shown them. The major, if not the sole, concern of the public authorities in providing for the dependent insane was to protect society against violence at their hands. The needs of the insane themselves went unheeded, largely because their needs were not yet known. When their illness manifested itself in violent behavior, the insane were ordinarily incarcerated in prisons like common criminals. When their illness was of a harmless type, they were likely to be treated as common paupers. Only in rare instances was mental disease recognized as such and its victims accorded therapeutic treatment.

An amendment of the Duke's Laws in 1665 provided for town unions when the care of "distracted Persons" who were "both very chargeable and troublesome" proved too burdensome for one town alone to bear. Advantage was taken of this provision in 1695, when the Court of Sessions of Kings County directed that "Mad James be kept by Kings County in General and that the deacons of each town within the said county doe forthwith meet together and consider about their propositions for maintenance of said James."[53]

What these propositions were we have been unable to discover, but this incident probably represents the earliest example of county care for dependents in New York.

A special structure was ordered to be built in New York City in 1677 for the confinement of Peter Paull, a "lunatick." Pending the completion of this one-man asylum, it was directed that the said Paull "bee confined into prison in the hold."[54] The records do not indicate whether this structure was ever completed. In later years the town jail was used for the custody of the violent insane. On April 5, 1725, the town marshal was paid two shillings and sixpence by the churchwardens of New York City "for to Subsist Robert Bullman & Madman in Prison." Usually the term of confinement was for the duration of the period of lunacy. In 1720, for example, the same town marshal was given the custody of one Henry Dove, "a Dangerous Madman, untill he shall Recover his senses."[55]

At times the harmless dependent insane were provided for in their own homes or lodgings like other classes of dependents. On May 20, 1720, the Mayor's Court directed the churchwardens to "pay to Mr. John Moere four Shillings Weekly to be by him laid out and Applyed to the use of Mrs. Schelleux Widdow (who is non Compos Mentis) toward her Support and Maintanance She being an Object of Charity." On October 10, 1721, the Mayor's Court of New York ordered the churchwardens to "supply Susan Commonly called Mad Sew with a good pair of Shoes & Stockings & other Necessary Warm Clothing She being Very Old Poor & Non Compos Mentis." An interesting instance where relief was provided in the form of a loan is recorded in 1712, when the churchwardens in New York City were ordered "to lend Philip Batten, butcher, thirty shillings, in order to go on with his trade (he being reduced to great poverty by reason of his wife being delirious) being an object of charity."[56]

A curious measure for preventing a possible suicide is revealed in the records of New York City for 1729:

Whereas Timothy Dally of this City Marriner is lately seized with a deep Melancholy and by intervals is perfectly distracted & non Compos Mentis so that it is feared he will lay violent hands upon himself if no Care be taken to prevent it. And he having a wife and four small children who cannot subsist without his labour it is Therefore Order'd that the Church Wardens pay to the wife of the said Timothy Dally Six Shillings p week towards subsisting The said Timothy Dally and his children during his illness they being Objects of Charity.[57]

One of the very rare instances of provision for medical care for mentally ill dependents occurred in Southampton in 1701, when the town trustees ordered Samuel Barbor to send his insane wife to "ye prison house" where she was to be maintained at town expense. At the same time one Captain Topping was directed "to speak to Dr. Wade to come and see her [Mrs. Barbor] and to administer that which is proper for such a Person according to his skill and cunning."[58]

MEDICAL AID TO THE POOR

The first general hospital in New York province was established in 1771 and was not opened until twenty years later. References to hospitals appear in the records of Albany and New York in the years immediately following the close of the French and Indian War in 1763, but these were military hospitals built and maintained temporarily for sick and wounded soldiers. In 1699 the Common Council of New York ordered that "the Mayor Agree with Some person for the keeping of an hospital for the maintenance of the poor."[59] It is uncertain, however, whether a hospital for the reception of the sick poor was intended, or merely a refuge for friendless and infirm poor, as the early English usage of the term "hospital" indicates. Most probably the latter was intended, inasmuch as the erection of a poorhouse or workhouse was being widely discussed during this period. At any rate, it is certain that neither hospital nor poorhouse was built at the time.

Practically the only means of providing medical aid to the sick poor during the provincial period was to contract with some private physician for attendance to the poor in their homes on a salary or visit basis. At an early date the services of a salaried municipal physician were made available to the needy in New York City. Dr. Johannes Kerfyle took office in 1687 and served at least two years, the city records show. In 1713 Jacob Provost became the city physician for the poor at a salary of eight pounds. Municipal medical care, however, was not limited to the services of the city physician. The minutes of the Mayor's Court include many items indicating that direct and indirect medical aid to needy individuals was often administered through other sources at city expense. For example: "August 23, 1715. Order'd The Church Wardens pay to Elizabeth Davis Three Pounds Current Money of New York towards paying her Doctor and defraying her Charges in the Cutting of her brest. She being an Object of Charity."[60]

In 1720 the churchwardens were directed to pay Mary Golding "for Nursing of Grace Pangborne" for three weeks. Nine years later the city treasurer was ordered to pay Dr. Jacob Moene three pounds "for Setting and Curing the broken Leg of A poor Saylor Named John who was an Object of Charity."[61]

Sick dependents were often boarded out in private homes during their illness. In 1719 the New York churchwardens were authorized to pay four pounds and eight shillings to Garrett De Bogh "for his Maintenance of Alexander Griggs a poor Sick man for Eighteen weeks." On other occasions the sick poor were sent to the dwelling hired as a poorhouse by the city. As has been noted, when the permanent poorhouse was opened in 1736, it included an infirmary intended not only for the inmates but for poor residents who fell ill.

That the city was quite generous on occasion is evidenced by the fact that on May 26, 1762, Dr. John Bard was paid seven pounds for delivering an almshouse inmate of a child. On March 17, 1773, Dr. Beekman van Buren was paid nearly thirty-eight pounds for attending and providing medicine to prisoners in the Bridewell and the New Gaol.[62]

The custom of appointing midwives for the service of the poor seems to have been practiced in the larger towns throughout the provincial period. It is interesting to note that a New York City ordinance passed in 1731 "for regulating Midwives" contained a prescribed oath in which the following provision was included: "You Shall swear, first that you Shall be Dilligent and faithfull and Ready to help Every Woman Labouring of Child As well the poor as the Rich; and that in time of Necessity you shall not for sake or Leave the poor Women to go to the Rich."[63]

Epidemics visited the province at frequent intervals, sometimes with disastrous results. Governor Cornbury was driven from New York City in 1702 by an epidemic of yellow fever which decimated the city. In 1731 a smallpox epidemic carried off about six hundred victims, and the churchwardens found it necessary to expend from their own purses nearly fifty pounds in addition to contributions from private citizens amounting to a considerable sum, for the relief and burial of victims. A contagious hospital was added, as already noted, to the almshouse building in 1739. Yellow fever accounted for more than two hundred deaths in 1742, in a population of less than eight thousand. In 1746 Albany was visited by an epidemic (probably of yellow fever) and lost forty-five inhabitants as a result. Both New York City and Albany learned to practice stricter segregation for victims of contagious diseases as time went on. An order of April 6, 1742, consigned John Tenbrook of New York to Bedloe Island as a smallpox patient. All persons were forbidden entry to the house where he lay or to houses where other smallpox patients were domiciled, except by order of the mayor. The city authorities of Albany resolved on October 11, 1756, that all smallpox patients should be sent from the city and that a convenient place should be found for their reception.[64]

In 1771 the first general hospital in the province, and the second in the American colonies, was founded in New York City. The movement leading to its establishment began in 1769 when Dr. Samuel Bard, in a commencement address at King's College (now Columbia University), reproached the city for not having a public hospital, "one of the most useful and necessary charitable institutions that can possibly be imagined." Describing the need for a hospital and the benefits it would bring, Dr. Bard declared:

The labouring Poor are allowed to be the support of the Community; their Industry enables the Rich to live in Ease and Affluence, and it is from the Hands of the Manufacturer we derive, not only the Necessaries, but the Superfluities of Life; whilst the poor Pittance he earns will barely supply the Necessities of Nature, and it is literally by the sweat of his Brow, that he gains his daily Subsistance; how heavy a Calamity must Sickness be to such a Man, which putting him out of his Power to work, immediately deprives him and perhaps a helpless Family of Bread!

Nor would the good Effects of an Hospital be wholly confined to the Poor; they would extend to every Rank, and greatly contribute to the Safety and Welfare of the whole Community."[65]

A campaign to raise funds for the hospital was begun and proved so successful that in 1770 Dr. Bard, together with Drs. Peter Middleton and John Jones, felt encouraged to present a petition to Acting Governor Colden requesting a charter of incorporation. The charter was granted by King George III on June 13, 1771, and twenty-six governors were designated to manage the institution which was incorporated under the name, "The Society of the Hospital in the City of New York in America." Provision for the sick poor was a primary consideration of the founders.

On September 12, 1771, the Common Council advanced municipal aid to this "usefull Undertaking, having for its object the Relief of the indigent & Diseased," in the form of a grant of land to serve as the grounds for the proposed hospital.[66] In the following year the provincial assembly voted to grant the hospital £800 annually for twenty years, the funds to be collected out of taxes on strong liquors retailed in the city. A condition of the grant was that the hospital should receive and treat without charge all sick indigents resident in any county of the province.[67] The city of New York withdrew its gift of land on June 16, 1772, and substituted for it an outright donation of £1,000, thus establishing the first publicly-supported institution providing medical aid to the poor in the province.

The project passed through many vicissitudes, however. Ground for the hospital was broken in 1773, but two years later, when it was completed, disaster overtook it in the form of a fire which practically destroyed the buildings. The assembly granted £4,000 toward the reconstruction of the hospital, but before the new group of buildings were ready for occupation the Revolution began and the project was halted. The hospital finally commenced operation in 1791, twenty years after its incorporation.

POOR RELIEF ASPECTS OF SLAVERY

The number of slaves in New York province averaged about 10 per cent of the total population. Their numbers were sufficient to keep the white population in a constant state of fear, in anticipation of possible insurrections, a fear reflected in the frequency and severity of the laws governing the conduct of slaves. This trepidation was particularly evident in New York City, where the so-called "slave conspiracies" of 1712 and 1741 resulted in the torture, hanging, and burning at the stake of a number of innocent Negro slaves.

It appears to have been a widespread practice for slaveowners to manumit aged or infirm slaves in order to escape responsibility for their care. The provincial authorities found it necessary, therefore, to place restriction on the practice of manumission. Records of 1750 in the Ulster County Court of Common Pleas show that Susanna Bond, conforming to the laws enacted by the assembly, appeared in court by attorney and offered security against the possibility that four slaves whom she desired to free would later become public charges. Her security was rejected as insufficient.[68] In 1773 an act of assembly penalized with a ten-pound fine any slaveowner who allowed his slaves to beg. This act would seem to indicate that some persons were not above letting the general populace help maintain their Negroes by charity in its commonest guise.[69]

CONCLUSION

Summarizing public welfare administration in provincial New York, we might say that its principal characteristic was the make-shift pattern and the lack of uniformity in poor relief throughout the province. Several generalizations can be made, however. The principal concern shown in poor-relief legislation was in preventing non-resident indigents from gaining settlement in the province. Measures for removing poor persons lacking settlement were very severe and were sometimes accompanied by corporal punishment as authorized by law. In general, the poor-relief pattern was modeled closely upon that existing in the mother-country. It was based primarily on local responsibility, although here and there county care was provided for. At first public welfare administration was vested in a mixed civil and ecclesiastical authority, but with the passage of time the secular influence became predominant.

Few institutions for the care of the poor existed in the province. Relief was usually provided in the home, in cash or in kind. All classes of indigents were customarily treated alike, special provision being rare. Dependent children, however, were usually disposed of through the system of apprenticeship or indentured servitude. Free education in general fell below the standards maintained during the

Dutch period. The violent insane were frequently incarcerated in prison and otherwise treated as common criminals. In the matter of providing medical care for the poor, New York City was particularly generous. The first general hospital was established toward the end of the colonial period, though it was not opened until 1791. Poor relief in the province operated, as a rule, within the framework of repression, although instances of generous provision for dependents are not wanting.

BIBLIOGRAPHICAL REFERENCES

1. *Docs. Rel. Col. Hist.*, III, 415.
2. Ellis H. Roberts, *New York: The Planting and Growth of the Empire State* (Boston, 1887), pp. 109, 232, 262, 343, 449.
3. David Gardiner, *Chronicles of the Town of Easthampton, County of Suffolk, New York* (New York, 1871), p. 40.
4. Oyster Bay, N.Y., *Oyster Bay Town Records, 1655–1763* (New York, 1916–31), I, 3, 4, 9. Hereinafter referred to as *Oyster Bay Town Records*.
5. *Records of the Town of Southampton*, V, 155.
6. Huntington, N.Y., *Huntington Town Records, Including Babylon, Long Island, N.Y.* (Huntington, 1887–89), II, 425–26.
7. W. S. Pelletreau, *History of Putnam County* (Philadelphia, 1886), p. 153.
8. *Oyster Bay Town Records*, VI, 367.
9. *Records of the Town of Southampton*, V, 81.
10. Sir George Nicholls, *A History of the English Poor Law* (rev. ed.; London, 1898), I, 341.
11. *N.Y.C., M.C.C., 1675–1776*, II, 330.
12. *Oyster Bay Town Records*, VI, 375.
13. *N.Y.C., M.C.C., 1675–1776*, I, 104, 113, 167.
14. *Ibid.*, p. 193.
15. *Ibid.*, p. 194.
16. *Ibid.*, p. 212.
17. *Ibid.*, p. 258.
18. *Ibid.*, p. 233.
19. *C.L.N.Y.*, I, 348–51.
20. *Ibid.*, pp. 507–8.
21. *N.Y.C., M.C.C., 1675–1776*, III, 52–53; *N.Y.C., M.M.C.*, March 24, 1713.
22. *N.Y.C., M.M.C.*, Nov. 8, 1720.
23. *New York Gazette or Weekly Post-Boy*, January 14, 21, 1754.
24. *N.Y.C., M.C.C., 1675–1776*, VII, 66.
25. *Eccles. Recs. N.Y.*, III, 1462.
26. *Ibid.*, p. 2148.

27. *Docs. Rel. Col. Hist.*, III, 823.
28. *Ibid.*, IV, 290.
29. *N.Y.C., M.C.C., 1675-1776*, III, 59-60.
30. *N.Y.C., M.M.C.*, August 31, 1714.
31. *Ibid.*, July 5, 1715.
32. New York City, *Charter (1730)* (New York, 1819), pp. 73-74.
33. *N.Y.C., M.C.C., 1675-1776*, IV, 240-41.
34. *Ibid.*, p. 308.
35. *Ibid.*, p. 309.
36. New York City Common Council, *Manual of the Corporation of the City of New York*, "Valentine's Manual" (New York, 1862), p. 658.
37. *Records of the Town of Southampton*, V, 67.
38. *N.Y.C., M.C.C., 1675-1776*, I, 348.
39. *N.Y.C., M.M.C.*, January 13, 1719.
40. *Ibid.*, May 24, 1720.
41. *Amenia Precinct Book for the Poor, A.D. 1760-1820* (MS), pp. 3-6.
42. *N.Y.C., M.M.C.*, December 13, 1726; July 20, 1725.
43. *Ibid.*, August 21, 1716.
44. *Ibid.*, July 15, 1735.
45. Baird, *History of Rye*, pp. 163-64.
46. William W. Kemp, *The Support of Schools in Colonial New York by the Society for the Propagation of the Gospel in Foreign Parts* (New York, 1913), p. 70.
47. C. F. Pascoe, *Two Hundred Years of the Society for the Propagation of the Faith in Foreign Parts* (London, 1901), II, 769.
48. *New York Mercury*, October 24, 1764.
49. *N.Y.C., M.C.C., 1675-1776*, III, 63-64.
50. *Ibid.*, IV, 74-75.
51. *History of the State of New York*, III, 76.
52. *C.L.N.Y.*, V, 689-92.
53. Gabriel Furman, *Notes, Geographical and Historical, Relating to the Town of Brooklyn* (Brooklyn, 1824), p. 101.
54. Stokes, *Iconography*, IV, 314.
55. *N.Y.C., M.M.C.*, July 5, 1720.
56. Thomas F. De Voe, *The Market Book* (New York, 1862), I, 91.
57. *N.Y.C., M.M.C.*, May 13, 1729.
58. *Records of the Town of Southampton*, V, 161-62.
59. Stokes, *Iconography*, IV, 418.
60. *N.Y.C., M.M.C.*, August 23, 1715.
61. *N.Y.C., M.C.C., 1675-1776*, III, 483.
62. *Ibid.*, VI, 289; VII, 411.
63. *Ibid.*, III, 121-22.

64. Munsell, *Collections on the History of Albany*, I, 104.
65. Samuel Bard, *A Discourse upon the Duties of a Physician with Some Sentiments on the Usefulness and Necessity of a Public Hospital* (New York, 1769), pp. 15–16.
66. *N.Y.C., M.C.C., 1675–1776*, VII, 311.
67. *C.L.N.Y.*, V, 367.
68. *Olde Ulster* (a periodical), I (1905), 11.
69. *C.L.N.Y.*, V, 533.

PART III

TRANSITION, 1776–1823

CHAPTER V

THE REVOLUTIONARY PERIOD, 1776–83

When the Declaration of Independence was promulgated in July, 1776, the authorities in a considerable part of New York province were already well prepared for a change of regime. For years a crystallization of sentiment had been taking place among the populace, and it was now divided into two active groups, the "patriots" and the "loyalists," while the "neutrals" stood awaiting developments. The patriots, consisting mostly of lower middle-class merchants, professional men, and the poorer classes, were determined to safeguard "the rights and liberties of the colonies" at all costs. The loyalists, comprising for the most part the propertied classes and the court party, vowed fealty to the British Crown and stood opposed to any movement aiming at separation or leading to possible armed conflict. The patriots, joined by some moderate loyalists, had sent delegates to the Continental Congress when that body convened at Philadelphia in September, 1774. While loyalist sentiment remained powerful in New York province to the very end of the Revolution, the patriot cause gained ground steadily. In May, 1775, a few weeks after the Battle of Lexington, a Provincial Congress was convened, taking over the powers of the assembly. The latter body had practically ceased to function. Meanwhile, local "committees of correspondence" and "committees of safety" were being organized in the counties, cities, and towns of the province to carry on the functions of civil government as extra-legal bodies.* At first the functions of these local committees centered primarily around military defense, including surveillance of suspected loyalists, seizure of arms, raising troops, concentration of supplies, and liaison with simi-

* Incidentally, this committee system of local government which was adopted in many of the colonies was no innovation in New York. It was already a time-honored tradition for communities to elect a committee to present their grievances to the proper authorities and to represent their interests in general. As early as 1689, when the abortive rebellion headed by Jacob Leisler took place, a "committee of safety" had been formed by the rebels to take over the functions of government.

lar committees throughout the colonies. But as the crisis became
more acute, the committees were forced to assume the functions of
civil government as well. Among the duties accepted by the Albany
Committee of Safety in 1775 were "the support of those made poor
by the war, the burial of their dead, and the helping of refugees."
The Schenectady Committee administered public relief of a general
nature as well as that arising from the military emergency.

Events moved swiftly after the establishment of the Provincial
Congress, despite the reluctance shown by the dominantly conservative elements among New York's political leaders to follow the
revolutionary path being blazed in other American colonies. It was
the irresistible force of circumstances together with strong pressure
from the lower classes, rather than the inclinations of the more
powerful political leaders, that forced the latter into a revolutionary
position which many of them found personally distasteful. On May
27, 1776, the Provincial Congress passed a resolution declaring the
colonial assembly dissolved, and maintaining that the people had
the right to form a new state government. In effect, this constituted
a virtual declaration of independence.

While the New York delegation to the Continental Congress cast
no vote on the Declaration of Independence when it was adopted on
July 4, 1776, it was indorsed five days later by the Provincial Congress. The following day (July 10) the same body voted unanimously that "the style or title of this House be changed from that of the
Provincial Congress of the Colony of New York to that of the Convention of the Representatives of the State of New York." The
Convention adopted as the law of the new state such parts of the
common and statute laws of England as were in force in the colony
of New York on April 20, 1775. A committee headed by Abraham
Yates and John Jay was appointed to draft a constitution. While
this committee was framing its report, the government was carried
on by the Convention, together with a Provincial Committee of
Safety and other revolutionary bodies. On March 1, 1777, a short
time before the state constitution was adopted, the Provincial Committee of Safety ordered the towns, precincts, manors, and districts
in each county to elect "supervisors, assessors and collectors" for
one-year terms. Among the officers elected at Schenectady were two
overseers of the poor.

The first constitution was adopted April 20, 1777. It provided for a state government following the provincial pattern closely, with the royal characteristics eliminated. The governor and lieutenant-governor were made elective officers. Provision was made for a popular assembly consisting of seventy members. In place of the previous Governor's Council, a Senate and a Council of Appointment and a Council of Revision were created. An undemocratic feature of the constitution lay in the high property qualifications it placed on suffrage, strictly limiting the number entitled to vote.* The old judicial system remained virtually unchanged under the new constitution, and the same was true of the form of town, city, and county administration.

The functions of the new state government, however, were greatly impeded, and its area of administration was highly complicated by the fact that considerable parts of its territory were occupied by the British at one time or another during the course of the Revolution, and some sections continued under British rule until the culmination of the war in 1783. New York City remained under British occupation and rule from 1776 to 1783, while campaigns by Burgoyne and St. Leger placed other areas of the state under British domination for varying periods of time. This factor must be kept constantly in mind in a review of poor-relief developments in New York during the Revolutionary period. A large part of the relief problems centered around aid to impoverished patriots compelled to flee from territory held by the British, and to loyalists who had to leave everything behind in flight from areas dominated by the patriot army.

This period is important in the development of public welfare primarily because it witnessed the first participation of the state in poor-relief administration. Four principal factors were responsible for bringing about this innovation.

1. The collapse of civil authority with the intensification of the crisis and the outbreak of armed conflict deprived many localities of the mechanisms for the collection and distribution of the poor rates. Even after temporary committees of safety and, later, permanent administrative systems were set up, the exigencies of the Revolu-

* The extent to which suffrage was restricted is indicated by the fact that in 1790 only 1,303 out of 13,330 male adult residents of New York City voted for governor.

tionary situation made it difficult, and in some cases impossible, for local authorities to carry out their functions with the smoothness and regularity possible under normal circumstances. Unable to meet relief needs, local authorities were compelled to call upon the state for material help.

2. The Revolutionary crisis resulted in an almost complete suspension of trade with Great Britain and her other colonies, disrupting a large part of the industrial and commercial activities in New York which were based on this trade, and resulting in unemployment and destitution.

3. Mass enlistment of able-bodied men in the Revolutionary Army left many families without means of support, thus forcing them into the ranks of public dependents. Local authorities felt justified in placing partial responsibility upon the state for the support of these dependents.

4. The most important public welfare problem created by the Revolution was to provide for refugees fleeing before advancing British troops, or from areas occupied by the British: many were propertyless, while others who possessed property were forced to leave it behind in their flight. In this emergency the harsh and stringent laws governing settlement and removal had to be suspended, since they were obviously inapplicable. The local communities in patriot-controlled areas were unable and unwilling to bear the burden of supporting the large number of nonresident refugees that streamed into them before the invading British and their Indian allies. The state was the only administrative unit that could properly be charged with the main support of patriot civilians and families fleeing from their places of settlement. On the other hand, as shall be seen, the British military authorities were faced with the problem of providing for loyalist refugees fleeing from patriot-held territory.

Emergency relief had to be provided for large numbers of refugees who fled from New York City to other parts of the state before and during the British occupation. But even before the city was threatened by the British, the provincial government was forced to come to its aid in providing for the poor. The winter of 1775-76 was a bitterly cold one and intensified the suffering of the poverty-stricken. Under the circumstances, the city authorities felt compelled to seek assistance from the Provincial Congress which was then meeting in New York. On December 16, 1775, this body passed a resolution empowering the Committee of Safety "to apply £1,000 to the relief of such indigent poor of the city of New York for whom the corporation may not have made provisions."[1] This action marked the first occasion where the state entered the public welfare field as a financing agency.

It appears to have been the original intention of the Provincial Congress to use the appropriation for "the employment of the industrious poor," and the entire sum was placed in the hands of John Ramsey, a woolen merchant, for this purpose. Ramsey agreed to devote his entire time to employing the poor in manufacturing linens and tow cloth, receiving for his services 5 per cent of all moneys turned over to him. But it soon became evident that home relief would have to be provided in addition to work relief. The Committee of Safety, which was empowered to act for the provincial legislature during its periods of adjournment, decided to extend direct relief to the city in a series of resolutions passed on February 3, 1776:

Ordered, That Comfort Sands purchase wood in small parcels as he may have opportunity, not to exceed in the whole the sum of 50 cords, and distribute the same among the very necessitous poor; and that he bring in the account to this Committee.

Ordered, That Mr. John Foster purchase all the good tow cloth which he can procure, on account of the Provincial Congress of this Colony, not to exceed 2s. per yeard in price; and that Mr. Foster send the same in small quantities, as fast as he can procure it, by safe conveyance to Mr. Peter T. Curtenius, at New-York. And

Ordered, That Peter Van Brugh Livingston, *Esqr.* as Treasurer of the Provincial Congress of this Colony, advance to Mr. John Foster, for the purpose of such tow cloth, the sum of £50 upon account, and take Mr. Foster's receipt for the same.[2]

On February 9, Comfort Sands reported to the Committee that a total of £130 had been spent on "wood, and other necessaries of various kinds, supplied to the poor," whereupon the Committee ordered that he be reimbursed out of the 1,000-pound fund which had been placed in the hands of John Ramsey. It was evidently the purpose of the Provincial Congress to use a part of the special poor fund for work relief as well as for home relief. On February 10 the Committee of Safety, noting that "the poor of this city are in great distress, and many of them unable to procure subsistence at this inclement season," ordered that £200 be placed in the hands of William Vandewater and Captain George Janeway "to be applied by them in purchasing barreled beef and ship bread, to be delivered in bags; turnips and potatoes, Indian corn meal and oak wood, for and towards the support of such poor inhabitants of this city as may stand in need of assistance for their immediate subsistence."[3] Messrs. Vandewater and Janeway were further ordered to convene the vestrymen of the city to distribute these articles of relief among the poor in each ward. (The vestrymen at this time were elected on a ward basis, each ward being represented by one vestryman.)

When the Provincial Congress convened in March, 1776, it was informed that the entire sum of £1,000 appropriated for the relief of the poor of New York City had been expended. Approximately one-third of the funds had been used for providing "wood, cheap provisions and other necessaries" to the poor; the remaining two-thirds had been spent in the work-relief program put into operation by Mr. Ramsey. The latter included employment of the "industrious" poor in "spinning, weaving and dressing flax, and manufacturing linen cloth . . . . in such manner as to support several hundreds of poor."[4] Mr. Ramsey complained that without additional capital he could not carry out the work-relief program on the extensive scale he had planned. Thereupon the Congress ordered on March 8 that a further sum of £1,300 be handed over to him by the treasurer, Peter van Brugh Livingston, "for the purpose of enabling him to employ the industrious poor in this city in spinning and manufactures." But even this comparatively liberal relief allowance soon proved inadequate to meet the desperate needs of the city's poor. Less than three months later the local vestrymen sent an urgent appeal to the legislature for a grant or loan of £5,000, explaining that this sum had been raised annually for poor relief in New York City in the past, and that it had several times proved inadequate. In the face of the acute distress occasioned by the "calamitous Circumstances of the times," the vestrymen were unable to raise sufficient poor funds. A large number of the well-to-do residents of the city who were

Tories had taken flight to British-controlled territory, and the collection of taxes for the poor rate seemed so impracticable under the circumstances that the vestrymen hesitated even to attempt it. Meanwhile, they pointed out in their memorial:

There are now at least four hundred Poor in the Alms house in this City & the Buildings adjoining which number will in all probability be encreased . . . . these Poor consist of the Blind & the lame; numerous helpless orphans, tender distressed Infants, Foundlings & decrepid old age in its last stage, the sick in body & distempered in mind, many of whom have by various means fallen into this city as well from different parts of this colony as from other colonies & countries.[5]

The Provincial Congress found the request for £5,000 too great a demand on its depleted treasury, but on June 10, 1776, it voted a loan of £1,500 to New York City to be expended for poor relief. At the same time it approved a loan of £100 to Queens County for the same purpose.[6]

The session of the Provincial Congress of July 9 was a historic occasion. It was this session that resolved unanimously: "That the reasons assigned by the Continental Congress for declaring the United Colonies free and independent States are cogent and conclusive; and that while we lament the cruel necessity which has rendered that measure unavoidable, we approved the same, and will, at the risk of our lives and fortunes, join with the other Colonies in supporting it." The Declaration of Independence, signed five days earlier, was ordered to be proclaimed "with beat of drum" in every county. It was further ordered that the name of the legislative body be changed from "Provincial Congress" to the "Convention of the Representatives of the State of New York," in conformance with the new independent status of the former colonies.

It is noteworthy that, immediately following the set of resolutions proclaiming the independence of New York from Britain, a resolution was adopted ordering Messrs. Banker, Brasher, and Paulding to constitute "a Committee to consider of and report the proper places for the reception and means of support of the poor inhabitants of the city and county of New York."[7] The situation of the city, in the face of a threatened invasion of the British troops under Howe, was already extremely serious. Residents, rich and poor, were evacuating the city in increasing numbers, and their rehabilitation in other districts became one of the major emergency problems confronting the new state.

By mid-August it became clear that the American patriot troops would not be able to hold New York City much longer against the sweeping advance of General Howe. On August 17, 1776, the State Convention received the following letter from General George Washington:

GENTLEMEN—When I consider that the city of New-York will, in all human probability, very soon be the scene of a bloody conflict, I can not but view the great numbers of women and children, and infirm persons remaining in it, with the most melancholy concern. When the men of war passed up the river, the shrieks and cries of those poor creatures, running every way with their children, was truley distressing, and I fear will have an unhappy effect on the ears and minds of our young and inexperienced soldiery. Can no method be devised for their removal? Many doubtless are of ability to remove themselves, but there are others in a different situation. Some provision for them afterwards, would also be a necessary consideration.

It would relieve me from great anxiety, if your Honourable Body would immediately deliberate upon it, and form, and execute some plan for their removal and relief, in which I will cooperate and assist to the utmost of my power. . . . .[8]

Acting promptly upon Washington's suggestion, the State Convention voted the same day to remove all women, children, and infirm persons from New York City. Messrs. Lott, Beekman, Berrien, and Campbell were appointed a committee to supervise removals, and the Convention pledged itself to pay the expenses incurred by the removal and maintenance of indigent persons. An advance of £200 was voted to the committee, which was directed to take a census of all "indigent and infirm persons whom they think entitled to the charitable exertions of this State . . . . to the end that this Convention may discharge the duty of faithful guardians of the public interest and happiness by relieving the complaints of the infirm and the wants of the indigent in the most humane and economical manner possible."[9]

Then began an exodus of the poor from New York which continued long after the city fell into the hands of the British on September 15, 1776. Hundreds of indigent families were evacuated from the city and maintained in upstate counties—mainly Westchester,

Dutchess, and Ulster—at state expense. Many former almshouse inmates were included among these refugees. The expense for their removal and support was sometimes charged to the city, but more often to the state. The local committees of safety were usually intrusted with the responsibility for placing refugee families in their several towns, precincts, or counties. In Ulster County, the refugees from New York were at first placed in New Windsor. On October 4, 1776, the State Convention voted more than £56 to Samuel Brewster, chairman of the Committee of Safety of New Windsor, for the removal and support of poor families sent from New York. Extracts from one of his accounts follow:[10]

STATE OF NEW YORK TO SAMUEL BREWSTER DR—

1776

August   26 To 2 Days Providing Places for ye poor Sent
           by this State........................ o– 12 0

October   2 3 Days myself and horse to Fishkills to Draw
           the cash for Sd Poor a 12/............ 1   16 0

Nobr   15 Cash to Mr. Hatfield to Leave this State... o   8 0

1777

Febr   6 3 lb. of thread Delivered to Sd Poor to make
           frocks and trowsers for the Contill Army
           a 18/.............................. 2   14 0

May   10 2 Days Spent in removing Sd Poor a 10/... 1   0 0

Within a short period the task of caring for refugees assumed such proportions that on November 12, 1776, the State Committee of Safety appointed a committee of three, consisting of Messrs. L'Hommedieu, Allison, and Adgate, authorized to take over the general superintendence of the poor supported by state funds, to receive and examine applications, to give directions to such persons as they might think proper for setting them at work, to issue orders to the several county committees for supplies, to bind out children of the "state poor," and to examine and audit all accounts of charges accrued by these means.[11] The committee was also empowered to remove all dependents belonging to New York from other states, "it being the design of this State to maintain their poor within the same." Furthermore, the committee was directed to request Governor Trumbull of Connecticut to remove to Dutchess County all the poor in that state who had legal settlement in New York. The scope of the committee's superintendence over the poor was specifically confined to "the poor removed from these counties now in possession of the enemy, and such poor the heads of whose families have been ordered removed from this State, as inimical to the cause of America." This Committee of Superintendence of the Poor may well be regarded as the first state body dealing exclusively with problems of poor relief, although its functions were necessarily of a temporary character.

To expedite the work of providing for the state-supported poor, the State Convention in May, 1777, appointed county commissioners for the general superintendence of indigent refugees in the counties of Dutchess, Westchester, Ulster, and Orange. These commissioners were authorized to remove dependents from one county to another or to various districts within the same county and to provide them with either home relief or work relief. It was specified that persons so removed from one county to another did not thereby gain the right of settlement.

The county commissioners were given the power

to bind out to trades or other occupations, the children of such of the said poor as were objects of the public charity, before they were driven from their habitations. . . . . And that they assist such persons who, before they were driven from their habitations as aforesaid, were not indebted to the public charity, but were able to support their families by their own means and industry, in putting out their children to such places and employments, for such time or times, as the said parents shall consent to.[12]

Thus an interesting distinction was made between those indigent refugees who were public dependents before their removal and those who were not. The county commissioners were given the right arbitrarily to bind out the children of the former group but had to obtain the parents' permission to bind out children of the latter. They were authorized to draw upon the state treasury for a sum not exceeding £500 for each county to enable them to carry on their work.

The commissioners appointed for Dutchess County resigned from their posts in 1778, and in June of that year the legislature enacted a bill naming Dirck Brinckerhoff, Jr., as commissioner to superintend the removal of the poor from New York City to Dutchess County. The same act (chap. 30, *Laws of 1778*) authorized the Commissioners of Superintendence of the Poor for the counties of Ulster, Westchester, and Dutchess to draw upon the state treasury for additional sums not exceeding £600 for each county, and fixed a salary of 16 shillings per day for the services of each commissioner. Chapter 31, *Laws of 1779*, provided further appropriations of £12,000 to the commissioners of Dutchess, Ulster, and Westchester for the maintenance of the poor removed to these counties from New York. It was voted at the same time to raise the salary of the Commissioners of Superintendence of the Poor to $20 per diem for each day served. In 1780 the unsettled poor in Ulster and Westchester were ordered removed to Dutchess County, where they were placed under the supervision of Samuel Dodge, who had been keeper of the New York City Almshouse and who returned to his post following the Revolution.* After the evacuation of the British troops from New York City, the patriot poor who had been removed thence were returned in triumph. It is estimated that during the years 1779–83 nearly £15,000 was spent by the state for their removal and maintenance.

In 1778 the legislature provided for the election of overseers of the poor in each locality, and chapter 68, *Laws of 1780*, ordered the county supervisors of Ulster, Westchester, Orange, Tryon, and Charlotte to fix the poor rates for each town, manor, district, and precinct within their several counties, on the basis of reports rendered annually by the local overseers.

Throughout the Revolutionary period, the authorities were deluged with petitions from destitute persons appealing for relief. For example, on March 14, 1776, the Provincial Congress received a petition from a jobless seaman of New York City stating that "your petitioner is well affected to the cause of his country, and is out of employ on Account of the distressed times, and [sees] no probable way to get into Business again, for to maintain his Wife & children until matters are accomodated." The petitioner asked that he be

---

* In 1782 the legislature named six state commissioners to take over the task of superintending the maintenance of poor refugees from New York City, Mr. Dodge having asked to be relieved of this responsibility.

given a commission in the military forces or employment as a mariner.[13] On June 8, 1776, one William Tillou, of New York City, an unemployed joiner, who explained that his wife was a "lunatic," petitioned the Provincial Congress to grant him a certificate directing the "Committee of Charlotte precinct Dutchess County that he may be permitted to reside in that precinct (as he is promised a good deal of Work there) and endeavour by honesty and application to maintain himself and small helpless family."[14] Among the petitions for relief received by the state authorities in 1777, an interesting, though somewhat informal, specimen may be quoted:

HONOURABLE CONGRESS: I take this opatunety to Let you No my Distrus I am hear Confined and Not Able to help my Self and If the Honourable Congress will Not take pitty on me hear Sun I must suffer and perris with hunger For I have got no money nor no way to get any hear For I am pour and Nedy god is good and grasus and I hope you are of the Same Fraim of pitty For my wife Cannot fead my pore children at home Now gentlemen I Lay to your mercy and Discresson For I have not one mouthful to support my Nature.[15]

Many petitions were also filed by resident soldiers disabled in the service of the Continental Army. For example, on April 25, 1777, the state legislature received an appeal from Robert Richardson, a weaver, who had served for two years in the Revolutionary Army until disabled "by a Cannon Ball striking his hand spike, and the one end of the hand spike broke the Rim of his Belly by which he is become Bursted, and has also Lost the use of his Arm by the Wind of a Cannon Ball." The petitioner asserted that a man who had rendered such service to the American cause should not be left destitute, and appealed for whatever relief the Convention might see fit to provide.[16] The Continental Congress had voted a pension scaled up to half-pay for all men in the Continental Army who suffered loss of limb or were otherwise disabled while engaged in active duty, depending upon the merit and need of each individual case. Soldiers disabled while on active duty and in need of relief were to be certified by proper officials to be named by the several states, and their names were to be forwarded to the federal authorities to be placed on the pension list. New York State was slow in acting upon this measure, and for several years seems to have provided for her own disabled troops without reference to the government's pension plan. But in April, 1779, an act was passed by the state legislature appointing commissioners to submit to the proper authorities names of disabled, needy soldiers eligible for government pensions.[17] In 1778 the state had authorized justices of the peace to provide food to needy families of soldiers serving in battalions raised within New York, the cost of such foodstuffs to be charged to the state. Later statutes provided for additional measures of relief for families of Continental soldiers disabled or killed in the line of duty.

Meanwhile the increasing distress among settlers along the state's northern and western frontiers, occasioned by invasions of the British troops together with the depredations of hostile Indians, compelled the state authorities to take measures for their relief, as they were already doing for the refugees from New York City. On August 9, 1777, the State Council of Safety adopted a resolution urging the authorities of Tryon and Albany counties to prevail upon the residents of their respective communities to lend all possible assistance to the refugees from the frontier settlements. It was further recommended that the county committees

prevent, as much as possible, any increase in the calamities of the sufferers, by impositions in the articles of house rent, firewood, provisions for themselves and cattle, and to put out and provide for, at the public charge of this State, all such poor persons and families refugees as aforesaid, as are not able to defray their own expenses; for which this Council doth hereby render the State of New-York responsible.[18]

The county committees promptly set about raising voluntary contributions for the relief of the refugees from the frontier settlements, but there appears to have been much confusion regarding methods of distributing the funds. An entry in the minutes of the Albany Committee for February, 1778, states:

The Legislature not having pointed out a mode for the distribution of the Donations for the Poor, and many of the Persons for which the said benefactions were given, are in the utmost distress. . . . .

Resolved That . . . . George Palmer, Esq. be requested to issue Provisions to said Persons to the amount or Value of Two hundred Pounds . . . . out of the moneys in his Hands collected for the maintainance and support of the ruined Settelers on the Frontiers of this State.[19]

Later in the same month, pursuant to chapter 6 of the *Laws of 1778*, the legislature appointed five state commissioners to collect and distribute the voluntary donations raised "for the relief of inhabitants of the frontier settlements who were forced to abandon their habitations."

In 1779 the legislature directed that £400 be placed in the hands of Frederick Fox of Tryon County, for distribution among certain indigent mothers whose husbands had been killed in action. Chapter 5, *Laws of 1780*, directed the Commissioners of Sequestration in charge of confiscated property and supplies for the same county, to supply distressed families with flour, meal, and milch cows. These directions were substantially repeated with application to Tryon and Westchester counties in statutes enacted during the last years of the Revolutionary War. It is interesting to note that in April, 1782, the state legislature passed a bill ordering payment of £118 to Dr. William Petry "for his Attendance and Medicine to a number of poor inhabitants of Tryon County, wounded by the Enemy at Sundry Times during the present War."

POOR RELIEF IN NEW YORK CITY UNDER BRITISH OCCUPATION

When the British defeated the American army at New York in September, 1776, and took possession of the immensely important "joint" between New England and the colonies to the south, complete British victory appeared to be merely a matter of weeks or of months at most. During the winter that followed, however, the army under Washington proved how far retreat is from flight. Sudden and decisive American victories at Trenton and Princeton tremendously affected the British morale. The outposts in New Jersey were drawn in, while along the Hudson, American partisans and spies became too active to permit the British military authorities to feel secure in that direction. Long Island presently began to be unsafe because of unexpected raids made by whaleboats from the Connecticut shore.

In 1777 it was expected that the invasions of Burgoyne and St. Leger, together with an expedition sent northward from Manhattan, would complete the work of cutting off New England and establishing an area from which the British might draw supplies and support for the suppression of the rest of the coastal colonies. But Oriskany was followed by Bennington, and Bennington by Saratoga. Confidence was lacking for a decisive British campaign in the lower Hudson. The result was that American sovereignty was re-established in the middle and upper Hudson and was gradually, though with no little difficulty, extended to the new state's northern and western frontiers. The lower Hudson, except for New York City, continued to be an area of strife and instability where neither British nor American sovereignty was certain.

New York City, securely held by the British for the duration of the war, became an island politically as well as geographically. It was an island of military royalism surrounded not only by Continentals and militia but also by bad-tempered countrymen who had stopped raising crops which could be seized. These citizens armed themselves with fowling pieces or muskets and were out to seize almost anything, whether persons or goods, that might prove valuable either to the American authorities or to themselves.

When New York City was captured by the British, so many of the people had left the town that the population was reduced to about 5,000; a population of 21,863 had been reported for 1771. But as the surrounding territory became more and more untenable for Tories, these friends of the king began to enter the city in large numbers. Before long a serious housing shortage developed, aggravated by a great fire which destroyed nearly a quarter of the town. This fire occurred September 20, 1776, starting in the vicinity of Whitehall Slip and spreading rapidly over a large area. At once there were three hundred destitute victims of the conflagration to be cared for at the almshouse, nearly as many as had been removed by the patriots prior to the British occupation. When this indigenous increase of dependents was supplemented by the entry of thousands of loyalist refugees, a large proportion of whom had fled their homes with little more than their most portable possessions and the clothes on their backs, the beleaguered authorities found themselves struggling with a relief problem of serious dimensions, a problem that was solved only with the end of the British occupation in 1783.

A second fire, which occurred in August, 1778, destroyed sixty-four houses and greatly intensified the problem of finding accommodations for the loyalist refugees who by that time fairly teemed in the city. The widespread destruction caused by the two conflagrations, together with the steady influx of British troops and civilian loyalists, placed housing space at a premium. Rents skyrocketed to 400 per cent above those prevailing before the occupation. Foodstuffs were difficult to obtain and profiteering was everywhere prevalent. Despite the efforts of the military authorities to fix prices and to punish violations by confiscation, prices of foodstuffs rose 800 per cent. Increasing numbers were forced to seek charity.

Actual privation extended at times even to high-ranking military officers, while the hardship suffered by the great mass of the poor was intense and prolonged. During the British occupation civil government was suspended and control of the city's affairs was assumed by the military authorities. Among the first measures taken to raise relief funds was the presentation of benefit theatrical performances. A theater was opened in January, 1777, to raise funds for relieving families of soldiers and sailors "who have fallen in Support of the Constitutional Rights of Great Britain in America."[20] Several special performances for the same purpose were given in subsequent months. The theater continued to do a considerable business during the years of occupation, but only a small proportion of the receipts went to the poor. Profiteering in bread was forbidden on January 10, 1777, and all profiteers' stocks were ordered seized for the poor. A year later the practice of raising money for the needy by lottery was adopted by permission of the British commander, General Robertson. The first beneficiaries of this enterprise were "the poor and distressed objects in the almshouse of this city." Among other voluntary efforts to relieve the poor was that of the Masonic Order, mentioned in the *New York Gazette and Weekly Mercury* of December 22, 1777, as being active in aiding the parish poor of Trinity Church. The same newspaper announced that forty poor widows with families were to be supplied with a quantity of beef and bread on Christmas Eve, through the generosity of a lawyer, John Coggil Knapp. Charity sermons continued to be preached in behalf of the pupils at the charity school, now considered as a parish enterprise.

In December, 1777, General Robertson published an announcement that, in the absence of an elected vestry, he had appointed several willing citizens to take responsibility for the care of the poor. These gentlemen were authorized "to solicit and receive the Donations of the Charitable and well disposed, and to appropriate the same to the Relief of the Poor according to their several Wants and Necessities."[21]

After collecting sufficient funds for temporary relief, the committee members formed into a vestry together with the magistrate of police, and their functions were thus given more stability. To their duties toward the poor was added the responsibility for seeing that the city streets, lamps, pumps, and other public-service equipment and facilities were maintained in good order. To provide a regular source of funds for their functions, the vestrymen were authorized to collect rents on houses belonging to patriots and not being used by the military population. At first this provision applied only to rents for the half-year ending May 1, 1778. On July 9, however, citizens petitioned Sir Henry Clinton to permit the vestry to collect such rents for another year.

Other dependable sources of income allocated to the vestry were tavern licenses, ferry rentals, lotteries, and fines and forfeitures. House and other building rentals totaled £35,281 between 1777 and 1782. Tavern licenses brought in £12,961, ferry rents £3,386, lotteries £10,314, and fines and forfeitures £1,474, during the same period.[22] More than half the total, or £35,732, was spent for the poor, the remainder being used for salaries, municipal maintenance, repairs, and miscellaneous purposes.

SUMMARY

The most important developments in public welfare during the Revolutionary period were: (1) the first participation of the state in the financing of poor relief, and (2) the creating of emergency state and county commissioners to administer relief to persons removed from their places of settlement because of the exigencies of the war. Implicit in this action was the recognition of a category that came to be known as the "state poor," that is, dependents who were not properly chargeable either to county or to local administrative units, but to the state. The stringent settlement laws were practically suspended during the emergency. This period also witnessed the operation for the first time of special forms of assistance to disabled veterans and to the resident families of soldiers wounded or killed in action.

BIBLIOGRAPHICAL REFERENCES

1. New York State Convention of the Representatives, 1776–77, *Journals of the Provincial Congress, Provincial Convention, Committee of Safety and Council of Safety of the State of New York, 1775–1776–1777*, I, 231. Hereinafter referred to as *Journals of the Provincial Congress.*

2. *Ibid.*, p. 282.

3. *Ibid.*, p. 290.

4. *Ibid.*, p. 348.

5. New York State Secretary of State, *Calendar of Historical Manuscripts Relating to the War of the Revolution in the Office of the Secretary of State, Albany, N.Y.* (Albany, 1868), I, 311. Hereinafter referred to as *Calendar of Historical Manuscripts Relating to the War of the Revolution.*

6. *Journals of the Provincial Congress*, I, 488–89.

7. *Ibid.*, p. 518.

8. *Ibid.*, p. 578.

9. *Ibid.*, p. 579.

10. New York State Comptroller's Office, *New York in the Revolution as Colony and State: Supplement* (Albany, 1901), p. 119.

11. *Journals of the Provincial Congress*, I, 709.

12. *Ibid.*, p. 916.

13. *Calendar of Historical Manuscripts Relating to the War of the Revolution*, I, 263–64.

14. *Ibid.*, p. 320.

15. *Ibid.*, p. 111.

16. *Ibid.*, II, 95–96.

17. New York State, *Laws of 1779*, chap. 30.

18. *Journals of the Provincial Congress*, I, 1032.

19. Albany Co., N.Y., Committee of Correspondence, *Minutes of the Albany Committee of Correspondence 1775–1778* (Albany, 1923–25), II, 1086.

20. Stokes, *Iconography*, V, 1043.

21. *Ibid.*, p. 1060.

22. Oscar T. Barck, *New York City during the War for Independence* (New York, 1931), p. 92.

CHAPTER VI

THE PUBLIC WELFARE SYSTEM UNDER
THE NEW STATE

The American Revolution set in motion a great wave of humanitarian reform that profoundly affected the treatment of the dependent and delinquent classes in many parts of the new nation, including New York State. Its influence, however, is hardly perceptible in the general poor laws of New York State during the first half-century of its existence. Not only were the harsh measures of the provincial period repeated, but others were added which in some respects were even more severe.

Peace had been signed, and the evacuation of New York City was several months past when the state legislature on April 17, 1784, enacted its first general law providing for "the Settlement and Relief of the Poor."[1] This statute repeated in substance the law of settlement and relief enacted in 1773 by the provincial legislators. There was one significant change, however, whereby the poor-law administrative system within the state was completely secularized. While the administration of local public welfare previously had been intrusted to churchwardens and vestrymen as well as overseers of the poor, only the last of these three groups was retained in the new act. The act specifically abolished the offices of churchwarden and vestryman in the southern counties—New York, Queens, Richmond, and Westchester—where these offices had been established a century before as active symbols of royal-ecclesiastic rule. Another departure in the law of 1784 reflected the democratic influence of the Revolution. It placed in the hands of "a majority of the freeholders and inhabitants, who shall be assembled at the annual district meetings," the right

to make prudential rules and orders for the sustenance of the poor, for binding out as apprentices the children of such parents as are unable to maintain them, and for compelling such persons to work as have not any visible means of gaining an honest livelihood; and at the same meetings to determine and agree upon

such sum and sums of money as they may think proper for the purposes aforesaid in the ensuing year. . . . .

The annual election of two overseers of the poor for each ward in
New York City was authorized by this statute. The overseers, in co-
operation with the Common Council, were empowered to exercise
the functions of the erstwhile churchwardens and vestrymen. Another section of the act vested in the trustees of the town of Kingston the powers exercised by overseers of the poor in other localities
throughout the state.

The act of 1784 erected the same elaborate barriers against obtaining a settlement as had appeared in the 1773 law and re-enacted
the severe penalties against those who violated its provisions. It
even narrowed the range of the local relief system, ordering the re-
division of districts formerly combined into parishes for joint support of their poor and directing that henceforth each district must
support its own poor.

The legislature of 1788 passed a second general poor law entitled
"An Act for the Better Settlement and Relief of the Poor," which
stated in its preamble that "the laws of this State for the settlement
and relief of the poor and for the removal of disorderly persons, have
by experience been found insufficient."[2] The very first section of the
new law laid down in simplest terms the principle of local responsibility: "Every city and town shall support and maintain their own
poor."

Like its predecessors, the new act dealt more with the problems of
settlement and removal than with those of relief. The requirements
for obtaining legal settlement were made far more stringent than
those prevailing in the provincial period. It was provided that settlement might be obtained by (1) renting and occupying a tenement in
a city or town of the yearly value of at least twelve pounds for two
years and actually paying such rent; (2) holding a public office or
charge in such city or town for one year; (3) being charged with and
paying the city or town taxes for two years; (4) having served as a
bound apprentice or servant in such city or town for at least two
years. Under the new statute the minimum rental required for gaining settlement was raised from five to twelve pounds per annum, and
the period of minimum tenancy was raised to two years instead of

forty days as formerly required. However, if a newcomer filed notice with two overseers of the poor within forty days after arrival and remained undisturbed in his new residence for twelve months, he thereby gained legal settlement. Children born out of wedlock were to be adjudged legally settled in the place of settlement of their mothers. Such children formerly had been settled in the town or city of their birth.

A newcomer suspected of being likely to become a public charge could be brought by an overseer of the poor before two justices of the peace for investigation. If an examination of the suspect convinced the justices that he was likely to become chargeable, they were empowered to order the stranger removed to the place of his settlement within a certain time. Upon failure of the stranger to obey such order, the justices were authorized to issue a warrant directing a constable to

convey or transport such stranger to the constable of the next city or town, through which such stranger shall have been suffered to wander and stroll unapprehended, and so from constable to constable, or in such manner, by the nearest and most convenient route, as the said justices shall think fit to direct, to the place of legal settlement of such stranger, if the same shall be within this State.

If the stranger had no legal settlement within the state or if his place of settlement could not be discovered, he was to be relayed from constable to constable to his place of last settlement or to a city or town beyond the state's borders. On the surface, this "passing-on" method of removal appeared simple and expedient, but in practice it proved to be most cumbersome and costly. An inveterate wanderer might be conveyed two or three times through the town whence he had been removed, in the course of retracing his circuitous route in the hands of constables, before finally reaching his destination. Suits to enforce acceptance of removed paupers or to prevent their being passed on to a certain district became regular features of relief administration in nearly every town along the highways of the state. The law provided that each constable engaged in the transportation of a removed stranger to his place of settlement must be paid for his services by his respective city or town. Before many years had passed a great outcry was raised against the iniquities and expense of passing on. We shall later have occasion to refer in some detail to this aspect of early poor-law administration.

Whipping was provided as a punishment for indigent strangers who dared to return to a community after having been removed. The statute of 1788, repeating the provision of 1721, declared that all such persons "shall, by every constable into whose charge such person shall come, if the justices . . . . shall think proper and so direct, be whipped, if a man not exceeding thirty-nine lashes, and if a woman, not exceeding twenty-five lashes, and so as often as he or she shall return, after such transportation." This provision, unsurpassed for harshness in the history of the state's poor laws, was to remain in effect for many years.

A fine of forty shillings was to be placed upon any inhabitant who should receive or entertain for fifteen days any person lacking settlement in the state, unless the inhabitant gave written notice within that period to an overseer of the poor "of the name, quality, condition and circumstances of the person so entertained, according to the best knowledge of such householder or inhabitant." The law authorized payment of half of the fine to anyone who should successfully sue an inhabitant or householder for violation of this section, thus placing a premium on informing against one's neighbor. If the stranger in question were discovered after remaining more than forty days with no written notice of his arrival, two justices of the peace might cause all who had entertained him without giving information of his presence to enter into bond to the amount of £100 against his becoming a public charge. If, however, it was decided that the residents involved were incapable of furnishing such bond, the justices were authorized to have the stranger conveyed out of the state in the direction of his last settlement.

As in 1773, the law permitted poor residents unable to find employment in their places of legal settlement to remove to other towns or cities within the state. There they could remain undisturbed in the pursuit of some honest employment, provided that they first procured a certificate of settlement from the overseers of the poor of their home town or district. Such certificates were to be delivered upon arrival to the overseers in the new place of residence. No person could obtain legal settlement in his new home by reason of such certificate, no matter how long he stayed. Settlement could be secured by certificated persons only (1) through the purchase of a freehold of the value of at least thirty pounds, or (2) the rental and occupancy for two years of a tenement of the annual value of at least twelve pounds, or (3) the execution of a local public office or charge for one whole year. A certificated person who failed to obtain settlement through these means could be transported back to his place of last legal settlement at any time that he became a public charge. If he should die or fall so sick as to make removal inconvenient, any public expenses arising from his burial or care were to be charged to the place of his legal settlement. The right of appeal was provided for in all cases, while penalties were to be imposed for "vexatious removals and frivolous appeals."

In contrast to the more stringent settlement requirements for other classes of newcomers, however, the new act contained an unusually liberal clause, providing that:

. . . . all marriners coming into this State and having no settlement in this State, or in any other of the United States of America; and every other healthy able-bodied person coming directly from some foreign port or place into this State, shall be deemed and adjudged to be legally settled in the city or town in which he or she shall have first resided for the space of one year.*

Behind this provision, evidently, was the desire to obtain a steady supply of trained sailors to man the growing merchant marine of the port of New York and a supply of skilled labor which might be profitably exploited in connection with the state's expanding commerce and industry.

Perhaps immigrants were favored over itinerant natives because, with land transport so difficult and a settled existence the rule, those who moved from town to town were generally suspected of being worthless.

While encouraging the settlement of able-bodied immigrants likely to augment the labor power within the state, the legislature built strong defenses against indigents and potential indigents from abroad by stringent regulations concerning entry of foreign-born

---

* An act of 1813 amended this provision in so far as it affected New York City, authorizing the Commissioners of the Almshouse and Bridewell to decide on the qualifications for gaining settlement in that city.

passengers at the port of New York. Within twenty-four hours of arrival at the port the master of a vessel was obliged to file with the mayor (or with the recorder in the mayor's absence) a written report, under oath, containing information as to the names and occupations of all persons brought into the state. The master was to forfeit twenty pounds for every passenger whose name was omitted and an additional ten pounds if that passenger were a foreigner. A householder who entertained a foreigner without reporting to the mayor or recorder was liable to a fine of five pounds. If a master of any vessel brought to the state "any person who cannot give a good account of himself or herself," or likely to become a public charge, he was obliged to transport or arrange for the transport of such person to the place of his embarkation within a month after his arrival in New York State. Each master was further obliged to post a £100 bond with the authorities of the port city against any of his passengers becoming public charges. Refusal to be bonded was punishable by commitment to jail until such bond was furnished. Apparently the inflow of indigents through the northern ports was too unimportant to warrant legislative safeguards at this time.

Having erected a formidable series of barriers against the acquisition of legal settlement by strangers likely to become public charges, and having arranged a judicial and constabulary system for their expulsion if unwanted and their punishment if they returned, the act finally turned to the problem of procedure for the actual disbursement of relief. The statute provided that persons in need of public relief must apply to one or more of the local overseers of the poor, who in turn were directed to bring the application to the attention of a local justice of the peace. An inquiry was then to be made by the justice, together with the overseer or overseers, into the condition and circumstances of the person applying for relief. If the case appeared to require public aid, the justice of the peace was to give a written authorization to the overseers of the poor to grant a certain allowance, weekly or otherwise, to the applicant. The overseers were forbidden to advance any relief beyond that authorized in the justice's order.

The act of 1788 contained the first provision in the state's history for the proper registration of all persons receiving public relief. The

overseers of each city and town were required to procure at public
expense "a book of good paper and well bound, wherein the names
of all poor persons applying for relief and being ordered to be relieved as aforesaid, shall be registered, with the day and year when
they are first admitted to have relief, the weekly or other sum or
sums of money allowed by the order for their relief, and the cause of
such necessity." No person was to be entered into the poor-books
unless an order authorizing his relief had first been obtained from a
justice of the peace. Overseers placing any person on the relief rolls
without receiving such an order were liable to a fine equivalent to the
sum expended for the relief of such person. The poor-books were
to serve as complete records, for accounting purposes, of all transac-
tions in public relief during the overseers' tenure of office. The overseers were ordered to present their accounts annually to the local
authorities for auditing.

Overseers of the poor were empowered to bind out children as apprentices or servants with the consent of the county justices of the
peace or of the mayor, recorder, and alderman, or any two of them,
in any city. All indentures or contracts for binding or placing out
children were to bear a clause stating: "That every master and
mistress to whom such child shall be bound as aforesaid shall cause
such child to be taught and instructed to read and write." The overseers were authorized to act as guardians of every bound child and
to see to it that the terms of the indenture or contract were observed, "and that such child be not ill used."

The statute provided a system of poor-relief administration
suited to the special needs of the city of New York. It authorized
the appointment by the Common Council of a body of twelve or
more to be known as "the commissioners of the almshouse and
bridewell," empowered to exercise the functions of overseers of the
poor. In pursuance of this act, the Common Council of New York
City appointed thirteen men to serve as commissioners. This step
marked an important departure in the relief policy of the city. In
1784 the Common Council had appointed thirteen commissioners to
manage the local bridewell (a combined jail and house of correction),
but the administration of poor relief had remained in the hands of
the Common Council aided by the local vestrymen. When the poor

law of 1784 abolished the office of vestrymen, the entire responsibility of poor relief fell on the Common Council. In 1785, upon petition of the municipal authorities, the state legislature enacted chapter 40, providing that "the power, duty and authority of overseeing and providing for the poor shall be vested in the mayor, aldermen and commonality of the said city, in common council convened, to be assisted by such commissioners as they have commissioned or appointed, or hereafter shall commission or appoint. . . . ." The commissioners chosen to assist the Common Council were those already serving as the managers of the bridewell, and the latter thenceforth became known as the Commissioners of the Almshouse and Bridewell. The poor law of 1788 raised the commissioners from the rank of assistants to the Common Council and placed the greater part of the administration of municipal public welfare into their hands.

Another section of the statute of 1788 provided that "in all cases where any of the present poor in any county of this State are maintained by the whole county, or by more than one town, such poor persons shall continue to be so maintained." This section applied primarily to areas where the population was so small and scattered that it became necessary for the county, rather than the local district, to act as the relief unit.

A very important section of the act contained a general authorization for the erection of almshouses in all towns and cities desiring to build such institutions. While the legislature had previously enacted laws permitting the erection of almshouses in specific localities, this was the first statute containing a general provision for this purpose. It declared that henceforth the overseers of the poor in any city or town within the state, with the consent and approval of the proper local authorities, could "build, purchase or hire" at the expense of the town or city "some convenient dwelling house or houses in such city or town, for the lodging and accommodation of the poor thereof."* They were further empowered

to purchase necessary materials for setting such poor persons to work; and there to keep, maintain and employ all and every such poor person, and to

* In the cities of Albany and Hudson, the consent of the Common Council was required; the overseers of the poor, together with any two county justices of the peace, of any town within the state might take this step with the "consent and approbation of the major part of the freeholders and inhabitants of such town."

take the benefit of the work, labour and services of any such poor person who shall be kept and maintained in any such house, for the better maintenance and relief of such poor persons, who shall there be kept and maintained, and thereof to appoint such person or persons, as keeper or keepers, from time to time, as they shall think proper; and in case any poor person, claiming relief of any city or town within this State, where such house or houses shall be so built, purchased or hired, shall refuse to be lodged, kept to work and maintained, in such house or houses, such poor person or persons refusing shall be put out of the book in which the names of the poor are by this act directed to be registered, and shall not be entitled to ask or receive any relief from the overseers of the poor of any such city or town.

Where towns were too small to establish almshouses independently, town unions were authorized for the purpose of maintaining an almshouse jointly. In such cases the overseers and justices of any two or more towns within a county might unite, with the approval of the freeholders, to plan jointly and put into operation a poorhouse. The authorities of towns operating poorhouses were empowered to contract with towns having none for the lodging and employing of the poor belonging to the latter towns. Indigent persons refusing to be lodged in the poorhouse of another town under these circumstances could be denied relief altogether.

The division of all counties into towns and the election of two overseers of the poor in each locality were ordered in another statute enacted in 1788.[3] As a result of this act many new towns sprang up during the ensuing quarter-century. Furthermore, the growth of population and other factors rendered it advisable for some towns to split into two or more towns. This process brought in its wake the problem of reapportioning public charges maintained in common in certain districts before the division took place. Numerous legislative acts were passed during this period providing for the "dividing of the poor" among newborn towns.

The work of dividing the poor after the erection of a new town or the division of an old one was no easy matter and often occasioned years of debate. An example of the problems arising out of the division of towns is afforded by the case of Hempstead, which was divided in 1784 into South Hempstead and North Hempstead. When the division took place, it was agreed that "the poor and the poorhouse (with its furniture) be equally divided between the two towns. . . . ."[4] A list of the poor belonging to each town was drawn up and agreed upon, each being assigned about twenty-four indigents. But the agreement proved more difficult to put into practice than it had been to put on paper. Three years later, representatives of North Hempstead and South Hempstead met "to Settle Some Arrearages Respecting the Poor of both Towns." These representatives were unable to arrive at a settlement until 1791, when they finally drew up a mutually satisfactory agreement. Among the arrears which the two towns agreed to pay jointly were the following:[5]

To the Widow Tredwell for Boarding and Nursing
an Indian Woman, the sum of.................. £ 3: 0: 0
Daniel Hewlet for Boarding Evans................ 11: 0:10
Black Charles for Nursing Negro Wench........... 3: 0: 0
Doctor Tredwells Ac't.......................... 2: 7: 6

It was also agreed that North Hempstead would thenceforth support one John Glass and his wife, in return for which it was to receive the sum of £16, while South Hempstead was to be paid £ 26 4s. 11d. for having previously maintained the Glasses. The articles of agreement further declared that "if John Hendersons Children is Liable to A support from these Towns by Virtue of a Certificate given by this Town before it was Divided, that North Hempstead Shall be at the Equal half of their Support if there should be a Lawsuit Commenced on the Occasion, the Expence to be Equal between the Two Towns." According to the agreement, if any person who had left Hempstead before that town's division returned without having obtained a legal settlement elsewhere and should become a public charge, then such person "shall be Supported by the Town where his last Settlement was in Either of the Two Towns."

The legislature in 1788 authorized the county boards of supervisors to levy poor taxes and to issue warrants to collectors, with the exception of New York City, where the Common Council was empowered to levy the poor rates.[6]

In 1801 the legislature again enacted a general poor law which repeated most of the provisions of the statute of 1788.[7] An important amendment to the poor law of 1801 was enacted eight years later, wherein it was ordered that when an indigent person lacking residence in any city or town within the state applied for relief in any locality and was too sick or disabled to be removed conveniently to his place of settlement, relief should be granted him by the local authorities. The accounts of funds expended for this purpose had to be recorded separately from the ordinary poor-books and were to be considered a county charge, "levied, collected and paid as other county charges are."[8] Thus nonresident public charges who could not be removed, owing to sickness or disability, were placed in the category of "county poor." This act represented what was probably the first step along the path which led ultimately to the establishment of state responsibility for nonresident indigents.

Another statute enacted in 1809 authorized the overseers of the poor of the several towns within the state to loan out at interest money placed in their hands for the relief of the poor, over and above the amount deemed necessary for the latter purpose. The accrued interest was to go into the general poor fund.[9]

In 1813 a general poor law was again enacted, comprising most of the provisions of the 1788 statute. The means for gaining settlement remained practically the same as before. However, the clause exempting New York City from the section regulating settlement requirements differed markedly from that contained in previous poor laws. It read:

Provided always, That the person or persons who may have, or hereafter shall come into the city of New York from any other state within the United States of America, shall not be deemed and adjudged legally settled under this section, unless the party shall first prove to the satisfaction of the commissioners of the alms-house and bridewell of the said city that after his or her arrival therein, he or she, as the case may be, shall have acquired such requisites to constitute a settlement, as are necessary in and by the laws of such state from whence he or she may have come as aforesaid.[10]

In the last clause we have an early indication of the principle of reciprocal treatment and also of the growing problem arising from the lack of uniformity in the settlement laws of the several states, a problem that continues to our own day.

The poor law of 1813 differed from its predecessors in another significant respect: it contained no provision for the corporal punishment of indigents returning to the place whence they had been removed. A harsh practice finally had been dropped from the statute books.

Settlement requirements were rendered far more stringent than ever before in a statute enacted in 1817 amending the act of settlement and relief passed four years earlier. According to the amendment, no person coming into New York State from any other state or from Canada could gain a settlement in any city or town unless (1) he purchased and paid for real estate in such city or town valued at $250, or (2) had rented and occupied a tenement of at least $100 rental annually for a period of four years or more (instead of a $30 minimum rental for two years, which had previously been sufficient for gaining settlement), or (3) had executed a public office in such city or town for three whole years (instead of one year), or (4) had been bound as an apprentice or servant and served as such for not less than seven years (instead of two years as formerly).[11] The requirements for gaining settlement as laid down in this amendment were the strictest ever to obtain in New York State.

Another section of the same amending act declared that the justices of the peace in any locality, after deciding that a stranger having no settlement anywhere in New York State was likely to become a public charge, might at their discretion order him "removed *directly* to the place where such person was last legally settled without this State." Implicit in this provision was the growing recognition of the evils and waste of the passing-on system commonly resorted to in removing nonsettled indigents, and an attempt was made to substitute direct removals, which were more humane and less costly. In 1821 the legislature further amended this provision, authorizing the local justices of the peace, after ascertaining that a stranger was likely to become chargeable, to order the latter's removal directly to his last place of legal settlement. Upon neglect or refusal to comply with this order, a warrant was to be issued ordering the local constable

to convey or transport such stranger to the constable of the first town or city, as the case may be, in the adjoining county; or if within the same county, to the town where the pauper was last legally settled, through which such stranger shall have been suffered to wander unapprehended, and so from the constable of one county to the first constable in the next adjacent county, and so from county to county by the nearest and most convenient route . . . . to the place of legal settlement of such stranger, if the same be within this state.[12]

If it appeared that the "said pauper" had first entered the state through the city of New York and that he had not acquired a settlement anywhere in the state, he was to be passed on to that city, there to be disposed of as the municipal poor-relief authorities saw fit.

The aforementioned statute of 1817 contained a provision aimed against a widespread practice of the time, the "dumping" of paupers by stealth upon one county or state by the authorities of another. The act provided that "if any person or persons shall bring or remove, or cause to be brought or removed, any poor or indigent person into any city or town within this state, and there leave such poor or indigent person, not having a legal settlement therein, and without legal authority so to do, such person or persons shall forfeit the sum of twenty-five dollars," together with the costs of the suit brought against the offender by the local overseers of the poor. This practice of illegal transportation of paupers will later be discussed at some length.

FINES AS A SOURCE OF POOR-RELIEF FUNDS

Besides raising poor funds through local taxation, the state continued the custom of assigning to local relief funds all or parts of fines levied for various offenses. Hawking and peddling, malicious trespass, excessive and deceitful gaming, Sabbath-breaking, profanity and drunkenness, violation of excise laws, export regulations, game-preservation laws, ferry regulations, inspection regulations for flour, meal, and sole leather, firing woods, cutting certain trees in the town of Schenectady, fire-limit violations in New York City and Albany, and fishing with nets in the Croton River, were some of the many offenses bearing fines which swelled the poor fund. Casks bearing false tare or brand marks were to be seized and sold, a moiety of ten pounds net to go to the poor. Such fines proved a fruitful source for financing poor relief.

SUMMARY

This period witnessed the completion of the process of secularization of poor-relief administration within the state. Responsibility for local relief functions passed entirely from the hands of ecclesiastic officials, churchwardens and vestrymen, into the hands of purely civil authorities, the overseers of the poor. In general, the settlement laws were made even more stringent than they had been during the colonial period, although the gaining of settlement was facilitated in the case of immigrant workers, farmers, and seamen who were willing to labor in the new land. Until the year 1813, corporal punishment was authorized in cases where indigent and other undesirable nonresidents dared return to a community from which they had been previously ejected. Among the provisions of the general poor law of 1788 was a section ordering the proper registration in poor-books of all persons receiving public relief. Power to bind out poor children as apprentices or servants was placed in the hands of local overseers of the poor. In New York City the functions of overseers of the poor were vested in a body known as the Commissioners of the Almshouse and Bridewell. The poor law of 1788 authorized the continuance of relief by the whole county or by "town unions" wherever it had existed heretofore, and included a general authorization of almshouse-building in all localities desiring such institutions. An act of 1801 provided that nonresident indigents too sick or disabled to be removed should be considered county charges, thus constituting one of the earliest groups to come under the category of "county poor." Indigent nonresidents were generally removed to their places of legal settlement through the passing-on system, being passed on by the constable of one locality to the constable of the adjacent locality until they reached their destination. In 1817, and again in 1821, justices of the peace were authorized to remove nonresident public charges directly to their places of settlement under certain conditions, instead of resorting to the prolonged, wasteful, and humiliating passing-on system. Besides taxes, court fines imposed for specified violations of the law were used for poor-relief purposes.

BIBLIOGRAPHICAL REFERENCES

1. New York State, *Laws of 1784*, chap. 35.
2. ———, *Laws of 1788*, chap. 62.
3. ———, *ibid.*, chap. 64.

4. Henry Onderdonk, Jr., *The Annals of Hempstead, 1643–1832* (Hempstead, 1878), p. 81.
5. *Records of North and South Hempstead*, VI, 279–80.
6. New York State, *Laws of 1788*, chaps. 65 and 67.
7. ———, *Laws of 1801*, chap. 184.
8. ———, *Laws of 1809*, chap. 90.
9. ———, *ibid.*, chap. 139.
10. ———, *Laws of 1813*, chap. 78.
11. ———, *Laws of 1817*, chap. 177.
12. ———, *Laws of 1821*, chap. 220.

CHAPTER VII

THE IMMIGRANT POOR

It has been said with much truth that the two grand themes of American history are the influence of immigration upon American life and institutions, and the impress of the American environment upon the ever-changing population. Certain it is that the course of events in New York has been profoundly affected by immigration. The principal factors focusing immigration upon this state were its geographic and economic position and its great harbor at the mouth of the Hudson offering natural access to the western lands.

Many who entered this harbor with high expectations found their dreams fulfilled. This is especially true of those who managed to reach the interior, where free lands were to be had in abundance, and where equal opportunity for the foreign born was no mere abstract ideal. But large numbers landing in New York City, without friends or funds, soon found themselves drawn into the slums, or even worse, the public almshouse. For them there was only disillusionment and despair.

To gain a foothold in the New World immigrants usually had to engage in the so-called "lowest" forms of work at correspondingly low rates of pay. The humble and ill-paid labors of its immigrant population were, however, vital to the development of the city as one of the great trade-centers of the world. As to the rest of the state, the Erie and other canals, and the first railroads linking New York City with the Mohawk Valley and the unfolding empire to the west were largely built by the hands of foreign-born workers. If the economic pattern of the time had involved a fair return for the great contribution of the immigrant, the number of foreign-born paupers would have been negligible.

Upon arrival, immigrant families generally had to eke out a precarious existence on a bare subsistence level. Unable to build up reserves and hence quickly pauperized when overtaken by unemployment, sickness, or the death of a breadwinner, they found it necessary to lean upon charity more heavily and more often, in proportion to their numbers, than members of the native population. This disproportion was discerned much sooner than were its causes, and for more than a century it evoked a great amount of condemnation and alarm, often coupled with a minimum of understanding.

We have seen in preceding pages how the infiltration of able-bodied immigrants skilled at some occupation was actually encouraged in legislation passed in New York both as a colony and as a state. We have referred to the clause in the general act of 1788 facilitating the settlement of foreign-born mariners "and every other healthy able-bodied person coming directly from some foreign port or place into this State." But for unfortunate foreigners, able-bodied or otherwise, who became public charges or were likely to "fall on the town," an unsympathetic attitude was usually displayed. By the year 1819, the Society for the Prevention of Pauperism—the leading welfare agency in the city of New York, having some of the most progressive citizens of the municipality among its active members—found itself constrained to list "emigrants to this city from foreign countries" at the head of nine sources of pauperism enumerated in its annual report for that year:

This inlet of pauperism threatens us with the most overwhelming consequences. From various causes, the City of New York is doomed to be the landing-place of a great portion of the European population, who are daily flocking to our country for a place of permanent abode. . . . . Many of them arrive here destitute of everything. When they do arrive, instead of seeking the interior, they cluster in our cities . . . . depending on the incidents of time, charity, or depredation, for subsistence. . . . . They are frequently found destitute in our streets; they seek employment at our doors; they are found in our alms-house, and in our hospitals. . . . . For years and generations will Europe continue to send forth her surplus population. The winds and the waves will still bring needy thousands to our sea-ports, and this city continue the general point of arrival. Over this subject can we longer slumber?

New York is the resting place and is liable to be devoured by swarms of people. . . . . Where is this evil to stop, and who can compass its magnitude?[1]

This "evil" was to become a progressively large problem in relation to poor relief in the state and particularly in the city of New York. It was to exert such pressure on welfare resources that it resulted in 1847 in what was probably the first permanent state-wide public welfare body in the United States—the New York State Board of Commissioners of Emigration.

Several fundamental questions arise at this point: Why was the contribution of immigration to the dependent population proportionately so great? What was its background? What effect did it have on the development of poor-law administration in New York? In view of the important historic influences of immigration on public welfare, we shall discuss at some length certain general principles involved and their specific application to this state.

Broadly speaking, two major factors determine the phenomenon of emigration: (1) discontent with home conditions, and (2) hope for improvement in some other country. Mass emigration is caused chiefly by unfavorable economic conditions. The flight from famine and the quest for food have steered countless shiploads of foreigners to these shores. Escape from religious and political oppression and hope for fuller freedom also brought great numbers of strangers who eventually made this land their own.

The relatively slight immigration during the first forty years of the Republic may be attributed to a number of circumstances acting as checks to mass immigration. Conditions in the "critical period" which followed the termination of the Revolutionary War, during which the newborn nation struggled to gain a foothold on this globe, could hardly be expected to attract throngs from other lands no matter how unfavorable the conditions were there. People will choose, ordinarily, to remain and suffer in familiar surroundings rather than to set their faces toward a dark and highly uncertain future elsewhere.

The early years of the nineteenth century witnessed a continuous state of intense hardship throughout Europe that provided strong stimuli to emigration. In the British Isles, the long process of converting farm land into pasture led to the dispossession and impoverishment of tenant farmers. In the factory towns that were rapidly springing up in England, starvation wages and irregular employment wrought heartbreaking consequences upon great masses of people. Oppressive conditions in Ireland had led to two abortive rebellions in 1798 and 1803. On the Continent, the Napoleonic Wars which disrupted Europe for more than a decade, 1803-15, resulted in still less tolerable situations.

This chain of circumstances would doubtless have driven many more thousands to migrate to America than actually landed here during those years, had it not been that counterbalancing forces acted as checks on both sides of the Atlantic. On the European side, the huge impressment of man power during the wars—added to the blockades established by the nations involved, which made oversea transportation an extremely hazardous venture—acted as an effective check on migration. On the American side, the cities along the seaboard, particularly New York, were experiencing troublous times. The Embargo Laws promulgated during Jefferson's administration had caused a virtual stoppage of shipping between the United States and the principal commercial countries of Europe. This suspension of ocean commerce had no satisfactory abatement in the years extending through the War of 1812, and, in consequence, New York City experienced a prolonged period of depression. In view of these restraining factors, it is surprising that even the few thousands who managed to enter the port of New York annually during these trying times had the fortitude to undertake the trans-Atlantic trip.

The termination of the Napoleonic conflicts in Europe and the Anglo-American War of 1812-15 resulted in the lifting of blockades, and thus the Atlantic once more became a peaceful highway of international traffic. At the same time the sudden demobilization of huge armies and navies participating in the European wars loosed hordes of penniless, unattached men on the countrysides of the Continent. It was several years before these people could be absorbed in normal pursuits. Meanwhile there was widespread suffering in the nations affected. This misery was greatly intensified by the succession of crop failures throughout Europe in 1816-17. No wonder that large numbers turned their eyes westward to the New World beyond the sea!

While Europe was passing through this period of accentuated hardships, letters from America, written by persons who had migrated to the States, were pouring into the old countries, particularly

Great Britain and the German states. In these letters, conditions in America were usually painted in glowing colors. Here are extracts from a specimen communication sent in 1818 by one Luke Bentley residing "40 miles West of New York City," to his brother in England:

We are all in good health and doing well. Any industrious person may do well here. Money is scarce but we get plenty of all the blessings of life. There are poor people here, but no hungry children crying for bread in vain, they all have enough and to spare. This is the promised land, flowing with milk and honey.

If an honest man is set naked on the American shore, he may soon make an independence. 'Tis the duty of those who have a number of children to place them where they can get a living—this is that place.[2]

This letter, like many others sent abroad and widely circulated in European countries, ends with an urgent exhortation to the writer's kinfolk and friends to come to America at once to partake of its bounty. As in later years, these epistolary sirens' songs found many willing ears. It would be difficult to overestimate their influence on the flow of immigration.

Here, then, were elements strongly conducive to America-bound migration, and the response was not slow in manifesting itself. No accurate immigration statistics are available for the period prior to 1819, but even if we accept the generous estimate of Seybert, the total number of foreigners arriving in all parts of the country from 1790 to 1810 averaged only 6,000 annually.[3] In 1817, however, more than 20,000 entered the United States, of whom more than 7,600 landed in the port of New York. Moreover, in the twenty months from March, 1818, to November of the following year, an estimated number of 28,000 arrived in this city.* It was this sudden increase in numbers that occasioned the alarm of the Society for the Prevention of Pauperism and caused it to issue its sharp warning against the invasion of "pauper hordes" from Europe. The economic depression of 1819–20 had the effect of slowing up the immigrant tide for a

* The influence of this sudden influx of foreigners on the population of New York is indicated in the city's rate of increase during the second decade of the nineteenth century. In 1810, the population was 96,373; by 1816 the total had increased little more than 4,000. But during the four years, 1816–20, the population grew to 123,700, a gain of 23,000.

time, but the number of arrivals picked up again in the late twenties and increased steadily in volume thereafter until it rose to a deluge a generation later.

They must have been hardy souls who braved and survived the long, weary, and extremely perilous voyage of those days. Judging from contemporary accounts of the trans-Atlantic passage via steerage, it must have seemed like an endless nightmare to those who endured it. This is how a passenger sailing to the United States from Belfast in 1795 characterizes the journey:

> The slaves who are carried from the coast of Africa have much more room allowed them than the immigrants who pass from Ireland to America, for the avarice of captains in that trade is such that they think they can never load their vessels sufficiently, and they trouble their heads in general no more about the accommodation and storage of their passengers than of any other lumber aboard.[4]

Unfortunately, this unflattering characterization was to remain applicable to immigrant carriers for decades to come. As in later years, most immigrants to America traveled in steerage. Cabin passengers were rare and even cabin accommodations in those days were not much better than the steerage of a century later. The poor traveler was left to the mercies of ship captains, agents, and other individuals who, more often than not, subscribed to that peculiarly widespread doctrine that the immigrant is fair game for all.

Not until about 1830 did ships come into use which were built especially for passenger service. Up to then passengers were considered as mere appendages to the cargo. It was customary for owners of vessels to enter into contracts with passenger agents whereby the latter, in return for a stipulated amount, were allotted a portion of steerage into which they might herd as many immigrants as could be induced to hazard the voyage. Obviously, the more he could crowd together into the steerage, the greater the agent's profit —and few agents of the period were burdened with scruples concerning the welfare of their clients.

The passage from Europe to New York sometimes consumed from three to six months. It was the rule for passengers to provide and cook their own food. The custom of having ships provide cooked food for passengers did not become general until well into the

thirties. Some who miscalculated the amount of provisions necessary for the long trip actually starved to death on the voyage.

Even more fearful to the immigrant poor than the specters of
hunger and starvation haunting the westward voyage, was the ever
present danger of an outbreak of the dread "ship fever" or typhus.
Many of the ships, as has been indicated, were unfit even for animal
transport; some had been abandoned as too unsafe for ordinary
cargo before being turned into immigrant vessels. The crowded steerage, the indescribable filth and dirt, the usual scarcity of wholesome
food, the use of stale and polluted water—in short, a total lack of
sanitation—all contributed to the generation of disease that made
the term "fever-ships" a notorious byword for immigrant vessels of
the nineteenth century.

In their efforts to evade the head tax, quarantine laws, and other
immigration measures, some captains showed no scruples about
smuggling in immigrants. Frequently, foreigners who had paid their
passage to New York City were landed at ports in near-by states
where the immigration laws were more lax, and the shipowners were
thus enabled to escape fees, quarantine inspection, and other port
regulations.* The passengers would then be sent on to New York.
They might be smuggled in by rowing them over under the cloak
of night and landing them in some out-of-the-way spot in the city,
or the captain might simply leave them to find their way to New
York as best they could. Many immigrants disposed of in this
manner and stripped of their last penny before or after landing would
wander into the streets of the city to add to the relief problems
of the harassed authorities.

In this formative period the solution of the question of responsibility for the relief of the foreign-born poor crystallized very slowly.
Both city and state had early begun to take steps toward damming
the flow of paupers from abroad by restrictive and protective enactments such as were contained in the general poor-relief law of 1788.[5]
By the terms of this statute, as has been noted previously, masters of
ships entering the port of New York were required to submit to the
mayor, within twenty-four hours after arrival, a report as to the

* Perth Amboy, in New Jersey, was a favorite landing-place for captains practicing
this ruse.

names and occupations of all passengers aboard. A fine of thirty pounds was fixed for each foreigner unreported. This measure, of course, was primarily intended to safeguard state and city against the "importation" of criminals and paupers. It was also provided that each householder must report all foreigners lodging in his or her house or family on penalty of a five-pound fine. Furthermore, each shipmaster was commanded to post a bond of one hundred pounds as an indemnity for any immigrant brought over on his ship who might become a public charge in any city or town within the state.

These measures met with little success. Vaguely worded and half-heartedly enforced, they could not check the inflow of poverty-stricken foreigners, nor could they effectively place the onus on the masters of immigrant ships for the pauperization of certain passengers after arrival.

Meanwhile the pressure of the foreign poor on the relief resources of New York City was increasing at an alarming rate. In consequence, a hue and cry was raised against the "pauper invasion," with the city turning toward the state for aid. As early as 1796, long before the great tidal waves of immigration had begun to roll into the growing metropolis, the Commissioners of the Almshouse and Bridewell made representation to the mayor and Common Council on the subject of alien poor. Expressing alarm over the "enormous and growing expense" of the upkeep of the Almshouse Department, the commissioners pointed out that this expense ($31,570 for the preceding year) arose "not so much from the increase of our own poor, as from the prodigious influx of indigent foreigners into this city." Of 770 paupers supported by the almshouse in the year 1796, the majority were foreign born, 148 having arrived from Ireland alone. Many of these persons, it was claimed, had been public charges since the time that they had debarked. The commissioners recommended that the city authorities appeal to the state legislature for help. This end might be accomplished either by creating more rigid barriers against indigents from abroad or by establishing state provision for their support:

. . . . for many of them having paid their last shilling to the captain, are landed destitute and emaciated, and we are sadly sensible of the effect of such numbers of these poor people huddling together in cellars and sheds, in and about the

Ship-Yards the last summer and fall; many of whom, as well as of our fellow-citizens in that quarter, fell a prey to the then destroying fever.[6]

The suggestion of the Commissioners of the Almshouse was acted upon by the city officials, who forwarded an appeal for state aid in relieving destitute foreigners. Earlier that year, Governor Jay, in a message to the legislature, had laid down the principle of state responsibility for the support of foreign poor:

The wisdom of our laws, has ordained that every place shall maintain its own poor. But . . . . a great number of persons are induced to come to this State without other resources than what the benevolence of our citizens or other adventitious circumstances may furnish. As these people do not properly belong to any particular place in this or the neighboring states, would it not be right to consider those of them who may be real objects of charity as the poor of the State, and to provide for them accordingly.[7]

Encouraged by the governor's attitude, New York repeatedly applied for state aid.

Some relief to the nonsettled poor in the city was given by the state in 1797. On December 18 of that year the city treasurer was ordered to receive from the state treasurer the sum of $2,000 granted by the legislature to aid in "the maintenance and support of such Poor in this City as shall not have gained any settlement in this State." It was not until 1798, however, that the state provided a means by which relief funds for this purpose might be supplied with some degree of permanence. In response to a petition from the Common Council of New York City, the legislature enacted chapter 89, *Laws of 1798*, which laid an additional tax of 1 per cent on goods sold at auction in the city, the proceeds of which were assigned expressly to the care of the foreign poor.

There was a particular reason why, in early American times, the auction duties could be depended upon to bring in a considerable revenue. Once the colonies were freed from British rule, and especially after 1815, British manufacturers began dumping goods in volume into the United States, often selling them below the cost of production in order to prevent the rise of American competition. Ordinary mercantile channels failing to provide an outlet for imports on such a scale, a host of auctioneers set up sales shops to relieve the congestion at the port of entry. Cries of anguish arose constantly against their enterprises, not only from native manufacturers who could not force their own products into the market, but from established merchants whose profit at times was reduced to zero by the glut. Nonetheless, the auction sales went on and great quantities of goods continued to be moved by this method. The revenue accruing from this measure averaged about $22,000 annually for the next twenty years and considerably eased the welfare burdens during that period. Later amendments to the act changed the share of the city's percentage of the auction duties from 1 per cent of the total sales, as originally provided for, to one-third of the total tax collected.

In the year 1816 the amount of the auction duties laid aside for the support of the foreign poor in New York City rose to $72,750, as compared with $32,450 the previous year. This unusually large revenue is explained by the fact that the post-war depression which had set in after the termination of the Napoleonic and Anglo-American wars forced large numbers of tradesmen to sell their merchandise at public auction. Notwithstanding the circumstances responsible for the huge increase in auction tax receipts, the relatively large sum turned over to the city evoked violent criticism and complaints from some upstate counties. The metropolis was receiving a disproportionate amount for the care of its foreign paupers, these counties claimed, while they got none at all. Districts along the Canadian frontier, and even centrally located ones, demanded that part of the auction duties be diverted to them so that the expense of supporting their foreign poor might be covered by the state.

The wave of protests resulted in legislative action toward the end of 1816, when a resolution was adopted directing the state controller to suspend payments of auction revenues for the time being.[8] After inquiry, the legislature had come to the conclusion that not more than half of the sums thus collected had actually been expended in support of indigent foreigners. It was claimed that the remaining half, if properly invested by the city at 7 per cent, could have yielded an annual income of $18,000 or more—"an ample fund for their [i.e., the foreign poor] future and *permanent* support."

In the port city the suspension of auction-duty payments met with a storm of disapproval. A memorial was drawn up by the city fathers setting forth in some detail New York's right to these moneys.[9] Among other things, the memorial pointed out (1) that the city's problem was unique in that the great majority of European emigrants entered through the port of New York; (2) that those least able to maintain themselves remained in the city, while the more desirable classes went on to the interior; (3) that those who failed in the attempt to earn a living were frequently passed on from town to town to New York; and finally (4) that the burden of supporting these unfortunates fell on New York, not because they had gained settlement there, but because they could be passed on no farther. For them, New York became the last stopping-place, the catch basin.

Furthermore, the memorialists stated, the unusually large sum received as New York's share of the public auction funds during the preceding year was not due to any happy circumstance but could be traced directly to the current economic crisis gripping the seaboard cities, which constituted an ill wind blowing a little good as far as destitute foreigners were concerned, in the form of increased auction sales and duties. At the same time this depression, depriving multitudes of regular employment, placed an additional strain on the city's poor fund. Statistics appended to the memorial show that of a total of 594 persons cared for in the almshouse, 458 were foreigners as against 136 natives.

A joint legislative committee to whom the memorial was referred found in 1817 that its representations were in the main well founded and recommended that the order suspending payment of auction duties be rescinded. A compromise resulted, and instead of receiving as before a percentage of the auction duties, New York was granted a flat sum of $10,000 annually for the support of her foreign poor.[10] This arrangement continued in force until 1850, when payments were again suspended.

DEVELOPMENT OF IMMIGRANT-AID SOCIETIES

Public provision for the relief of sick and destitute foreigners constantly lagged behind the needs of the time. As in other phases of social welfare, private agencies were forced into being to answer the need with which the slow processes of social legislation failed to cope. In New York, the earliest societies formed for the purpose of serving immigrants in need were composed of foreign-born persons or their descendants, who banded together for the assistance of new arrivals from the old country.

The first of these organizations in New York was founded in 1784 by thirteen Germans.* The modest size of its membership list did not deter the organization from keeping abreast of the time by choosing an impressively elongated name, "The German Society in the State of New York for the encouragement of emigration from Germany, the assistance of needy emigrants, and the dissemination of useful knowledge among their countrymen in this State." The aim of the Society was to give advice, protection, and, wherever possible, financial assistance to German immigrants. At first its activities were limited almost exclusively to furnishing information to new arrivals from Germany. But in time the Society's functions were extended, and later it was largely instrumental in protecting the immigrant from fraud and imposition before and after arrival. One of its early concerns was the protection of "redemptioners," that is, persons who contracted with ship captains to be sold into servitude for a certain number of years in lieu of their passage money. Upon landing in port, it was customary to place redemptioners at public sale on the auction block and to bind them out to the highest bidders for a stipulated term of service.† The redemptioner was exposed to many forms of crooked dealing on the part of both the seller and buyer, and cases are recorded where individuals were forced into a lifetime of slavery. Like its prototype in Pennsylvania, the German Society constantly worked toward the elimination of the evils attending this system of white servitude.

Since the Irish, with the Germans, constituted the major proportion of immigrants in New York, it was natural that associations

* The New York St. Andrew's Society, established earlier in 1756, was a benevolent organization of persons of Scotch birth or derivation for the aid of fellow-Scotchmen: it was not primarily a society for immigrant aid.

† The redemptioner system never developed in New York to the extent it did in Pennsylvania. Selling immigrants for passage money came to an end in New York about 1819.

should arise to render advice and assistance to newcomers from Ireland. In the second decade of the nineteenth century at least two such organizations were to be found in the city—the New York Irish Emigrant Society and the Shamrock Society. In their advisory capacity, one point was emphasized by both, namely, that Irishmen seeking homes here should shun the seaboard cities, especially New York, and go to the interior where better opportunity awaited them. A document issued in 1817 by the Shamrock Society, entitled "Hints to Emigrants from Europe," points out that while artisans were better paid here than in Europe and generally enjoyed far more comfort,

> There are not many of the laborious classes, whom we would advise to reside or even loiter in great towns, because as much will be spent during a long winter as can be made through a toilsome summer, so that a man may be kept a moneyless drudge for life. But this is not perhaps the worst; he is tempted to become a tippler, by the cheapness and plenty of liquors, and then his prospects are blasted forever.[11]

Taking the same position, the Irish Emigrant Society in 1818 submitted a memorial to Congress requesting that a portion of unsold lands be set aside for the colonization of Irish newcomers on terms of extended credit. Calling attention to the "helpless and suffering condition of the numerous foreigners flying from a complicated mass of want and misery," the memorialists pointed out that the Irish, owing to the peculiar pressures existing in their native country, were flocking here in great numbers. But "for want of guides to their steps and congenial homes, where all their honest efforts might be called into activity," many were being dammed up at the fountain-head—the ports of entry—where they remained "perplexed, undecided and dismayed." And so, the memorial went on dolorously, "the very energies which would have made the fields to blossom make the cities groan."[12]

This oft-repeated advice not to tarry in New York City but to "go West" was well founded. After surviving the hardships of the average voyage by steerage, the immigrants found themselves in a strange world which was for the most part indifferent to their fate. Representing predominantly agricultural peoples, many found themselves facing new types of problems in an urban environment with which they could hardly be expected to cope successfully. Here they were herded into tenements and "shanty towns" with the chances of escaping the demoralizing, disease- and pauper-breeding environment strongly against them.

SUMMARY

Mass immigration and dependency were closely interrelated during this period and remained so in subsequent years. A large majority of the foreigners landing in the port of New York were extremely poor; some were perilously close to the pauper line upon arrival. Many of them continued westward where they prospered in an environment of splendid opportunities. As a whole they made an invaluable contribution to the building of America. Those who remained, for various reasons, in the eastern seaboard cities, found the going far more difficult, and large numbers became public dependents. The state welcomed and encouraged the settling of skilled foreign workers and farmers, but placed various restrictions upon the settlement of unskilled laborers. In the 1790's the New York City authorities grew so disturbed over the increasing number of foreign poor in the almshouse that they made an urgent request to the state for aid. In 1796 Governor John Jay laid down the principle that the support of nonsettled indigents was properly the responsibility of the state, rather than of any locality within its territory. The following year the legislature made a lump-sum appropriation to New York City toward the support of "such Poor in this City as shall not have gained any settlement in this State." In 1798 a statute was passed creating a permanent means of state aid to the nonsettled poor in New York City, laying aside for this purpose a certain percentage of the auction duties collected in the city. This period also witnessed the rise of several immigrant-aid societies, notably Irish and German.

BIBLIOGRAPHICAL REFERENCES

1. Society for the Prevention of Pauperism in New York City, *Second Annual Report* (New York, 1819), pp. 18 ff.
2. Edith Abbott, *Historical Aspects of the Immigration Problem* (Chicago, 1926), pp. 42–43.

3. Adam Seybert, *Statistical Annals* (Philadelphia, 1818), p. 28.
4. Samuel T. Orth, *Our Foreigners*, "Chronicles of America Series" (New Haven, 1920), XXXV, Part I, 111–12.
5. New York State, *Laws of 1788*, chap. 62.
6. New York City Commissioners of the Almshouse and Bridewell, *Minutes* (MS), February 1, 1796.
7. New York State Governors, *Messages from the Governors* (Albany, 1909), II, 365. Hereinafter referred to as *Messages from the Governors*.
8. New York State Senate, *Journal* (40th sess. [Albany, 1816]), pp. 26, 29.
9. New York City Common Council, *Minutes of the Common Council, 1784–1831* (New York, 1917), VII, 765–67. Hereinafter referred to as *N.Y.C., M.C.C., 1784–1831*.
10. New York State Assembly, *Journal* (40th sess., 2d meeting [Albany, 1817]), pp. 245, 246, 247.
11. Shamrock Society of New York, *Hints to Emigrants from Europe*, reprinted in John Melish, *Travels through the United States of America* (Belfast, 1818), Appendix, p. 629.
12. New York Irish Emigrant Society, "Encouragement to Irish Emigrants, Communicated to the Senate, February 16, 1818," in U.S. Congress, *American State Papers, Class 10, Miscellaneous*, Doc. No. 449, pp. 489–90.

CHAPTER VIII

TREATMENT OF DEBTORS AND VAGRANTS

The great humanitarian movement that spread over the Western world in the late eighteenth century manifested itself in New York State mainly in three directions: reform of the penal code, the rise of private philanthropic societies, and the establishment of institutions devoted to special classes of dependents. While some of these reforms originated in New York, most of them were inspired by developments already under way in Philadelphia or in England and were modeled upon the same lines. This is largely attributable to the fact that the Friends, who played a prominent part in the contemporary reform movement in this state, maintained a steady flow of correspondence with their fellow-Quakers elsewhere and were constantly apprised of reform developments in other cities and countries.

The attention of the reformers was early directed to the problem of humanizing the harsh penal laws then prevailing. The Quakers, notably John Howard of England, were among the first to initiate organized protests against the cruel treatment which society meted out to those who broke its laws. Severe punishment, the progressives declared, far from acting as a deterrent, only hardened the people in general and consequently tended to increase rather than to diminish crime. Even more important, they argued, was the fact that contemporary penal practices were incompatible with the spirit of the Enlightenment, with the new concept of human dignity and justice.

In New York, up to the final years of the eighteenth century, it was customary to resort to either capital or corporal punishment in the treatment of convicted offenders. Persons found guilty of felonies were usually hanged; the penal code provided a death penalty for thirteen different offenses. Those convicted of lesser crimes were ordinarily subjected to corporal punishment such as whipping, placing in stocks or the pillory, and ear-cropping. It was not until

1796—the great penal-reform year in New York—that the first state prison was established.

The jails of the time were used primarily for the detention of persons awaiting trial and for insolvent debtors, while the workhouses and houses of correction received vagrants and disorderly persons. Such correctional institutions, however, were rare during the colonial period. New York City had no separate penal institution until 1756. In earlier years a part of the city hall had been set aside for prison quarters. Ordinary offenders were confined in the basement, dangerous characters in the subbasement, and debtors in the garret. The city erected a separate jail about 1756 and a house of correction or bridewell, as it was called in England, in 1775. The latter institution was reserved for misdemeanants as well as for those felons fortunate enough to escape execution, while the jail was used almost exclusively for the confinement of debtors.

RELIEF FOR POOR DEBTORS

The imprisonment of insolvent debtors was a practice sanctioned by centuries of common law prior to the settlement of the American colonies and was carried over to the New World by the early colonists. The practice was common in the Dutch as well as in the English settlements in the New York colony. For example, when the court at Kingston ordered a prison to be built "for drunken savages and Christians" in 1680, it specified that burghers imprisoned for debt should be confined in the loft of the church, which had been set aside for that purpose—a rather unusual place for a public prison![1]

The practice of imprisoning debtors constituted one of the harshest features of the legal system. Debtors owing insignificant sums and unable to discharge their debts could be thrown into jail on demand of their creditors and, under certain circumstances, could be held there indefinitely. Most of the imprisoned debtors were completely impoverished. A man actually able to discharge a debt would hardly choose instead indefinite confinement in a crowded, vermin-infested, disease-breeding jail. The poor debtor imprisoned by his creditor found himself shut off from the opportunity for gainful employment that might permit him to discharge his obligations, while his family was rendered helpless and his debts continued to pile up, thus prolonging his period of enforced idleness. Furthermore, the imprisoned debtor was in far more difficult straits than his fellow-inmates, since there was no public provision for furnishing him with food or fuel. These necessities had to be purchased by himself or furnished by his family, friends, or private citizens, or else he had to depend upon the jailer to supply them on credit. If an imprisoned debtor happened to be penniless, as was often the case, his plight was indeed a desperate one.

It was not unusual for philanthropic individuals to band together occasionally and hold public entertainments for the benefit of these debtors, even in colonial times. For example, the *New-York Mercury* of January 11, 1768, reported that "a concert is given at Burns' 'long room' for the benefit of poor debtors in gaol."[2] When a charity collection yielding £87 was taken up by a church in New York City in 1772, £30 of this sum was handed over for the relief of imprisoned debtors and their families. Debtors in jail used to hang old shoes and bags from their cell windows as a means of soliciting the alms of passers-by.[3] It was not unusual to find in the newspapers of the period advertisements such as this:

The debtors confined in the Gaol of the City of New York, impressed with a grateful sense of the obligations they are under to a respectable publick for the generous contributions that have been made to them, beg leave to return their hearty thanks .... because they have been preserved from perishing in a dreary prison, from hunger and cold.[4]

Beginning with 1730, when an act was passed for the partial relief of insolvent debtors, sporadic efforts were made to ameliorate their condition. After the successful culmination of the war for independence, the harsh treatment of imprisoned debtors evoked sharper criticism than ever, for it was markedly incompatible with democratic institutions and ideals. Finally, in January, 1787, a group of ten public-spirited citizens, led by Matthew Clarkson, formed themselves into the "Society for the Relief of Distressed Debtors."*

Its objects, as stated in the constitution, were: "To administer to

* It is worthy of note that the establishment of this society preceded by several months the formation of a similar group in Philadelphia, called the "Philadelphia Society for Alleviating the Miseries of Public Prisons."

the comfort of prisoners, by providing food, fuel, clothing and other necessaries of life. To procure the liberation of such as were confined for small sums, and were of meritorious conduct, by discharging their debts."[5]

This simple and well-conceived program the Society proceeded to carry out with an admirable degree of efficiency. In December, 1788, the Society presented a memorial to the legislature, describing the plight of debtors in prison and urging the passage of legislation in their behalf. Among other things it was stated:

In prosecuting the purposes of their association the memorialists have, with unspeakable regret, observed a large number of persons confined within the jail, deprived of the comforts of their families, prevented from the opportunity of obtaining the means of subsistence by their industry, and liable to become use-less, if not pernicious, members of society, from the great danger they are in of acquiring habits of intemperance.[6]

The memorialists pointed out that in less than two years there had been 1,162 commitments to the jail for debt in New York County alone; that 716 of these had been for small sums recoverable before a justice of the peace; and that many of the imprisoned debtors owed less than twenty shillings.

The memorial of the Society, supported by a considerable amount of sympathetic public opinion, won the consideration of the legislature and was largely responsible for the passage of chapter 24, *Laws of 1789*, ordering the liberation after thirty days' confinement of debtors imprisoned for sums of less than £10, provided that the debtor took oath that he was without property to settle his obliga-tions. While this act constituted a long step forward in the relief of imprisoned debtors, their condition still remained most deplorable. In 1790 the debtors incarcerated in the Albany jail (then located in a part of the city hall) signalized the Fourth of July by calling atten-tion to the fact that in the fifteenth year of American independence men were still being imprisoned for the crime of owing money. Their toast was: "May the time come when no honest man shall be con-fined for debt."[7] In 1794 the imprisoned debtors of the same city petitioned the legislature for a law compelling their creditors to sup-port them during their confinement. But the legislative committee

Thy Assured Friend
Thomas Eddy

to whom the petition was referred reported that the act of 1789 provided sufficient relief for this class of prisoners.[8]

Meanwhile, the Society for the Relief of Distressed Debtors was carrying on its ministrations in New York City. It was uncommonly successful in obtaining donations in cash and in kind, for popular sympathy was strongly attracted to the imprisoned debtors. On May 11, 1789, the Society announced the receipt of fifteen hundred pounds of fresh beef over a ten-week period from an anonymous donor. In November, 1789, it received a contribution of £50 from President Washington, who had been inaugurated in New York City on April 30 of that year.* The grateful debtors inserted an advertisement in a local paper several days later: "The prisoners confined for debt in the city of New York most respectfully beg leave to return their grateful thanks to the President of the United States, for his very acceptable donation on Thursday last."[9]

A public notice appearing two years later extends thanks to Joseph Winter for "the seasonable relief he has afforded them (the imprisoned debtors) by his timely supply of a whole Bullock, and a proportionable quantity of Bread," and expresses the hope "that the affluent will follow so laudable an example."[10]

In subsequent years the New York Society's scope of charitable work was gradually widened to include several spheres of interest quite beyond its original purposes. Its concern for imprisoned debtors led the Society to investigate the state of the jail in which they were confined, and thence to the whole question of penal reform. Noting that whiskey was openly sold in the city jail, the Society in 1791 prevailed upon the state legislature to enact a law forbidding the sale of spirituous liquors in the jails of New York or Albany.[11] About the same time a broader movement was started for the liberalization of the penal code in general, in which members of the Society played a leading role. Most prominent in this movement was a Quaker merchant of New York City, Thomas Eddy, who was an active figure in most of the humanitarian reforms of his day. Eddy, with the aid of Philip Schuyler, Governor John Jay, and State Senator Ambrose Spencer, was largely instrumental in ob-

---

* New York City was then the capital of the United States, as well as of New York State.

taining the passage of a new penal code in 1796. Several years earlier
he had made a study of the Pennsylvania criminal code, then the
most advanced in the country, and upon his return to New York
he launched the movement which culminated in the legislative act of
1796. This statute abolished capital punishment for all crimes except
treason, murder, and stealing from a church, and substituted life
imprisonment for all other felonies previously punishable by death.[12]
It also abolished whipping as a form of punishment.* The same act
authorized the establishment of two state prisons, one to be erected
in New York City and the other in Albany, and provided a series of
regulations for these prisons based on the Pennsylvania system,
which was then considered the most humane in existence. Only the
prison at New York was constructed, however. Located at Greenwich Village, it was opened in 1797 and remained the sole state
prison in New York until the opening of the Auburn institution
twenty years later. Thomas Eddy supervised its building and acted
as its first "director" or warden. The discipline inaugurated at the
first state prison at New York and under the later "Auburn system"
appears barbarous in the light of modern standards. Nevertheless,
the establishment of these early state prisons marked a most important step forward in penal reform, since it symbolized the acceptance of a new principle in the treatment of the criminal—reformation instead of retribution. The application of the new principle,
of course, proved a far more difficult task than its formulation; its
realization remains incomplete to this day.

To return to the Society for the Relief of Distressed Debtors, the
scope of this organization expanded in still another direction. In the
beginning, it had rationed out only unprepared foodstuffs to its beneficiaries, leaving it to the prisoners to find some means of cooking
the food themselves. Finding this method wasteful and inefficient,
the Society in 1802 decided to open a "soup-house" near the jail,
where food could be cooked and served hot to the prisoners. When
hard times came in ensuing years, the Society decided to furnish soup
to the poor people of the community at a reduced price. Finally its

---

* This provision was not strictly observed. The general poor law of 1801, for instance, retained a clause authorizing whipping as a punishment for strangers who returned to a locality whence they had been previously removed.

ministrations were extended to the "general poor" of New York City as a permanent policy. Relief in kind was afforded to "worthy" dependents on an increasing scale. In 1803 the organization changed its name to Humane Society, and later its scope of activities was still further extended to include the "resuscitation of persons apparently dead from drowning," in imitation of the Royal Humane Society established some years earlier in London. The interest of the Humane Society in the poor debtor continued unabated. Acting in concert with other progressive organizations and individuals, the Society succeeded in obtaining occasional legislative relief for this group. Improvement of the poor debtor's lot proved a slow process, however. As late as 1815, a notice appeared in an Albany newspaper to the effect that the "poor debtors confined in prison in this city are in a suffering condition," and that "the public charity, and that of individuals, if dispensed in their favor, would be received with gratitude and thanks."[13]

The movement against imprisonment for debt led to the passage in 1817 of an act "for the relief of persons imprisoned for debts less than twenty-five dollars, in the city and county of New York." This statute provided that all such debtors should be set at liberty upon oath before a judge or justice that "his personal or real estate does not exceed, in value, the sum of twenty-five dollars over and above such articles as are by law exempt from seizure by execution."[14] The act further provided that no person thus discharged could again be imprisoned for the same debt.

With the rise of the common man in subsequent years, the movement against the undemocratic practice of imprisoning debtors gained added vigor. The fight was waged on a national scale for many years, with United States Senator Richard M. Johnson of Kentucky taking a leading part. In 1817, and several times thereafter, Martin Van Buren, who later became governor of New York State and president of the United States, introduced a bill in the state legislature to abolish imprisonment for debt, but his efforts proved unsuccessful. Meanwhile the laboring class, particularly in New York City, was throwing its growing strength into the struggle. The Working Men's Party, which was founded in 1829, made this issue one of the major planks of its platform and was a vital factor in the successful climax of the movement in 1831, when the Stillwell Act put an end to most of the glaring abuses of the practice of imprisonment for debt.*

THE VAGRANT PROBLEM

In spite of repeated efforts on the part of state and local authorities to check the incoming tide of vagrants, they continued to roam the highways of New York in ever increasing numbers. Then as now, those loosely classified as vagrants comprised several diverse groups. Many were honest laborers seeking employment in new places; some were itinerant workers; others were foot-loose adventurers or social misfits; still others were members of families stranded in a destitute condition while searching for a place to settle down. There were also a considerable number of runaway slaves and bond servants included under this classification.

The problem of vagrancy was particularly acute in New York City, which, because of its location and its rapid rise to the status of metropolis, naturally attracted vagrants of all types. At the end of the Revolution, the municipal authorities viewed vagrancy with considerable alarm and anxiously sought methods to cope with it. An area within the city called "Canvass Town," a huddle of shelters pitched at the foot of Broad Street among the ruins left by the great fire of 1776, was a particularly notorious haven for disreputable persons and a hotbed of crime. So alarming did the situation become, that on June 16, 1784, Mayor James Duane discussed it at great length in a communication to the Common Council, setting forth a plan "for the better Government of the Alms House and Bridewell or House of Employment in the City of New York." Pointing out that the number of public dependents had greatly increased as a result of the ravages of war, Mayor Duane declared:

Ever since the Evacuation of this District by the British Forces, the tranquility of the Inhabitants hath been disturbed by an idle and profligate Banditti

---

* The Stillwell Act did not abolish imprisonment for debt entirely, and the practice continued for many years after. Like other legislation of a similar character, some of its provisions were repealed or vitiated by subsequent statutes. As late as 1881, Governor Alonzo B. Cornell revealed the wide prevalence of imprisonment for debt, contrary to the popular view that it had been abolished long before. "The county jail in the city of New York is never free of prisoners detained for debt . . . . instances of imprisonment for claims as small as $20 are not infrequent. Cruel hardship is constantly inflicted in this manner."

who continue to rob and steal in defiance of the vigilance of the Magistrates and the severity of frequent and exemplary Punishments and by other abandoned Vagrants and Prostitutes whom the ordinary Process of Justice hath not awed nor reclaimed and it is conceived that the Discipline of the Bridewell or House of Employment vigorously administered will alone be effectual to correct and restrain those shameful Enormities.[15]

The plan drawn up by the Mayor included a recommendation that the administration of the municipal poor-relief system be taken out of the hands of the Common Council, which was already over-burdened with other municipal business, and placed under the authority of a group of commissioners. The state legislature embodied this suggestion in a statute enacted the same year which transferred poor-relief functions from the Common Council to the Commissioners of the Bridewell and Almshouse. Among other directions, the commissioners were admonished by the mayor to be "Vigilant in enforcing the Law against Vagrants or otherwise."

It was the custom of the time to pay a bounty to law-enforcement officials for each vagrant apprehended by them. In 1785, when the bounty on vagrants was 4s. each, the city treasurer was ordered to pay certain constables £20 12s. for arresting and conveying one hundred and three vagrants to the bridewell. Apparently the harvest gathered by the constables was a plentiful one, for in November, 1786, the bounty was lowered to 2s. 6d. In January, 1788, police officers were paid £45 18s. for bringing in vagrants.[16]

Throughout the colonial period it was customary to apply corporal punishment such as whipping, stocks, pillory, ear-cropping, and branding, to convicted vagrants. Nearly every town had its "public whipper." Usually this functionary was employed on a piecework basis, receiving a set fee for each whipping he administered on behalf of the town. At times he was granted a bonus for performing his duties with particular skill or vigor. In 1762, for example, the Common Council of Albany voted an extra sum of 5s. 6d. to the public whipper, Rick Van Toper, "for the due and wholesome manner in which he laid the lash upon the back of Tiberius Haines."[17] A year later the city of Albany purchased James Nox, a bond servant, from his master for £9, so that he might serve as a public whipper for the remainder of his term of service. The whipping post was abolished in Albany in 1796.[18]

Occasionally the town authorities would content themselves with simply "warning out" vagrants without administering corporal punishment. Vagrants might also be sent to the bridewell or to the poorhouse in towns possessing such institutions. In the fall of 1784 the state legislature passed a bill authorizing the Common Council of New York City to confine at hard labor vagrants and other petty offenders, instead of subjecting them to corporal punishment as heretofore. This bill, however, was vetoed by the Council of Revision. But in March, 1785, the legislature enacted a similar law permitting the Common Council, in cases where it was empowered to inflict corporal punishment, to substitute

a confinement of the offender in the house of employment or bridewell . . . . to be kept at hard labour therein, or at any work or employment, within any part of the jurisdiction of the said city and county, for a longer or shorter period, according to the nature of the offence: And also to confine and set to hard labour . . . . all idle and disorderly vagrants, not having visible means of a livelihood.[19]

No person coming under this statute could be confined for a term longer than six months.

The problem of providing suitable labor for imprisoned vagrants proved a very difficult one. Various expedients were adopted with indifferent success. Early in 1787 vagrants from the bridewell were put to work preparing the almshouse ground for grass seed. In the same year the keeper of the bridewell, William Sloo, introduced the novel idea of taking his charges to the river banks during the fishing season and providing them with nets with which to catch shad for the inmates of the almshouse and bridewell. The Common Council showed its appreciation by presenting Sloo with £20 "for his Assiduity and good management in employing the Vagrants under his Care during the fishing Seasons in taking such Quantities of Shad for the Use of the Bridewell & Almshouse as to create a great saving in the Articles of Provisions provided for those Institutions."[20] This policy was continued for several years, with Keeper Sloo being rewarded by a £20 grant annually in addition to his salary. During this period vagrants were also employed at filling up low-lying areas and in manufacturing nails.

A large number of vagrants were committed to the almshouse, to the annoyance of the pauper inmates and the institutional authorities. In November, 1789, the Commissioners of the Almshouse and Bridewell complained to the Common Council that the poorhouse had

become too much of a common Receptacle for idle intemperate Vagrants, many of whom of right have no lawful residence in this Place and who by pretended Sickness or otherwise, often impose on the Magistrates of the City, by which Means the House is overcrowded with numbers of abandoned Characters greatly incommoding those who are really objects of Charity as well as imposing on the industrious part of the Community.[21]

Overcrowding in the municipal almshouse, occasioned in large measure by the commitment of vagrants there, became so intolerable that the city authorities in 1794 decided to build a new institution. Early in 1795 the almshouse officials reported that the institutional population had reached 622, including 259 children "mostly under nine years old," 14 blind persons, 25 persons suffering from "lunacy, insanity and idiotism," besides a large number of aged people. The institution, it was declared, could comfortably accommodate only about half the existing population.[22] In keeping with the custom of the time, funds for erecting the new almshouse were raised by a public lottery, permission to raise £10,000 by this means having been given to the city by a special act of the legislature, chapter 51, *Laws of 1795*. The new almshouse, a four-story building located in City Hall Park, was completed in 1796.

Meanwhile, repeated efforts were being made to establish an institution distinct from either the almshouse or the bridewell, a workhouse similar to those instituted in England centuries earlier, where vagrants and other minor offenders and able-bodied paupers could be kept at hard labor. The combined "Poor House, Work House and House of Correction" erected by the city in 1735 had failed to fulfil the expectations of its promoters. Within a short time the latter two-thirds of the title was quietly dropped and the institution was thenceforth referred to simply as the almshouse. Later attempts to establish a workhouse in the city also met with failure. In 1789 the Common Council approved a plan submitted by the Commissioners of the Almshouse and Bridewell, proposing that a part of the bridewell be set aside as a workhouse for "idle, intemperate vagrants" and for disorderly inmates of the poorhouse. This plan was never carried out, however.

Finally, in 1816, a new institution known as the penitentiary was erected by the city. It was placed under the jurisdiction of the combined poor-relief and penal authorities who were now called the Commissioners of the Almshouse, Bridewell and Penitentiary. This practice of placing the administration of charitable and correctional institutions into the hands of a single public authority was typical of the period, as indeed it remained for decades to come.

Situated in the Bellevue area near the East River, the penitentiary was intended exclusively for the confinement at hard labor of vagrants and other petty offenders, and of intractable paupers at the almshouse. Some of the penitentiary inmates were employed on the city roads, others in the garden or at housework, and a considerable number were set to work picking oakum. But many more were left in idleness; the problem of finding regular and profitable employment for all the inmates still continued to plague the commissioners. Shortly after the erection of the penitentiary, the attention of these officials was attracted to a new method of labor inaugurated in the workhouses of England, a method which was gaining wide approval as the best solution to the problem of most effectively punishing vagrants and disorderly persons. The new plan involved the "tread mill, or stepping mill," a device invented by William Cubitt of England and first used at Bury prison in 1818.

THE TREADMILL

The treadmill was built on the common principles of the ordinary treadwheel run by water. It consisted mainly of a huge revolving drum attached by a shaft to a machine for grinding grain. The revolving drum was usually about five feet in diameter and twenty-four feet in length, sufficient for some sixteen men to stand on. Treadboards, or steps, were formed along the length of the wheel, and a hand rail was fixed above it to permit the men to retain their upright position while the wheel revolved. It was operated in the following manner: the prisoners ascended at one end of the wheel by means of the steps, and when the requisite number were ranged upon it, the wheel commenced its revolutions; the men continued to step upward in unison as if ascending an endless flight of stairs, their combined weight acting upon each successive stepping-board precisely as a stream of water upon a water wheel. This operation was maintained without stop throughout all the hours of labor, and replacements were made at regular intervals without bringing it to a halt. As the wheel revolved, each man gradually advanced from the side at which he mounted toward the opposite end. Having reached this position, he descended for a rest, while another prisoner mounted at the other end as he had done, going through the same procedure until his turn came to descend for a rest. The gearing of the wheel was so fixed that a bell struck every half-minute as a signal for the end-man to descend and for another to mount. Thus, twenty-four prisoners might be assigned to one wheel, permitting sixteen to operate the mill at a time, while eight were resting. Each man would be on the wheel eight minutes and off four, allowing twenty minutes of rest in every hour.

The establishment of a stepping-mill at the penitentiary was first suggested to the Commissioners of the Almshouse and Bridewell by several members of the New York Society for the Prevention of Pauperism,* who had read glowing accounts of the device in pamphlets issued by philanthropic societies and individuals in England, and who expressed the opinion that its introduction in New York City would be efficacious "both as a punishment and a source of profit." The instrument was hailed as a great achievement and was confidently expected to solve the problem of vagrancy. In those prisons in England where the treadmill was in use, it was claimed that the number of recommittals had been diminished by one-half. James Hardie, who was for a time gatekeeper at the penitentiary, described the advantages of the stepping-mill in a pamphlet written in 1823:

1st. No skill or time is requisite to learn the working of it.

2nd. The prisoners cannot neglect their task, nor do it remissly, as all must work equally, in proportion to their weight.

3rd. It can be used for every kind of manufactory to which water, steam,

* This society had been formed in December, 1817. Its activities profoundly influenced social welfare developments in New York during its brief but active existence and will be discussed at greater length in a subsequent chapter. A letter to Mayor Stephen Allen, advocating the erection of a treadmill, from Thomas Eddy, a leading member of the Society, was also influential in winning the attention of the authorities to the new medium for exacting hard labor from prisoners.

wind or animal power is usually applied, and especially to the grinding of grain, for which every prison is at a great expense.

4th. As the mechanism of a Tread-Mill is not of a complicated nature, the regular employment which it affords is not likely to be often suspended for want of repairs in the machinery, and should the supply of grain at any time fail, it is not necessary that the labour of the prisoners should be suspended; nor can they be aware of the circumstance; the supply of labour may therefore be considered as unfailing.

5th. It is constant and sufficiently severe; but it is its *monotonous steadiness* and not its *severity* which constitutes its terror, and frequently breaks down the obstinate spirit.[23]

Still another advantage set forth by Hardie was the possibility of setting women prisoners to work on the treadmill, since its operation required weight rather than brawn. This aspect appealed also to Mayor Stephen Allen, who, on October 28, 1822, presented a plan for the erection of a treadmill to the Common Council, in which he noted:

There are always a numerous class of Prisoners in the Penitentiary and Bridewell consisting of female Prostitutes and vagabonds for whom little or no employment could be provided; but it has been found by experience that the operation of the women on the tread wheel in proportion to their weight is equally useful as that of the men; there is then this additional advantage arising from the erection of the Mill that this class of Prisoners will now be made to earn their bread by the sweat of their brow.[24]

The project proposed by Mayor Allen was accepted by the Common Council, which authorized the appropriation of $3,000 for the purpose. The treadmill was put into operation at the penitentiary in September, 1823. It was originally intended to instal three tread-wheels, but only two were finally built. Thirty-two prisoners were assigned to each wheel, sixteen operating it at a time while an equal number rested; each spent eight minutes on the wheel and eight minutes off. About forty bushels of grain were thus ground daily for the use of the city's charitable and correctional institutions, saving an estimated amount of $1,900 annually to the city.

But the labor of operating the treadmill proved so grueling and monotonous, and its effect on the prisoners' physical and mental health so damaging, that protests against its continued use soon arose from progressive individuals and groups. Time also proved the treadmill a failure, in so far as one of its primary purposes was concerned, that is, as a deterrent to vagrancy. In fact, despite the acknowledged terrors of the treadmill, vagrancy continued to increase at an alarming rate. Finally, in October, 1826, the Common Council passed a resolution ordering its Police Committee "to enquire and report on the propriety of discontinuing the use of the Tread Mill in certain cases, and that until such report be made no females be placed upon the Tread Mill under any pretence whatever."[25] The treadmill was entirely discontinued shortly after and passed into history as an interesting phase of the treatment accorded to vagrants and other petty offenders.

SUMMARY

This period was featured by a great movement toward penal and prison reform in which the Quakers played a prominent role. The movement resulted in the humanization of the penal code, the abolition of the death penalty for all but three categories of crime, and the substitution of prison terms and the establishment of the first state prisons. The reforms extended to the treatment of insolvent debtors who were often imprisoned for long periods of time for failure to pay debts of insignificant amounts, and who frequently had to obtain the means of subsistence during their imprisonment from private charitable sources, since no public provision was made for their food and fuel. Amelioration of their condition was obtained gradually, largely due to the persistent efforts of the Society for the Relief of Distressed Debtors, organized in 1787 (later the Humane Society), and the work of Thomas Eddy and other individuals. Punishment of debtors lessened in severity and in time imprisonment for debt was almost entirely abolished.

The problem of vagrancy was far more difficult of solution. Despite ingenious efforts to cope with it, the number of vagrants in the state continued to grow steadily. The most ambitious attempt to cope with vagrancy during this period was the establishment of the treadmill in New York City, which proved a complete failure within a few years of its inception.

BIBLIOGRAPHICAL REFERENCES

1. *Olde Ulster*, II (1906), p. 39.
2. Stokes, *Iconography*, IV, 781.

3. Philip Klein, *Prison Methods in New York State* (New York, 1920), p. 33.

4. Elizabeth Dike Lewis, *Old Prisons and Punishments*, "Half Moon Series" (New York, 1898), II, No. 3, 98.

5. *A Sketch of the Origin and Progress of the Humane Society of the City of New York* (New York, 1814), p. 3.

6. *Ibid.*, pp. 4–5.

7. Munsell, *Annals of Albany*, II, 302.

8. *Ibid.*, III, 118–19.

9. Quoted from the *New-York Journal*, December 3, 1789, in Stokes, *Iconography*, V, 1257.

10. New York *Daily Advertiser*, December 27, 1791.

11. New York State, *Laws of 1791*, chap. 39.

12. ———, *Laws of 1796*, chap. 30.

13. Munsell, *op. cit.*, VI, 111.

14. New York State, *Laws of 1817*, chap. 260.

15. *N.Y.C.*, *M.C.C.*, *1784–1831*, I, 48–49.

16. *Ibid.*, pp. 176, 263, 347.

17. George R. Howell and Jonathan Tenney (eds.), *History of the County of Albany, 1609–1886* (New York, 1886), p. 467.

18. Reynolds, *Albany Chronicles*, p. 260.

19. New York State, *Laws of 1785*, chap. 40.

20. *N.Y.C.*, *M.C.C.*, *1784–1831*, I, 302.

21. *Ibid.*, p. 505.

22. New York City Commissioners of the Almshouse and Bridewell, *Minutes* (MS), February 2, 1795.

23. James Hardie, *The History of the Tread-Mill* (New York, 1824), pp. 17–18.

24. *N.Y.C.*, *M.C.C.*, *1784–1831*, XII, 541.

25. *Ibid.*, XV, 662.

CHAPTER IX

EARLY EMERGENCIES: DEPRESSIONS
EPIDEMICS AND WAR

The young state was beset with a long series of emergencies during the first half-century of its existence. There were economic crises, disease, epidemics, and a war, 1812–15. These periods of stress brought to the surface new problems of poor-relief administration and occasionally resulted in the adoption of new techniques and procedures.

New York State came out of the Revolution as one of a confederation of colonies which had broken the hold of England south of the Great Lakes, but which was not to be bound under a federal constitution until 1789. The intervening years (1783–89) have been called "the critical period," and for many sections of the population this was no misnomer. The post-war crisis struck New York City with particular severity. The end of the Revolution found a good part of the city in shambles, owing largely to the disastrous fires of 1776 and 1778. The British had made no effort to rebuild the affected area during their occupation.

The city was mainly dependent on its shipping for well-being. In 1784 the British West Indies' ports were closed against American trade, and during the next two years New York's shipping activities fell off 33 per cent. In 1785 the New York legislature received two or three petitions in bankruptcy once or twice a week; in 1786 it received from five to thirty-five petitions day after day for weeks together. Newspapers of the middle and upper Hudson areas printed more insolvency notices in 1788 than in 1787, though the depression was supposed to have been over in the previous year.

Generally, 1786 is regarded as the blackest year of the period. The state's few manufacturing plants were closing their doors, owing largely to the systematic dumping of goods by British manufacturers who aimed to keep the United States a market for the motherland. By 1787 shipbuilding had ceased. Mechanics were out of work in large numbers. The same year New York City merchants petitioned the legislature for relief. They declared that they had lent large sums to the American government, but that the government's depreciated currency now prevented their meeting bills presented by British creditors. Lawyers became a hated breed, as through legal processes the property of some businessmen was cleverly transferred to the asset lists of others.

Rent was high; money was scarce. "Cash! Cash! O Cash!" exclaimed one contemporary, "why hast thou deserted the Standard of Liberty! and made poverty and dissipation our distinguishing characteristic?"[1] Commerce and agriculture were at a standstill. Disaffection grew rife as ruin confronted large sections of the population. The successful outcome of the Revolution seemed to many to represent only a Pyrrhic victory. In neighboring Massachusetts the desperate condition of the farmers resulted in the outbreak of Shays's Rebellion in 1786. For a time it seemed that the seeds of rebellion would spread to New York. "There are a great proportion of the people who are ripe for confusion and war," wrote a New Yorker in March, 1787. "This is not because they are discontented under their own government but because they are so embarrassed in their affairs that they believe no disturbances can make them worse."[2]

Opportunely, as the period wore on, a crop shortage developed in Europe which necessitated large imports of American farm products and helped relieve the distress of the agricultural areas. New York State was predominantly agricultural and was to remain so for many years. Its population at the end of the Revolutionary War totaled about 234,000, ranking sixth in population among the states. By 1790 its population had increased to 341,000, less than 20 per cent of its inhabitants living in urban districts.*

Although the bottom of the post-Revolutionary depression was not reached until 1786, extraordinary relief measures had to be resorted to much earlier. In 1784 the legislature authorized the raising of £6,000 annually for the support of the poor and the maintenance of public roads in the city and county of New York. This sum proved insufficient, and on February 5, 1785,

* The U.S. Census of 1790 showed a population of 33,132 in New York City, with about 6,000 in Albany and Poughkeepsie.

Mr. Lawrence Embree & others of the Commissioners of the Alms House attended the Board & informed them that there were a great number of families in this City in the greatest possible Distress for want of the Common Necessaries of Life & that it was not in the Power of Commissioners to furnish them with any Relief Whereupon it was determined by the Board to request that the Clergy of the different Denominations will be pleased on Sunday, that is toMorrow Week, to impress their Congregations with a due Sense of the deplorable Circumstances & urgent Wants of the Poor at this severe Season & to sollicit Contributions for their Relief. . . . .[3]

In conclusion the Common Council ordered that £150 be advanced at once to the commissioners for relief purposes, to be replaced out of the money collected in the churches.

At the same time it was ordered that upward of £50 be dispensed from the city treasury for outdoor relief in the seven wards. The peak of the depression was reached in 1786, but extraordinary relief measures continued for several years after. In November, 1785, the inmates of the almshouse numbered 301, including 99 boys and girls. In May, 1787, the almshouse population had risen to 426, with 149 children included.[4] Special outdoor-relief orders were still being issued in 1789. Many orders for payment for the delivery of firewood to the poor appear in the city records, and there are numbers of instances where individual petitioners were granted relief from city funds.

With the end of the "critical period," public welfare administration resumed its normal tenor for a few years. Then, in the middle nineties, an extraordinary drain on the public welfare resources of New York City manifested itself from a new direction. The last decade of the century witnessed the beginning of a series of yellow-fever epidemics mostly centered in New York City, which were to prove an intermittent scourge to the city and state for many years.

In 1794 a number of cases of yellow fever had broken out, arousing the apprehension of the populace and authorities. The disastrous plague which had decimated the population of Philadelphia in 1793 was still vivid in the public mind. The legislature in that year had passed a law prohibiting passengers from Philadelphia to land in any New York port, and Albany and New York City had taken stringent measures to enforce this ban. In 1794 the legislature enacted a statute empowering the mayors or recorders of Albany and

Hudson to execute the act prohibiting the landing of passengers from plague-stricken ports, and authorized the state treasurer to spend £1,000 annually to finance enforcement of the interdictions. The act also provided that Governors Island should be used for quarantine purposes.[5]

Warned by the state of the need for isolation facilities for fever patients, New York City in 1794 obtained a lease having six years to run on about five acres on Kip's Farm, at a site known as Belle Vue. Ownership of this section was vested at the time in Brookholst Livingston. The city paid £2,000 for the lease and acquired ownership in fee simple in 1798. In October, 1794, erection of buildings was begun at Belle Vue for the reception of fever patients. These structures were at first called "the hospital at Belle Vue," a name later contracted to Bellevue Hospital.

The first serious epidemic in the post-war period occurred in 1795. Its first victims were two sailors who were removed to Belle Vue from a ship docked at Whitehall on May 29.[6] The number of sick increased as the summer wore on. A special payment of £100 to the Commissioners of the Almshouse and Bridewell was ordered on September 29 for the "relief of families become distressed & necessitous by reason of the present epidemic Fever in this City." Larger expenditures soon became necessary. On October 6, a welcome draft for $7,000 was received from the city of Philadelphia for the relief of these sick poor. An accompanying letter from the mayor explained that the citizens of that community had raised the sum in grateful recollection of the donation of $5,000 received from New York in 1793. In November the Common Council authorized the city treasurer to negotiate two loans totaling $9,000 to meet the drain on its financial resources occasioned by the epidemic. Meanwhile many citizens had fled the city in terror, and business was at a standstill. The plague toll of dead for the year was 732 out of a total population of about 50,000. On February 1, 1796, the city appropriated £400 of the funds received from Philadelphia to relieve "families become indigent and distressed from the late Epidemic Fever."[7]

In 1796 the state reimbursed Albany in the amount of £255 and New York in the amount of £3,311 for expenses incurred during the epidemic. It also took measures against further epidemics. An act of 1796 provided for the appointment of a health officer and of commissioners of the health office in New York City. All vessels arriving at the port of New York were made subject to quarantine, as well as those on which a person was ill with fever or had died of fever and those arriving from ports where infectious diseases prevailed. The same act provided for the erection of a lazaretto at a maximum cost of £2,000 on Nutten (Governors) Island, or on another island if it were deemed more practicable, for the reception of persons arriving in vessels subject to quarantine and persons actually ill from infectious ailments.[8]

Difficulties lay in the way of locating a lazaretto on the island designated,* however, and in June, 1796, Governor John Jay wrote to the mayor of New York City proposing that the state purchase Bedloe Island as a site for the institution. The city responded by granting the site in question to New York State "for the purpose of erecting such lazaretto and for such other purposes as the legislature shall from time to time direct." Certain buildings on Bedloe Island belonging to the French Republic were purchased and prepared for temporary isolation purposes. On September 5, 1796, the commissioners of the health office informed the Common Council by letter that the Bedloe Island lazaretto was ready for the reception of patients, and that therefore the hospital at Belle Vue was no longer needed. After several changes of plans, however, the lazaretto project was abandoned, and under chapter 19, *Laws of 1799*, the commissioners of the health office were directed to purchase a tract on Staten Island and there erect a marine hospital instead. The brunt of the hospitalization of epidemic victims fell upon Belle Vue Hospital.

During 1796 and 1797 the city was practically free from infectious disease. But the summer of 1798 brought the most disastrous attack of yellow fever that the city had ever suffered. On June 12, Belle Vue was opened as a fever hospital. The health office took such measures as seemed likely to guard against the disease, one of which, submitted August 27 to the Common Council, prohibited for a time the

---

.* A garrison of federal troops was stationed on Governors Island, which was then far smaller than it is today, and it was found impossible to locate the lazaretto at a satisfactory distance from the garrison.

retail trade in oysters and also prohibited the sale of country fruit or vegetables in or about markets or stands after twelve o'clock noon, except on Saturdays. On September 10 a standing committee of aldermen, with Gabriel Furman acting as chairman, was appointed to aid the commissioners of the health office for the duration of the emergency. More accommodations were needed at Belle Vue, especially as under existing conditions the convalescent patients had no place apart from the sick and dying. Two new buildings were ordered erected, each sixty by twenty feet, one of which was two stories in height. So swiftly did the workmen labor on these structures that both were completed in eight days. In all, 389 patients were admitted from August 1 to November 29, 1798, of whom 205 died.

The New York Dispensary had its full share of fever cases. Of a total of 418 patients admitted during this period, 270 were yellow-fever victims. Of these, 235 survived—an astonishing record, far better than that of Belle Vue and attributable in part to the probability that the patients were sooner treated after being attacked, and that their illness generally was less severe than that of the patients at Belle Vue. By far the greater majority of the epidemic victims received treatment outside of institutions. The available hospital space, even with the addition of two buildings at Belle Vue, could accommodate but a small proportion of those stricken with the plague. The task of providing medical aid to the sick poor who were cut off for one reason or another from hospital attention proved a formidable problem for the health committee appointed by the Board of Aldermen. There was a serious scarcity of physicians in the city. Many members of the profession had fled with their families upon the outbreak of the plague, and those who remained had a great many more patients on their lists than they could possibly attend. The situation of indigent patients became most distressing, and to relieve it somewhat the aldermanic committee employed three physicians to administer to the sick poor of the city. Visiting nurses paid from public funds were also supplied to indigent sufferers.

Another serious problem faced by the public authorities was that of providing material aid to the sick poor and their families, and also to the abnormal number of destitute inhabitants. Business activities throughout the city remained virtually suspended during the epidemic. Those who had the means rushed from the city to safer distances upstate. Numbers of workers were thrown out of employment and were forced to seek public relief. Many women were widowed and children made orphans by the heavy toll taken by the plague. As a partial solution to the problem the aldermanic committee advertised that they would attend the almshouse seven hours daily "to receive the applications of the sick, the widow and orphan, or their friends in their behalf, and to grant such relief as the liberality of the Common Council of the city had directed."[9] When it appeared that the money borrowed by the city for the purpose of relieving the sick poor would soon be exhausted, John Murray, Jr., a prominent merchant, offered to guarantee a further loan of $10,000 if it should be needed. However, the liberal donations of food and money sent from other parts of the state and from New Jersey and Connecticut caused the city authorities to decide that a further loan was unnecessary.

Three food stations, or "repositories and cook shops" as they were called, were established. There, we are told, "the needy were liberally supplied with soups, boiled meat, bread, candles, and other proper and necessary articles suitable to their situation."[10] The historian of the epidemic, James Hardie, declares that from sixteen hundred to two thousand persons received their daily subsistence at these cookhouses. In addition, eight hundred persons were supported in the almshouse. Most of the food, which came as contributions from various parts of the country, was deposited in a store which stood opposite the almshouse. More than five hundred families were supplied from time to time with these provisions, which mainly included beef, pork, mutton, flour, poultry, Indian meal, and potatoes. At times relief in cash supplemented relief in kind to needy families. Several women who had lost their husbands through the epidemic received public assistance in removing with their children to the homes of relatives or friends in the country.

It is interesting to note that the committee charged with public aid to the indigent during the epidemic hired a staff of relief investigators whose duties included visits to the homes of applicants to inquire into their circumstances and to report accordingly to the authorities. They were authorized

to visit the indigent sick, to examine into their situations, to represent their cases, to relieve their immediate wants out of money entrusted to them for that purpose, and in short to do everything which they might be directed by the Committee, or their own prudence might suggest, toward the mitigation of the sufferings of individuals, or to stop the progress of the deadly pestilence.[11]

May we not regard these temporarily employed persons as the first social case workers in public welfare in New York City and State?

The cost of financing care, relief, and preventive measures proved an extraordinary strain on the municipal purse. In 1799 the legislature passed an act authorizing New York City to borrow on the credit of the state the sum of $45,000 to be applied "towards discharging the expence incurred in relieving the distresses of that city occasioned by the late epidemic which has prevailed there."[12]

Though no exact figures are available, the mortality toll of the epidemic was undoubtedly large. Estimates of the deaths directly due to yellow fever between July and November, 1798, vary from 1,500 to 2,000. Between a third and a half of the population of about 55,000 fled the city during the plague, and some two or three hundred of these are said to have perished. Besides, about 1,000 died of illnesses complicated by attacks of yellow fever.[13]

The calamity stimulated speculation regarding the source of the epidemic. Noah Webster, the lexicographer, suggested a connection between epidemics and comets, atmospheric conditions, and other phenomena. Referring to an earlier epidemic, he said: "The pestilential state of the elements was strongly marked . . . . by the poorness of the shad brought to market in New York." The celebrated Philadelphia physician, Benjamin Rush, who engaged in a bitter controversy on the nature and cause of yellow fever, argued that the epidemic of 1793 was due to the putrefaction of a quantity of damaged coffee which was left exposed on a wharf.[14] Dr. Richard Bayley, health officer, connected the outbreak of the epidemic of 1798 with a flood of rain water which had lain stagnant in Lispenard's meadow, near the Hudson, until drained by order of the Common Council. This was a close guess, lacking only the explanation of swamplands as breeding-places for the carriers of the deadly disease germ. A Quaker merchant who volunteered as a visitor of the sick in 1798 also attributed the plague to stagnant water. He proposed that its presence should be prohibited, that persons with wet cellars should be made to keep them dry and clean by pumping, and that docks and slips should be filled in, at least in so far as they furnished traps for standing water. It was noted that the first fever cases appeared near unfilled land at Coenties Slip.

Probably the most popular theory among the medical men of the time was that the epidemic rose from miasma, or foul vapor emanating from stagnant pools, privies, decaying matter, filthy streets, and swampland. "Ought it to be a matter of surprise," Dr. Samuel L. Mitchill of Columbia College wrote to James Hardie, "that during a moist and hot season venom should be produced, rise into the air and render it too foul and poisonous to support life?"[15]

A lesser attack of yellow fever in 1799, together with the recollection of the epidemic of the preceding year, kept the problem of preventing further disastrous visitations uppermost in the minds of many citizens. A joint committee representing the Common Council, the Chamber of Commerce, the Medical Society, and the commissioners of health reported in January, 1799, that many lives might have been saved among the poor during the epidemic of 1798 if a supply of tents had been available for use as dwellings at sites remote from the stricken zones. It was proposed that, in anticipation of future emergencies, tents should be secured sufficient to accommodate five thousand persons. These tents, according to the committee, might also be used for military needs, thus serving a double purpose.[16]

Governor John Jay's message to the legislature in 1800 suggested that the plague might represent the prosecution of unknown moral purposes by Providence, but he proposed to give the city further powers to deal with the problem of prevention on the chance that it was due rather to unsanitary conditions. Laws passed in the spring of 1800 empowered the city to buy up certain sites and structures deemed dangerous to health and to impose stringent sanitary regulations. In May of the same year the Common Council directed that £100 be expended on the erection of two small buildings near the marine hospital for the accommodation of poor persons from the city stricken with yellow fever.[17]

The epidemic of 1798 remained for many years the worst to occur

in New York City or State. However, outbreaks of notable proportions occurred on several occasions in the first three decades of the
nineteenth century. The epidemic of 1803 took off more than six
hundred victims. In 1809 yellow fever attacked Brooklyn with such
serious results that a proclamation was issued in New York City
prohibiting all intercourse and communication with the affected
districts of Brooklyn. In 1819 New York City experienced a major
epidemic, when four thousand persons were brought down with
yellow fever. Three years later the city was again visited by the
deadly plague, which took a toll of two hundred and forty lives.

These visitations of disease had the effect of stimulating progress
in sanitation and more stringent quarantine laws. A municipal
Board of Health was created in 1805, mainly as a result of the recurring plagues. In the same year, which witnessed an economic
depression together with a mild outbreak of yellow fever, the municipal authorities ordered the filling of the Collect Pond, a large swamp
area in the city. The work on the Collect Pond, which had provided
a perfect breeding-place for the disease-carrying mosquito, was a
signal contribution to the salubrity of the city, though the authorities who conceived the project never dreamed of the true relationship
between the swamp and yellow fever. The task of filling the Collect
Pond continued slowly until 1808, when its completion was made a
work-relief project during an unemployment crisis. New York experienced several such unemployment relief situations in the early
years of the nineteenth century.

The winter of 1804–5 was a severe one, and the poor in New York
City underwent intense suffering. The extreme cold weather,
coupled with an unusual amount of unemployment, led to the adoption of a number of emergency measures. One of the most difficult
problems centered around the matter of supplying much-needed fuel
to the poor. In January, 1805, the state legislature enacted an unusual law permitting the municipal authorities "to take down and
remove the wooden bastions at the battery and Rhinelander's wharf,
within the said city, and appropriate the same for fuel for the use of
the poor."[18] On April 1, 1805, the Common Council resolved to allow the Society for the Relief of Poor Widows with Small Children
to return to the almshouse "244 loads of good Oak wood charged to

the said Society in the account rendered by the Superintendent of the Alms-house in full discharge of the said account." Later in the year, the city controller reported that "from the unusual severity of the last winter, which called into exercise every charitable emotion, and a corresponding disposition to relieve the distresses of the poor, the Corporation took a lively interest in affording them relief, which occasioned the expenditure of a large sum of money." The controller added that the municipal treasury had been unable to meet the extraordinary demands for public relief funds.[19]

The winter of 1805–6 also saw an unusual amount of distress in New York City. In February, 1806, the Humane Society applied to the Common Council for the use of a building to serve as a soup house for the poor. Several weeks later the city authorities ordered that a maximum of $600 be appropriated for the erection of the desired soup house. This soup house was still doling out food late in 1806.

THE EMBARGO AND THE DEPRESSION OF 1807–9

In 1807 France and Great Britain were locked in the throes of that long-drawn-out conflict which was to find its culmination years later at Waterloo. Each country had declared blockades against the other, to the great detriment of American commercial interests engaged in European trade. American vessels sailing with cargoes for England were being seized by French warships, and ships bound for France were being seized by the British. Besides, the British were busy impressing American seamen into the Royal Navy. In retaliation Jefferson led Congress to pass the Non-importation Act, closing American ports to certain categories of British goods. This act proved ineffectual, however, and in December, 1807, Congress passed the Embargo Act prohibiting all shipping between American ports and Europe. This act reflected primarily the determination of Jefferson and his adherents to maintain peace at any price. In his deep desire for peace, Jefferson had determined to keep America out of the European conflict. But the effect of Jefferson's well-intentioned act was disastrous to American commerce and ushered in a two-year depression of extraordinary severity. The chief sufferers were the ports along the eastern seaboard. New York City felt the

force of the embargo immediately. Not only was shipping at a standstill, but the city's growing manufacturing industry was also seriously affected since it depended largely upon foreign markets for prosperity. Thousands of laborers and marine workers were thrown out
of employment. The sudden transformation in the economic conditions of the city as a result of the passage of the Embargo Act is
graphically described by a contemporary, John Lambert, in his book
of travels in America. Lambert visited New York in the fall of 1807
and found the city astir with business activity, the docks bustling
with longshoremen, clerks, and sailors, while a large number of ships
were being loaded with goods going abroad. But what a different
scene he found upon returning five months later:

> Everything wore a dismal aspect at New York. The embargo had now con-
> tinued upwards of three months. . . . . Already had 120 failures taken place
> among the merchants and traders, to the amount of more than 5,000,000
> dollars; and there were above 500 vessels in the harbor, which were lying up use-
> less and rotting for want of employment. Thousands of sailors were either
> destitute of bread, wandering about the country, or had entered into the British
> service. The merchants had shut up their counting-houses, and discharged their
> clerks, and the farmers refrained from cultivating their land, for if they brought
> their produce to market, they either could not sell at all, or were obliged to dis-
> pose of it for only a fourth of its value.[20]

On January 4, 1808, a committee recommended to the Common
Council that the city use such means as were in its power, "particularly at this inclement season, to alleviate the evils which must
result from a suspension of the ordinary avocations of the laborious
part of the Community in this City."[21] Four days later a large group
of unemployed seamen of the city decided to take time by the fore-
lock and start something in the direction of their own relief. They
published a notice in the *Daily Advertiser* inviting all seamen to
assemble in the park fronting the city hall at eleven o'clock the day
following "for the purpose of enquiring of [the mayor] what they are
to do for their subsistence during the Winter."

The mayor called a special meeting of the Common Council, at
which he was requested to publish in the daily papers and handbills
an announcement that "the mayor decidedly disapproves the mode
of application . . . . to be pursued by the Sailors of this port for
relief," and that the Corporation would "provide for the wants of

every person without distinction who may be considered proper objects of relief." In conclusion the Board advised the sailors and other citizens not to attend the meeting which had been called.[22]

The next day the demonstration took place and the assembled seamen presented a memorial to the mayor:

Our situation is not only distressing but truly alarming. The Embargo lately levied upon our shipping has not only destroyed all employment by Sea, but rendered it impossible to gain a subsistence by our labor on shore. Our humble petition to you Sir, is to know how we are to act in this case, and to beg of you to provide some means for our subsistence during the winter, should not the embargo be immediately taken off. . . . .

The greatest part of the wages due us from our last voyage is already expended, and more, we are already indebted for our boarding. By what means shall we discharge these debts? Should we plunder, thieve or rob, the State prison will be our certain doom.

. . . . You tried to dissuade us from our purpose, mentioning that provision was made for objects of pity. We are not objects of pity yet, but shall soon be, if there is not some method taken for our support. We are for the most part hale, robust, hearty men, and would choose some kind of employment rather than the poorhouse for a livelihood. We humbly beg therefore, you will provide some means for our subsistence or the consequences may not only prove fatal to ourselves, but ruinous to the flourishing Commerce of America, as we shall be necessitated to go aboard foreign vessels.

On January 11 the mayor laid before the Board of Aldermen the memorial presented him by the seamen's assembly. It then developed that the Board's Ways and Means Committee had already taken action in the matter, indicating that the seamen's demonstration had the desired effect of stimulating the city to action in their behalf.

The Committee reported that it had conferred with Captain Chauncey of the navy yard and that he had agreed to receive the unemployed seamen for service at that place. The municipality was to pay the cost of their maintenance at twenty cents a day, and the seamen were to sign articles and be under navy discipline but were to be permitted to terminate their service at their own pleasure. The Committee recommended this arrangement to the Common Council, "as thereby every Sailor in distress will be comfortably supported, and being removed from town, and subject to the orders and discipline of the Navy no ill consequences can result to the peace

of the city, from their tumultuous associations." To provide for
other classes of the able unemployed the Committee reported it had
asked the street commissioners for figures on the number of workers
who could be employed to advantage in filling the Collect Pond in
the low-lying ground on the site of the present Tombs prison and its
immediate vicinity. The Committee further suggested that the improvement of certain highways and streets in the city could provide
useful types of public works projects.

For the needy who were unable to labor or for whom work was not
available, the Committee proposed to issue rations of soup and meat
four times weekly. A soup house was being set up at the almshouse,
and in the few days' interim, pending its completion, "partial supplies" were being provided. The Board adopted a resolution empowering the Committee to put its program into effect.

A week later it was reported that no profitable labor had yet been
provided, owing to the inclemency of the weather. The Committee
of Ways and Means gave notice, however, that applicants for work
who should be in actual need might apply at the almshouse for
rations for themselves and families. A statement for the week
showed that 2,951 rations had been issued; the daily issue had risen
from 243 to 1,049. The cost had been $265.59, at 9 cents per ration,
and cash relief for distressed families had totaled $89.29. The Com-
mittee assured the Board that economy would be "rigidly observed"
in the distribution.[23]

The Building Committee in charge of the construction of the new
city hall reported progress in the struggle with depression. By reducing the daily wage of twenty stone-cutters from $1.25 to $1.00,
they had been enabled to employ five more men at the work with no
increase in total expenditures. This undoubtedly represents one of
the first applications of the "share the work" idea. As might be
expected, the superintendents of the project willingly co-operated in
extending this form of relief. They suggested that more men might
be employed in the shops where the stone was prepared, on the same
basis. "Thus," said the Committee, "a two-fold good would result,
the employment of our citizens who are in distress, and their labor
obtained at a reduction of 20 per cent from the usual rate of wages."[24]

A week later it was reported that the rations issued for the past four days had totaled 8,345. With $115.21 which had been given in cash to distressed families, the total cost for the week was $866.26. Fifty-nine laborers had been employed on the Collect Pond project at a total cost of $105.27. Contracts with carmen had been made, which would result in an expected cost of $395.73. The Committee asked for and obtained $2,000 to meet its obligations.[25]

On February 8 it was reported that twenty-one seamen had been admitted for service at the navy yard between January 16 and February 6. Eighty laborers, it was further reported, had been employed on the Collect Pond project, but "as this labour is not very profitable, and as means of employment will be afforded at Governor's Island the Committee had concluded that it will be best to discharge these Labourers, and have given the Street Commissioner orders accordingly."[26] The work at Governors Island consisted in the construction of fortifications. Castle William, the round fort at the corner of the Island nearest Manhattan, was built during this period, as was the twin work off the Battery—Castle Garden—which is now the city aquarium. The total rations for the week had been 19,306 at a cost of $1,737.54. Cash relief for distressed families amounted to $108.76. The Committee declared itself convinced that impositions were being practiced on a considerable scale and proposed to adopt measures to prevent abuses.

On March 3 a gathering of laborers petitioned the Common Council for increased rations, and four days later a committee of laborers visited the city hall to inform the Common Council of the distress of their families, owing to inadequate relief and lack of jobs. They were directed to meet the Committee of Ways and Means the day following.[27] Meanwhile, the drive to reduce relief was continuing. A bill successfully introduced by the city's representatives in the legislature at this time provided that no person from any other state should be considered legally settled in any New York city or town unless he or she "shall have acquired such requisites to constitute a settlement, as are necessary in and by the laws of such state, from whence he or she may have come."[28]

In an effort to obtain federal aid in the unemployment crisis, the city authorities urged the War Department to initiate a public works program in New York. On March 21 it was announced that the

Secretary of War had agreed to co-operate with the city in providing work for the unemployed. Five days later the state legislature passed a joint resolution requesting the state administration to bring to the notice of the federal government the exposed situation of the port of New York. Besides urging military protection for the harbor, the resolution emphasized the destitute condition of the seamen and the danger of their migrating to foreign ports and service if they were not adequately cared for at home.[29] It is evident from this communication that the attempt to care for the seamen at the navy yard had been largely unsuccessful.

On April 4 the Committee of Ways and Means announced it had stopped the distribution of emergency relief rations and had directed the navy yard to discharge the few seamen remaining there. Subsequently the Committee reported that expenditures for relief, including sundry equipment and services for the entire season, amounted to $14,228.[30] It is interesting to note that the Committee, which two months previously had felt that abuses were widespread in the distribution of relief, now reported that they "have been less than could reasonably be expected."

The winter of 1808–9 showed no improvement in the conditions of unemployment and destitution. Mayor De Witt Clinton wrote the Secretary of War in December, 1808, suggesting that laborers on the fortifications around the city be continued at work. The secretary replied that there was no objection to keeping on the job as many workers as could be employed to advantage on reasonable terms. By mid-January the superintendent of the city almshouse thought it necessary to call the attention of the Common Council to the large and increasing number of outdoor poor. An appropriation was granted for the emergency. Early in February, 1809, a petition from a large number of citizens informed the Common Council that the severity of the winter and the abnormal unemployment had led them to organize a committee to collect donations for the relief "principally though not wholly, of those of the poor whose distress does not usually obtrude itself upon the public." The Committee felt that the distribution of all public charity should be under the direction of the Board of Aldermen, owing to the inefficiency of distribution by many independent groups and persons. The petitioners recom-

mended that the legislature be requested to authorize a special tax
to reimburse advances made to meet the emergency need. On February 13, however, the Finance Committee of the Board stated
that a special tax would be "inexpedient," expressing the belief
that the public distress had been greatly mitigated by the formation
of a number of associations for benevolent purposes, and that the
pressure of applicants at the almshouse was less than in the previous
year. Fewer rations were being issued.[31]

Another private philanthropic body arising out of the emergency
period was the Assistance Society organized in December, 1808, by
a "number of friends of humanity," with the object of "relieving and
advising sick and poor persons in the city of New York." Its founders aimed, specifically, "to supply the deficiencies of other charitable
societies, as far as their resources will admit." They also expressed
the opinion that public relief did not go far enough in meeting the
needs of the poor. "Popular charities in general," they declared, "go
no farther than the communication of temporal benefits," and fail
"to bestow on the sons and daughters of affliction counsels of prudence and religion, which, if followed, under the influence of grace,
would not fail to produce their welfare in future life and their eternal
and immeasurable felicity."[32]

The Assistance Society raised relief funds by printed appeals and
by house-to-house solicitation. Its high point of activity was reached
in the week ending March 1, 1809, when it extended relief to 827
families. Thereafter its ministrations fell rapidly, until there were
only nine families receiving relief from its treasury at the end of
April. More than $3,300 had been disbursed by the Society up to
April 26. Relief was dispensed in kind, food, clothing, and fuel, almost exclusively, while cash was offered in only a few cases. Applicants were rigorously investigated by the Society's visitors before
being granted relief, and the organization was able to boast that it
had been "deceived" in very few instances, although at times it had
been faced with the dilemma of whether to extend or withhold assistance to families in which the "guilty" or "undeserving" were
found along with the "innocent" or "deserving."[33]

On April 3, 1809, the Commissioners of the Almshouse and Bridewell reported that from January 6 to March 31 they had expended

$12,785.95 in the relief of the outdoor poor. Rations had totaled more than 76,000; loads of wood about 1,800; extra salaries, $215.25; cash relief, $602.77. Each relief ration cost ten cents, an increase of one cent over the previous year, and included one pound of bread, a half-pound of pork, and one quart of bean porridge. Pointing out the persistence of street begging, which continued despite public and private provisions for relief, the commissioners urged that beggars should be "discountenanced," since they represented a disgrace to the city and a scandal to strangers, who might conclude from appearances that little was being done for the alleviation of the plight of the poor.

Before the next winter ended, the expenditures of William Mooney, erstwhile superintendent of the almshouse, came under investigation. Mooney, founder of the Society of St. Tammany, was one of Tammany's first representatives to hold a municipal office. Apparently he had made the most of his tenure of office, which was terminated under pressure. On October 30 the investigating committee reported that expenditures at the almshouse for the year ending July 31, 1809, had greatly exceeded those of any previous year, and were nearly double those of the year ending July 31, 1804. It had been found that the ratio of increase in expenditures was much greater than the increase in the number of paupers. The greatest increase in goods consumed had been in those "articles which are used as the gratifications of luxury or intemperance, while the use of some articles which might contribute to the comfort of the sick or feeble has been diminished or discontinued." Liquor consumption at the almshouse, the committee found, amounted to upwards of twelve hundred gallons in one year.[34]

The War of 1812 brought a degree of profitable activity to the marine interests of New York City. Many privateers were fitted out in the city's shipyards and numbers of them returned to dispose of prizes taken in battle. As the British blockade tightened, however, the masses found not only food but even fuel difficult to procure. During the winter of 1813–14, a Fuel Association was formed which distributed 1,315 loads of wood in the course of the season. Concerts and entertainments were held to raise funds for charitable purposes.

The Common Council voted a special fund of $2,000 for the relief of distress in the ten wards of the city. Meanwhile the blockade had brought a further degree of inertia to merchant shipping. In September, 1813, it was calculated that nearly 150 seagoing vessels were laid up at the docks along the Hudson. Along the northern and western borders of the state considerable damage from invasion was incurred during the war. The legislature, through chapter 16, *Laws of 1814*, appropriated $50,000 for the relief of the sufferers in Niagara and Genesee counties on the western frontier. The Common Council of New York City voted a fund of $3,000 for the same purpose and resolved that February 2, 1814, should be a day of fasting, humiliation, and prayer throughout the city. The churches of the city raised $1,300, and private contributions within the municipal area totaled more than $5,000.

Early in 1814 it was reported that the increased cost of maintaining the almshouse and bridewell in New York under war conditions made it necessary to instal facilities for putting all able inmates usefully to work. A new almshouse was built at a cost of $90,000. Distressed families relieved outside the almshouse in the year ending April 1, 1814, comprised 12,592 persons. The almshouse population had increased to 1,201. Total costs of relief for the year were $21,-541.29, including both indoor and outdoor poor.[35]

On November 14, 1814, the superintendent of the almshouse told the Board of Aldermen that he had reason to believe that, because of the distresses occasioned by the war, the number of outdoor poor would be greatly increased. He asked for 1,750 loads of wood for fuel to distribute among six of the city's wards, the poor living in the other wards to be supplied from the stock at the almshouse.

The records for the years immediately following the war show that the city of New York appropriated funds quite frequently in aid of associations for the relief of widows and orphans. One thousand dollars was granted from the municipal treasury in October, 1815, to the House of Industry for the Employment and Support of Indigent and Distressed Females. It appears that this agency had furnished employment for 500 poor women during the year of its existence, enabling them to support large families of children and relieving pressure on the public purse and the propertied class. In December the Society for the Relief of Poor Widows with Small Children petitioned the city authorities for aid, reporting that it had relieved 217 widows and 538 small children during the preceding year. So heavy had been the demands on the Society's resources that it was in debt for wood distributed the previous winter. The Board of Aldermen resolved to appropriate $750 in aid of the Society. Earlier in the year the French Benevolent Society (established in 1809) had been helped to the extent of $750 by the city.[36]

The post-war years witnessed mild recurrences of economic depression but brought forth no new public welfare developments of importance.

SUMMARY

The emergency situations that occurred in this period evoked a number of interesting and, in some respects, important developments in the welfare field in New York. The repeated epidemics were certainly a decisive factor in the establishment of quarantine and preventive measures of increasing stringency, in the improvement of hospitalization for immigrants, seamen, and residents, and finally in the construction of the first substantial permanent hospital on the present site of Bellevue Hospital in New York City. The improvement of sanitation as a preventive step was another important aspect of the movement against recurring plagues.

Economic depressions during this period brought forth the first definite advance of private philanthropic bodies into the field of general outdoor relief. As hard times became intensified under the Embargo, New York City witnessed the first considerable mass demand within the state for relief—significantly, it was for *work relief*. In the attempt to provide this type of relief, the federal authorities co-operated with the city on a welfare project for the first time.

Though the city's own works projects were soon abandoned, the federal program for fortifying the port was continued to some purpose and in part at least represented a federal work-relief enterprise. An innovation was the wage-cutting, spread-the-work movement initiated under municipal auspices among the workers building the new city hall.

One of the most notable public welfare developments in the War of 1812 was the resumption by the state of the practice of appropriating public funds for the relief of families distressed through invasion, a practice first introduced in Revolutionary times.

BIBLIOGRAPHICAL REFERENCES

1. Henry P. Johnson, "New York after the Revolution, 1783–1789," *Magazine of American History*, XXIX (1893), 305.
2. Orin G. Libby, *The Geographical Distribution of the Vote of the Thirteen States on the Federal Constitution, 1787–8* (Madison, Wis., 1894), pp. 54, 60.
3. *N.Y.C., M.C.C., 1784–1831*, I, 115.
4. *Ibid.*, pp. 185, 291.
5. New York State, *Laws of 1794*, chap. 53.
6. Robert J. Carlisle (ed.), *An Account of Bellevue Hospital* (New York, 1893), pp. 11–15.
7. *N.Y.C., M.C.C., 1784–1831*, II, 180, 181, 200, 201, 212.
8. New York State, *Laws of 1796*, chap. 38.
9. James Hardie, *An Account of the Malignant Fever Lately Prevalent in the City of New York* (New York, 1799), pp. 54, 56.
10. *Ibid.*, pp. 57–59.
11. *Ibid.*, p. 60.
12. New York State, *Laws of 1799*, chap. 93.
13. Hardie, *op. cit.*, pp. 13–14.
14. Francis R. Packard, *History of Medicine in the United States* (New York, 1931), I, 129–31.
15. Hardie, *op. cit.*, p. 17.
16. *N.Y.C., M.C.C., 1784–1831*, II, 498–99.
17. *Messages from the Governors*, II, 451.
18. New York State, *Laws of 1805*, chap. 3.
19. *N.Y.C., M.C.C., 1784–1831*, III, 716; IV, 55.
20. John Lambert, *Travels through Canada and the United States of North America in the Years 1806, 1807 and 1808* (2d ed.; London, 1814), pp. 62, 294–95.
21. *N.Y.C., M.C.C., 1784–1831*, IV, 693.
22. *Ibid.*, p. 699.
23. *Ibid.*, pp. 702, 714.
24. *Ibid.*, p. 719.
25. *Ibid.*, pp. 728–29.
26. *Ibid.*, p. 751.
27. *Ibid.*, V, 40, 46.
28. New York State, *Laws of 1808*, chap. 192.

29. *N.Y.C.*, *M.C.C.*, *1784–1831*, V, 59; New York State Senate, *Journal* (31st sess. [Albany, 1808]), p. 207.
30. *N.Y.C.*, *M.C.C.*, *1784–1831*, V, 79, 123.
31. *Ibid.*, pp. 375, 397, 414, 429.
32. Lilian Brandt, *Glimpses of New York in Previous Depressions* (New York, 1933), pp. 27–28 (mimeographed, confidential).
33. *Ibid.*, p. 29.
34. *N.Y.C.*, *M.C.C.*, *1784–1831*, V, 494, 714–26.
35. *Ibid.*, VII, 660, 741.
36. *Ibid.*, pp. 82, 121, 319, 359.

CHAPTER X

A HALF-CENTURY OF CHILD WELFARE, 1784–1823

Indenture and apprenticeship constituted the chief features of the child welfare pattern of the period, as had been the case in pre-Revolutionary times. The first statute of the new state covering this subject, chapter 15 of the *Laws of 1788*, defined at length the intent of the law. It legalized indentures entered into by minors with the consent of parents or guardians; children of Indian women were excepted, as these might be bound out only with the certified consent of a justice of the peace. In New York City, Albany and Hudson, dependent children or minors found begging in the streets might be bound out by "the mayor, recorder and aldermen or any two of them," without consent of the parents. In accordance with traditional practice, the maximum age limit for indentured service was fixed at twenty-one years for males and eighteen years for females. Attempts by employers to prevent apprentices from setting up shop for themselves after the expiration of their terms, or to exact or take any payment for this privilege, were prohibited under penalty of a forfeiture of £40.

Recalcitrant apprentices or servants were to be confined in the bridewell, house of correction, or common jail. Runaway apprentices or servants, excepting those whose apprenticeship was paid for, were compelled to serve double the period of their absence unless they could provide other means of satisfying the master or mistress. Other sections in the act afforded legal protection for the apprentice or servant against ill-usage by the master. Poor-law officials were required to see that the terms of indenture or similar agreements were fulfilled, that no bound child was misused, and that grievances arising in this connection were redressed according to law.

A supplementary act, chapter 20 of the *Laws of 1796*, provided that minors without parents or guardians might validly bind themselves out with the consent of the town overseers or the justices of the peace or any judge of the Court of Common Pleas in the county where they resided. When the father of a child was not in legal capacity the mother was given the right to bind out the child, and the same right was extended to Indian mothers deserted by their husbands.

The general poor law of 1788 (chap. 62) included a section marking a significant step forward in the development of the laws pertaining to apprentices and servants. This section provided that every indenture or contract binding out a child as a servant or apprentice must thenceforth contain a clause to the effect, "that every Master and Mistress to whom such child shall be bound as aforesaid, shall cause such child to be taught and instructed to read and write." While some educational provision had been included in indenture forms for many years previously, this statute constituted the first general legislative enactment providing for the kind of education to be given to poor apprentices.[1]

Dependent boys were usually apprenticed to learn the "art and mystery" of such crafts as were commonly followed by the blacksmith, cordwainer, cooper, carpenter, farmer, mason, mariner, etc., while girls were usually apprenticed to learn housewifery, which included sewing, knitting, and spinning.

The records of this period indicate a growing concern on the part of poor-law officials for the well-being of apprentices bound out by them. Complaints from apprentices charging abuses were submitted with greater frequency and were given more consideration by the authorities. In November, 1791, for example, the Commissioners of the Almshouse and Bridewell of New York City, having decided that a boy bound out by them two years earlier to a resident of Ulster County was being subjected to ill-treatment, made arrangements to take the boy from his master and to apprentice him to Cadwallader Colden, Jr., also of Ulster, with the provision that he should be taught the clothier's trade.[2] The problem arising from binding out dependent children to persons living in districts removed from the supervision of local authorities was already manifest. A significant item appears in the minutes of the Commissioners of the Almshouse and Bridewell for December 3, 1792:

Whereas complaints hath frequently been made that some of the poor Children, placed at a distance in the County, have been very illy treated by the persons with whom they live, therefore Resolved that no person be permitted to take a child into the Country from the Almshouse without first obtaining leave of the board.[3]

Children composed a large proportion of the almshouse population at the time. In February, 1795, of the 622 paupers on the books of the New York City almshouse, 259 were children, mostly under nine years of age. The policy pursued by the authorities was to bind out as many of these children as possible. With recurring regularity, the minutes of the Board of Commissioners of the Almshouse and Bridewell end with the following notation: "After binding out several children, the board adjourned....." In 1794 a total of 94 children at the almshouse were bound out by the commissioners.[4]

It appears that some of the earliest manufacturing firms turned to the almshouse as a source of labor supply, as may be inferred from an entry of July 28, 1794:

Consented .... that the 10 following boys may be bound to Andrew Stockholm & Co. at the Cotton Manufactury in this County, To wit, Willm. Brickly, Willet Pearcy, Joseph Pearcy, John Marchant, Willm. Anderson, Peter Conklin, Thos. Waling, James McIntosh, Thos. Hill and John Woods.[5]

With the rapid growth of New York City as a seaport, the apprenticing of dependent boys as seamen became increasingly popular. In a section devoted to the care and treatment of pauper children, listed among the "Rules for the Government of the Almshouse" adopted by the Common Council in the year 1800, it was recommended:

When the children arrive at proper ages, great care should be taken to furnish them with suitable places, that they may be instructed in some useful trade or occupation; and as the Commerce and Navy of the country are becoming of great importance, it would be well if there was a power of binding to the sea-service, when it should be judged most advantageous.[6]

Thereafter, over a period of many years, a large proportion of the boys at the almshouse were bound out to service in the merchant marine. Chapter 75, *Laws of 1816*, extended the right to bind out poor children to grandparents, even in cases where the father or mother of such children were alive.

FREE SCHOOLS FOR POOR CHILDREN

Free education during the provincial period and for long after was conducted mainly by private groups as a charitable enterprise. Occasional attempts to provide a free public-school system during the colonial era had failed, and, aside from a few schools operated by the more progressive towns, the only institutions furnishing free instruction were the charity schools established by the churches.

The eighteenth-century Enlightenment popularized the idea of free, public, secular education as an integral part of democratic society. A milestone along the path toward the realization of this ideal in New York State was the founding in 1786 of the African Free School for the children of Negro slaves by the New York Society for Promoting the Manumission of Slaves. This school, though a private undertaking, later received financial support from the public treasury.

Meanwhile, a trend toward the establishment of a state system of free common schools was gaining ground. As early as 1782, Governor George Clinton had declared in his opening message to the legislature that it was "the peculiar duty of the government of a free state . . . . to endeavor by the establishment of schools and seminaries, to diffuse that degree of Literature which is necessary to the due discharge of public trusts."[7] In a report submitted in 1787, the Regents of the University of the State of New York, organized three years earlier to supervise higher and secondary education in the state, concluded that "the erecting of public schools for teaching reading, writing and arithmetic is an object of very great importance which ought not to be left to the discretion of private men, but be promoted by public authority."[8] This constituted the first explicit declaration by an official body advocating a public-school system in this state. The same recommendation was repeated in subsequent reports of the Board of Regents, with Governor Clinton's powerful support. In 1791 the legislature passed a bill authorizing a group of men headed by Robert Livingston to receive moneys from the excise fees and fines collected in Clermont, Columbia County, and to build and maintain a school with these funds. This diversion of money normally assigned to the poor was authorized for the establishment and maintenance of common schools by a number of towns throughout the state.

The first act leading to the establishment of a state common-school system was passed by the legislature in 1795. Entitled "An Act for the Encouragement of Schools," it authorized the appropriation of £20,000 from the state treasury annually for five years,

for the purpose of encouraging and maintaining schools in the several cities and towns of this State, in which the children of the inhabitants residing in the State shall be instructed in the English language or be taught English grammar, arithmetic, mathematics and such other branches of knowledge as are most useful and necessary to complete a good English education.[9]

The beneficial results of the statute of 1795 soon became apparent. Within three years 1,352 common schools had been organized throughout the state and were attended by 59,660 pupils. Sixteen academies for secondary education had also been incorporated. Unfortunately, however, this annual appropriation was not renewed after the five-year period specified in the law of 1795, and financial support on a state-wide basis was permitted to lapse until 1812.

On September 23, 1796, the Common Council of New York City voted to distribute £944 out of the state and city school fund among the charity schools and religious societies of the municipal area. Lacking authority to establish free common schools, the municipality resolved at the same time to petition the legislature for a special law granting such permission. In 1797 the legislature enacted chapter 34, authorizing the city to expend a limited sum for the establishment of common schools. However, free elementary education continued to depend mainly on sectarian charity schools until 1805, when the Society for Establishing a Free School in the City of New York, founded largely through the initiative of Thomas Eddy and other Quakers, was incorporated "for the education of poor children who do not belong to or are not provided for by any religious society."[10]

A private subscription started by the Society was supplemented by a state grant of $4,000 to be paid out of the city's excise revenues to the organization's trustees to enable them to erect a school building. An annual appropriation of $1,000 by the state was also voted by the legislature.[11] The Society's first school was opened in 1806 and immediately proved to be a great success, meeting a long-felt need. By 1824 the Society had six of these schools in operation in New York City, with over five thousand pupils in attendance.[12] Meanwhile in Albany a school building had been erected in 1804 through the contributions of charitable persons. About twenty-three poor children were instructed there in "reading, writing, and plain work and in the strict observance of every Christian and moral duty."[13]

NEW YORK FREE SCHOOL NO. 2, 1808

The first school for the poor in Brooklyn was established in 1813, when a group of women organized the Loisian Seminary for the purpose of "teaching poor children reading, writing, arithmetic, knitting and sewing." The school was conducted for five years by volunteer teachers in the homes of members, and was then converted into a public school.[14]

The opening of the first free school under the auspices of the Free School Society in 1806 marked the beginning of the public-school system in New York State. Instruction first confined to the poor gradually extended to all classes, as, with the improvement in public facilities, those in good circumstances overcame their reluctance to send their children to the common schools. An act providing a permanent system of common schools was passed by the legislature in 1812. Each township was to be divided into school districts. Three commissioners of common schools were to be elected by each town as financial officers to handle the funds to be distributed among the districts. The offices of trustee, clerk, and director were created for each district, as well as the office of state superintendent of common schools. In 1813, chapter 52 authorized the appointment of five commissioners of school money in New York City who were in turn empowered to distribute school funds to the trustees of the Free School Society, the Orphan Asylum Society, the Economical School, the African Free School, and "such incorporated religious societies in New York City as now support or shall hereafter establish charity schools in said city."

The appropriation of local funds for the support of schools, in addition to the state school fund, was left to the discretion of the inhabitants of each town. An amendment was passed in 1814, however, making it compulsory for each town to raise a sum equal to its allotment from the state school moneys. Failure to levy the requisite sum was to be penalized by forfeiture of the right to the corresponding state allotment. The first distribution of money under these provisions was made in the year 1816. The availability of state funds greatly stimulated the establishment of schools all over the state. By 1828, 55 counties, divided into 8,298 school districts, reported 441,856 children attending school.[15] Many legislative acts liberalizing the common-school system were enacted in subsequent years, although it was not until 1867 that the common schools in this state were made entirely free.

INSTITUTIONAL CARE: THE ESTABLISHMENT OF ORPHAN ASYLUMS

Until the establishment of the first orphan asylum in 1806, the almshouse remained the only type of charitable institution in New York State for the reception of dependent children. In spite of the preference for indenture, a great many needy children found their way into the common poorhouse; a census of the New York City almshouse in 1795 showed that over 40 per cent of its inmates consisted of children under nine years of age.

Judging from reports of the Commissioners of the Almshouse and Bridewell, as well as other contemporary documents, the almshouse children in New York City at the turn of the nineteenth century appear to have been treated with a large degree of liberality and intelligence. The "Rules for the Government of the Almshouse" adopted by the Common Council in 1800 contained a nine-point program for the care of the child inmates, which is so progressive in the light of the time that it deserves to be quoted in full:

1. Care shall be taken to provide healthy and proper nurses for such of the children as may require them; and where this can be done out of the house, it shall be preferred.

2. Such children as have arrived at a suitable age, shall regularly attend the school provided for them, and shall be instructed in reading, writing and arithmetic.

3. The girls shall be taught plain work and knitting by a proper person to be provided for that purpose, and shall be employed therein at least three afternoons in every week.

4. Care shall be taken that the children are kept clean and neat; that they receive their food regularly, and that they behave themselves in a decent and orderly manner. They shall be allowed such sports and pastime as may contribute to their health, but always in the presence of some discreet and sober person; and shall be kept as much as possible from any intermixture with the other paupers.

5. If any of the children distinguish themselves by their good behavior and capacity, the board will direct their being instructed in the higher kinds of learning, and will take measures that they may profit thereby in their future situations in life.

6. The children shall be kept in separate apartments, according to their different sexes.

7. The schoolmaster, or some proper person, shall twice on each Sunday, read to the children and such of the adult paupers as may choose to attend, proper prayers and sermons, with some passages or parts of the Bible, or some other religious book.

8. When any of the children arrive at proper ages, they shall be bound out to suitable trades or occupations, and provision shall be made in their indentures for their due maintenance and instruction.

9. If any of those who shall have been so bound out, shall be injured or ill-treated, the superintendent shall consider it as his duty to procure them redress. They are to be considered, in every respect, as the children of the public, under his care.[16]

It is noteworthy that this set of rules was embodied in its entirety in an ordinance passed by the Common Council five years later, indicating that it represented more than an isolated gesture on the part of the poor-relief authorities.[17] Unfortunately, contemporary poor-relief documents relating to almshouse conditions in other parts of the state show that the enlightened attitude of the New York City officials toward the treatment of dependent children was exceptional rather than typical. In other sections, little if any distinction was made between dependent children and other classes of dependents. Even in the case of New York City, a sharp distinction must be made between theory and practice in the development of poor relief. Although the New York almshouse rules relating to children were surprisingly progressive, the actual condition of the poorhouse children fell far below the standards set by the authorities. Continued overcrowding made impossible a satisfactory separation of children from the adult inmates; educational facilities were very limited (as, indeed, they were outside the almshouse); the regime was harsh and often cruel, and there were other unfavorable factors inherent in the very concept of the mixed almshouse. A movement leading toward the establishment of separate institutions for child dependents was inevitable and became manifest at the end of the eighteenth century, culminating in the founding of the first orphan asylum within the state.

The series of yellow-fever epidemics in the last decade of the century had taken a considerable toll among breadwinners in New York City, leaving numbers of penniless widows and orphans in their wake. Many of them could find relief only in the common almshouse. Moved by the plight of these dependents, a group of women in 1797 established a charitable organization which they named the Ladies Society for the Relief of Poor Widows with Small Children (incorporated by chap. 99, *Laws of 1802*). A leading spirit in the founding of this society was Mrs. Isabella Graham, who served as its first directress. The Society devoted its efforts particularly to widowed mothers who worked for a livelihood, but whose earnings were too meager to support themselves and their children. Its aim in such cases was to supplement the widow's income with small monthly allowances. Relief was given only in kind, except in very unusual instances, when a rigidly limited cash allowance was permitted. The means, character, and circumstances of each applicant were investigated with minute care by the Society's agents before relief was granted. Help was denied to widowed mothers who failed to meet the strict moral standards set in the Society's by-laws. Except in very rare instances, no relief was granted to widows who refused to agree to place out as servants or apprentices such of their children as were judged eligible, or to place the younger ones at a charity school.

During the first winter (1797–98) of its existence, the Society granted relief to 98 widows with 223 children. By 1800 the number of beneficiaries on the books of the organization had grown to 152 widows with 420 children under the age of twelve. An interesting feature of the Society's activities was its work-relief program. The conviction was expressed in its report for 1800 that its clients "would rather eat their own bread, hardly earned, than that of others with idleness." It set widows to work making shirts and other articles of clothing in their own homes, supplying nearly three thousand yards of linen, besides other materials, for this purpose in one year.[18]

A comparatively large grant of public funds was made to the Society in 1803, when a yellow-fever epidemic greatly increased its scope of activities. Chapter 68 of the *Laws of 1803* authorized the city of New York to raise $15,000 by lottery, to be turned over to the Society in aid of its work.

Similar organizations, such as the Society for the Relief of Indigent Women and Children in Albany (incorporated 1804) sprang up elsewhere, but the New York Society must be credited with the founding of the first orphan asylum in the state. During the Society's early years its officers had been confronted with the problem of disposing of the children of deceased widows who had been recipients of its relief. They bound out as many of these children as they could, but there were some orphans who could not be disposed of in this manner. At first the officers succeeded in placing out such children in the homes of members of the Society, thus saving them from commitment to the common almshouse. But this expedient soon reached the point of saturation, and the Society had to seek another way out of the dilemma. About this time there fell into the hands of Mrs. Joanna Bethune, a prominent member of the Society and a daughter of Mrs. Graham, a copy of the *Life of Francke*, containing a history of the orphan house founded by the latter at Halle, Germany. The inspiration for the establishment of an orphan asylum seems to have originated from the perusal of this volume. At any rate, members of the Ladies Society for the Relief of Poor Widows with Small Children set about early in 1806 to found an orphanage. A public meeting took place on March 15, 1806, at which the New York Orphan Asylum Society was organized, with Mrs. Sarah Hoffman chosen as first directress.*

As with the parent-organization, membership in the new society was open only to women. A two-story frame house in Greenwich Village was hired as temporary quarters for the asylum, and a "pious and respectable man and his wife" were employed as superintendent and matron.[19] Twelve orphans were received during the first six months of the asylum's existence. This was the fourth orphan asylum to be established in the territory now comprising the United States. At the time of its opening, only one other such institution— that located in Charleston, South Carolina—was still functioning.

"The Orphan Asylum Society in the City of New York" was incorporated by chapter 179 of the *Laws of 1807*. Admittance to the asylum was to be restricted to orphans deprived of both parents. The constitution stated:

The orphans shall be educated, fed and clothed at the expense of the Society and at the Asylum. They must have religious instruction, moral example, and habits of industry inculcated on their minds. As soon as the age and acquirements of orphans shall, in the opinion of the Board of Directors, render them capable of earning their living, they must be bound out to some reputable persons or families for such object and in such manner as the Board shall approve.

Boys were to be bound out only to farmers or mechanics, girls to "respectable families."[20]

---

* Mrs. Hoffman had been serving as second directress of the Society for the Relief of Poor Widows with Small Children before taking over the direction of the new organization.

The officers of the Society were given the right, by special act of the legislature, to bind out their charges directly. A permanent institution was begun in July, 1807, intended to accommodate two hundred orphan inmates. The cost of building the asylum forced the organization deeply into debt, causing it to petition the legislature early in 1808 for a grant-in-aid of its work. The legislature responded with a rather unusual provision authorizing the Board of Health of New York City to raise by lottery $5,000—in addition to a sum of $25,000 previously authorized—and to hand over the first-mentioned sum to the Orphan Asylum Society.[21] It was specified, however, that lottery tickets for the asylum's benefit must not be sold until all lotteries previously authorized should be disposed of. This restriction occasioned a considerable delay, and seven years passed before the Society collected its lottery money. Meanwhile, in 1811, the legislature voted a grant to the Society of $500 annually to be paid by the state treasurer out of the fund arising from auction duties which had been earmarked by act of the legislature in 1798 for the foreign poor in New York City.[22] The Orphan Asylum Society continued until 1853 to receive yearly grants from this fund.* Finding this annual appropriation insufficient, the Society repeatedly petitioned the municipal authorities for additional financial aid. Its appeals were regularly turned down until 1824, when the Common Council voted a special grant of $500 to the Society. It was made clear at the time that the appropriation was not to be regarded as setting a precedent, and that the Council did not thereby commit itself to "any future contributions."[23]

Another orphanage opened in New York State during the period under discussion was the Roman Catholic Orphan Asylum in the City of New York. It was established in 1817 as the Roman Catholic Benevolent Society in the City of New York and was intended for the care and education of orphans of the Roman Catholic faith. Like the Orphan Asylum Society, it began to receive state grants regularly soon after its opening. A similar institution, the Roman

* A detailed account of the development of the fund appropriated to the foreign poor of New York City out of moneys arising from auction duties may be found in chapter vii, pp. 134–36.

Catholic Orphan Asylum in the City of Brooklyn, was founded in 1826 and incorporated eight years later. The St. Vincent's Female Orphan Asylum of Albany dates its beginning from the year 1828, when three Sisters of Charity arrived in that city from Emmitsburg, Maryland, and established a day school for dependent orphan girls, which later developed into an orphanage. It was not until 1849, however, that the St. Vincent's Orphan Asylum Society in the City of Albany was incorporated.

The 1830's saw the rise of a number of special institutions for dependent children throughout the state. All were established under private auspices, and most of them were aided financially by grants from the state or local treasuries. The following institutions were opened during this decade: the Society for the Relief of Orphan and Destitute Children in the City of Albany (later known as the Albany Orphan Asylum, and since 1933, as the Albany Home for Children) founded in 1829 and incorporated in 1831; the Orphan Asylum Society in the Village of Utica founded in 1830 and incorporated the same year by chapter 267; the Leake and Watts Orphan-House founded and incorporated in New York City in 1831; the Orphan Asylum Society of the City of Brooklyn founded in 1832, incorporated 1835; the Troy Association for the Relief of Destitute Children established in 1833, incorporated in 1835 as Troy Orphan Asylum; the Orphan Asylum of St. John's Church in Utica in the County of Oneida founded in 1834, incorporated in 1837; the Society for the Relief of Half-Orphan and Destitute Children in the City of New York founded in 1835, incorporated in 1837; the Asylum for Relief of Children of Poor Widowers and Widows, New York City, incorporated in 1835 (merged with the Roman Catholic Orphan Asylum in the City of New York, 1852); the Buffalo Orphan Asylum founded in 1836, incorporated in 1837; the Rochester Orphan Asylum (later Hillside Home for Children) organized in 1836, incorporated in 1838; and the Association for the Benefit of Colored Orphans in the City of New York (since 1884 name changed to Colored Orphan Asylum and Association for the Benefit of Colored Children in the City of New York) founded in 1836, incorporated in 1838.

SUMMARY

During the period 1776–1823 the public care of dependent children in New York State continued to fall under three major categories: (1) maintenance in the local poorhouse; (2) relief in their own homes; and (3) the system of indenture and apprenticeship. The period saw the rise of a number of private organizations devoted to child welfare. Out of such organizations arose the first institutions for the care of dependent children—the orphan asylums —established under private auspices and aided by public funds, state or local (sometimes both). It also witnessed the rise of common schools for poor children. These schools were founded for the most part as private charitable undertakings, developing gradually into a state-supported and finally into a state-controlled public-school system, removed from the province of public welfare as we conceive it today. The rise of the first institution for juvenile delinquents, as well as institutions for deaf and blind children, occurring toward the end of this period, will be described in subsequent chapters.

BIBLIOGRAPHICAL REFERENCES

1. Robert F. Seybolt, *Apprenticeship and Apprenticeship Education in Colonial New England and New York* (New York, 1917), p. 87.
2. New York City Commissioners of the Almshouse and Bridewell, *Minutes* (MS), November 7, 1791.
3. *Ibid.*, December 3, 1792.
4. *N.Y.C., M.C.C., 1784–1831*, II, 125.
5. New York City Commissioners of the Almshouse and Bridewell, *Minutes* (MS), July 28, 1794.
6. *N.Y.C., M.C.C., 1784–1831*, II, 663.
7. *Messages from the Governors*, II, 183.
8. Charles E. Fitch, *The Public School: History of Common School Education in New York from 1633 to 1904* (Albany, 1904), p. 15.
9. New York State, *Laws of 1795*, chap. 75.
10. ——, *Laws of 1805*, chap. 108: "An Act to incorporate the Society instituted in the City of New York, for the establishment of a free School for the Education of poor Children, who do not belong to or are not provided for by any religious Society."
11. ——, *Laws of 1807*, chap. 20.
12. Fitch, *op. cit.*, p. 22.
13. Munsell, *Annals of Albany*, IV, 317.

14. Henry R. Stiles, *A History of the City of Brooklyn* (Brooklyn, 1867–70), III, 11–13.
15. Samuel L. Knapp, *Life of Thomas Eddy* (London, 1836), p. 132.
16. *N.Y.C., M.C.C., 1784–1831*, II, 671.
17. New York City, *Laws and Ordinances of 1805*, chap. 6.
18. *Constitution of the Ladies Society, Established in New York, for the Relief of Poor Widows with Small Children* (New York, 1800), p. 13.
19. Mrs. Jonathan Odell, *Origin and History of the Orphan Asylum Society in the City of New York, 1806–1896* (New York, 1896), I, 9.
20. *Ibid.*, p. 16.
21. New York State, *Laws of 1808*, chap. 240.
22. ———, *Laws of 1811*, chap. 86.
23. *N.Y.C., M.C.C., 1784–1831*, XIV, 100.

CHAPTER XI

CARE OF SPECIAL DEPENDENT CLASSES

During the fifty-year period following the successful conclusion
of the Revolution, there came into being a number of agencies and
institutions dedicated to the care of special classes of dependents.
Several of these have been mentioned in preceding chapters. Coin-
cident with the development of these services was the steady extension of state aid in social welfare. In some fields it acted merely
as a subsidizing agent, in others its participation was more direct
and comprehensive. One of the most important developments during this period was the expansion of medical services to the poor,
initiated chiefly by private organizations with the encouragement
and financial assistance of the state.

MEDICAL AID

The evolution of Bellevue, the first public hospital in the state
devoted primarily to the reception of poor patients, has been briefly
traced in the discussion of disease epidemics in chapter ix. Beginning as an infirmary room in the New York City almshouse in
1735, it became a separate entity in 1825.

Meanwhile the New York Hospital, a semipublic institution, was
opened in 1791. In 1792 the annual state grant to the hospital,
which had previously been set at £800, was raised by the legislature to £2,000. Three years later it was increased to £4,000, and
again in 1796 to £5,000. An annual allowance of $12,500, payable
out of the auction duties in New York City, was voted by the legislature in 1800. This annual state grant continued until 1857. In
1799 the governors of the hospital entered into an agreement with
the United States Treasury Department whereby the sick and disabled seamen of the port of New York were to be received in the
hospital. The cost of care was to be paid out of funds set aside for
that purpose by the federal collector of the port. This arrangement
lasted for decades. Through an act passed by the New York legis-

lature in 1796, the hospital also became the beneficiary of fines collected by harbor masters at the port of New York for violation of certain harbor regulations.[1]

The New York Hospital was intended mainly for the reception of the sick poor, although its facilities were open to all ranks of society. No figures are available as to the number of patients admitted during its first year of operation, but in the year ending February, 1793, the admissions totaled 236. This number was

EASTERN DISPENSARY
Incorporated April 25, 1832

doubled the next year, and by 1804 more than 1,000 patients were being admitted annually.[2]

Almost simultaneously with the opening of the New York Hospital, another type of nonprofit-making medical institution commenced operation in New York City. The New York Dispensary, organized in 1790 largely through the efforts of the Medical Society of the County of New York, was opened February 8, 1791, with Isaac Roosevelt serving as the first president.* Samuel Bard, who had played an important role in the founding of the New York Hospital, was appointed one of the senior physicians. According to its

* The idea for this institution may have been suggested by the existence of a dispensary which had been established in Philadelphia in 1766.

articles of incorporation, approved by the legislature in April, 1795, the purpose of the dispensary was "relieving such sick poor persons as are unable to procure medical aid at their own dwellings and are so circumstanced as not to be proper objects for the Alms House or [New York] Hospital." At first, patients seeking admission to the institution had to procure a certificate signed by a contributor, stating that "such person is a proper object to be relieved." All restrictions on admission were subsequently removed. Explaining its new policy a dispensary report stated:

No questions are asked to wound the sensitiveness of poverty, and no re-proofs offered to drive away the vicious. This is not our business. They suffer or they would not come for aid; and while we do not measure out our benefi-cence with a censorious hand, we know that we are doing good, securing the common weal, and we are speacking to the hearts of all by showing that a common interest still unites the different classes of the community, and bridges over the immense gulf which, at first sight, seemed to separate them.[3]

At a still later period this liberal attitude toward applicants for treatment was modified, requiring patients to attest to need.

In October, 1798, a subscription was initiated by the well-known physician, David Hosack, to raise funds for the building of a lying-in hospital in New York City, "an asylum for the reception of women in a state of pregnancy, who are unable to procure the necessary medical assistance and nursing, during the period of their confine-ment." Nearly $5,000 was raised for the project, and in March, 1799, the Society of the Lying-in Hospital of the City of New York was incorporated by the legislature. A building was secured on Cedar Street, but the available funds proved insufficient to carry through the plan for a separate institution, and in 1801 an agree-ment was made between the Society's officers and the New York Hospital whereby the existing funds of the former were paid into the latter institution on condition that a lying-in ward should be established there.[4]

PROVISION FOR THE MENTALLY ILL

In colonial times poorhouses and prisons afforded the only types of institutions available for the care, or rather confinement, of the insane. The suspicious attitude toward these unfortunates and the repressive treatment accorded them are well reflected in the first legislative measure for the insane enacted in New York. Chapter 31, *Laws of 1788*, significantly entitled "An Act for apprehending and punishing disorderly persons," contained a section relating to "persons who by lunacy or otherwise are furiously mad, or are so far disordered in their senses that they may be dangerous to be permitted to go abroad." The statute empowered any two justices of the peace to direct the local constables and overseers of the poor "to cause such persons to be apprehended and kept safely locked up in some secure place within such city, or within the county in which such town shall lie . . . . and (if such justices shall find it necessary) to be there chained." Nonresident insane persons were to be sent to their last legal place of settlement and there "locked up or chained" on the authority of two local justices of the peace. Nothing in this act was to be construed as restraining friends or relatives of "such lunatick" from taking him under their own care and protection if they desired to do so.

The act of 1788 relating to the insane was taken almost verbatim from an English law (2 George II, Stat. 17, c. 5) with a similar title enacted forty years earlier. Its repressive nature was typical of public provision for the mentally ill in that period throughout Europe and America.

In New York City the only institutional provision for the insane consisted of "strong-rooms" in the common poorhouse and cells in the municipal bridewell. In 1785 an attempt was made by the authorities to segregate the insane in the bridewell from the other inmates, when the Common Council directed the Commissioners of the Almshouse and Bridewell to "partition off as many Rooms in the Attick Store in the Bridewell not exceeding five as they may conceive Necessary for the Confinement of lunatic & mad persons."[5]

A milestone in the treatment of the mentally ill was reached in September, 1792, when the newly opened New York Hospital admitted its first mental patient—the first instance of such hospital care in this state. The founders of the New York Hospital had planned provision for mental patients many years earlier. In 1774, while construction of the hospital buildings was in progress, they had voted "to appropriate the cellar part of the North wing or such part of it as they may judge necessary into wards or cells for the reception of lunatics."[6] The cells for mental patients were located in the basement of the completed hospital. Custodial care rather than curative treatment was accorded to the insane in the beginning. To the hospital's credit, however, it should be noted that the early records indicate that chains and similar means of mechanical restraint so commonly used in the contemporary treatment of the insane were not in use at the New York Hospital.

The mentally ill were admitted to the hospital in ever increasing numbers, new apartments being converted into cells for their reception. Accommodations for their care were soon taxed to the utmost, and the inevitable condition of overcrowding set in. More than two hundred mental patients were received into the hospital between the years 1797–1803. By the latter year the inadequacy of existing facilities became so alarming that a third story was added to the institution to accommodate the insane. Even this addition could not meet the growing need, and it was decided to erect a separate building for mental patients. The governors of the hospital applied to the state legislature for further aid. Their petition was favorably received, and in 1806 a law was passed extending the annual appropriation of $12,500 to the hospital until 1857, thus assuring the institution of a permanent fund.* It is interesting to note that the long-term appropriation was specifically granted for the purpose of encouraging the hospital authorities to "provide suitable apartments for the maniacs, adapted to the various forms and degrees of insanity," a provision indicating the early recognition of the need for classification in institutions for the mentally ill.[7]

A separate building, close to the main structure and capable of accommodating eighty patients, was soon erected at a cost of $56,000. Known as the Lunatic Asylum, it was opened in July, 1808, under the superintendence of Dr. Archibald Bruce. During the same month an agreement was entered into between the authorities of New York City and the governors of the New York Hospital arranging for the removal of mentally ill persons from the city almshouse to the Lunatic Asylum, where they were to be maintained at a charge of two dollars per week per patient to be paid by

* Previously an annual appropriation of the same amount, first voted in 1800 and renewed in 1804, had been made on a five-year basis.

the city.[8] Most of the insane poor continued to be confined at the almshouse and bridewell, only the most hopeful cases being sent to the asylum for curative treatment. The cost of maintaining insane paupers chargeable to New York City from July 15, 1808, to May 1, 1809, amounted to a little over $2,500. On May 15, 1809, a report to the Common Council showed that there were thirty-five patients being maintained in the Lunatic Asylum at the city's expense.[9]

An important step in public provision for the mentally ill was taken in 1809, when the legislature passed a law authorizing the overseers of the poor of each city or town within the state to contract with the New York Hospital for the maintenance and care of insane paupers belonging to their respective localities, the cost of such maintenance to be paid out of the local poor funds.[10] This was the first legislative enactment to recognize the insane poor as a distinct group. It was intended to encourage local poor-law officials to send mentally ill paupers who were deemed curable to the asylum for therapeutic treatment. Unfortunately, however, the new law did little to affect the condition of the insane poor. In the first place, the capacity of the asylum was limited to a few score patients, and private pay patients were preferred to charity cases. Even more important was the unwillingness of many overseers of the poor to send their charges to the asylum, a procedure involving transportation and maintenance expenditures which they were anxious to avoid. It was cheaper to keep the insane in local almshouses and prisons or to neglect them entirely.

Meanwhile a great reform movement in the treatment of the mentally ill was manifesting itself in Europe. This movement was to affect profoundly the development of institutional treatment in this country, particularly in New York. In the last decade of the eighteenth century, two men, a French physician named Philippe Pinel and an English Quaker named William Tuke, had introduced systems of humane treatment of mental patients that contrasted sharply with prevailing methods. In 1792 Pinel, newly appointed physician at the Salpêtrière in Paris, abolished the systematized brutality whereby the insane inmates of the Salpêtrière had been chained, whipped, and generally treated worse than criminals. He introduced instead a system based on the proposition (then little understood) that the insane were not pariahs or criminals but sick people entitled to humane, curative treatment. In the same year William Tuke founded the Retreat for the Insane at York, where harsh methods of restraint were likewise superseded by humane care.

We have already alluded to the constant intercourse of ideas through correspondence that went on between humanitarian reformers in Europe and America, particularly among the Quakers, during this period. It was through such an interchange that the first separately operated mental hospital in New York State came into being. The Lunatic Asylum, situated close to the main building of the New York Hospital, had become overcrowded soon after its opening in 1808. The officers of the hospital began to consider the advisability of erecting a new and larger asylum on a more spacious site, possibly some distance from the city proper. Among the leading advocates of this idea was Thomas Eddy who was serving at the time as treasurer of the New York Hospital. Eddy had learned of the Retreat at York from his friend, Robert Murray, a philanthropic Quaker merchant who had removed permanently from New York to old York upon the outbreak of the Revolutionary War. In some manner a copy of an important little book, *Description of the Retreat near York*, published in 1813 by Samuel Tuke, a son of the founder, fell into Eddy's hands. Greatly impressed by the description of the "moral treatment" instituted at the Retreat, Eddy entered into correspondence with Samuel Tuke, who stimulated his desire to have similar methods adopted in New York. In 1815 he brought before the governors of the New York Hospital a plan for a new asylum operated under the system of moral treatment in use at the York Retreat. His plan was accepted, and a petition was brought before the state legislature applying for a grant to permit the New York Hospital authorities to erect a new institution for the insane.[11] In 1816 the legislature responded favorably, voting an appropriation to the hospital of $10,000 annually in addition to the $12,500 annual grant that had been made previously.[12]

This liberal appropriation enabled the governors to put into effect their plan for providing the mentally ill with humane care. A plot comprising seventy-seven acres was purchased on the Bloomingdale Road overlooking the Hudson River, between six and seven miles north of the city hall, where Columbia University is now situated. A building with a capacity of two hundred patients was begun in 1817 and was ready for occupancy in 1821. Because of its location on the Bloomingdale Road (now Broadway), the institution was called the Bloomingdale Asylum.* Eddy urged the "complete elimination of corporal punishment, chains, and the rule of terror" prescribed by some of the most prominent authorities of the time.[13] A lay superintendent, Laban Gardner, was given charge of the administrative work of the institution, except for the medical details, which were intrusted to Dr. James Eddy, a son of Thomas Eddy. The Bloomingdale Asylum, which operated as a department of the New York Hospital, received only pay patients, although low rates were arranged as before for paupers sent by poor-relief officials from various parts of the state.

RELIEF FOR THE PHYSICALLY HANDICAPPED

In the year 1807 Rev. John Stanford, who later served as official chaplain to the public institutions of New York City, began to preach occasional sermons at the municipal almshouse. There his attention was attracted to a group of deaf-mute inmates, who appeared to be beyond the pale of human communication. Touched by their plight Stanford organized several of them into a class and started to instruct them in reading and writing. Owing to changes in the almshouse administration, however, he was soon obliged to discontinue this class.[14] But Stanford did not lose his interest, and some years later he played an important part in the establishment of the first institution for deaf-mutes in this state.

In 1816 Thomas H. Gallaudet, founder of the Connecticut Asylum for the Education and Instruction of Deaf and Dumb Persons at Hartford—the first institution of its kind in this country—came to New York City to raise funds for his project and succeeded in arousing wide public interest in the subject of educating the deaf.

* The hospital retained the name, Bloomingdale, until 1936, although it had been removed to White Plains in 1894. It is now known as the Westchester Division of the New York Hospital.

Later in 1816 William Lee, formerly the American consul at Bordeaux, brought to New York a communication from a French instructor of the deaf named Gard, urging the establishment of schools for deaf-mutes in America. This communication, addressed to the "Philanthropists of the United States," was placed in the hands of Dr. Samuel L. Mitchill, a noted scholar of the period, Dr. Samuel Akerly, Rev. Mr. Stanford, and several other public-spirited citizens of New York. These gentlemen, after a conference at Stanford's home, decided to call a public meeting at Tammany Hall. A committee appointed at this meeting to undertake a census of deaf-mutes in New York City presented a report in January, 1817, showing a total of sixty-six deaf-mutes in seven of the city's ten wards. It was thereupon decided to establish an institution where deaf-mutes could be "restored to those social, intellectual and religious privileges from which their misfortune had cut them off." Many persons objected to this project on the ground that the institution then being completed at Hartford had ample facilities to cover the needs of the whole country. The promoters of the enterprise continued with their work, however, and on April 15, 1817, the New York Institution for the Instruction of the Deaf and Dumb was incorporated.* The school, located at first in one of the rooms of the city hall, was formally opened on May 12, 1818, with four pupils attending. Within a month this number rose to eleven, only two of whom paid for their instruction. It was originally intended that the school should be supported solely by private subscriptions, but when this plan proved infeasible, the directors applied to the Common Council for financial aid. The council responded in July, 1818, by voting to permit the use of a room in the old almshouse building for the school. At the same time it made an outright grant of $500 out of public funds to the institution and authorized its trustees to receive ten deaf-mutes "in needy circumstances and unable to pay the expence of their instruction," to be paid for by the city at an annual rate of $40 each.[15] This provision made possible the admission of more students to the school; by the spring of 1819 forty-seven pupils were being instructed there.

* By an interesting coincidence, the school for the deaf at Hartford was opened on the very day that the New York institution was incorporated.

NEW YORK INSTITUTION FOR THE DEAF AND DUMB

Erected in 1829 at Fiftieth Street and Fifth Avenue, New York City

Finding their resources too limited to support the expanding institution, the board of trustees decided to send Dr. Akerly to Albany to request financial aid of the legislature. Accompanied by the principal of the school, Abraham O. Stansbury, and eleven pupils, Dr. Akerly gave a demonstration of the work of the institution, which impressed the legislators so favorably that they enacted two bills in April, 1819, rendering state aid to the school. The first act granted the institution a moiety of all fines and forfeitures imposed in New York City in cases of forging and counterfeiting public lottery tickets; the second provided an outright state grant of $10,000.[16] A considerable part of the institution's income for the next fourteen years was derived from its share of lottery fines. An additional state grant of $2,500 was awarded to the institution in June, 1821, and in the following year an act was passed authorizing state support for a maximum of thirty-two indigent state pupils at the rate of $150 each per annum. Each Senate district was entitled to send four deaf-mutes to the school to be maintained and taught at state expense.[17] No pupil could be supported at the expense of the state for more than three years. The state also undertook to provide partial support for pupils whose parents were able to pay only a portion of the expense involved. The act of 1822 authorized the county supervisors to send to the institution at county expense any deaf-mute not provided for by the terms of the statute. As the New York institution had no building of its own, the legislature in 1827 appropriated $10,000 for the erection of an asylum, provided that the directors could raise a like amount through private subscription. This provision was met, and a building was erected and opened in 1829 at Fiftieth Street and Fifth Avenue, New York City. The number of state pupils authorized by the legislature was frequently increased in subsequent years, until it reached a total of nearly two hundred. In 1855 the legislature removed all restrictions as to the number of state-supported pupils. With the expansion of the school and the gradual encroachment of business buildings on all sides, it was deemed advisable to remove the institution to a more secluded location; in 1853 the cornerstone of a new structure was laid at a beautiful site on Washington Heights, where the institution still stands.

A short-lived institution for deaf-mutes was established in 1823 in the town of Canajoharie, in Montgomery County. Incorporated as the Central Asylum for the Instruction of the Deaf and Dumb, it was planned to provide for deaf-mutes in parts of the state removed from New York City. The act of incorporation, chapter 189 of the *Laws of 1823*, contained a provision for a state grant of $1,000, part of which was to be used toward the erection of a suitable building and the remainder for the support of indigent pupils. The structure was used only as a school, the pupils being boarded out in neighboring farmhouses at the rate of one dollar each per week. Chapter 166, *Laws of 1825*, ordered the state treasurer to take over all the debts of the institution up to the sum of $800 and authorized the directors to receive two indigent pupils from each Senate district, to be supported by the state at an annual rate of $80 each. The enterprise proved a failure, however, and in 1836 the Central Asylum terminated its existence, the indigent pupils being transferred to the New York Institution for the Deaf and Dumb at state expense.[18]

PUBLIC AID TO REFUGEES

Relief to refugees constituted the earliest form of state aid in New York, as has been noted in connection with the support of patriot refugees during the Revolutionary War. Several occasions for similar action arose during the post-Revolutionary period. The most notable instance of this type of relief arose out of an influx of French refugees from San Domingo in the last decade of the eighteenth century. The great Negro uprising in San Domingo led by Toussaint L'Ouverture resulted in the flight of hundreds of French residents from that island. Large numbers who took passage on American ships arrived in this country destitute, having left all their worldly goods behind in their precipitate flight. In July, 1793, a ship bearing sixty-three refugees, men, women, and children, anchored in New York harbor. The inhabitants throughout the state responded with openhanded generosity to the appeals made in behalf of these destitute people. A relief committee organized under the sponsorship of the Chamber of Commerce of New York City soon raised $11,000 from private contributions. Finding this sum insufficient for the needs of the French refugees, the Citizens' Relief Committee sent a petition to the legislature urgently requesting state aid. In its petition the Committee asserted that since July 20, 1794, it had been providing an average of three hundred and thirty persons with lodging, bedding, food, firewood, and clothing. In response the legislature enacted chapter 58 of the *Laws of 1794*, allocating £3,500 for the support of the *émigrés* from San Domingo.[19]

In November, 1796, Governor John Jay, noting that the funds appropriated by the legislature two years before were now exhausted, recommended an additional appropriation for relieving the sufferers. Significantly enough, the principle expounded by Jay earlier in the same year to the effect that the alien poor should be considered wards of the state, a principle alluded to in chapter vii, was repeated in his message in November relating to the San Domingo refugees: "They cannot with propriety be considered as the poor of any particular district, their fate is peculiar as well as distressing, and they appear to me as having become by the dispensations of Providence the poor of the State."[20] Two months later the legislature authorized an appropriation of $2,500, to be expended under the governor's direction, for the San Domingo sufferers.[21]

Meanwhile the Common Council of New York City also took steps to furnish aid to the indigent refugees. In November, 1796, the council voted a loan of $300 to Richard Lawrence, one of the almshouse commissioners, to be applied toward their relief. When a number of *émigrés* appealed for further aid in May, 1798, the council granted permission for them to be received and maintained at the almshouse. A second petition received the same month resulted in an appropriation of $100 by the council, to be distributed among eight refugee families at the rate of one dollar weekly per family. Destitute French refugees from San Domingo and other West Indian islands continued to arrive in New York during the ensuing years and on numerous occasions were granted special relief funds by the city authorities. In 1805 the Common Council voted a grant of $500 to petitioning refugees from San Domingo; six years later $200 was voted for the aid of French *émigrés* from both San Domingo and Cuba.[22]

On several other occasions in early American times the state took measures to render aid to foreign refugees. Under chapter 58, *Laws of 1784*, and chapter 67, *Laws of 1786*, the commissioners of the State Land Office were authorized to allot sections of public land for the ownership and use of Canadian refugees. Land was again allotted to refugees from Canada during the War of 1812.

STATE AID TO MANUMITTED SLAVES

Antislavery sentiment found fertile soil in New York during the early years of American independence. In fact, John Jay, who drafted the state constitution in 1777, included a clause in that document calling for the abolition of slavery, which failed of adoption only by a narrow margin. Slaves formed a comparatively small proportion of the state's population, and the evolution of Northern economy was unfavorable to the exploitation of slave labor. In 1776 there were some 22,000 slaves in New York, constituting less than 12 per cent of the total population. By 1790 the slave population had decreased in the face of a great increase in the general population, and, thereafter, with the introduction of gradual abolition, the number of slaves in New York fell steadily, until in 1830 there were only seventy-five enumerated in the census.

Reference has been made in chapter iv to the colonial laws placing restrictions upon the manumission of slaves. These were intended to check the widespread practice of manumitting old and infirm slaves in order to escape responsibility for their support. Owners desiring to free slaves were required by law to post security against their becoming a charge upon the town.

In 1785 the restrictions against manumission were somewhat liberalized by a statute permitting masters to free slaves under the age of fifty and apparently able to support themselves without posting security, provided that they received the written consent of the local overseers of the poor and two peace justices in a town, or of the mayor or recorder and any two aldermen in a city. In other cases the owner had to give bond that the freedman would not become a public charge.[23] An interesting permit for manumission issued under this law at New Rochelle in 1787 reads:

We the subscribers do hereby certifie agreeable to an act of the Legislature. . . . . Passed the 12th of April 1785 that a certain Negroe Man named Michael late the property of Charles Heroy and Hester Heroy of the County of Dutches

. . . . is under the age of fifty years and of sufficient Ability to provide for himself Abram Guion Evenezar S. Burling justices of the Peace, Theodocius Barto Leonard Lispenard oversears of the poor December 22d 1787.[24]

The year 1785 also witnessed the establishment of the "New York Society for Promoting the Manumission of Slaves and protecting such of them as have been or may be liberated." Among the early members of the Society were John Jay, who served as its first president, John Murray, Matthew Clarkson, and Thomas Eddy. The Society pursued three major aims:

1. To effect, if possible, the abolition of slavery in this state, by procuring gradual legislative enactments.

2. To protect from a second slavery such persons as had been liberated in the state of New York, or elsewhere, and who were liable to be kidnapped and sold to slave dealers in other places.

3. To provide means for educating children of color of all classes.[25]

In 1787 the Society opened the African Free School in New York City with about forty pupils, most of them the children of slaves. The Society in subsequent years took a leading part in the abolition movement in this state and in advocating improved conditions for slaves and the Negro people generally.

Through an interesting chain of circumstances a certain category of manumitted slaves came to be recognized as "the State's poor" and paupers entitled to support at state expense. In 1784 the legislature enacted a bill providing for "the speedy sale" of estates forfeited to the state "by attainder or conviction in the progress of the late war." Slaves were included in the seized property of Tories, many of whom were very wealthy. Chapter 64, *Laws of 1784*, provided that the commissioner or commissioners appointed to effect the speedy sale of forfeited property

shall, out of the monies which may come into his or their hands for rents, make suitable provision for the support and maintenance of any slave or slaves who may be found unable to support themselves, and who belonged to, and have not been disposed of by any person or persons, whose respective estates have become confiscated or forfeited to the people of this state.

An important amendment of 1786 manumitted all slaves taken over by the state as parts of the forfeited property of attainted persons. It further ordered the several commissioners of forfeitures "to

provide for the comfortable subsistence of all such slaves so forfeited in their respective districts as by age or infirmity are become
unable to gain a subsistence, at the expence of the people of this
State."[26] In this provision the state clearly acknowledged responsibility for the support of aged and infirm manumitted slaves formerly
owned by attainted persons, the second class of dependents to be
recognized as "the State's poor," the first having been patriot refugees in the Revolution.

On March 29, 1799, the legislature enacted its first law providing
for the gradual abolition of slavery in New York State. By this
act any child born of a slave within the state after July 4, 1799,
was deemed to be born free, with the proviso that such child should
be the servant of the legal owner of its mother until the age of
twenty-eight if a male and until twenty-five if a female, under the
same conditions as children "bound to service by overseers of the
poor." However, the slave-owner might abandon his or her right
to the services of such child within one year after its birth, by
written notification to the town clerk. Such an abandoned child was
to be considered a pauper of the town or city where the owner of
the child's mother resided and was liable to be bound out by the
overseers of the poor on the same terms as other dependent children. It was further enacted that "every child abandoned as aforesaid shall be supported and maintained till bound out by the overseers of the poor . . . . at the expence of the State," at a maximum
rate of $3.50 per month for each child.[27] Thus another category of
"State's poor" was created, the state assuming responsibility for
the support of abandoned children of slaves born after July 4, 1799,
in the interval between "abandonment" by their mothers' owners
and their being bound out as paupers by the local overseers of the
poor. An amendment to this statute enacted in 1802 restricted the
sum to be paid out of state funds for these children to two dollars
each per month. Such state support was not to be provided after
the child reached the age of four years, unless it appeared "that
such pauper is either so descripid or infirm that it will be impracticable to bind out such pauper."[28] A later amendment (chap. 40,
Laws of 1804) permitted the abandonment of children born of slaves
after July 4, 1799, after such children reached the age of twenty-one

if males and of eighteen if females, provided that the owner first received a certificate from the overseers of the poor denoting the apparent ability of the abandoned person to provide for himself or herself. Subsequent acts reflect repeated efforts to force masters to maintain and support slaves grown old in service instead of turning them out to become burdens upon the public at large.

SUMMARY

The post-Revolutionary period was notable for the assumption by the state, of total or partial financial responsibility for increasing categories of social welfare activity. Besides the aid extended to the foreign poor lacking settlement in any district within the state and to certain societies engaged in child welfare—aspects which have been treated in previous chapters—the scope of state support during this period (1784–1823) included: (1) grants and annuities to the New York Hospital in recognition of the treatment of poor patients below cost or free of charge; (2) financial assistance toward the erection and maintenance of the Bloomingdale Asylum, the first institution exclusively for the care of the mentally ill in this state; (3) subsidies to institutions for the physically handicapped (deaf-mutes); (4) full state responsibility for the support of certain classes of manumitted slaves and children of slaves; and (5) special appropriations toward the relief of the San Domingo refugees in New York. The decades that followed were to see a rapid expansion of the scope of state participation in social welfare work.

BIBLIOGRAPHICAL REFERENCES

1. *An Account of the New-York Hospital* (New York, 1811), p. 5.
2. New York State Senate, *Journal* (28th sess. [Albany, 1804]), pp. 46–50.
3. New York State Board of Charities, *Annual Report for the Year 1897* (New York, 1898), I, 620.
4. *An Account of the New-York Hospital* (New York, 1820), p. 6.
5. *N.Y.C., M.C.C., 1784–1831*, I, 185.
6. Albert Deutsch, *The Mentally Ill in America* (Garden City, 1937), p. 98.
7. New York State, *Laws of 1806*, chap. 54.
8. *N.Y.C., M.C.C., 1784–1831*, V, 216.
9. *Ibid.*, pp. 536, 548.
10. New York State, *Laws of 1809*, chap. 90.
11. Knapp, *Life of Thomas Eddy*, pp. 26–29.

12. New York State, *Laws of 1816*, chap. 203.

13. Deutsch, *op. cit.*, p. 99.

14. Charles G. Sommers, *Memoir of the Rev. John Stanford* (New York, 1835), p. 292.

15. *N.Y.C., M.C.C., 1784–1831*, IX, 738–39.

16. New York State, *Laws of 1819*, chaps. 206, 238.

17. ———, *Laws of 1821*, chap. 250; *Laws of 1822*, chap. 234; *Laws of 1827*, chap. 97.

18. ———, *Laws of 1836*, chap. 511.

19. ———, *Laws of 1794*, chap. 58.

20. *Messages from the Governors*, II, 384.

21. New York State, *Laws of 1797*, chap. 6.

22. *N.Y.C., M.C.C., 1784–1831*, II, 306, 436, 438, 442, 466, 473, 478, 576, 607, 629, 691, 742; III, 476, 487, 557, 629, 655, 662, 665; V, 574, 655; VI, 502, 516, 525; VIII, 307, 361.

23. New York State, *Laws of 1785*, chap. 68.

24. New Rochelle, N.Y., *Records of the Town of New Rochelle, 1699–1828*, transcribed, translated, and published by Jeanne A. Forbes (New Rochelle, 1916), pp. 363–64.

25. Samuel L. Mitchill, *The Picture of New York* (New York, 1807), p. 113.

26. New York State, *Laws of 1786*, chap. 58.

27. ———, *Laws of 1799*, chap. 62.

28. ———, *Laws of 1802*, chap. 52.

CHAPTER XII

THE STATE-WIDE POOR-LAW SURVEY OF 1823

An unprecedented interest in poor-law problems was manifested in New York State during the early decades of the nineteenth century. This concern, which was particularly intense in New York City, may be attributed to three major factors: (1) the occurrence of economic depressions of unusual severity during the first twenty years of the century, causing widespread suffering and dependency; (2) an alarming rise in relief expenditures, owing in large measure to the depression periods and to the rapidly increasing population of the state; and (3) the contemporary stir over the poor-law question in Great Britain featured by many inquiries into the nature, causes, and relief of dependency, and culminating in the great poor-law reform of 1834. The developments in England had the effect of stimulating similar inquiries in America, particularly in New York, where leading reformers kept in close communication with their fellows abroad.

As early as 1809 an investigation into the "sources of vice and misery" in New York City was conducted by the Humane Society. This organization had grown out of the Society for the Relief of Distressed Debtors, founded in 1787. Significantly enough the committee of inquiry was headed by Thomas Eddy, whose close contact with humanitarian reformers in England has already been discussed. Also significant is the fact that this inquiry was initiated at a time when New York City was still in the throes of a prolonged depression, the worst it had experienced hitherto. Matthew Clarkson, president of the Society, presented the report of the committee to the public in December, 1809, with these words:

Associated for the purpose of relieving the indigent, our attention has been naturally drawn to the causes which produce the extreme poverty and misery, which have so much increased among our labouring poor. . . . . To obtain more perfect information in relation to these subjects, we lately appointed a committee to investigate them; and their report . . . . we now lay before you, hoping that when your attention shall be awakened to a consideration of the evils which it details you will concur in endeavouring to effect a radical reform.[1]

The report drawn up by Eddy and the other members of the committee reflected perfectly the prevailing tendency in America to attribute poverty and dependency mainly to moral factors. In spite of the existing depression, the report nowhere makes any reference to economic factors as possible causes of pauperism. Its keynote was sounded in the dictum: "By a just and inflexible law of Providence, misery is ordained to be the companion and the punishment of vice." Intemperance was first and foremost among the causes of pauperism in the committee's opinion, a viewpoint that was shared by most contemporary students of the subject. According to the report the chief stimulation to intemperance in New York City was the excessive number of taverns operating therein. More than seventeen hundred tavern licenses had been issued by the mayor during the preceding year, while eighteen hundred licenses to liquor retailers were issued annually by the excise commissioner. On the basis of these figures the inquiry committee concluded that "no existing evil requires a more prompt and effectual remedy than the excessive number of licenses for retailing spirituous liquors which are annually granted in this city."[2]

A more comprehensive survey of dependency and its causes was made in 1818 by the Society for the Prevention of Pauperism in New York City, an organization founded the preceding year by John Griscom, Matthew Clarkson, Divie Bethune, Thomas Eddy, and other public-minded citizens. Its primary objects, as stated in its constitution, were to

investigate the circumstances and habits of the poor; to devise means for improving their situation, both in a physical and moral point of view; to suggest plans for calling into exercise their own endeavors, and afford the means for giving them increased effect . . . . and as far as possible, prevent mendicity and street begging.[3]

The committee appointed to draft the Society's constitution at the founding meeting in December, 1817, was also delegated to draw up "a statement of the prevailing causes of pauperism, with suggestions relative to the most suitable and efficient remedies." In its report on this subject, completed several months later, the committee enumerated the chief causes of poverty and pauperism in New York City. These causes, with explanatory remarks, were listed in the following order:

1st. IGNORANCE, arising either from inherent dullness, or from want of opportunities for improvement. . . . . The influence of this cause, it is believed, is particularly great among the foreign poor that annually accumulate in this city.

2nd. IDLENESS. A tendency to this evil may be more or less inherent. . . . .

3rd. INTEMPERANCE IN DRINKING. This most prolific source of mischief and misery drags in its train almost every species of suffering which afflicts the poor. This evil, in relation to poverty and vice, may be emphatically styled the *Cause of Causes*. . . . .

4th. WANT OF ECONOMY. . . . .

5th. IMPRUDENT AND HASTY MARRIAGES. . . . .

6th. LOTTERIES. The depraving nature and tendency of these allurements to hazard money is generally admitted by those who have been most attentive to their effects. . . . .

7th. PAWNBROKERS. The establishment of these offices is considered as very unfavourable to the independence and welfare of the middling and inferior classes. . . . .

8th. HOUSES OF ILL FAME. The direful effects of those sinks of iniquity upon the habits and morals of a numerous class of young men, especially sailors and apprentices, are visible throughout the city. . . . .

9th. THE NUMEROUS CHARITABLE INSTITUTIONS OF THE CITY. . . . . Is not the partial and temporary good which they accomplish, how acute soever the miseries they relieve, and whatever the number they may rescue from sufferings or death, more than counterbalanced, by the evils that flow from the expectations they necessarily excite; by the relaxation of industry, which such a display of benevolence tends to produce; by that reliance upon charitable aid, in case of unfavourable times, which must unavoidably tend to diminish, in the minds of the labouring classes, that wholesome anxiety to provide for the wants of a distant day, which alone can save them from a state of absolute dependence, and from becoming a burden to the community? . . . .

LASTLY. Your Committee would mention WAR, during its prevalence, as one of the most abundant sources of poverty and vice, which the list of human corruptions comprehends. . . . .[4]

After listing the causes of pauperism the committee made several recommendations for its alleviation and prevention. The first suggestion was to divide the city into districts, to each of which two or three members of the Society were to be assigned as visitors. These visitors were to make frequent house-to-house inspections within their district, to keep a careful record of the character and financial condition of all residents, to give them the benefit of their friendly advice and criticism, and to stimulate a spirit of self-dependence and sobriety in order to fend off pauperism. The district visiting idea did not materialize at the time, but many years later it served as a basic principle of the Association for Improving the Condition of the Poor and similar societies. Other recommendations made by the committee were: to encourage and assist the laboring classes to save their earnings by the establishment of a savings bank; to prevent the access of paupers who were not entitled to settlement in the city; to suppress street begging; to aid in furnishing employment to those unable to procure it by establishing houses of industry and by supplying materials for domestic labor; to promote the increase of churches and Sunday schools; and to further the suppression of liquor shops in the city.[5]

The Society continued its inquiries into the causes of dependency in subsequent years, devoting a part of each annual report to this subject. Its findings on the etiology of dependency differed from time to time. In 1819, for example, its list of "the present sources of pauperism" comprised: (1) emigration to the city from foreign countries; (2) emigration from other counties and other states; (3) intemperance; (4) lawsuits in our criminal courts; (5) defects of the penitentiary system; (6) gambling houses; (7) want of cleanliness; (8) disregard of religious worship and religious institutions; (9) ignorance.[6] The emphasis on emigration from other states and countries reflected the great influx of immigrant poor during the preceding year, with its consequent drain on the municipal relief funds.

In its report for 1821 the Society included among the ascribed causes of pauperism several new factors, namely, "criminal prosecutions," "conditions of prisons," "pardons," and "want of employment."[7] The last-mentioned item was included in the list of causes for the first time, evidently as a result of the post-war depression. The Society in its search for the causes of dependency was by this time also giving increased consideration to the relationships between crime and poverty. Its attention was being drawn particularly to the subject of juvenile delinquency. Investigation convinced the Society that the penal institutions in the city where young and old offenders were thrown together indiscriminately were breeding places for crime and that pauperism was an inevitable end-result of criminal careers. Ultimately it arrived at the conviction that the reformation of juvenile delinquents constituted the greatest single preventive measure against pauperism. In 1824 the organization was dissolved and a new one was founded under the name, Society for the Reformation of Juvenile Delinquents; simultaneously the new Society established the first juvenile reformatory in America. The founding and early history of this institution will be described at greater length in a subsequent chapter.

Meanwhile demands were being raised for a state-wide inquiry into poor relief to be conducted under public auspices. Over a period of several years, culminating in 1823, the legislature was frequently petitioned by individuals and groups of citizens from various parts of the state, particularly from New York City, to launch an inquiry leading to a fundamental change in the poor-law system. At the same time the legislators were showing keen interest in the great controversy over the poor law then raging in England. In that country it was widely believed that poverty and pauperism were created by the very laws enacted to ameliorate these conditions. This theory was not entirely without justification in fact. Contemporary English poor-law administration was featured by the "allowance system" dating back to the Gilbert Act of 1782 and again embodied in the so-called Speenhamland Act of 1795. Through the allowance system the poor-law authorities of each locality were charged with the relief of all working people receiving less than a fixed subsistence wage. However laudatory its purpose might have been, this plan proved disastrous in effect. Employers lost no time in utilizing the system to depress wages below the subsistence level, knowing that the additional income necessary to keep the worker alive would be forthcoming from the public purse. Thus a vicious circle was created: The wage-cutting policy resulted in widespread poverty leading in turn to ever increasing expenditures for poor relief. These expenditures rose from about £2,000,000 in 1798 to the staggering total—for that time—of £7,780,801 in 1817. More basic etiological factors in the increase of dependency—such as the Industrial Revolution—were generally overlooked or minimized in contemporary discussions of the poor law. The prevailing opinion was that the poor law itself was the prime cause of dependency.

The debates in England were followed with great interest in America. When an unusually severe economic depression made itself manifest in New York following the Napoleonic and Anglo-American wars, this interest became sharper than ever, and efforts were made to utilize the lessons learned from the English experience. In the process there developed a tendency to apply English observations to the American scene, where conditions were not at all analogous to the situation in the mother-country except for some surface similarities. In his message to the legislature in 1818, Governor De Witt Clinton sounded the call for a radical change in the state poor laws. "Our statutes relating to the poor," he declared, "are borrowed from the English system. And the experience of that country as well as our own, shows that pauperism increases with the augmentation of the funds applied to its relief."[8] While his alarm was partly justified by the situation in New York, his message clearly indicates the impress of the opinions current in England. The English influence was also reflected in the report of a joint legislative committee appointed in 1819 to study the state poor laws and to suggest recommendations for amending them. In its preamble the committee observed:

That the increase of pauperism in this country, and the expense to the honest and industrious portions of the community, in consequence thereof, is truly alarming, more especially when they turn attention to that country whence this part of our civil policy is derived. Our ancestors, influenced by the same pure and benevolent principles which governed the parliament of Great Britain, and before the effects of the system had fully developed themselves, adopted the principles of the poor laws of that country.[9]

The legislative committee attributed the great rise in dependency and relief expenditures to the fact that the poor laws made no discrimination between "deserving" and "undeserving" indigents and to the ease with which public relief was obtainable. "Once fed on the public bounty," the report stated, "many despised the habits of their ancestors, and preferred beggary, without labor, to independence supported by industry." While casting doubt on the very principle of mandatory public relief for paupers, the committee was not prepared to recommend a total abolition of public relief and contented itself with pointing out the more serious defects in the system. Referring to the confusion and expense involved in the prevailing methods of settlement and removal, the committee recommended facilitation of local-settlement requirements so that the expense of litigation and removals in cases of nonsettled poor might be reduced to a minimum. On the other hand, relief should be extended only to the "virtuous" poor whose dependent condition could be traced to infirmity, disease, or other disabling cause.

The idle, the vicious and intemperate can have no claims of right on the public bounty, and they should therefore be excluded from its enjoyment. Better leave them to the exercise of individual charity, which is more discriminating; the dispensers of which will feel strong inducements to impress on the mind of the receiver the necessity of reformation.

Since intemperance was a great source of pauperism, the poor law should contain provisions to restrain it. These recommendations were embodied in a bill which failed to become law. In 1820 an assembly committee brought in another bill drastically amending the poor laws, but the bill was so vague and confusing that it was fortunately defeated also, although it embodied several progressive features.[10]

Several legislative committees were appointed in succeeding years to investigate the poor law and to draw up proposals for amending it, but these did little more than repeat the observations and suggestions of the committee of 1819, with little of practical import resulting therefrom. Finally, however, in 1823 a concurrent resolution was adopted by both houses authorizing the secretary of state

to collect from the several towns, cities and counties of this state, such information as may be necessary to give a distinct view of the expenses and operation of the laws for the relief and settlement of the poor; and also such information from other states, with respect to their poor laws, as may show the effect of those systems, and suggest improvements in our own; and that he communicate a digest or abstract of such information to the legislature.[11]

He was also instructed to prepare, with the collaboration of the attorney-general, a new poor law in line with recommendations resulting from the inquiry.

A report "on the relief and settlement of the poor" was submitted to the legislature by Secretary of State John V. N. Yates in February, 1824. Based on replies to a questionnaire sent to the poor-law authorities in every district in the state, together with miscellaneous statistics and opinions gathered from various states and foreign countries, the Yates *Report* presents an invaluable picture of the poor-relief system of the time.* Largely as a result of the recommendations it contained and of the bill based on its findings, the entire poor-relief policy of New York State underwent a profound modification.

The *Report*, representing the first comprehensive survey of poor relief to be made in the United States, consisted of two parts: the first contained a digest and interpretation of the data gathered by the secretary of state together with his proposals for improving the poor-relief system; the second part constituted an Appendix entitled, "Documents Accompanying the Report of the Secretary of State on the Subject of Pauperism." About ten times the length of the *Report* proper, the Appendix consisted mainly of abstracts from the communications of poor-law authorities in this and other states and countries referring to the incidence of pauperism, methods and costs of poor relief, and theories as to the nature, cause, and prevention of dependency.[12]

On the basis of returns from 367 cities and towns of New York, Secretary Yates reported a total number of 22,111 recipients of public poor relief throughout the state out of a total population of approximately 1,500,000. These he divided into two classes: the "permanent" poor, comprising all who were supported at public expense continuously through the entire year and the "occasional" or "temporary" poor, who received relief for temporary periods only. Of the total number Yates estimated that 6,896 were permanent paupers while 15,215 were occasional paupers. Included in the permanent classification were 446 idiots and lunatics, 287 blind persons,

* Three years earlier (1821) a legislative committee headed by Josiah Quincy had submitted a report on the pauper laws of Massachusetts to the general court of that state. Its conclusions, based on a state-wide survey, were almost identical in substance with those of the Yates *Report*. It is interesting to note, also, that the Quincy *Report* contained frequent allusions to the contemporary poor-relief discussions in England. The scope of the Quincy *Report*, however, was in no wise comparable to that of Secretary Yates.

928 aged and infirm, 2,604 children under fourteen years of age, and 1,789 able-bodied adults. Of the total number of public dependents (both permanent and occasional) 16,228 were natives and 5,883 were foreign born, while nearly 40 per cent (8,753) of the total were children. The distribution of indigents was very unequal throughout the state, ranging from 1.3 per thousand inhabitants in Erie and Seneca counties to 70 per thousand in New York City. On the whole the proportion of paupers was lowest in the least populated counties and highest in those most densely populated. The counties bordering the ocean and the Hudson, comprising one-third of the state's population, had more than one-half of all public dependents, New York City alone accounting for about three-sevenths of the total.

Comparing the incidence of pauperism in various states, Secretary Yates estimated that New York averaged one permanent dependent for every 220 inhabitants; Massachusetts, one for every 68; Connecticut, one for every 150; and Pennsylvania, one for every 265. Rhode Island, Delaware, and Virginia all showed a smaller proportion of public dependency than New York, a fact attributed by Yates to the employment of the poorhouse system in the aforementioned states. It may be noted at this point that although the Yates investigation was ostensibly an impartial inquiry into the nature, extent, and relief of pauperism, it was actually intended in large part to discover how much opposition existed to the establishment of a system of poorhouse relief throughout the state, with a view to abolishing public outdoor relief entirely. The questionnaire sent out by Secretary Yates was heavily weighted in favor of the poorhouse system, and so was the ensuing report, as we shall see.

Statistics cited in the *Report* show that poor-relief expenditures in the state had risen from $245,000 in 1815 to $368,645 in 1819 and $470,582 in 1822, an increase far out of proportion to the population increase during the same period.[13]

Affirming the opinions of previous inquiries into the nature of dependency, Secretary Yates advanced the belief that intemperance had produced more than two-thirds of the permanent dependents and more than half of the occasional. His view was fairly representative of the opinions presented in the communications of poor-law officials. Some officials had even more emphatic views on the relationship between drink and dependency. The supervisor of the poor in Elmira stated:

From what personal observations I have been able to make in regard to the poor, I am satisfied that their disability to maintain themselves has arisen from *intemperance*. This appears to be the great evil of all evils, and one of the great destroyers of the human family, and the source from which almost all their misfortunes flow.[14]

One local official wrote rather cryptically:

Please to set down in your mind the number of paupers generated by spirituous liquors in this state, and then combine all the misfortunes that human nature is subject to, and see what they will produce. Strike the balance and see which is the most prolific in creating paupers.[15]

To intemperance some poor-law officials added "idleness" and "sin" as potent sources of pauperism. A Poughkeepsie overseer of the poor stated: "From all the observations I have been able to make respecting pauperism, I am decidedly of the opinion that a great portion of the paupers are *voluntary*, in consequence of drunkenness, idleness and vice of all kinds."[16]

While the great majority of poor-law officials replying to the Yates questionnaire stressed moral factors as the dominant causes of dependency, several gave some consideration to economic factors. The supervisor of the manorial town of Taghkanic in Columbia County suggested that anachronistic relationships between landowners and tenants contributed greatly to poverty in his area. Here the manorial system had in effect been preserved. The land around the town was held by tenants on short leases for a few years—in some cases for two or three years. The short tenure gave them no incentive to make improvements and no opportunity to better their condition. Any property they might accumulate could be sold to cover their defaults in rent. Such dislodged tenants, devoid of any means, would frequently become objects of charity.

A peculiar situation existed in Cazenovia, Madison County, where the houses and lands of farmers forced into bankruptcy were rented out to poor persons; only the poorest would be willing to rent the land, as people of means would prefer to purchase it outright. The supervisor complained that in accordance with the state's settlement laws payment of a six-penny tax entitled these poor persons to apply for relief, a privilege they were not slow to exercise.

In Cambria, Niagara County, the burden of poor relief resulted mainly from the building of the Erie Canal, which passed through the town. The work had concentrated at that point some two thousand to three thousand "adventurers and transient families," mostly foreigners, whose only means of subsistence were the wages they received from day to day. Since the contractors were legally free from responsibility for injury sustained by workingmen, many who suffered disabilities in the course of their labor became public charges.

That the economic effects of the factory system were already making themselves felt is indicated in the report of the supervisor of Newport, Herkimer County, who declared that "cotton and woolen manufactories have a tendency to increase the number of paupers in the town in which they are situated."[17]

CONTEMPORARY MODES OF POOR RELIEF

The Yates survey revealed a wide variation of poor-relief methods employed by the several localities in New York State. Those in general use may be divided into four main categories:

1. Almshouse relief
2. Home relief
3. The "contract system," whereby all the poor of a town were placed under the care of one or more householders at a fixed rate per year, month or week
4. The "auction system," whereby the care of the town's poor was "auctioned off" to the lowest bidder or bidders, individually or collectively

Scattered throughout the state were some thirty poorhouses operating under different types of administrative plans. Rensselaer County was the first to boast of a county poorhouse, which it called "House of Industry" to emphasize the principle that all inmates were expected to work according to their abilities. It was established in 1820 under a special legislative act which extended to other counties the right to erect county poorhouses whenever their boards of supervisors voted to do so.[18] This statute represented a significant step toward the recognition of the county as an administrative unit in poor relief. Some towns, like Rye and Harrison in Westchester County, operated a poorhouse jointly under the town-union plan. Most of the poorhouses, however, were operated independently by cities and towns such as New York, Albany, Brooklyn, Hudson,

Schenectady, Poughkeepsie, Plattsburgh, and Goshen. The secretary of state estimated that these institutions together maintained about two thousand inmates.[19] Some towns owned farms that were leased to tenants who maintained the town poor at a low rate; others hired private dwellings to house the poor, with a superintendent in charge.

Many communities resorted to the contract system of public relief. Frequently all the town's poor were placed under the superintendence of a single "contractor" (usually a resident farmer); in other instances the poor were distributed among several "contractors." The contractor was generally granted the right of putting his charges to work and of appropriating for himself the fruits of their labor. The town of Beekman in Dutchess County reported that it had used the contract system since 1820, paying a fixed rate of $32 annually for the care of each pauper over twelve years of age and $16 each for those under twelve. In the town of Amsterdam all the poor were kept by a certain farmer, under contract, at a fixed rate of $350 annually; apparently the farmer contracted to receive all paupers sent by the town for this sum.

Even more widespread than the contract system was the practice of auctioning off the poor to the lowest bidder or bidders. It was believed by the proponents of this practice that aside from the economies effected the humiliation and fear involved in standing for "sale" at a public auction deterred many from applying for relief. Here and there successful bidders had to give bond to insure satisfactory care, but even this device could scarcely protect the auctioned poor from the privation which was the logical consequence of the low prices paid for their keep. Because of its wide use throughout the northeastern states, this practice was known to contemporaries as the "New England system." Thus a letter to Secretary Yates from Cazenovia, Madison County, explained: "Our overseers of the poor have, for several years past, practiced after the *New-England method* of setting up the poor *at auction.*"

In many cases the successful bidders at "pauper auctions" were themselves on the fringe of dependency, bidding extremely low in a desperate effort to avoid applying for relief themselves. As a result the town could credit itself with a special saving, being spared the support of a potential dependent and his family. The poor who were auctioned off were supposed to work for their bidders according to their varying abilities. This was a potent factor in determining the "purchase price," as illustrated in the letter from the supervisor of Greenville in Greene County:

This town for a few years past, have sold their paupers at public auction, on the day of the town meeting, and those who purchase give in proportion to the supposed ability of the paupers for labor. There are some, however, who are entirely incapacitated for labor, in consequence of disease; there are others again, capable of occasional labor, probably enough to earn their bread.[20]

But the consequences both to the bidder and to the poor, as a contemporary pointed out, were often far from satisfactory. In an address delivered in 1820 before the Westchester County Agricultural Society, a leading citizen of that county, Abijah Hammond, graphically described the operation of the auction system:

Notwithstanding the large amount raised in this county, for the support of the poor, they are neither fed, clothed, nor treated like human beings. . . . .

Most of the parish poor are now *sold*, as the term is, that is, *bid off*, to those who agree to support them on the lowest terms, to purchasers nearly as poor as themselves, who treat them in many instances more like brutes than like human beings; and who, instead of applying the amount received from the poor-master, for the comfort of the pauper, spend it to support their families, or, which is too often the case, in purchasing ardent spirits; under the maddening influence of which, they treat these wretched pensioners, and not unfrequently their own wives and children, with violence and outrage.[21]

It appears that poor persons were sometimes auctioned off to their own relatives. Thus the supervisor of Hunter, Greene County, related the following incident to Secretary Yates:

N.T. is husband to an active woman, who is able and willing to support him. She has living with her two sons by a former husband, who own and manage the farm upon which they all live. These sons contrived to have old N.T. thrown upon the town, and last year they kept him themselves at a dollar per week. This year he was bid off [*sic*] by another man (as the sons wish to get a greater sum). The man who bid him off went the next day with his team to get old N.T. but the sons and wife refused to give him up, alledging *there was no law to separate man and wife!* and that they had concluded to keep him themselves for a dollar a week![22]

The supervisor added, with a note of triumph: "Our overseers are prudent enough to keep aloof from them, and leave them *as they ought to do, to support him themselves.*"

In spite of these shocking defects in the auction system it was staunchly defended by many town authorities who employed it, mainly on the grounds of expediency and economy. The town of Chazy, Clinton County, reported that for several years past it had "sold at public sale all the poor of the town; this mode has been the means of reducing the expenses for the support of the poor for the year 1817 at least two-thirds." Local officials reporting from the counties of Dutchess, Greene, Madison, Oneida, Onondaga, Otsego, Albany, Queens, and Columbia also expressed satisfaction with the plan. Many years were to pass before the auction system finally disappeared from New York State.

CONTEMPORARY PROBLEMS OF SETTLEMENT AND REMOVAL

The prevailing laws of settlement and removal, according to the almost unanimous opinion of the poor-law officials, constituted one of the worst features of the poor-relief system. The varied and complicated methods by which settlement might be gained, as outlined in chapter vi, created the greatest confusion in the minds of those administering relief. As Secretary Yates observed in his *Report:* "The qualifications necessary to constitute a settlement are so technical, numerous and complicated, if not obscure, that even eminent counsel are often at a loss to determine questions arising upon this branch of our pauper system." Reports to the secretary of state showed that the expenses arising out of litigation over legal settlement, fees to constables and justices for removals, and the like, amounted to nearly one-ninth of the entire poor-relief cost in the state. In one county, Oswego, the costs of settlement and removal proceedings had actually been greater than the total cost of supporting the poor. It was estimated that the removal of 1,796 indigent persons in New York State in 1822 had cost more than $25,000, enough to support 2,833 paupers for a whole year, while the sum of $13,500 expended in 127 court appeals involving settlement disputes would have been sufficient to provide institutional care for 450 dependents.[23]

Determination of the legal settlement of a dependent person frequently involved expensive litigation between towns, some of which did not hesitate to stoop to fraud and disgraceful tricks to avoid the burden of relief. In a communication to Secretary Yates an

Albany overseer of the poor, evidently a man of unusual intelligence and broad humanity, expressed condemnation of the prevailing frauds and impositions and referred specifically to "the common practice of procuring paupers to be set down in cities or towns, when they have no settlement." This was the practice of ridding towns of indigent nonresidents, particularly those who through mental illness or mental defect were unable to give a coherent account of themselves, by carrying them to another town and leaving them there. The overseer of Albany cited a case that had occurred in his own city:

A poor unfortunate lunatic, of the age of eighteen or twenty years, was left in our streets in the winter, and in the night, whose feet were in consequence badly frozen; he could give no intelligent account of himself, but from all the circumstances, there was too much reason to believe that this was one of the tricks frequently resorted to by towns, to free themselves of paupers. This young man was of necessity sent to the alms-house. . . . .[24]

A similar instance was reported by the supervisor of Franklin in Delaware County. It concerned the fate of an aged man who "fell sick and was partially deranged" while traveling through the town of Franklin. After some superficial inquiry the local officials concluded that the old man resided in New Berlin, and he was removed to that town. It developed that he was not legally settled there, and Franklin had to bear the expense of his maintenance together with the costs of an unsuccessful appeal and bringing him back.

The Franklin supervisor wrote:

On a re-examination, it was thought he might belong to the town of Williamstown, in Massachusetts, and their existing laws laying heavy penalties on any person bringing poor persons to that place, gave rise to the propriety of taking him there in a clandestine manner. He was decoyed there in the night, and left, the lord knows where, *old, deranged and infirm!*[25]

The expense and cruelty involved in executing the settlement laws led many supervisors to suggest that all nonresident poor should be provided for by the county in which they became dependent instead of having them removed to their places of legal settlement. It was felt by the proponents of this plan that an obligation to support every poor person in the county, no matter what his settlement status was, would impel the local authorities to exercise vigilance toward all those likely to become public charges and would also result in great savings in removal costs.

Another source of confusion and irritation traceable to the prevailing poor laws was the method of relieving nonsettled alien paupers. In a lengthy communication to Secretary Yates, Mayor Stephen Allen of New York City complained that, while the state was contributing only about $10,000 annually to New York City for the relief of alien poor through the auction duties, the cost to the city for relieving nonsettled dependents actually amounted to approximately four times that sum. Expenditures for the New York almshouse, bridewell, and penitentiary during 1823 had been about $85,000, more than half of which was expended on persons lacking settlement in the city.[26] Mayor Allen thereupon strongly suggested that the state advance a greater share of the auction duties. Although shipmasters were required to give bond against the possibility of passengers becoming public charges in New York, they often evaded this requirement by landing destitute passengers at points in near-by New Jersey or Connecticut, leaving them to find their way into the city. On the other hand, several of the counties along the Canadian border demanded that they be allotted a share of the auction duties on the ground that they too were supporting many alien paupers. Officials in Oswego County complained that destitute persons arriving there from the Canadian provinces were seriously draining the poor funds in that county. The towns of Louisville in St. Lawrence County and Sacketts Harbor in Jefferson County also called attention to the undue number of alien paupers they were supporting.

GENERAL CRITICISMS OF THE POOR LAW

In general the Yates survey disclosed a number of major defects in the poor-law system of New York. These were numerated by Yates as follows:

1. That our present poor laws . . . . lead to litigation of the most expensive and hurtful kind, in appeals and law suits concerning the settlement, maintenance and removal of paupers, exhausting nearly one-ninth of the funds intended for their relief, in the payment of fees of justices, overseers, lawyers and constables, and are at the same time productive of much cruelty in the

removal of paupers, frequently at inclement seasons of the year, regardless of the claims of age, sex or condition. . . . .

2. The poor, when farmed out, or sold, are frequently treated with barbarity and neglect by their keepers. . . . . The British parliament, the Massachusetts legislature, and almost every writer on the subject of pauperism, have condemned these modes of providing for the support of the poor as being wasteful in regard of economy, and cruel in regard to the paupers themselves.

3. The education and morals of the children of paupers (except in almshouses) are almost wholly neglected. They grow up in filth, idleness, ignorance and disease, and many become early candidates for the prison or the grave. . . . .

4. There is no adequate provision for the employment of the poor throughout the state, and no industrious habit can be effectually inculcated under our present system. . . . .

5. The poor laws tend to encourage the sturdy beggar and profligate vagrant to become pensioners upon the public funds. The facilities afforded them in being placed upon the pauper list operate as so many invitations to become beggars. . . . .

6. These laws also hold out encouragement to the successful practice of street beggary.

7. Idiots and lunatics do not receive sufficient care and attention in towns, where no suitable asylums for their reception are established.

8. There is an evident want of economy in the disbursement of the public funds, appropriated for the support of the poor in several towns and counties. In one county particularly (Oswego), the monies raised by tax for the fees of officers and appeals exceeded the amount raised for the support of the poor.[27]

PROPOSED CHANGES IN THE POOR-RELIEF SYSTEM

As possible solutions to the defective poor-law system, Secretary Yates posed two alternatives: (1) That the system be abolished entirely, leaving the support of the poor exclusively to private charity; and (2) that the prevailing system be modified so as to bring it to the point of maximum effectiveness. The secretary of state, while impressed by the arguments in favor of the first alternative, concluded that the second would be more expedient. He then proceeded to outline a ten-point plan for the improvement of the poor laws, which included these recommendations:

1. The establishment of one or more houses of employment in every county, with a farm connected to each institution. Here paupers could be maintained at county expense, and employed at labor, chiefly agricultural, according to their abilities. The children of paupers should receive proper education and be bound out at suitable ages.

2. A workhouse or penitentiary should be built in connection with each county poorhouse, for the reception of beggars and vagrants.

3. Poor relief funds could be raised by an increase in the excise duties and a special tax on owners of distilleries of whiskey and other ardent spirits.

4. One year's residence in a county should constitute a settlement, with the exception of certain specified cases, in place of the confused and complex requirements for gaining settlement under the prevailing laws.

5. All orders of removal should be abolished. Persons entitled to relief should receive it in the county where they became sick or infirm; able-bodied vagrants should be returned to their county of settlement, or be sent to the workhouse upon refusal.

6. No able-bodied male between the ages of eighteen and fifty years should be placed on the pauper list, or be maintained at public expense.

7. Severe penalties should be inflicted on all those apprehended in bringing to, or leaving in, a county any indigent person not chargeable to it.

8. Street beggary should be prohibited, and beggars should be sent to workhouses immediately.

9. The expense of erecting each house of employment, or poorhouse, should be borne by the county out of tax monies.

10. Persons imprisoned on civil process, together with their families, should be supported if necessary at county expense, inasmuch as there was no legal provision at the time for the support of needy persons (such as debtors) imprisoned in towns where they had no legal settlement.[28]

Three great changes were anticipated in this plan: (1) indoor relief was to become the chief form of public poor relief in place of the hitherto predominant outdoor relief; (2) the almshouse was to be made the center of the poor-relief system; and (3) the county was to be made the major administrative unit instead of the town.

The views of Secretary Yates on the establishment of a county poorhouse system were supported by the great majority of officials replying to his questionnaire. Many arguments were advanced in favor of the plan. It was widely believed that such an institution would serve as an effective deterrent to application for relief. "The bare name of a county workhouse," wrote one official, "appears to strike a dread on paupers. When sent to the house they stay there only for a short time."* It was also claimed that the poorhouse,

* The terms "workhouse," "house of industry," "house of employment," and "poorhouse," were used indiscriminately by some poor-law officials. Secretary Yates used "poorhouse," "house of industry," and "house of employment" as synonyms meaning institutions for the "deserving" poor, while a "workhouse" was a distinct institution receiving vagrants, beggars and other disorderly persons. This latter distinction, of course, was the correct one.

while helping those entitled to support, would weed out those receiving aid under false pretenses, since only those in most desperate need would accept the restrictions and humiliation entailed in such institutionalization. Those able to labor would prefer to work for themselves outside rather than to work for others within the institution. Besides, under the immediate supervision of a prudent overseer, the vices of the poor would be checked and their morals improved; drunkards would be cut off from their source of liquor supplies and, together with the idle, would be guided toward industrious habits through compulsory labor.

The question of the comparative cost of outdoor and indoor relief occupied a prominent place in the discussion. Most of the poor-law officials agreed that institutional relief would be cheaper, though there were several dissenting opinions. Some even went beyond the prediction of Secretary Yates that the introduction of a state-wide system of county poorhouses would cut relief costs at least 50 per cent. Yates presented statistics indicating that in properly managed poorhouses the annual per capita cost would not exceed $35, while outdoor relief averaged about $65 per capita annually. He added that expenses for medical and nursing care, which entailed a considerable part of contemporary relief costs, would be drastically reduced when all dependents were gathered together under one roof.

Sentiment in the legislature favorable to the establishment of county poorhouses was greatly strengthened by the *Report* of the secretary of state, and in 1824 a bill was enacted embodying his major recommendations, namely, the establishment of a state-wide system of county almshouses to serve as the main centers of relief and the abolition of removals. But while the principles espoused by Yates were left intact, the statute as finally passed contained so many exceptions and exemptions as greatly to vitiate the practical application of these principles. Despite its weaknesses, however, the act of 1824 resulting from the Yates survey marked a most important milestone in the history of public welfare in this state. The provisions of this act will be described at length in the following chapter.

BIBLIOGRAPHICAL REFERENCES

1. Humane Society of New York, *A Report of a Committee of the Humane Society, appointed to inquire into the number of Tavern Licenses and other sources of vice and misery in this City* (New York, 1810), p. 3.

2. *Ibid.*, p. 6.

3. Society for the Prevention of Pauperism in the City of New York, *First Annual Report of the Managers* (New York, 1818), p. 25.

4. *Ibid.*, pp. 14–18.

5. *Ibid.*, pp. 19–23.

6. Society for the Prevention of Pauperism in the City of New York, *Second Annual Report of the Managers* (New York, 1819), pp. 17–18.

7. ———, *Fourth Annual Report of the Managers* (New York, 1821), p. 6.

8. *Messages from the Governors*, II, 914–15.

9. New York State Assembly, *Journal* (42d sess. [Albany, 1819]), p. 607.

10. New York State Legislature, *Legislative Documents* (43d sess. [Albany, 1820]), Docs. 123, 124.

11. New York State Assembly, *Journal* (46th sess. [Albany, 1823]), p. 937; New York State Senate, *Journal* (46th sess. [Albany, 1823]), pp. 360–61.

12. The report proper was published in the Senate *Journal* (47th sess. [Albany, 1824]), pp. 95–108; the accompanying documents were published as Appendix A to the same *Journal*, comprising 154 pages. The *Report* and Appendix may also be found in the Assembly *Journal* for 1824 (pp. 386–99 and Appen. B). They were reprinted in the New York State Board of Charities, *Annual Report for the Year 1900* (Albany, 1901), I, 937–1145.

13. New York State Senate, *Journal* (47th sess. [Albany, 1824]), pp. 96, 99.

14. *Ibid.*, Appen. A, p. 71.

15. *Ibid.*, p. 21.

16. *Ibid.*, p. 20.

17. *Ibid.*, pp. 14, 27, 33, 46.

18. New York State, *Laws of 1820*, chap. 51.

19. New York State Senate, *Journal* (47th sess. [Albany, 1824]), p. 99.

20. *Ibid.*, Appen. A, pp. 19, 25, 33, 38.

21. *Ibid.*, p. 77.

22. *Ibid.*, pp. 11, 25–26.

23. *Ibid.*, pp. 99, 101–2.

24. *Ibid.*, Appen. A, p. 4.

25. *Ibid.*, pp. 17–18.

26. *Ibid.*, pp. 41–42.

27. *Ibid.*, pp. 101–2.

28. *Ibid.*, pp. 100, 104–5.

PART IV

THE TREND TOWARD INDOOR RELIEF, 1824–66

CHAPTER XIII

RISE OF THE COUNTY POORHOUSE

The four decades between 1824 and 1866 saw great changes in the economic and social life of New York State and of the country. This period marked the transition from a preponderantly agricultural to an increasingly industrial economy. Industry not only became intrenched in the East but sent its outposts into the West as well.

New York was rapidly becoming the foremost state in the Union. The wilderness of the western and northern counties was gradually converted into agricultural communities; scattered frontier communities at the beginning, they were settled districts long before the end of this period, participating fully in the social, economic, and political life of the state. The crude hardship of pioneer life on the isolated farms was gradually giving way to conditions of comparative comfort. Postal service was increasing; facilities for popular education were expanding.

The most powerful impetus to the further development of the state was the extension of the means of transportation and communication. In 1825 the Erie Canal was successfully completed, opening vast new areas for commerce and stimulating a canal-construction movement which lasted into the mid-thirties. Six additional state canals were built within a decade.

The development of the railroads in the thirties and forties added further stimulus to the development of the state. A series of railroads linked New York and Buffalo. Early in the fifties the Erie Railroad reached the lakes at Dunkirk. The counties of the southern tier were brought into closer touch with New York City, thereby gaining a readier market for their commodities. Even greater were the benefits accruing to the mercantile and financial interests of the city. New Orleans, which had long served as the main market for the produce of the Northwest, gave place to New York, and the trade of the country bordering on the Great Lakes fell under the control of New York financiers.

Beginning with the 1820's internal trade between the states gained in importance even beyond that of the trade with foreign countries. The inner market provided a sufficient outlet for the wealth of agricultural products. Differences in soil and climatic conditions in various parts of the vast country, with the steady growth and improvement of transportation facilities, led to localization of agricultural production and made exchange of produce among different sections both practicable and necessary.

Because of its strategic location, New York City soon became the exchange center for the produce of many regions. In 1831 Massachusetts was still ahead of New York in the quantity of export trade; by 1841 the exports of New York were three times those of Massachusetts. The supremacy of New York City over all other American ports was by this time securely established.

Industry was rapidly developing in parts of the state convenient to shipping facilities and raw supplies. New manufacturing towns sprang up, and part of New York's farming population joined immigrant masses in wage labor in the growing manufacturing industries. Raw material could easily be brought by way of the canals. The census of 1830 showed New York leading the Union in manufactured products. The opportunity which it afforded in the way of amassing wealth drew to it a large number of ambitious, wide-awake, restless men and women from all parts of the country, especially from New England. Meanwhile, following the Napoleonic wars, immigration increased rapidly, nearing the half-million mark annually in the forties.

The population of both state and city grew steadily. The census of 1825 showed a population of 1,616,458 in New York State and 166,086 in New York City. By 1850 the population had increased to 3,097,394 in the state and 515,547 in the city; in 1860 the census figures stood at 3,880,735 for the state and 813,662 for the city.

The changing social and economic forces had varying effects on the people. To some sections of the population they brought comfort and prosperity, to others extreme poverty and dependency. Depressions of increasing severity, evils attendant upon rapid urbanization—ill-housing, overcrowding, poor factory conditions, unemployment—these were some of the negative aspects of the changing socio-economic scene. It was in the midst of these developments that public welfare administration evolved during this period.

THE COUNTY POORHOUSE ACT OF 1824

When the historic Yates *Report* was submitted to the legislature in 1824, it was accompanied by a model bill embodying the principal recommendations made by the secretary of state. This bill was adopted, with some important modifications, as chapter 331 of the *Laws of 1824:* "An act to provide for the establishment of county poorhouses." Although based on the broad principles espoused by Yates, the bill as finally enacted contained so many exceptions to his major recommendation, the mandatory establishment of an almshouse in each county, as nearly to nullify it in practice. The statute made it the duty of the board of supervisors of each county—with thirty-eight out of fifty-four counties excepted—to direct at their next meeting the purchase of one or more tracts of land and to erect thereon one or more county poorhouses. To defray the cost of purchase and building, a special tax not exceeding $7,000 was to be levied by the county. The county supervisors were directed to appoint annually not less than five superintendents of the poorhouse to be charged with the management and discipline of the institution.* The latter, in turn, were authorized to employ a keeper of the poorhouse.

All persons thereafter applying for relief within a county coming under the terms of this act, upon receiving proper certification of need from a justice of the peace and an overseer of the poor, were to be removed forthwith to the county poorhouse unless sickness or infirmity rendered such removal dangerous. With the approval of the superintendents, disorderly persons might be committed to the poorhouse for periods not exceeding six months, at hard labor. Children found begging in the streets might also be sent there by local overseers of the poor, to be discharged at the discretion of the county

---

* Later amendments permitted the appointment of three superintendents, and in certain cases even one, instead of five as required in this statute.

superintendents.* Every poorhouse inmate able to work was required to perform such service or labor as the keeper might order. Inmates refusing or neglecting to obey the rules and regulations of the almshouse, as prescribed by the superintendents, could be placed by the keeper in solitary confinement, on bread and water.

All expenses for maintaining the institution and supporting its inmates were to be defrayed by the county out of tax funds. Deficits remaining at the end of the year, however, were to be covered by special taxes prorated among the towns "in proportion to the number and expenses of paupers the several towns respectively shall have in the said poorhouses."

Turning to the question of removal, which had received extended discussion in the Yates *Report*, the statute of 1824 prohibited the removal of paupers from any city or town in one county to a city or town in another, no matter what his settlement status might be. Each county was to be charged with the support of all nonsettled dependents within its borders. Removal from one city or town to another within the same county, however, was not precluded by the act.

Finally, the law contained a provision authorizing boards of supervisors of exempted counties to establish a county poorhouse whenever they should vote to do so at an annual meeting. Thus the establishment and maintenance of a county poorhouse was made mandatory in the case of sixteen of the fifty-four existing counties and permissive in the remaining thirty-eight.

The act of 1824 marked a historic step in the state poor-law development. It established the principle of indoor relief; it made the county poorhouse the center of the public relief system; it advanced the principle of county responsibility for all poor persons lacking settlement, thus superseding for a time state responsibility for the alien poor; it sought to abolish outdoor relief; it prohibited removals of indigent persons across county lines; and, finally, it introduced the system of exclusive county responsibility for the poor in nearly

* Chapter 20 (Title II) of the *Revised Statutes of 1827* empowered any justice of the peace to commit a child to the county poorhouse or other place provided for the poor upon complaint and proof that such child was found "begging for alms, or soliciting charity from door to door, or in any street, highway, or public place."

one-third of the counties. It marked a profound though not complete break with the tradition of local responsibility handed down from the Elizabethan age.

The act, however, could not stand unsupported for any length of time; to carry out its implications a thoroughgoing revision of the poor law was needed. Another serious weakness of the act was the establishment of a dual poor-relief system in the state whereby certain areas operated on the principle of county responsibility while others maintained the practice of local responsibility. Some counties, desiring neither complete county responsibility nor complete local responsibility, asked for legislation permitting a compromise between the two. Such a compromise was effected in 1826, when the legislature enacted a bill authorizing the establishment of a poorhouse in the county of Schenectady. According to the provisions of this act, the support of each pauper sent to the county poorhouse was to be a charge upon the city or town to which he belonged unless he came under the classification "county poor," in which case he was to be supported by the county. But while each town and city was to pay for the support of its own poor, "all the expenses incident to the establishing, keeping, maintaining and governing said county poorhouse" were to be a charge upon the county.[1] Each city and town was required to support its own poor, and it was made mandatory for them to send all their poor to the county almshouse. Certain exceptions to this rule were allowed; justices of the peace could, after examining the condition and circumstances of an applicant, grant him temporary or outdoor relief instead of sending him to the poorhouse. The *Revised Statutes of 1827* extended the right to afford temporary relief to certain applicants, with the approval of one or more justices of the peace, to all other parts of the state.

Several special acts were passed by the legislature in ensuing years authorizing certain counties to abolish the distinction between town and county poor, that is, to give the county sole responsibility for the support of all public dependents. By virtue of chapter 146 of the *Laws of 1826*, Genesee County was the first to be added to the eighteen counties originally covered by the act of 1824. The statute of 1826 also contained this provision:

All such monies as shall be received by the several towns in said county for excise, fines, penalties, or from any other source whatever, as have been heretofore applied to the support of the poor in said towns, shall be paid . . . . into the hands of the treasurer of said county to be paid by him to the superintendents of said county poorhouse, to be applied and accounted for in the same manner as other monies received by them for the support of the poor in said county.

Chapter 166 of *The Laws of 1827* authorized Saratoga County to abolish the distinction between town and county poor, specifying that "all paupers in the said county shall be considered county paupers." Another act of 1827 extended the same authority to the counties of Washington and Warren, with the added provision that Cayuga, Herkimer, and Ontario counties might also adopt the county responsibility system whenever a majority of their respective boards of supervisors would determine to do so. An interesting provision in this act permitted superintendents of the county poorhouse, with the approval of the supervisors, to provide for the support of "idiots and lunatic paupers" outside the poorhouse whenever such a course seemed desirable.

Certain counties coming under the law of 1824 were petitioning the legislature to be exempted from the provision imposing the county system upon them. Thus, in 1826, Niagara, Steuben, and Wayne counties petitioned for exemption from the application of the county poorhouse act and their petitions were granted. From time to time other counties submitted similar petitions which met with varying reactions on the part of the legislature.

There were now three different poor-relief systems operating in New York State: (1) in some counties all the poor were considered county charges and all poor-relief expenditures were defrayed by the county; (2) in others all the poor (with certain exceptions receiving temporary relief) were maintained in the county poorhouse, with the support of each inmate being charged to the town where he belonged; (3) some counties had no county poorhouse, each town supporting its own poor in local almshouses or otherwise. The lack of uniformity in the operation of these systems was certain to create some confusion and controversy. An important source of friction was the clause in the law of 1824 prohibiting removals of indigents beyond county lines, which came into direct conflict with settlement provisions in the general poor law of 1813.

An opportunity to clarify and consolidate the various laws respecting settlement and poor relief came with the revision of the statutes in 1827 and 1828. The poor law as amended was embodied in chapter 20 of the *Revised Statutes of 1827*. Title I of this chapter, "Of the Relief and Support of Indigent Persons," repeated in substance some of the major existing provisions for poor relief and revised others.

The *Revised Statutes of 1827* made sweeping changes in the settlement requirements. Property qualifications for settlement were dropped completely. One year's residence in any town was deemed sufficient to gain settlement for any person of full age. A married woman was to have the same legal settlement as her husband. A minor could obtain settlement as follows: (1) if a female minor, by being married and living with her husband for one year, in which case she was to have her husband's settlement; (2) if a male minor, by being married and residing for one year separately from the family of his father; (3) by being bound as an apprentice and serving one year by virtue of such indenture; and (4) by being hired and actually serving for one year as a wage-earner.

No inmate of a poorhouse could gain settlement in the town where it was located by virtue of residence in such institution.*

The new law placed a ban on removals even more stringent than that enacted in 1824. Not only was the removal of poor persons from county to county prohibited, but also removals from one city or town to another within the same county. In counties where local responsibility prevailed, the dependent person was to be granted relief by the town in which he became poor, sick, or infirm. If he had a legal settlement in another town within the same county, the local overseers of the poor were directed to give written notice to the overseers of the place of settlement, requiring them to provide

---

* Chapter 190 of the *Laws of 1825* had already provided that children born in county poorhouses could not thereby claim settlement in the town where the poorhouse was located. Unless the father of such child, if legitimate, or the mother, if illegitimate, already had a settlement in the town previous to its birth, the child was to be considered a county pauper until such time as it could acquire legal settlement of its own.

for the support of such pauper. If the latter overseers wished to dispute the matter of settlement, they were directed to arrange for a hearing before the county superintendents of the poor within a specified time. Upon written notice the county superintendents were to convene at a stated date to determine the controversy over settlement, their decision being final.

A dependent person lacking a settlement in any town within the county where he became a public charge was in all cases to be supported at the expense of the county. In places where the distinction between town and county poor had been abolished, all poor persons, of course, were to be considered county charges regardless of their place of legal settlement.

In counties where a county poorhouse was located, all paupers were to be maintained therein with certain exceptions. In cases where examination into the condition and circumstances of an applicant convinced a justice of the peace that temporary relief should be extended to such applicant instead of sending him to the poorhouse, the law directed the justice to make out a written order for such relief, specifying the amount of money required. This order was to be drawn upon the county treasurer should the applicant be a county charge; if not, the cost of support was to be charged to the town where relief was afforded. It was further provided that "no greater sum than ten dollars shall be expended or paid for the relief of any one poor person, or one family, without the sanction in writing of one of the superintendents of the poor of the county, which shall be presented to the county treasurer with the order of the justice." In places where there was no county poorhouse, the overseers of the poor were required to examine into the condition and circumstances of an applicant with the assistance of a justice of the peace and to prepare a written order "for such allowance, weekly or otherwise, as the said justice and one of the said overseers shall think required by the necessities of such poor person."

In the matter of financing poor relief it was ordered that in counties where the distinction between town and county poor had been abolished the local commissioners of excise and other officers were to pay over to the county treasurer all moneys "which shall thereafter be received for licenses to tavern keepers, retailers or grocers, and all monies which shall be recovered as penalties for violating the excise laws, or any other laws, and which are directed to be paid to the overseers of the poor." The major source of county poor funds, of course, remained the special tax on real and personal estates.

Forfeitures and fines still supplied a large part of the poor moneys. The revised statutes directed that forfeitures for violating regulations of auctioneers' sales were to be paid over to the county treasurer for the use of the county poor. A moiety of the penalty for selling improperly branded flour and meal was to go to the use of town or city poor. Penalties imposed for violation of the law regulating inspection of flour and meal, beef and pork, pot and pearl ashes, fish, fish oil, lumber, culling of staves and heading, flaxseed, sole leather, and other commodities not specially mentioned, were to go to the city or county treasurer for the use of the poor. License fees of various kinds, or a moiety thereof, also went to the poor.

Persons illegally removing paupers were to be deemed guilty of a misdemeanor, liable upon conviction to a sentence not exceeding six months or a fine not exceeding one hundred dollars or both.

One important provision of the *Revised Statutes* declared:

It shall be the duty of superintendents of the poor of every county, during the month of December in each year, to report to the secretary of state, in such form as he shall direct, the number of paupers that have been relieved or supported in such county the preceding year, listing the number of county paupers from the number of town paupers, if any; the whole expense of such support, specifying the amount paid for transportation of paupers, and any other items, etc.

The secretary of state, in turn, was directed to lay before the legislature each year an abstract of the said returns and reports. Thus was laid the basis for a regular state-wide system of poor-law statistics. Unfortunately, however, the lack of co-operation on the part of many of the local and county poor-law authorities resulted in serious inaccuracies in these annual statements over a period of many years.

The revisers of the statutes of 1827 vigorously affirmed the opinions expressed by Secretary of State Yates three years earlier. They remarked in their explanatory notes:

After having done the best we could to improve and simplify the existing laws, we have yet come to a decided conviction in our own minds, that a simple system embracing the county poor-houses and the principle of making all the poor a county charge, is by far the most practicable and economical. . . . . We cannot forbear from remarking that the *principle* of the English laws is that each parish shall support its own poor. In adopting their laws, we have extended it to towns, which include many parishes; why it should not be still further extended to counties we are unable to perceive.[2]

One of the revisers went so far as to declare that, as a result of the revised statutes, "what remained of the English system of poor laws is almost entirely abolished."[3]

The trend toward the establishment of county almshouses and the abolition of the distinction between town and county poor progressed rapidly during the ensuing years. By 1832 poorhouses had been erected in forty-eight counties, and the distinction between town and county poor had been abolished in thirty-five counties.[4] Three years later all but four of the existing fifty-five counties in the state had poorhouses, while county responsibility for all the poor was observed in forty counties.[5]

A major reason for the rapid adoption of the county poorhouse system was the impressive economy apparently effected wherever it was put into practice. It was evidently much cheaper to gather all public dependents in a central institution than to scatter them in many places. Quite as important was the theory that it acted as a deterrent to prospective applicants for relief.

To contemporaries it seemed that the state had at last hit upon the perfect poor-relief system. In his annual message to the New York legislature in 1832, Governor Enos T. Throop gave expression to the widespread satisfaction with the new system as follows:

The county poor-house system has been voluntarily assumed by so many counties that we are permitted to hope that no compulsory legislation will be necessary to ensure its universal adoption. It has had the effect of providing more effectually and comfortably for the needy, and of repressing idleness; and when in complete operation, it will save to the people of the State, in poor rates alone, an amount equal to one-half, and probably much more, of the ordinary expenses of administering the government.[6]

Enthusiasm for the new system continued to mount, and in his annual report on poor-relief statistics for 1837, the secretary of state recommended that a law be enacted making it mandatory for every county in the state to establish a poorhouse and to adopt the principle of county responsibility. The extent to which county support had grown by this time is indicated in the poor-relief statistics for 1839. These figures showed that of a total of 48,713 persons receiving public relief in New York during that year, 45,899 were classified as "county paupers" and only 2,814 as "town paupers."[7] The figures for the following year are even more impressive, showing 52,764 persons receiving relief from the counties as compared with only 3,797 town paupers.[8]

It appeared that the principle of county responsibility for all the poor, with its administration centered around the county poorhouse, was now established on a permanent basis in New York State. But it was not long before the new system began to disintegrate. A strong tide of opposition against the county plan was rising, a tide that was to carry the policy of local responsibility to the pre-eminent position it had formerly occupied. Among the chief objections raised against the county system were these:

1. Under the new system, local poor-law officials were empowered to grant temporary relief at county expense. It was charged that many officials were granting temporary relief too readily and too generously, in the knowledge that all expenditures would be met by the county instead of the town.

2. It was also charged that local poor-law officials were being paid too highly for their services (the pay of overseers of the poor varied in the several counties, averaging between $1.50 and $2.50 per day on days when they were called upon to perform their functions).

3. Evidences of gross overcrowding and shocking treatment of county poorhouse inmates were becoming manifest, leading to demands for the abolition of such institutions along with demands for their improvement.

As early as 1838 the state assembly directed its Committee on the Internal Affairs of Towns and Counties to make an investigation of alleged abuses existing in county poorhouses. The Committee presented its report, based on correspondence with the superintendents of the poor of each county, in two separate sections, one dated March 30, 1838, and the other April 18, 1838. The first section dealt almost exclusively with a detailed description of the shocking conditions prevailing in the Genesee County poorhouse. This institution consisted of three buildings—a main building of brick which was "badly constructed," a low wooden building "so much out of repairs that it is worthless except as a present shelter from the weather," and a second wooden building which had been erected primarily for the confinement of insane and feeble-minded paupers, which was also "in bad repairs." The report revealed a terrible degree of overcrowding in the poorhouse, with indiscriminate herding of the paupers. One room, 18 feet by 17, held five beds occupied by twelve women and children; another of the same size had six beds occupied by fifteen women and children. The garret of the main building, which was neither lathed, ceiled, nor heated, had five beds for twelve lodgers. The garret of one of the wooden buildings was divided into two rooms, the first occupied by fourteen men and the second by twenty-five men and boys crowded into eleven beds. But the most indiscriminate herding was evidenced in the garret of the second wooden building, which had "ten beds and was occupied by 19 persons, two married men and their wives, one very old man, one aged colored woman, two male idiots, and eleven children."[9] Insane and feeble-minded persons were lodged in the same rooms with mentally normal inmates. A room that had originally been set aside for lying-in women was occupied by two married couples and three children sick with the measles. Since every room in the institution contained some sick inmates, a woman who had been delivered shortly before was placed in a room with a dying consumptive and his wife, one other woman, and several sick children. The indiscriminate crowding had resulted in widespread disease and suffering among the inmates. So intolerable had the situation become that the superintendents of the county almshouse appealed to the local overseers "to abstain from sending any more [poor] to the poorhouse, but to provide for them at home."[10]

In a lengthy communication to the secretary of state, the county superintendents of the poor declared that they had made repeated requests to the county supervisors for an adequate appropriation to permit enlargement and repair of the institution, only to be met by refusal in each instance.

A similar situation was disclosed with reference to the Mont-

gomery County poorhouse in the second section of the report by
the Committee on Internal Affairs. Here, too, an extraordinary degree of overcrowding was found to exist, with one hundred and fifty-
five inmates jammed into fourteen rooms and unmarried adults of
both sexes indiscriminately lodged in the same rooms.[11] The Committee also noted a number of complaints received from county
superintendents of the poor regarding the administration of temporary relief by town officials. The county authorities charged that
the latter were piling up unnecessarily large expenditures for temporary relief, and some suggested that the poor law be amended so
that all outdoor or temporary relief should be charged to the towns
rather than to the counties.

As a result of the unsatisfactory operation of the new system in
Genesee, the authorities of that county petitioned the legislature
in 1839 for permission to restore the distinction between town and
county poor. The legislature responded favorably by enacting chapter 121 of the *Laws of 1839*, authorizing the town overseers of the
poor to care for paupers locally or to send them to the county poorhouse where they were to be maintained at town expense. This was
the first serious check to the trend toward state-wide adoption of
the county system. In 1840 five counties—Chemung, Essex, Franklin, Greene, and Steuben—petitioned the legislature for "power to
sell their poorhouses . . . . and to provide for the support of the poor
upon the same footing as before the present system was adopted."
This time, however, the legislature, upon the recommendation of its
Committee on Internal Affairs, rejected the request of the petitioners. Similar petitions presented the following year by Essex and
Franklin counties and some inhabitants of Warren County were
likewise rejected.[12]

Nevertheless, resistance to the counter-movement toward local
responsibility was short-lived. In 1842 the supervisors of Lewis
County were authorized to restore the distinction between town
and county poor, and the same right was extended to Herkimer,
Saratoga, and Tioga counties in 1843, to Cattaraugus, Chautauqua,
Jefferson, Otsego, and Steuben counties in 1844, to Dutchess, Essex,
and Oneida counties in 1845, and to the counties of Allegany,
Broome, Cortland, Franklin, Livingston, Onondaga, Orange, Seneca,

Sullivan, and Ulster in 1848. Finally, in 1849, the boards of county supervisors throughout the state were authorized to abolish or restore at their own discretion the distinction between town and county poor.[13] This act struck the finishing blow to the system of county responsibility and heralded the official return to the principle of local responsibility laid down in the Elizabethan poor law of 1601.

DEVELOPMENTS IN MUNICIPAL RELIEF ADMINISTRATION

New York City had been exempted from the provisions of the county poorhouse act of 1824. For many decades the city had granted both indoor and outdoor relief, the latter proving indispensable in depression periods. To be sure, the municipal authorities were strongly in favor of indoor as opposed to outdoor relief, and urban New Yorkers were largely instrumental in promoting the movement which led to the passage of the law of 1824. Nevertheless recurrent economic depressions, hard winters, epidemics, fires, and wars caused large-scale suffering and dependency of a type necessitating some public provision for temporary outdoor relief. The situation was aggravated by the ever increasing numbers of newcomers of low economic status. Moreover, the city almshouse was often so overcrowded that in times of stress the misery of the poor could be alleviated only by the use of outdoor relief. Opposed though the authorities were to this method, they were forced by circumstances to practice it with more or less consistency and at times to apply it widely to the local situation.

Public outdoor relief, however, was not systematically organized. Tolerated as an unavoidable evil, it was resorted to only in cases of urgent need, and care was taken to keep it within certain limits. Voices against its extension were constantly heard. The alarm was greater and the voices louder when expenditures increased. Objections to this form of relief were based mainly on the contentions that it involved larger expenditures than support in the almshouse, that the conditions of urban life and the lack of adequate means of investigation made it possible for large numbers of people to secure relief undeservedly, and that the certainty of obtaining relief from the city led many to relax their industry.[14] In short, it was opposed both as uneconomical and as tending to increase pauperism. Expenditures for outdoor relief in New York City rose steadily during the second quarter of the century, amounting to $43,739 in 1845. The expenditure of this sum, considered huge in that day, naturally attracted much attention and comment. It became increasingly apparent to those who studied the problem that the loose administration of poor relief, with responsibility and control divided between thirteen commissioners of the almshouse and bridewell besides the board of aldermen and the mayor, required drastic correction. An effort to provide a solution was made in 1845, when the state legislature passed a law abolishing the offices of the thirteen commissioners and creating a special almshouse department as an independent part of the city administration. The department was placed under the charge of a paid commissioner to be elected for a term of one year at a minimum salary of $2,000 annually, thus centralizing responsibility for relief in one person.[15]

Those who hoped that the change would lead to lower costs, particularly in outdoor relief, were quickly disappointed. The city expenditures for outdoor relief rose to over $65,000 in 1847 and to $95,000 in 1848. Outdoor relief during the latter year was granted to 44,572 persons, constituting about one-ninth of the whole city population. Even more alarming was the estimate made by the commissioner of the almshouse that the outdoor poor aided by both public and private funds in 1848 had totaled nearly 100,000, or one-fourth of the entire population. The commissioner saw no remedy for the situation unless suitable employment with adequate pay could be furnished to the poor. A demand for a change arose, and in 1849 the legislature enacted a bill abolishing the office of commissioner and placing the almshouse department under the management and control of a board consisting of ten persons to be known as the "governors of the almshouse." Complete charge of charitable and penal institutions operated by the city and county of New York, with certain exceptions, was vested in this board.[16]

The steady growth of public charitable institutions and the extension of municipal aid to private agencies led to another important change in administration in 1860 with the creation of a city Department of Public Charities and Correction. The new Department was headed by four commissioners appointed by the city controller for five-year terms* and charged with the direction of all the institutions formerly managed by the board of governors, including the city almshouse, workhouse, and the "nurseries" for destitute children, the county "lunatic asylum," potter's field (the burial ground for paupers), the penitentiary and city prison, and the hospitals connected herewith.

Several changes were made in the poor-relief administration of Albany during this period. Albany County had come under the provision of the law of 1824 making mandatory the establishment of a county poorhouse. A special legislative act in 1832 abolished the distinction between town and county poor in Albany. It was further provided in the act:

Every poor person entitled to support, according to law, in the said city and county of Albany, shall . . . . be supported and maintained by the mayor, aldermen and commonalty of the city of Albany, at the expense of the county; and all poor persons . . . . shall be removed by the overseers of the poor of the several towns, and the overseers of the poor of the city of Albany to the said county alms-house, at the expense of the several towns and the said city . . . . and thereafter the necessary expenses of the removal of any poor person from any town in the said county to the said alms-house shall be paid on the certificate of the keeper of the alms-house by the chamberlain of the City of Albany.[17]

This statute was to remain in effect for only five years, but its provisions were subsequently extended by special acts. The almshouse was placed under the charge of the mayor, aldermen, and commonalty of the city of Albany, authorized to appoint a county superintendent of the poor. The office of the county superintendent was abolished by chapter 207, *Laws of 1849*, but was revived at a later date.

THE POOR-LAW SURVEY OF 1856

In 1856 the state senate, responding to increasing public dissatisfaction with the operation of the poor laws and a demand for inquiry into public charities, appointed a committee of three to investigate "all charitable institutions supported or assisted by the State and all city and county poor and workhouses and jails."†

* The first group of commissioners were to serve for only five years, those appointed thereafter for six.

† In the fall of 1853 a series of twenty-three open letters, signed by "Franklin" and addressed to the secretary of state, appeared in the *Columbia Republican*, published

The duties and powers assigned to the committee were of a sweeping character. It was specifically instructed

to examine into the condition of the said establishments, their receipts and expenditures, their method of instruction, and the government, treatment and management of their inmates, the conduct of the trustees, directors or other officers of the same, and all other matters whatever pertaining to their usefulness and good government.[18]

The resulting investigation, which was the most thoroughgoing survey of its kind since the Yates inquiry of 1823, took five months to complete. The committee, consisting of Senators Mark Spencer, George W. Bradford, and M. Lindley Lee, handed in its report on January 9, 1857. The two-hundred-and-seventeen-page report contained a detailed account of the condition of scores of charitable and penal institutions in the state—"poorhouses, workhouses, hospitals, jails, orphan and lunatic asylums," among others. Only that part of the committee's report dealing with almshouses will be discussed here; other aspects will be treated in the following chapter.

According to the committee, there were throughout the state fifty-five almshouses exclusive of those in Kings and New York counties which, for some reason, were not included in the general report. These fifty-five almshouses maintained 4,936 inmates, including 1,307 children, 837 "lunatics," 273 "idiots," 25 deaf-mutes, and 71 blind persons.* The committee declared:

The poorhouses through the State may be generally described as badly constructed, ill-arranged, ill-warmed and ill-ventilated. The rooms are crowded with inmates; and the air, particularly in the sleeping departments, is very

---

at Hudson. These letters consisted mainly of a critical survey of the operation of the poor laws and public charitable institutions in New York State together with recommendations for improvement, and bear evidence of careful study and intelligent analysis, although nothing is known of their author apart from his pseudonym "Franklin." They contain a wealth of material on contemporary poor relief and were included in the annual report of the secretary of state for 1855. Their publication and the widespread comment and discussion they aroused were largely instrumental in bringing about the legislative inquiry of 1856 (see New York State Senate, *Documents* [78th sess. (Albany, 1855)], Vol. III, Doc. No. 72).

* Statistics appended to the report show that there were 1,365 inmates in the Kings County poorhouse, while the population of the New York City almshouse and workhouse totaled 1,757, exclusive of poor persons maintained in the city lunatic asylum, the Bellevue establishment, and other public charitable institutions operated by the city and county of New York.

noxious, and to visitors, almost insufferable. In some cases, as many as forty-five inmates occupy a single dormitory, with low ceilings and sleeping boxes arranged in three tiers one above another. Good health is incompatible with such arrangements. They make it an impossibility.

Most poorhouses examined by the committee lacked hospital accommodations for the ailing; in some cases inmates sickened and died without any medical attention whatever. Proper classification of inmates was neglected, and the moral atmosphere was so low as to lead the committee to suspect that a number of the 292 children born in almshouses during the previous year were "the offspring of illicit connections" formed in the institutions. Food furnished at the poorhouse was generally insufficient and poor, while there were many instances of severe suffering because little or no fuel was provided in the winter. Educational facilities for almshouse children were usually very poor. Little effort was made to provide work for able-bodied inmates, while enforced idleness brought about a breakdown of morale. Treatment of the mentally ill and feeble-minded inmates was particularly shocking, the committee reporting:

The cells and sheds where they are confined are wretched abodes, often wholly unprovided with bedding. In most cases, female lunatics had none but male attendants. Instances were testified to of the whipping of male and female idiots and lunatics, and of confining the latter in loathsome cells and binding them with chains. . . . . The cells were intolerably offensive, littered with long accumulated filth of the occupants, and with straw reduced to chaff by long use as bedding, portions of which, mingled with the filth, adhered to the persons of the inmates and formed the only covering they had.[19]

Summarizing its impressions, the committee bluntly declared that the great majority of poorhouses inspected by its members were most disgraceful memorials of the public charity, and that the inmates in some of them were treated less humanely than criminals or even animals. The committee further charged that the gross neglect of the most ordinary comforts and decencies of life it had witnessed, if published in detail, "would disgrace the state, and shock humanity." And the details it did provide in an appendix to its report were quite sufficient to support its charges.

Chief among the recommendations of the committee was the return to outdoor relief. "Worthy indigent persons should, if possible, be kept from the degradation of the poor house, by reasonable supplies of provisions, bedding, and other absolute necessaries, at their own homes." This was a remarkable statement of policy for 1857, completely counter to the strongly dominant trend toward institutionalization, and anticipating the home-relief policy officially adopted in New York State with the passage of the Public Welfare Law of 1929. Contrary to the prevalent belief that the poorhouses were filled with the worthless and vicious only, the committee found among the inmates "persons of great worth and respectable character, reduced to extreme poverty, not by any vice or fault of their own, but by some inevitable loss of property, or of friends and relatives who, if living, would have supported them in their age and infirmities."

Another major recommendation made by the committee was that all children be removed from poorhouses and placed in orphanages and similar institutions for their special care. In this recommendation the committee anticipated the principle adopted in the Children's Act of 1875, directing the removal of all children between the ages of three and sixteen from poorhouses. A third major recommendation urged the removal of insane paupers from almshouses and the building of state hospitals for their reception.

Legal requirements for the better regulation of almshouses, with the erection of more suitable buildings and adequate arrangements for warmth, ventilation, bathing, classification of the inmates, occupation, instruction, and medical attendance, such as "decency, health and sound morals demand," were also recommended.

Most important of the committee's recommendations was that a law be enacted providing

for a more efficient and constant supervision of all the charitable and reformatory institutions which participate in the public bounty, or are supported by taxation; and a commission of well qualified persons, to be appointed by the Governor and Senate, with such arrangement of the terms of service as will constantly secure experience, appears to be the best mode of effecting the purpose.[20]

To accomplish the ends suggested the existing poor laws would have to be thoroughly revised, and a committee was forthwith appointed by the senate to draft such a revision.[21] But nothing concrete came

out of the draft of the Committee of Revision, and it was not until
1867 that the major recommendation of the investigating committee—that pertaining to the establishment of a state supervisory
board of public charities—was finally written into law, thus marking
a new period in the public welfare history of New York.

SUMMARY

The early years of the period 1825–67 witnessed a steady trend
toward acceptance of the county as the administrative unit in the
poor-relief system of New York State. This movement, beginning
with the passage of the county poorhouse act of 1824 and culminating in the establishment of almshouses by all but four counties and
the adoption of complete county responsibility for the poor by forty
counties, was checked about the year 1840, when the pendulum
started to swing backward toward town responsibility. The county
poorhouse remained, however, the center of the poor-relief system
throughout this period. Settlement requirements were simplified;
property qualifications were abolished and one year's undisturbed
residence in a county was deemed sufficient to gain a legal settlement. A new category of poor-law official—the county superintendent of the poor, whose primary function was to manage the county
almshouse—was created. A regular state-wide system of statistics-
gathering in poor relief was established, but operated with indifferent success during the early decades.

Another important trend was that toward institutionalization
of dependents, together with discouragement of public outdoor relief. The county poorhouse received all types of public dependents—
young and old, sane and insane, infirm and able-bodied. While the
poorhouse dominated the public relief system, however, special types
of institutions—for the insane, the feeble-minded, destitute and delinquent children, etc.—also were established, some under state
auspices. These will be discussed in the following chapter.

BIBLIOGRAPHICAL REFERENCES

1. New York State, *Laws of 1826*, chap. 147.
2. ———, *The Revised Statutes of the State of New York, as Altered by the Legislature* (Albany, 1836), III, 547.
3. ———, *Notes on the Revised Statutes of the State of New York* (Albany,
1830), p. 35.

4. New York State Assembly, *Documents* (56th sess. [Albany, 1833]), Vol. II, Doc. No. 38.

5. ———, *Documents* (58th sess. [Albany, 1835]), Vol. III, Doc. No. 185.

6. *Messages from the Governors*, III, 378.

7. New York State Assembly, *Documents* (63d sess. [Albany, 1840]), Vol. VIII, Doc. No. 332.

8. *Ibid.* (64th sess. [Albany, 1841]), Vol. VII, Doc. No. 277.

9. *Ibid.* (61st sess. [Albany, 1838]), Vol. VI, Doc. No. 310.

10. *Ibid.*

11. *Ibid.*, Doc. No. 360.

12. *Ibid.* (63d sess. [Albany, 1840]), Vol. VI, Doc. No. 267; *Ibid.* (64th sess. [Albany, 1841]), Vol. VII, Doc. No. 265.

13. New York State, *Laws of 1849*, chap. 194.

14. *N.Y.C., M.C.C., 1784–1831*, XIX, 638.

15. New York State, *Laws of 1845*, chap. 283.

16. ———, *Laws of 1849*, chap. 246.

17. ———, *Laws of 1832*, chap. 45.

18. New York State Senate, *Journal* (79th sess. [Albany, 1856]), p. 165.

19. New York State Senate Select Committee to Visit the Charitable and Penal Institutions of the State, "Report," in Senate *Documents* (79th sess. [Albany, 1856]), Vol. I, Doc. No. 8.

20. *Ibid.*, p. 22.

21. New York State Senate, *Journal* (80th sess. [Albany, 1857]), p. 940.

CHAPTER XIV

PUBLIC WELFARE IN EMERGENCY PERIODS. I

A series of emergency situations occasioned by epidemics, economic crises, and civil war, and complicated by unparalleled waves of immigration, created great strains in the relief organization of the state and occasionally resulted in important innovations in public welfare administration.

EPIDEMICS

While yellow-fever epidemics had caused great ravages during the decades following the Revolution, its occurrence in the period under discussion was negligible, no serious outbreak having occurred from 1822 to 1870. On the other hand, cholera and typhus epidemics became increasingly frequent.

Asiatic cholera was pandemic in the year 1832, taking a high toll of lives throughout the world. It made its appearance in New York State in the summer of that year and in less than two months it accounted for thousands of victims. Its greatest impact was felt in New York City where more than 3,500 persons died of cholera in July and August.[1] The dread disease claimed 401 victims in Albany that summer, out of a total population of about 26,000.[2] Buffalo was also hard hit, as were Troy, Poughkeepsie, Hudson, and other large towns lying along the waterways of the state.

On June 21, 1832, a few days after the first outbreaks of cholera had been reported in this state, Governor E. T. Throop sent a message to the legislature pointing to the lack of health and quarantine regulations outside of New York City and recommending legislation that would enable the various communities to take steps against the spread of contagious and infectious diseases.[3] The very next day the legislature passed an act "for the preservation of the Public Health." In every city and incorporated village of counties lying along the lakes, rivers, or canals of New York where a board of health was not already in existence, the authorities were directed to organize such a body immediately. Any other town or village in the state was empowered to create a health board whenever it should decide to do so. Each board was to consist of not less than three nor more than seven persons, with a physician acting as health officer.[4] Overseers of the poor were to serve as members of the local health boards. Among other duties the boards were empowered to prescribe regulations concerning sanitation, segregation and treatment of nonsettled persons, intercourse with infected places, and quarantine of persons and of ships. All expenses incurred by the several boards in the execution of the act were to be charged to their respective counties. Superintendents of county poorhouses were authorized to remove any of their charges to special "pest-houses" in case of outbreak of a contagious or infectious disease.*

Outbreaks of cholera in almshouses were frequent during this year and exacted a heavy toll. Within one week eighty-five out of two hundred and twenty inmates of the Poughkeepsie almshouse were stricken with the disease; fifty died.[5] The mortality from cholera at the New York City almshouse was likewise heavy; this was due in part to the fact that many already suffering from the disease were sent there, available hospital space being hopelessly inadequate to meet the crisis. Between five hundred and six hundred inmates of the Albany poorhouse were moved to newly erected buildings at the height of the epidemic.[6] In all the large cities of the state various public buildings, such as city halls and schoolhouses, were requisitioned as emergency hospitals. Little was known at the time of the causes, prevention, or cure of cholera, there being almost as many theories of the disease as there were physicians. Nevertheless, in the face of a pressing necessity, heroic efforts were made to check its spread. These measures sometimes were founded on good common sense and resulted in permanent improvement of sewage systems and of general sanitation. More often the methods adopted were pitifully futile. We are told that in Albany "quantities of tar [were] burned in the streets, creating gloominess, with the hope of abating the plague."[7] In New York City and other places bags of camphor

* This act was to be effective for only one year, but it was renewed annually until 1835. It was revived in 1849 when a particularly severe cholera epidemic again broke out.

were worn around the neck to ward off the disease—an impotent device that has survived to our own day. Many individuals, including physicians, doubted whether any positive measures to check an epidemic should be taken at all, on the ground that a plague was a form of God-sent punishment and should not be interfered with until God saw fit to end it. Proclamations setting days of prayer, fasting, and humiliation were issued everywhere.

A large amount of suffering was caused by the difficulty of obtaining water in some of the temporary hospitals in New York City. This proved an important factor in the decision made that year to build the Croton Aqueduct, to provide the city with a plentiful supply of pure water from a source many miles distant.

Motivated by a desire to allay unnecessary fears, to disseminate accurate and useful information, and to stimulate public officials to take prompt and intelligent action, a group of progressive physicians in New York City early commenced publication of the *Cholera Bulletin* which was issued thrice weekly from July 6 to August 31, 1832. The very first issue contained a letter urging that immediate provision be made for hospitalization of poor persons stricken with the disease. The editors also sharply rebuked the municipal authorities, including the health officials, for their failure to take adequate measures to prevent and treat cholera. An editorial in the *Bulletin* of July 20 declared that providing the needy with sufficient clothing, proper food, and better housing, constituted one of the most important preventive measures. The editorial insisted that such help should come from public sources rather than from private philanthropy:

It is truly surprising that with all the resources of New York there should be so few comforts for the poor at this alarming period. . . . . Ward meetings have been held in different parts of the city for the purpose of adopting measures by which the distresses of the poor may receive the necessary attention. But all this should have been done long ago by the Corporation, who are the legitimate fathers of the poor of this city. The public voice has been in favour of supplying the wants of the needy—the members of the Corporation have been repeatedly urged to give all their attention to this important consideration, and yet, nothing has been effected.[8]

The cholera found most of its victims among the poor, concentrated as they were in the most crowded and least sanitary areas.

Soon the disease made its way into the residences of the comfortable. A great strain was exerted on local relief funds as breadwinners were taken off by the epidemic, leaving whole families destitute. This stress was substantially alleviated in some cities and towns where boards of health took over many of the relief functions ordinarily exercised by the poor-law officials. Substantial portions of the special health appropriations were often used for relief purposes. The cholera orphaned many children, a fact reflected in a resolution adopted August 6, 1832, by the Board of Aldermen of New York City appropriating $1,000 to the several orphan asylums "to aid in the support of the orphans who have been sent to these establishments during the present epidemic."[9] Hardships were increased by the flight of many merchants and manufacturers from the afflicted cities and towns into the country, closing their places of business until their return. Workers virtually locked out of their places of employment were rendered destitute. The *New York Evening Post* of August 6, 1832, estimated that nearly 100,000 inhabitants—more than one-third of the total population—left the metropolis at the height of the epidemic.

A milder recurrence of the cholera plague broke out in various parts of the state in 1834; but in 1849 a pandemic cholera struck with a severity paralleled only by the 1832 outbreak. Commencing in May it spread rapidly to nearly every large town along the waterways of America. By presidential proclamation, August 3 was observed as a day of fasting and prayer because of the cholera.[10] The toll was heavy throughout New York. In Buffalo the Board of Health reported 2,505 cases and 858 deaths. Albany reported 2,109 cases, of whom 834 died. The mortality reached 5,070 in New York City.[11] In a survey of the cholera epidemic of 1849, Dr. James Wynne noted that in New York City "the inhabitants of those parts of the town where the disease was most fatal, were universally poor and destitute; wretchedly clad, miserably fed, and worse lodged. . . . ."[12]

Soon after the epidemic made its appearance the legislature enacted chapter 364 of the *Laws of 1849*, authorizing the governor to revive the law of 1832 which had provided for the creation of local boards of health in the towns and cities with broad powers.* Governor Hamilton Fish issued a proclamation to this effect on June 5, reviving the law for one year.[13]

In New York City a "Sanatory Committee" of the Board of Health was organized and vested with the full powers of the Board. One of its first actions was to provide medical advice and attendance for the poor of the city by appointing physicians to be in constant attendance at the police stations. Two physicians were assigned to each station-house, available to all residents of the district seeking prompt assistance.[14] Public schoolhouses throughout the city were requisitioned as emergency cholera hospitals, over the opposition of many individuals who protested against the use of educational institutions for this purpose. Besides, in certain districts where the cholera was particularly virulent, physicians were assigned to visit the poor in their homes and to proffer needed medical aid. Later, visiting nurses were also provided for the poor in their homes. A report on the expenditures of the "Sanatory Committee" to the Board of Aldermen in December, 1849, shows that a substantial part of the $55,372 expended by the Committee during the course of the epidemic went into special services for the poor.[15]

Cholera again visited the state in epidemic form in 1854, killing more than 2,500 persons in New York City. Typhus was also a frequent visitor, particularly at the port of New York during the great waves of immigration beginning in the late forties.

THE ECONOMIC CRISIS OF 1837–43

The great depression of 1837 was preceded by several years of distress in New York City. In the year 1834 a recurrence of the cholera epidemic, combined with a short-lived but severe financial panic, caused widespread suffering among the poor of the city. The following year a great fire, unprecedented in the history of the country, broke out in the business section, laying waste a vast area and resulting in property damage of more than $10,000,000. For months many business houses were closed while reconstruction went

---

* The legislative authorization of 1849 was later declared unconstitutional, whereupon chapter 324 of the *Laws of 1850* was passed, providing for the establishment of permanent boards of health in the cities, towns, and villages of the state. The boards of health of New York City and Brooklyn were made the subject of a special act (*Laws of 1850*, chap. 275).

on. Hundreds of workers were thrown out of employment and the offices of the relief authorities were crowded with applicants. Relief funds came pouring into the city from all parts of the United States and from several Canadian cities, but it appears that a major portion of these contributions was utilized in relieving merchants whose stores had been destroyed and also insurance companies which were threatened with bankruptcy, rather than in aiding the laboring poor.

The year 1836 was a "boom" year throughout the country. The wild speculation in land and canals that had started several years earlier reached a dizzy height. Building projects were carried on everywhere. Commodity prices soared to new highs. Widespread failures in wheat crops, chiefly due to the Hessian fly, sent the price of bread well beyond the reach of thousands of poor families. Flour was scarce; in Troy, which was a great depot for that commodity, there were only 4,000 barrels as against 30,000 the previous year. The price of flour rocketed from seven dollars to twelve dollars a barrel. Prices of other foodstuffs—and of rent and fuel—rose sympathetically.

Then came the great crash, ushering in a depression period of six years' duration. Hundreds of business houses caught in the swirl of the speculation mania went bankrupt. Over six hundred bank failures were recorded in a few months. Money became tight; specie payment was suspended in nearly every part of the country. The bottom fell out of the cotton market.[16]

Widespread discontent among the laboring masses manifested itself early in 1837, particularly in New York City where suffering was intense. On February 10, placards were posted all over the city announcing a mass meeting to be held three days later under the auspices of the Equal Rights, or Loco-Foco party, a radical group with a considerable following among the working class in New York.* At the head of the placard was the inscription: "Bread, Meat, Rent, and Fuel! Their prices must come down."[17] A great crowd numbering about 5,000 persons attended the demonstration at City Hall Park. Following the meeting an unauthorized speaker jumped on the platform and, declaring that 53,000 barrels of flour were stored in one of the largest warehouses in the city, urged the

* Founded in 1835 and disbanded at the end of 1837, this party represented one of the earliest attempts to establish a farmer-labor party in this country.

crowd to march to the warehouse and demand that the flour be sold at a reasonable price. Several hundred persons responded to the suggestion, and there occurred the well-known "flour riots" during which the warehouses of two prominent flour merchants were broken into by mobs and hundreds of barrels of flour taken out.[18]

As distress became acute, public meetings of the unemployed and other groups were held to discuss the hard times and formulate measures for relief. The most notable of these gatherings was held at City Hall Park on May 3, 1837, again under the auspices of the Loco-Foco party. An assemblage of between 4,000 and 5,000 persons attended this meeting and adopted a number of resolutions, including one which urged the Common Council "to employ, in the present scarcity of occupation, as many laborers as might well be, in the construction of the works for bringing water to this city, and other public works in progress."[19] It was also proposed that a part of the money paid into the city treasury by foreign emigrants should be applied to facilitate their removal to the west; that the Common Council be invited to set an example of retrenchment in reducing the city salaries, and that a committee of five persons be appointed in every ward to attend to the condition of destitute emigrants and others who may desire to remove to the country.

On the same day a resolution was presented to the Board of Aldermen taking note of widespread suffering among unemployed workers and their families and authorizing the street commissioner to hire as many of the unemployed on street work as he might deem expedient. No action was taken on the resolution; on May 8 it was laid on the table "together with a petition on the same subject," which probably embodied the resolutions adopted at the City Hall Park meeting on May 3.[20]

Nothing came of the persistent efforts of the unemployed and their public-spirited sympathizers to have the city fathers adopt a work-relief program in 1837, although several attempts to set up such a program were made.

Mayor Clark's annual message, presented to the Common Council on May 22, called attention to the growing relief needs developing out of the depression:

The coming winter will find our citizens not less charitable in feeling, but far less able than formerly, to continue their private subscriptions and contributions, and the Common Council will doubtless be solicited for greater aid than has usually been given for the support of all the charitable institutions; the out-door poor will be increased, and will be more than usually earnest in their intreaties.[21]

But the mayor offered no concrete suggestions for meeting the emergency, confining himself to a recommendation that the Council investigate the problem. A week later a select committee of the Board of Aldermen was appointed to consider a petition presented by one James Howel "in behalf of the unemployed operatives, for relief."[22] In its report, submitted on June 7, the committee noted that the economic crisis had increased the almshouse population by at least one-third; that applications for outdoor relief were multiplying; that many of the applicants belonged to the "new poor" and merited special attention; and that a public works program would afford an expedient means of relieving unemployment and distress. It was suggested that public works undertaken for this purpose should be carried on by contract rather than through direct employment of workers by the city. Pointing out that municipal public works costing $250,000 had already been authorized by law, the committee recommended that these projects should be started immediately through contractors, together with any other projects that might be designated by the Common Council.[23]

The proposals for relief through public works came to naught, however, partly through the refusal of contractors to bid on projects upon the terms of payment offered by the city, and partly because the finance committee of the Board of Aldermen reported that the municipal treasury was too depleted to permit the allocation of funds for the employment of the "necessitous poor."[24]

As frequently happens in depression periods, relief measures were sought which would place the burden on the laboring class rather than on the taxpayers. On July 5, 1837, the Board of Aldermen directed its Committee on Street-cleaning to inquire into the expediency of reducing the wages of the street sweepers and cartmen so that more men could be employed without increasing the total expenditures.[25] The records of the Board do not indicate whether or not this plan for sharing work and wages was put in operation.

While neither the state legislature nor the municipal authorities took any appreciable emergency measures to help the unemployed, energetic measures were taken to aid bankers, merchants, brokers, and other middle-class groups affected by the crisis. This sort of favoritism served to embitter large sections of the laboring population against the public authorities. " 'Millions to benefit landowners and shippers, but not a dollar for the unemployed hungry!' exclaimed the Anti-Monopolists."[26]

Meanwhile, with the approach of winter, unemployment and privation continued to increase. The inaction of the public authorities resulted in great strains on the resources of private welfare agencies. Some that had been receiving subsidies from the municipal treasury petitioned for larger grants, while many organizations not previously in receipt of financial aid made applications for special subsidies. Spontaneous citizens' relief groups sprang up in several wards of the city. On December 1, 1837, a meeting was held to formulate plans for city-wide private relief on an organized basis.[27] As a result of this meeting a relief committee was formed for each ward, headed by a central committee with the mayor as chairman. Each ward was districted, a block usually constituting a district. Representatives were assigned to each district to make house-to-house visits for the combined purposes of soliciting donations in kind or in cash and investigating relief needs in their districts. A central depot was provided for each ward where contributions in kind were received and distributed to the needy. Relief was afforded only on the approval of the district representatives. Cash was given in special cases, although very infrequently and in small amounts.

But the situation was far too serious for private philanthropy to cope with. In his weekly, the *New Yorker*, of January 20, 1838, young Horace Greeley painted a pessimistic picture of conditions in the city. Estimating that fully one-third of the 200,000 wage-earners were wholly or in large part unemployed, he added:

> Some of these subsist on the scanty earnings of former days, some are aided by relatives or personal friends, and some manage to avoid starvation with the few shillings which partial and precarious employment or still more uncertain beggary afford them; but there are still thousands—we estimate them from some personal observation at not less than ten thousand—within the limits of our city who are in utter and hopeless distress, with no means of surviving the winter but those afforded by the charity of their fellow citizens.[28]

The almshouse and all charitable institutions were "full to over-flowing," he noted, and the exhaustion of the resources of the private welfare agencies had left thousands of needy without provision of any kind. At least $50,000 must be raised to aid adequately these needy thousands, Greeley estimated. Himself an active member of the citizens' relief committee of the Sixth Ward—the "squalid, poverty-stricken Sixth"—Greeley observed at firsthand the terrible suffering created by the economic crisis and the ineffectiveness of the measures taken to meet it. What he saw made a deep impression on his social outlook. His biographer, James Parton, tells us that his observations of the plight of the poor during this depression led him to an enthusiastic espousal of Fourierist socialism.[29] While lauding the work of the district committees in his editorial of January 20, Greeley suggested that more efficacious methods of aiding the unemployed should be utilized in the future. Impressed by the fact that the great majority of the needy who had come under his observation had demanded work rather than alms, he proposed the establishment of a central employment office which should seek and distribute work for the jobless and serve as the pivotal point for philanthropic endeavors:

There ought to be a regular and permanent organization of all the benevolent and good in our city, with others throughout the land, for the extinction of mendicity and suffering from want, and for purposes of universal philanthropy. Such an organization should ever exist, and its first aim should be to afford or procure employment on some terms for every person who might desire it. We believe it need cost but a trifle to do this—to say to every able-bodied individual who could find no other means of subsistence—You shall at least have a living if you will accept the place we offer you, or enter our manufactory, work-shop or other service.

Another prominent feature of Greeley's preventive program was the "education of the children of the destitute, and a regard to the moral and intellectual improvement of the poor." By these means, Greeley declared, beggary and destitution might be prevented at far less cost than was required to relieve them. To the unemployed and the newly arrived immigrant he repeatedly cried: "Go West!"—west to the land of opportunity, the land of hope.

The secretary of state's annual abstracts of poor-relief statistics showed that the number of persons relieved or supported during the year ending December 1, 1837, totaled 51,266, while the total expenditures for public relief amounted to $495,095. These figures represented an increase of about 35 per cent over the number of relief recipients in the previous year, and 25 per cent in total expenditures.[30]

If the relief expenditures in New York State reached unprecedented heights in 1837, they were to mount even higher in 1838. Statistics for this year showed expenditures amounting to over $570,000 as compared with $495,095 the previous year. Even more significant was the steep rise in the number of persons receiving public relief from a total of 51,266 in 1837 to 105,216 in 1838.[31] It will be noted that while the number of relief recipients more than doubled, the total amount of expenditures increased only 15 per cent. The cities were hardest hit by the depression, as the relief figures show. In New York City alone, 80,696 persons received public support in 1838 at a cost of $209,452.* Albany County had 1,810 persons on its relief rolls, maintained at an expense of $30,416.[32]

The Albany authorities adopted a work-relief measure which was frequently resorted to in subsequent depression periods throughout the country. An ordinance was passed by the Common Council toward the end of 1838 laying aside a large area of city land for the cultivation of vegetables by such inmates of the almshouse as were capable of work. The products of this land were to be sold and the income turned over to the poor fund.[33] But this plan was hardly calculated to provide immediate relief for the unemployed. In his message to the Common Council on January 1, 1838, Mayor Teunis van Vechten observed that no adequate relief for the suffering poor had yet been afforded or even suggested. The almshouse was full and the existing provision for outdoor relief was not meeting the needs of temporary dependents. The establishment of soup houses would help relieve the needy, he said, but the major aim of the community should be to provide work for the jobless. "It is then our duty . . . . to furnish employment to the poor . . . . by projecting and directing improvements calculated to effect that object."[34]

---

* The number of public dependents in New York City rose from less than 30,000 in 1837 to over 80,000 in 1838, but the relief expenditures increased little more than $10,000 during the same period.

It does not appear that any effective action was taken on the mayor's recommendation for a public works program. Resort was again made to the establishment of a soup kitchen as a palliative. A public soup house was opened in the basement of the Albany city hall on January 18, 1838, and continued to operate until April 7 of the same year. Soup rations were supplied by the city to 291 families, comprising about 1,450 persons. A daily ration of a pint of soup was doled out to each person, together with "a large piece of bread" for each family. The expenses connected with the city soup house totaled $1,098, averaging less than one cent per day for each person receiving rations.[35] The city again operated a public soup house in the winter of 1839.[36]

There was a slight economic revival in 1839, followed by a recession and depression that lasted until 1843. Both public and private relief agencies were heavily taxed throughout this period. Their failure to cope adequately with relief problems arising out of the protracted depression led to serious questioning of welfare methods. It was the opinion of many influential citizens that the aid given the poor during the course of the depression served to break down their morale and was responsible for the increase of mendicancy and able-bodied pauperism. They held that relief methods should be based on the moral regeneration of the poor rather than on their material relief. An outstanding exponent of this theory—which may be easily recognized as a revival of the concepts developed by the Humane Society and the Society for the Prevention of Pauperism in the early years of the nineteenth century—was Robert M. Hartley, who served during the depression years as secretary of the New York City Temperance Society.

THE FOUNDING OF THE NEW YORK ASSOCIATION FOR IMPROVING THE CONDITION OF THE POOR

In the winter of 1842–43 Hartley brought together a group of citizens who appointed a committee to examine the poor-relief situation in New York City. This committee, headed by Hartley, found four major flaws in the existing relief system: (1) lack of discrimination in dispensing relief; (2) isolated and independent action among the private almsgiving societies of New York, which then numbered between thirty and forty, making it easy for "unworthy" charity-seekers to receive support from more than one agency; (3) lack of provision for personal contact with the recipients of alms at their homes, thus depriving them of personal counsel and sympathy aimed toward character-building; (4) public charity, having no special reference to eliminating causes and tending to increase the incidence of pauperism because of its impersonal mass approach to the problem.[37]

Further discussions of this group led to the organization in 1843 of the New York Association for Improving the Condition of the Poor. In an "Address to the Public" (1844), announcing its establishment and soliciting support, the Association declared the measures to be employed in its work would be preventive rather than remedial in nature:

Its primary and direct action . . . . is to discountenance indiscriminate alms-giving; to visit the poor at their habitations; to give them council; to aid them, when practicable, in obtaining employment; to inspire them with self-reliance and self-respect; to inculcate habits of economy, industry and temperance; and whenever it shall be absolutely necessary, to provide such relief as shall be suited to their wants.[38]

The primary emphasis of the Association was on moral assistance; the constitution declared that "its design is the elevation of the moral and physical condition of the indigent; and so far as is compatible with these objects, the relief of their necessities." Unity of action was one of the leading features of the plan proposed by the Association. Through a careful division of labor and responsibility in this city-wide general organization, "the chances of imposition are diminished; the exact amount of charity given to each individual may be ascertained; and a judicious administration of alms secured."[39]

In carrying out its work, the Association divided the city into sixteen districts corresponding to the sixteen wards. Each district, in turn, was subdivided into sections comprising about twenty-five families. An advisory committee was formed for each district and a visitor was assigned to each section. At the top was a central office which co-ordinated the work on a city-wide basis and served as a fountainhead for the diffusion of information. Material relief was to be granted sparingly and only in small quantities. An applicant could receive relief only through the visitor assigned to the section where he resided. Executive power was vested in the office of agent or director. Robert M. Hartley was appointed the first corresponding secretary and agent, serving in this capacity until 1876.

The Brooklyn Association for Improving the Condition of the Poor was established March 26, 1844, with Seth Low as its first president and Stephen Crowell as corresponding secretary and general agent. Its plan of organization was identical with that of the New York A.I.C.P., and its constitution and visitor's manual were copied literally from those of its New York prototype.[40] Similar societies sprang up in various parts of the country in subsequent years.

In giving rise to the Association for Improving the Condition of the Poor, the depression of 1837 left a permanent mark on the development of social welfare in this state and country.

BIBLIOGRAPHICAL REFERENCES

1. Citizens' Association of New York, *Report by the Council of Hygiene and Public Health upon Epidemic Cholera and Preventive Measures* (New York, 1865), p. 12.
2. Reynolds, *Albany Chronicles*, p. 491.
3. *Messages from the Governors*, III, 393–95.
4. New York State, *Laws of 1832*, chap. 333.
5. *Cholera Bulletin* (New York), August 10, 1832, p. 124.
6. *Ibid.*, August 6, p. 107.
7. Reynolds, *op. cit.*, p. 491.
8. *Cholera Bulletin*, July 20, 1832, p. 52.
9. New York City Board of Aldermen, *Proceedings, 1832* (New York, 1835), III, 168.
10. Reynolds, *op. cit.*, p. 561.
11. *Abstract of Report by James Wynne, M.D., on Epidemic Cholera, as It Prevailed in the United States in 1849 and 1850*, published in Great Britain General Board of Health, *Report on the Epidemic Cholera of 1848 and 1849* (London, 1850), Appen. C., pp. 28, 39, 43.
12. *Ibid.*, p. 38.
13. *Messages from the Governors*, IV, 486–70.
14. New York City Board of Health, *Report of the Proceedings of the Sanatory Committee of the Board of Health in Relation to the Cholera as It Prevailed in New York in 1849* (New York, 1849), p. 26.

15. New York City Board of Aldermen, *Documents, 1849–50* (New York, 1850) Vol. XVI, Doc. No. 19.
16. Willard L. Thorp, *Business Annals* (New York, 1926), p. 121.
17. F. Byrdsall, *The History of the Loco-Foco or Equal Rights Party* (New York, 1842), pp. 100 ff.
18. James Grant Wilson, *Memorial History of the City of New-York* (New York, 1892–93), III, 345; "Communication from Mayor Clark," N.Y.C. Bd. of Aldermen, *Documents, 1838–39* (New York, 1839), IV, Doc. No. 29, p. 303.
19. *New York Evening Post*, May 4, 1837.
20. N.Y.C. Bd. of Aldermen, *Proceedings, 1836–37* (New York, 1837), XII, 605, 628.
21. ——, *Documents, 1837–38* (New York, 1838), IV, Doc. No. 1, p. 9.
22. ——, *Proceedings, 1837* (New York, 1838), XIII, 50.
23. ——, *Documents 1837–38*, Vol. IV, Doc. No. 4.
24. *Ibid.*, Doc. No. 9; N.Y.C. Bd. of Aldermen, *Proceedings, 1837*, XIII, 112–13.
25. *Ibid.*, p. 186.
26. Gustavus Myers, *History of Tammany Hall* (New York, 1917), p. 109.
27. Brandt, *Glimpses of New York in Previous Depressions*, p. 46.
28. *New Yorker*, January 20, 1838.
29. James Parton, *Life of Horace Greeley* (Boston, 1893), pp. 165–67.
30. New York State Assembly, *Documents* (61st sess. [Albany, 1838]), Vol. VI, Doc. No. 311.
31. *Ibid.* (62d sess. [Albany, 1839]), Vol. III, Doc. No. 146.
32. *Ibid.*
33. Albany Common Council, *Minutes*, January 1, 1838, p. 417.
34. *Ibid.*
35. *Ibid.*, April 16, 1838, p. 55.
36. *Ibid.*, January 21, 1839, p. 318; February 18, 1839, p. 337; and March 4, 1839, p. 358.
37. New York Association for Improving the Condition of the Poor, *First Annual Report* (New York, 1845), pp. 15–16. Hereinafter referred to as N.Y.A.I.C.P.
38. N.Y.A.I.C.P., *Address to the Public, Constitution and By-Laws, and Visitor's Manual of the Association for Improving the Condition of the Poor* (New York, 1844), p. 7.
39. *Ibid.*, p. 6.
40. Stiles, *History of Brooklyn*, II, 275; Brooklyn Association for Improving the Condition of the Poor, *Fourth Annual Report, 1847, Containing the Constitution, By-Laws, Visitors' Manual, List of Officers* (Brooklyn, 1847).

CHAPTER XV

PUBLIC WELFARE IN EMERGENCY PERIODS. II

A period of growing prosperity from 1848 to 1853 was suddenly interrupted by another severe depression. Beginning with the summer of 1854 industrial activity declined rapidly. Feverish speculation in the autumn brought on financial panic, and scores of financial and commercial companies went into bankruptcy. Construction projects were halted. Employment fell precipitately, particularly in New York City, and wage-rates declined as the demand for labor diminished. At the same time commodity prices rose, partly due to failures in the wheat and cotton crops. Rent and food were especially high. In an attempt to halt the fall of wages workers resorted to strikes, but the condition of the laboring population worsened steadily. An unusually severe winter aggravated the situation in New York City.

By the onset of winter large numbers of New Yorkers who had never before sought aid were forced to apply for relief at private and public welfare agencies. "The most remarkable feature in the general distress," it was observed in a contemporary report, "was the respectable character of many of the applicants."[1] According to the Association for Improving the Condition of the Poor, which was the outstanding private relief agency in New York City, destitution reached "an extent before unknown in the city." It was estimated by the Associated Working Men's Committee, a pressure group arising spontaneously out of the depression, that there were 195,000 men, women, and children in absolute want during the winter of 1854-55, most of whom had never experienced dependency before.[2]

The period was featured by a remarkable degree of organized effort on the part of the unemployed to obtain either jobs or relief. In Robert M. Hartley's detailed description of the crisis in the A.I.C.P. *Report* for 1855, he relates that numerous demonstrations in the cause of adequate unemployment relief took place in City Hall Park, Washington Square, and other public places. Parades of the jobless were also frequent. The city authorities were bombarded by petitions of labor groups demanding action to alleviate the distress. The insistence of these pressure groups was reflected in the opening message of Mayor Fernando Wood to the Common Council on January 1, 1855:

Surely we are admonished that if this rate of taxation be continued, more of it should be devoted to the relief of the poor, whose industry bear most of its burthens, and who are now ringing into our ears their cries of distress. Labor was never so depressed as now. . . . .

This is the time to remember the poor! . . . . Do not let us be ungrateful as well as inhuman. Do not let it be said that labor, which produces everything, gets nothing, and dies of hunger in our midst, whilst capital, which produces nothing, gets everything, and pampers in luxury and plenty. . . . .[3]

The pressure of the unemployed groups did much to stimulate private and public agencies to unusual exertions in providing relief. Lectures and concerts were held for the benefit of the needy. Contributions were received from distant parts of the country. Even more significant was the speedy organization of "ward relief committees," along the same lines as those which existed during the depression of 1837–43. There were ward relief committees functioning in twelve of the twenty-two wards of the city. Some of the committees co-operated with the A.I.C.P., turning over their funds to the latter for distribution, but most of them operated independently. As a result friction developed between them and the A.I.C.P. which had opposed the organization of ward committees from the first, holding that they were unnecessary and that the Association was big enough to handle the problem of private relief alone.

Claiming that the hasty organization of the ward committees was contrary to "the rigid laws of economic times" and that they were unable to provide relief judiciously and discriminately, the A.I.C.P. also charged that their existence served to divert contributions which otherwise would have been made to the Association. It was further alleged that the committees were actually fostering a tendency among the unemployed to rely upon charity and that the office of the A.I.C.P. Board of Managers where relief was never dispensed "was crowded by clamorous beggars who had been sent there by ward committees."[4] Moreover, the committees were entirely too generous in granting relief and were teaching the unemployed that relief was due them "as a right and not as a favor." The A.I.C.P. observed with alarm that one committee had perpetrated the "indefensible indiscretion" of passing a resolution advising the poor not to pay their rent and had "appointed a vigilance committee to protect them in refusing." During the winter soup kitchens had been set up in different parts of the city by ward committees. This form of relief drew the strong condemnation of the A.I.C.P. on the ground that it was a "recognized principle among sound social economists and philanthropists that the poor should not be aided in promiscuous masses in soup kitchens, but by personal visits at their homes." Thanks to the attitude fostered by the committees, the A.I.C.P. allegation continued, the city was "overrun by an unmanageable crowd of men, women and children . . . . seemingly in great wretchedness . . . . who often manifested much asperity and bitterness if they did not get all they asked."[5]

No figures are available as to amount of emergency aid rendered by the ward relief committees during the depression, which ended in the summer of 1855. The New York A.I.C.P. reported that it had relieved 15,549 families, comprising 62,396 persons, at a total cost of $95,018 in the year ending November 1, 1855. Its relief load for that year was 260 per cent greater than the average of the four years immediately preceding it.[6]

A number of substantial grants-in-aid were made by the Common Council to private organizations, including the A.I.C.P. and the ward committees. On February 19, 1855—four days after receiving a petition from "the Committee of Unemployed Workingmen"—the Board of Aldermen voted an appropriation of $500, to be distributed among the several ward relief committees. A week later it voted a grant of $11,000 to these committees, together with an appropriation of $15,000 to the A.I.C.P.[7]

The expenditures of the Almshouse Department of the city for 1855 totaled $797,142, an increase of nearly $200,000 over the previous year. The superintendent of outdoor poor* reported that

---

* The Board of Governors of the Almshouse Department had created a separate "Department for the Relief of the Out-Door Poor" under the immediate direction of a paid superintendent, a forerunner of the home-relief bureau in present-day welfare departments.

"the great distress which existed during the last winter, owing to the stagnation of business, increased the demands of this department to an extent never before equalled, and compelled many who had been able to support themselves by their labor, to become applicants for relief."[8] Public outdoor relief in cash or in kind during 1855 had been granted to a total of 85,136 persons, an increase of 43,000 over the previous year. Expenditures for outdoor relief amounted to $121,861, over $38,000 more than in 1854.

Corresponding increases in relief figures were shown for the state as a whole. In his annual report on poor-relief statistics for 1855 the secretary of state estimated that 204,161 persons had been relieved at a total of $1,379,959.[9] Comparable figures for the previous year showed only 137,347 persons relieved, with total expenditures of $1,121,904.[10] The number of persons receiving temporary or outdoor relief rose from 95,986 in 1854 to 159,092, an increase of more than 60 per cent.[11]

THE CRISIS OF 1857–58

Like the economic crisis of 1854, the depression of 1857 came unexpectedly after a short period of prosperity. The year 1856 and the first half of 1857 were described by a contemporary as a time of "overflowing plenty, peace and prosperity." Business was booming, an abundant harvest had been gathered, and the granaries of the country were filled to capacity. The demand for labor was greater than the supply and wages were on the rise. The nation appeared to be headed for even more prosperous times.

The crash came like a bolt from the blue. Defects in the credit system had permitted unlimited expansion which in turn stimulated unsound speculation. A slight contraction of credit apparently was sufficient to work havoc with the system. The startling failure of a large corporation hitherto regarded as entirely safe initiated a process of contraction. Money became extremely tight, and a steady stream of bankruptcies of railroads, banks, mercantile and industrial firms followed. By the end of December, 1857, 985 mercantile establishments failed in New York City with liabilities exceeding $120,000,000, and many more failures were recorded later.[12] A run on the banks forced the New York legislature to suspend specie payments for one year. The wheels of industry throughout the country almost ceased turning, and thousands of workers were thrown out of employment.

With the intensification of the crisis through the winter, suffering became acute. Meager savings were soon eaten up and destitution overtook many thousands who had always been self-supporting and independent. "To the unemployed poor," one relief agency observed, "it was as if the wealth and resources of the country had been swallowed up by some overwhelming catastrophe."[13] The plentiful grain crops harvested in the West were lying idle in granaries for want of capital to defray the cost of shipping them East. The great depression paradox was not overlooked by the poet Walt Whitman, who wrote in the *Brooklyn Daily Times:* "The granaries of the land are filled with harvests of the year, and, strange to tell, the philanthropic are everywhere meditating by what means famine shall be kept from our doors."[14]

As usual, New York City experienced the severest shocks of the depression. In the fall of 1857 Mayor Wood estimated that 30,000 workers had already been thrown out of their jobs, and that thousands more would be unemployed during the next few months. Hunger stalked the streets of the city; many died of starvation. Pressure groups, consisting of the jobless and their allies among the laboring class, sprang up spontaneously for mutual defense. Displaying a remarkable degree of militancy, they launched a series of actions that brought their plight dramatically to the attention of the municipal authorities and forced the latter to give them prompt and serious consideration. "Hunger meetings" and parades of the unemployed became daily occurrences in New York. . . . . The slogan of "Work or Bread" became popular. The unemployed showed unmistakably that they preferred jobs to relief. In numerous petitions to the Common Council they raised the issue of "the right to work," claiming that in the emergency situation it was incumbent on the public authorities to create jobs by launching public works projects at once. They also shocked the city fathers by demanding relief as a right.

A militant hunger meeting of the unemployed was held in Tompkins Square on election day, November 4, at the end of which the participants tore down the wooden fences around the Square and carried them home for fuel. An even greater demonstration, attended by about 5,000 persons, was held the next day in the same Square. Raising the slogan of "Work or Bread," the participants adopted resolutions demanding that the city authorities immediately institute large-scale public works, including construction and improvement of streets and sewers, the building of a new reservoir, and improvement of Central Park, which had been purchased by the city in 1853. Petitions embodying these demands were drawn up at the meeting in the name of the "Working Men's Association," claiming to represent 50,000 unemployed "mechanics and workingmen" in the city, and were presented the following day to the Common Council.

Revolution and riots were predicted by some of the speakers if unemployment-relief measures were not promptly instituted by the authorities. One speaker, a blacksmith, was reported to have said: "Go to Wall Street and make the moneyed men shell out. Let them know that the poor will have bread or will use the musket."[15]

The ominous mood of the unemployed made a deep impression on the authorities, who were quick to express sympathy and extend promises. As early as October 8 a resolution had been introduced in the Common Council recommending that needed public works, such as the improvement of Central Park and the building of the new reservoir, be set in operation during the winter months so as to alleviate the condition of the unemployed and save public funds that would otherwise have to be expended in direct relief.[16] On October 22 Mayor Fernando Wood sent to the Council a communication on the unemployment situation similar in tenor to the remarks made in his message of January, 1855. Estimating that there were then 30,000 workers thrown out of employment, and that this number would increase to 50,000 by January, he warned the Common Council that the jobless were in a desperate mood and expressed the fear that "not a few will resort to violence and force" rather than submit to the humiliation of relief from public or private charity.[17]

As a means of reducing unemployment Wood recommended a public works program along the lines that had already been urged by other sources, including the unemployed themselves. A distinctive feature of Wood's plan was a proposal that the city purchase 50,000 barrels of flour and corresponding quantities of corn meal and potatoes, to be distributed among public works laborers in lieu of 75 per cent of their wages, the remaining 25 per cent to be paid in cash. Expenditures would be defrayed by the issuance of public construction stock bearing 7 per cent interest and redeemable in fifty years. The mayor's message together with the workingmen's petition of November 5 was later referred by the Board of Aldermen to its Committee on Finance.

On November 7 the unemployed held a huge meeting which was climaxed by a "hunger march" on the city hall and a threat on the part of the demonstrators to force their way into the aldermanic chambers in order to present their demands en masse. The mayor was warned by the jobless that their patience had been exhausted and that they would not be content to starve silently. Another great demonstration was held on the morning of November 9. So belligerent was the temper of the crowd that the mayor threw a guard of two hundred policemen around the city hall, and the United States Assistant Treasurer telegraphed to Washington asking for troops to guard the subtreasury building in Wall Street.* The agitation of the jobless on this occasion brought immediate results, stimulating the Common Council to unusual activity relating to the unemployment-relief problem.[18]

That very day the Finance Committee of the Board of Aldermen submitted its report on the mayor's message and the workingmen's petition which it had had under consideration. The Committee indorsed the proposal for the immediate beginning of work on Central Park, and also recommended an increase of $50,000 in the annual street-building appropriation for 1858. It declared, however, that other types of emergency-works projects urged by the unemployed were impracticable, owing to legal restrictions. It also opposed the mayor's suggestion that part of the wages on public works should be paid in kind, on the ground that such a measure would involve competition with private tradesmen. In the course of its report the

* More than one hundred armed soldiers and marines were stationed at the Customs House the following morning in readiness "to repel any attack on the sub-treasury." (*New York Evening Post*, November 10, 1857.)

Committee took occasion to denounce the frequent demonstrations and parades of the jobless, counseling them to be patient.[19]

The same day (November 9) an ordinance authorizing an appropriation of $250,000 for Central Park improvements, which had lain on the table of the Board of Councilmen for nearly three weeks, was voted upon favorably and was signed at once by the mayor.[20] The councilmen adopted a resolution requesting the commissioners of Central Park to employ immediately from 1,500 to 2,000 workers, whose wages would be provided for by the Common Council.

Aldermen and councilmen adopted resolution after resolution expressing their deep concern over the plight of the unemployed, recommending methods of alleviating the situation, and explaining at length why they felt themselves unable to comply with all the demands of the jobless. Most of the resolutions were of the "pass-the-buck" type, vigorously urging *other* bodies to take action. The councilmen proposed that the federal government build a new post office in the Central Park area, and a joint committee of the Common Council was forthwith appointed to push this project. The city controller was urged to expedite the financing of contemplated street construction and improvement. Contractors were requested to proceed as rapidly as possible with their work for the city, so as to provide more employment for the jobless. City authorities and contractors were urged to give preference to men with families when hiring laborers. A special committee of the Board of Aldermen was appointed to confer with the poor-law authorities, the philanthropic associations, and the citizens generally as to the best methods of providing unemployment relief.* The governors of the almshouse were asked "to purchase and store flour, corn-meal, and other provisions,

* A conference of private welfare agencies had already been held to discuss methods of coping with the unemployment situation. This conference appears to have concluded that the best means of alleviating the situation was to encourage the unemployed to leave the city, taking their families with them. As a practical measure they agreed on a campaign of advertising throughout the country for farmers and manufacturers willing to employ jobless residents of New York City. In a circular published in the *New York Times* of November 4, Robert M. Hartley made a plea for nation-wide co-operation in this campaign, offering as an inducement to prospective employers the cheapness of labor during the emergency period. The campaign proved a total failure; the A.I.C.P. *Report* for 1861 notes that only about ten employers responded to the widely circulated plea of the New York charitable agencies (N.Y.A.I.C.P., *Eighteenth Annual Report* [1861], pp. 36–37).

in anticipation of extreme destitution among the laboring population." They were also requested to consider at once "the expediency of quickly organizing an efficient corps of out-door visitors for the suffering poor, so that prompt relief may be afforded in all cases where it may be needed."[21]

The concrete results arising from this day of uncommon activity proved very meager, however. Work on the new reservoir was barred by reason of existing litigation. Street construction and improvements were also checked by legal restraints. Those who had placed high hopes in the Central Park project as a measure for alleviating unemployment were greatly disappointed. On November 19, 1857, the Central Park Commission had authorized the employment of 1,000 men as soon as funds were received from the bond issue.[22] But so much time was consumed in the issuance and sale of the municipal bonds for the Central Park public works that large-scale work began only when the emergency period was well-nigh over.

Meanwhile acute suffering continued through the winter. It was estimated that within three months more than 41,000 homeless persons received night shelter in the police stations of the city. On November 19 the Board of Aldermen voted to permit the unemployed poor to occupy a municipally owned building known as Platt Hall.[23] Several days later the councilmen adopted a resolution noting that a large number of destitute persons seeking lodging in the police stations were being turned away because there was no room for them, and recommending that suitable rooms or buildings be procured in each ward to accommodate the overflow from the station houses.

No citizens' emergency-relief committees such as those organized on a ward basis in the depressions of 1837–42 and 1854–55 functioned during this crisis. The opposition of the A.I.C.P. evidently was a potent factor in preventing their establishment. Soup kitchens were also rare, as that Association noted with satisfaction in its annual report for 1858.[24] At the height of its activities, in January, 1858, the A.I.C.P. extended relief to 9,665 families, totaling nearly 38,000 persons. The number of persons receiving relief from that agency in the year ending October 1, 1858, was about 60 per cent more than the total for the previous year.[25]

Public outdoor relief rose sharply in the city with the onset of the depression. On November 17 the governors of the almshouse directed a committee to consider without delay the advisability of applying to the Common Council for an appropriation of $50,000 in addition to the $30,500 for outdoor relief requested in their budget estimate for 1858. This additional sum was "to be applied solely for the purpose of affording temporary relief to those who are in destitute circumstances and unable to obtain employment, or are otherwise incapable of gaining their livelihood during the coming winter."[26] The governors declared that "applications for temporary relief have already increased to an unprecedented extent" and could be expected to increase still more in the coming months. They believed that the extension of temporary relief would deter many from seeking refuge in the already overcrowded charitable institutions of the city. In his report for 1858 the superintendent of the outdoor poor stated that a record number of applications for temporary relief had been received as a result of the crisis. Expenditures for public outdoor relief amounted to $138,583 in 1858, an increase of $30,000 over the previous year and of $43,000 over 1856.[27] In all, 130,150 persons were relieved or supported at public expense in New York City at a total cost of $490,883.[28]

The number of relief recipients in New York City amounted to nearly half the total number supported throughout the state in 1858. According to the poor-law statistics, 261,155 persons, representing 7.4 per cent of the total population were granted relief in New York State in 1858 at a cost of $1,491,391.* While the number relieved represented an increase of nearly 90,000 over that of 1857, the expenditures advanced only $137,000, indicating that the per capita allowance was much lower than that of the previous year.[29]

While relief in New York City naturally showed the highest rate of increase during the depression period, other communities in the state were noticeably affected. This was particularly true of the large towns and cities. In Albany relief expenditures for the year

* These figures are exclusive of Albany County, which had abolished the office of superintendent of the poor and therefore was not required to report on poor-relief statistics to the secretary of state.

ending November 1, 1858, amounted to $57,139, as compared with $43,159 the previous year.[30] The cost of maintaining the almshouse was $39,672, an increase of about 20 per cent over 1857. At that time the institution was owned and operated by the city, which was paid by Albany County for the support of the inmates on a per capita basis.

Perturbed by the pronounced rise in almshouse expenditures, the County Board of Supervisors and the Common Council of Albany appointed a joint committee in 1859 to investigate the subject. The committee chose to confine its inquiry to the period November 1, 1857, to May 1, 1859. Differences among the committee members resulted in the submission of separate reports in December, 1859. That of the Supervisors' Committee condemned the almshouse administration, charging it with inefficiency and extravagance. Majority and minority reports were rendered by the Committee of the Common Council. The majority report agreed in the main with the conclusions of the Supervisors' Committee; the minority report defended the almshouse superintendent and attributed the unusual rise in expenditures to general economic conditions beyond his control.[31] In a brief submitted in his own defense, William Hurst, the superintendent, explained that the period covered by the investigating committee had been a most unusual one in the history of the almshouse administration. This was particularly true of the depression winter of 1857–58, when "hundreds of respectable mechanics and honest laboring people were, without any fault of their own, suddenly deprived of the means of obtaining a livelihood by their own industry." Attacking the findings of the majority group in the Committee of Inquiry, Superintendent Hurst posed several categorical questions:

Did it not occur to their [the committee's] philanthropy to remember that the inmates received at the institution that winter were not only largely increased in numbers, but were of a very different class from the general character of the inmates? that they were respectable mechanics, accustomed to all the comforts of life, used to earning their $2 per day, and who would scorn charitable relief but for the universal distress that then pervaded all classes and conditions? and did not charity dictate that such a class of unfortunates should be provided with better kind of clothing, and a better quality of food, and that thus additional expenditures should necessarily be incurred?[32]

The Common Council was deadlocked on the question of proper action on the reports, and the mayor was finally authorized to appoint a committee to consider the advisability of removing the almshouse superintendent from his post. Repeated efforts to effect this removal failed, however, and the superintendent kept his job in spite of the serious charges made against him by members of the council.[33]

In Kings County, which included the city of Brooklyn, the recipients of outdoor relief during the year ending July 31, 1858, totaled 32,940—more than double the number temporarily relieved in the previous year. This increase was attributed by the county superintendents of the poor to "the financial revulsion, and the almost unprecedented stagnation in the different branches of trade and industry during the memorable fall and winter months of 1857–58."[34] Expenditures for temporary relief amounted to $33,260 —nearly twice the amount expended for the same category in the fiscal year 1856–57, and a record figure for Kings County up to that time.[35] It is interesting to note, however, that the aggregate expenses for all categories of poor relief in Kings County—including maintenance of the county almshouse, hospital, "lunatic asylum," and nursery, together with temporary relief, amounted to $192,079, about $41,000 less than the expenses incurred in the fiscal year 1856–57. The cost of almshouse care during the depression year declined by nearly $43,000 from that of the previous year, in spite of the fact that the average number of inmates increased by 155 over the 1856–57 average of 1,340.[36] The superintendents of the poor attributed this decrease to a more efficient system of purchasing supplies that had been installed that year.

The extent of outdoor relief in other counties in New York in 1858 furnishes a significant index of the effect of the depression elsewhere in New York State. For example, in Erie County, where Buffalo is located, the number of temporary relief recipients in the year ending December 1, 1858 was 5,915, representing a rise of more than 100 per cent over the previous year, and Oneida County, which includes Utica, extended temporary relief to 7,062 persons, nearly twice as many as received such relief in 1857.[37]

CIVIL WAR RELIEF PROBLEMS

The emergency-relief problems created by the outbreak of the Civil War in 1861 were of a different character from those arising out of economic depressions, and, in grappling with them, different administrative methods had to be employed. Four hundred thousand men from New York State served in the Union army and navy during the course of the war. More than 53,000 died in service, and many thousands more were disabled by wounds.[38] Aid had to be provided for families deprived of their breadwinners through enlistment or draft, for the disabled soldiers, and for the widows and orphans of those who died in service.

On April 12, 1861, Fort Sumter was fired on by the South, marking the beginning of the long bloody conflict. Two days later an emergency meeting of New York State officials and legislators took place in Albany, where it was decided to draft a bill providing for the enrolment of 30,000 volunteer militia and appropriating $3,000,000 to meet the expense of organizing and outfitting the volunteers. This bill became law on April 16. On the previous day the president had issued a proclamation calling forth the militia of the several states, New York's quota being 13,280 men.[39]

Since enlistment did not proceed as rapidly as had been hoped, it was necessary for the public authorities to devise measures to stimulate the process. Many millions of dollars were paid by state, county, city, and town governments in bounties and other inducements. Eligible men showed a reluctance to enlist unless they were assured that some provision would be made for the support of their families. The city of New York acted early in trying to solve this problem. On April 23, 1861, the Common Council created a fund of one million dollars to fit out regiments and to aid such soldiers as needed assistance. The fund was placed in the hands of the Union Defense Committee of New York City for disbursement. Organized on April 20, this Committee comprised about thirty prominent citizens, together with the mayor and controller of New York City and the presidents of the boards of aldermen and councilmen.*

* The membership of the Union Defense Committee included John A. Dix, Hamilton Fish, Simeon Draper, Abiel A. Low, William M. Evarts, Alexander T. Stewart, and James S. Wadsworth, among others. The Committee adjourned sine die in the spring of 1864.

Its expressed purpose was "to represent the citizens in the collection of funds, and the transaction of such other business in aid of the movements of the Government as the public interests might require."[40] Relief to soldiers' families was distributed by the Committee through ward committees consisting of four persons in each ward who were required to check applications carefully in order to prevent fraud. Of the original appropriation of $1,000,000, which was almost exhausted by the end of June, $230,000 was expended in relief to nearly 12,000 needy families.[41]

On July 1 the Common Council adopted a resolution expressing disappointment at the failure of the Union Defense Committee to lay aside at least half of the million-dollar fund for the relief of needy families of volunteers. In its resolution the council urged the citizens to "call a public meeting, or to take such measures as they may deem necessary to relieve the families of the soldiers and to suggest some plan whereby the poor worthy and needy laboring classes may obtain some kind of employment." Another resolution recommended the appointment of a joint committee of both branches of the Common Council to consult with prominent citizens as to the best means of providing relief for the poor families of soldiers.[42]

An ordinance was passed on July 15 appropriating $500,000 to be known as the Volunteer Family Aid Fund of the City of New York. Instead of turning over the money to the Union Defense Committee, however, the Common Council designated the city controller as treasurer of the fund. He was directed to appoint one assistant treasurer in each senatorial district of the city who was authorized to make disbursements to applicants entitled to relief through ward committees in his district. These committees were to consist of the alderman and councilmen of each ward together with citizens appointed by the Union Defense Committee. The maximum weekly allowance was to be $2.00 for each family head, $1.00 for the oldest child, and 50 cents for every additional child. Not more than $5.00 weekly were to be paid to any one family. Relief was to be granted only to dependents of soldiers in active service who had been residents of the city prior to May 1, 1861. Each ward committee was authorized to employ a visitor to investigate applicants at a wage of $1.50 per day.[43] A further appropriation of $500,000 was voted by the Common Council for the same purpose on December 5. The ordinance authorizing the appropriation virtually repeated the provisions of the measure of July 15, with several modifications making the requirements for obtaining relief more stringent. The new ordinance also raised the daily wage of visitors to $2.00 and reduced the maximum weekly relief per family to $4.00.[44]

A third appropriation of $500,000 for the relief of families of volunteers was voted by the Common Council on June 12, 1862. Several days later the mayor sent a message to the council explaining that he had been reluctant to sign the ordinance appropriating the money and had done so only because he had been unwilling that through any act of his "the families of our brave soldiers, now periling their lives on the battle-field in defense of the Union, should be driven to the necessity of appealing for alms to our institutions of public charity."[45] He charged that the amount of relief allowed to families was too generous and suggested that an amendment be adopted reducing the maximum.* His most serious objection to the ordinance was that it made a political football of relief by giving the aldermen and councilmen a dominant place on the ward relief committees. As a remedy he urged that the law be amended so as to place the distribution of the fund in the hands of "private citizens of high character, on whom no suspicions may rest of political favoritism in the performance of this delicate duty." This recommendation was indignantly turned down by the council. Further appropriations for the relief of soldiers' families were made from time to time during the ensuing years. It was estimated that the total amount expended by the city for this type of relief exceeded $6,000,000 by the end of the war.

Measures for the relief of soldiers' families similar to those taken in New York City were adopted in other communities throughout the state. A special committee of the Albany Common Council was appointed to consider the problem on April 19, 1861, a few days

---

* The maximum relief allowance specified in the ordinance was twelve dollars a family per month.

after the outbreak of hostilities. The report of the committee, submitted on April 23, was keyed in a highly emotional strain:

> Our common country is struggling amid calamity; our national capital is in danger; our great government is beleaguered by foes, and its laws set at defiance. It calls upon its people for aid . . . . the people are willing and eager to go to its call, but patriotism is confronted by helpless wives and children. Who shall maintain the families of those whose daily labor supplies to them their daily bread? The danger is imminent, and prompt action is required. Volunteers will swarm to their country's rescue if they can only feel that their wives and their children shall not be permitted to suffer. . . . . The Federal and State governments provide for the soldier but they do not provide for the soldier's family. Who, then, shall keep his family from want? . . . . Should it not be done at the common expense?[46]

The committee recommended the immediate establishment of a Volunteer Relief Fund through an initial appropriation of $5,000. A committee to be appointed by the Common Council would have supervision over the fund and would divide the city into districts, appointing one or more subcommittees to take charge of relief in each district. Applicants were to be scrupulously investigated by these district subcommittees, which would determine the amount of relief required in each case. The Common Council responded favorably to the report, modifying it only in one important particular by giving the mayor the power of appointing the central committee. A Volunteer Relief Committee, consisting of five aldermen, was forthwith appointed by Mayor George H. Thacher.[47] Soon after its establishment the Volunteer Relief Committee began negotiating with a citizens' relief committee which had been organized under private auspices. As a result of these negotiations it was decided that both committees should act together in extending relief to soldiers' families under the name Joint Military Relief Committee. The city was divided into eight districts, each under the special charge of two or more members of the Joint Committee, whose duty it was to investigate personally every application for relief in their district. Relief payments were to be made weekly.[48] During the first year of activity the Joint Committee disbursed $50,609, of which $30,000 had been appropriated by the Common Council, the remainder representing contributions from private sources. An average number of 435 families were relieved each week.[49] A report of disbursements during the week ending June 3, 1861, indicates that the highest amount allowed to a family was six dollars weekly, with the great majority of families receiving between two and four dollars a week.[50] The Joint Military Relief Committee disbanded in the spring of 1862. On June 16 of the same year the Common Council appointed a new Military Relief Committee consisting of the entire Board of Aldermen, each alderman to have charge of relief in his own ward. An initial sum of $5,000 was placed at the disposal of the new committee.[51] An additional $1,000, to be disbursed by the same committee among families of soldiers killed in action, was voted on October 20, 1862.[52]

The system of dispensing relief through the aldermen proved unsatisfactory, probably because of the political implications involved. On January 26, 1863, the Common Council appropriated $5,000, which it placed in the hands of the mayor and the city overseer of the poor to be disbursed by them in cash or in kind among soldiers' families in need of relief, at a rate not exceeding two dollars weekly per family. This sum was exhausted in less than six weeks.[53] No special provision for the distribution of relief to soldiers' families was made thereafter, such relief being handled by the overseer of the poor as a part of his general relief functions.

Vast sums of money were expended by other communities throughout the state for the relief of needy families of soldiers. Appropriations for such relief usually were made simultaneously with the granting of bounties to the soldiers themselves. Scores of acts were passed by the legislature in the war period enabling county, city, and local authorities to raise funds for these purposes. On May 17, 1863, the legislature enacted a law declaring that the supervisor, town clerk, and justices of the peace in each town and the Common Council in each city should constitute a board of relief for their respective localities. The boards of relief were vested with power to extend aid to the indigent families of soldiers, whether volunteer or drafted, the cost of such relief to be a local charge.[54]

Figures presented by the State Bureau of Military Affairs in its annual report for 1867, based on incomplete returns from county, city, and town authorities, show that during the war a total of over $7,600,000 in public funds was expended for the support of soldiers' families.[55] This represented a huge outlay for those times. The whole amount paid by state, county, city, and town authorities up to December, 1865, for "bounties, fees and expenses, interest on loans, and for support of soldiers' families" reached the staggering sum of $114,212,000.[56]

Considerable sums were also raised and disbursed by private charitable organizations in connection with various aspects of war relief. In all parts of the state, as elsewhere in the Union, ladies' aid societies were formed to furnish bandages, shirts, blankets, and other supplies for the soldiers at the front. It is interesting to note that the work of the Women's Central Relief Association of New York, organized in April, 1861, led to the creation of the United States Sanitary Commission in June, 1861. The Sanitary Commission was a national society enjoying semipublic status, although supported entirely by private funds. Its major task was to co-ordinate the work of voluntary agencies in giving medical aid to the army, supplementing the work of the Army Medical Department, and to advise the government authorities on sanitary problems connected with the conduct of the war.[57] Bazaars and fairs for war charities were held everywhere. Concerts, exhibitions, and large-scale collection campaigns constituted other methods of raising funds.

AID TO WOUNDED AND DISABLED SOLDIERS

As the war progressed the public authorities were confronted with the increasingly serious problem of providing care for wounded and disabled soldiers returning from the front. A considerable number of these men, discharged from the army because of wounds or sickness, were unable to perform any work. While in service they had been drawing pay and their families usually could obtain special relief. Both these sources of aid were now withheld from them.

To be sure, the Congress of the United States in 1861 had passed an act entitling any volunteer wounded or disabled in the service to all the benefits enjoyed by persons disabled in the regular service. Unfortunately, however, Congress had neglected to implement this act with an appropriation. In order to alleviate the situation, the state legislature appropriated in 1862 the sum of $30,000 for the transportation, care, and hospital needs of the sick and wounded soldiers of the state.[58] Of this amount only $15,000 was spent the first year. Most of the money was used in adapting the Albany military barracks to hospital purposes and in fitting up the Central Park barracks in New York and quarters at Rikers' Island in the East River for the reception of sick and wounded soldiers.

An additional sum of $15,000 for medical aid was appropriated in 1863. But the number of sick and wounded soldiers was increasing to such an extent that later in the year the state legislature appropriated $200,000 to provide transportation to and from their homes for sick, wounded, and discharged soldiers. The appropriating act authorized the governor to appoint agents to have charge of these functions. These agents established offices at key points throughout the state, with the main office located in New York City. Here a "Soldiers' Depot" was opened for the accommodation of volunteers passing through the city. More than 110,000 men received relief at this one agency alone.[59]   A further appropriation of $200,000 for this purpose was made in 1865.[60]

A large number of disabled soldiers upon returning from service found themselves without friends or means of subsistence and were forced to seek refuge in the almshouses. Many states recognized their duty to provide for the men disabled in defense of the Union and were furnishing asylums for them. The first attempt to establish such a soldiers' home in New York State was made in the year 1863, when the legislature incorporated an organization headed by General Winfield Scott, for the purpose of erecting and maintaining an institution for officers and soldiers unable to support themselves because of wounds or other disabilities received while in the army. This home was never erected, however, the trustees discovering upon investigation that there were but very few soldiers in the state whose friends were willing to allow them to become inmates of an asylum. In 1865 the Common Council of Albany offered to the state government the building known as Ira Harris U.S.A. General Hospital, to be used as a temporary home for destitute and disabled soldiers until the legislature should provide for the establishment of a permanent institution.[61] This offer was accepted, and in March, 1866, the legislature enacted a law placing the "Temporary Home" in Albany under the direct supervision of the governor of New York and appropriating $70,000 for its maintenance. Additional appropriations totaling several hundred thousand dollars were made in ensuing years.[62] This institution continued in operation until June, 1869, when its inmates were transferred to the National Home for disabled soldiers in Maine.[63]

Meanwhile the New York State Department of the Grand Army of the Republic (which had been organized in 1866) was exerting constant pressure for the establishment of a permanent home for destitute and disabled veterans in New York. Owing largely to its agitation, the legislature passed chapter 873, *Laws of 1872*, incorporating the New York Soldiers' Home, to be managed by a private corporation. This institution never materialized, however, and in 1876 an act of incorporation was granted to the "Grand Army of the Republic Soldiers' Home of New York." The management of the home was placed in the hands of a self-perpetuating board of trustees acting as a corporate body, with the governor and controller of New York and the commander of the State Department of the Grand Army of the Republic serving as ex officio members.[64] According to the articles of incorporation the institution was to be built

for the reception, care, maintenance and relief of soldiers and sailors who served in the union army or navy during the war of the rebellion, from the State of New York, and received an honorable discharge therefrom, who from any cause stand in need of the care and benefits of a soldiers' home.

A site for the home was selected at Bath, in Steuben County, and funds were raised by private subscription to finance building operations. On March 11, 1878, the legislature enacted a law changing the name of the institution to the New York State Soldiers' and Sailors' Home and transferring its control to the state. The governor was authorized to name a new board of trustees, with the advice and consent of the senate. The board was to consist of nine members with the governor and attorney-general serving ex officio. Trustees were to be appointed for revolving terms of three years, all vacancies to be filled by the governor.[65] An initial appropriation of $82,361 was voted by the legislature in May, 1878, to pay off the existing indebtedness of the home, to complete and furnish the buildings, and to provide for the maintenance of its inmates.[66]

The Civil War orphaned thousands of children in New York State and created a grave problem in child welfare. A number of new orphanages were established under private and public auspices, and older institutions were expanded, as a result of the war havoc. It became necessary for the state to make large increases in appropriations to child-caring institutions. This aspect of public welfare will be treated in detail in a subsequent chapter on child care.

SUMMARY

Three different types of emergencies have been discussed in these two chapters—epidemics, depressions, and war. The great cholera epidemic of 1832 resulted in the creation of temporary health boards in many towns with local overseers of the poor serving on each board. These boards were vested with certain poor-relief responsibilities during the epidemic period. Certain local health boards created upon a temporary basis were continued as permanent bodies because of the 1832 crisis. The Buffalo board may be cited as an example. A serious poor-relief problem was created by the sickness and death of thousands of breadwinners, depriving families of their source of subsistence. Important sanitary improvements affecting the condition of the poor grew out of the experience of 1832 and later epidemic years. In general, the division of work between poor-law and health authorities in these emergencies remained ill-defined.

The depressions of 1837–43, 1854–55, and 1857–58 resulted in few permanent changes in the public welfare machinery in New York State. In the city of New York, which was hardest hit by epidemics and economic crises, ward committees of private citizens were formed during the 1837 crisis as a major instrumentality for relieving the "new" or "depression" poor. Embittered by their desperate plight a group of the unemployed staged the famous "flour riots," during which certain flour warehouses were sacked. Petitions were sent to the Common Council urging the institution of public works as an emergency measure, but little was accomplished along these lines. Soup houses constituted a favorite method of relieving the poor. The indiscriminate mass character of public outdoor relief during this period was a determining factor in inducing a number of citizens of New York City to establish the Association for Improving the Condition of the Poor in 1843. The aim of the new society was to organize relief on a personal basis with emphasis on moral rather than on material aid. It is interesting to note that the state, which took no action in behalf of the unemployed, was very active in providing various kinds of relief to merchants, bankers, and brokers, a fact which created great bitterness among the poor. Horace Greeley and others raised the slogan, "Go West!" in connection with the crisis. The unemployed were urged to move into the interior with their families, where greater opportunities awaited them.

The depression of 1854–55 was featured in New York City by a clash between the A.I.C.P. and citizens' relief committees organized on a ward basis. Sharp criticism of the ward committees was expressed by the Association on the grounds that they granted relief indiscriminately, that they tended to weaken and disrupt its own systematic work, and that they fostered the spirit of pauperism among the poor. Large grants were made by the Common Council of New York City to the ward relief committees and the A.I.C.P. Again the unemployed demanded the setting-up of public works projects, and again they met with disappointment.

The crisis of 1857–58 saw a remarkable upsurge of class-consciousness among the unemployed, especially in New York City. Pressure groups of the jobless raised militant slogans and demands, among which were "the right to work" and "the right to relief." Demonstrations and parades of unemployed workers and their allies, sometimes reaching huge proportions, became almost daily occurrences, and the public authorities expressed fear of riots or even of revolution. There is no doubt that the militant character of the workers' demonstrations forced public officials to give serious consideration to the problems of the unemployed and to their proposals for public works as a means of solving them. The Common Council made several provisions for public works, including an appropriation of $250,000 for work on the recently purchased Central Park, but owing to legal technicalities most of these efforts went for naught.

Public relief rolls increased considerably throughout the state during these depression periods, particularly in the large towns. Expenditures for poor relief also rose, although not in the same degree as the relief rolls, indicating a lesser per capita allowance for relief during hard times.

Millions of dollars were spent by counties, cities, and towns in New York State for the relief of indigent families of soldiers during the Civil War. Methods of dispensing such relief varied. In New York City a special fund for this purpose was created by the Common Council and at first was disbursed through a private organization, the Union Defense Committee. Later appropriations for the relief of soldiers' families were distributed through ward committees consisting of the alderman and councilmen of each ward acting jointly with citizens appointed by the Union Defense Committee. Objections were raised against this method of dispensing relief on the ground that it lent itself to manipulation for political purposes by the elected officials who controlled it. In Albany a Volunteer Relief Fund was created by the Common Council and was administered by a joint committee including aldermen and members of a private citizens' committee. Later the Fund was administered solely by the Common Council, each alderman having charge of relief in his own ward. Objections to this system led to the transfer of disbursing power to the mayor and the overseer of the poor, and subsequently this form of relief was placed in the hands of the overseer alone, along with other categories of relief.

Beginning with 1862, the state legislature appropriated several hundred thousand dollars to provide transportation and care of sick and wounded discharged soldiers to and from their homes. The governor was authorized to appoint agents for this purpose, and agencies were established in key points throughout the state. The main agency was located in New York City, which alone afforded relief and care to more than 110,000 men. Many state laws were passed during the war enabling localities to raise funds for the relief of sick, destitute, and disabled ex-soldiers.

Long before the war reached its conclusion the public authorities were faced with the problem of special institutional care for destitute and disabled veterans mustered out of service. Efforts to organize a State Soldiers' Home in New York State failed in 1863 after articles of incorporation had actually been legislated. In 1865 the city of Albany offered to place at the disposal of the state a hospital building to be used as a temporary home for soldiers until a permanent institution should be established. This offer was accepted, and the "Temporary Home" in Albany was operated under state auspices until 1869, when its inmates were transferred to a National Home in Maine. A Soldiers' Home under private auspices was again incorporated in 1872, but failed to materialize. Four years later the activities of the Grand Army of the Republic led to the establishment of a similar corporation, which selected a site for the institution at Bath, New York, and commenced building operations. The institution was transferred to state control in 1878, under the name, New York State Soldiers' and Sailors' Home.

BIBLIOGRAPHICAL REFERENCES

1. N.Y.A.I.C.P., *Twelfth Annual Report* (New York, 1855), p. 21.
2. *Ibid.*, p. 18.
3. N.Y.C. Bd. of Aldermen, *Documents, 1855* (New York, 1855), Vol. XXII, Doc. No. 1.
4. *Ibid.*, p. 29.
5. *Ibid.*, pp. 33, 34.
6. *Ibid.*, p. 43.
7. ———, *Proceedings, 1855* (New York, 1855), LVII, 294, 327, 386–87.
8. N. Y. C. Superintendent of Out-Door Poor, "Report," in N. Y. C. Governors of the Almshouse, *Seventh Annual Report, 1855* (New York, 1856), pp. 189–90.
9. New York State Assembly, *Documents* (79th sess. [Albany, 1856]), Vol. V, Doc. No. 214.
10. New York State Senate, *Documents* (78th sess. [Albany, 1855]), Vol. III, Doc. No. 72.
11. New York State Assembly, *Documents* (79th sess. [Albany, 1856]), Vol. V, Doc. No. 72.
12. N.Y.A.I.C.P., *Fifteenth Annual Report* (New York, 1858), p. 17.
13. ———, *Fourteenth Annual Report* (New York, 1857), p. 44.
14. Brandt, *Glimpses of New York in Previous Depressions*, p. 63.
15. *New York Times*, November 6, 1857.
16. N.Y.C. Bd. of Aldermen, *Proceedings, 1857* (New York, 1857), LXVIII, 51–52.
17. *Ibid.*, pp. 156–61.
18. *New York Times*, November 9, 1857.
19. N.Y.C. Bd. of Aldermen, *Proceedings, 1857*, LXVIII, 271–79.

20. N.Y.C. Bd. of Councilmen, *Proceedings, 1857*, LXVIII, 1004-6.
21. N.Y.C. Bd. of Aldermen, *Proceedings, 1857*, LXVIII, 266, 279; N.Y.C. Bd. of Councilmen, *Proceedings, 1857*, LXVIII, 956, 1003, 1004, 1007, 1009, 1345.
22. N.Y.C. Bd. of Commissioners of the Central Park, *Minutes, 1857–58* (New York, 1858), p. 88.
23. N.Y.A.I.C.P., *Fifteenth Annual Report*, p. 29; N.Y.C. Bd. of Aldermen, *Proceedings, 1857*, LXVIII, 340–41; N.Y.C. Bd. of Councilmen, *Proceedings, 1857*, LXVIII, 1110–11.
24. N.Y.A.I.C.P., *Fifteenth Annual Report*, p. 27.
25. *Ibid.*, pp. 57–58.
26. N.Y.C. Bd. of Governors of the Almshouse, *Minutes, 1857* (New York, 1857), pp. 631–32.
27. N.Y.A.I.C.P., *Fifteenth Annual Report*, p. 279.
28. New York State Assembly, *Documents* (82d sess. [Albany, 1859]), III, Doc. No. 101, p. 7.
29. *Ibid.* (81st sess. [Albany, 1858]), Vol. I, Doc. No. 10; *ibid.* (82d sess. [Albany, 1859]), Vol. III, Doc. No. 101.
30. Albany City Chamberlain, *Report to the Common Council* (Albany, 1857), pp. 10, 15; *ibid.*, 1858, p. 6.
31. *Alms House Affairs: Reports of the Committee of the Supervisors (with the Evidence Taken), the Majority and Minority Reports of the Committee of the Common Council, and the Petition of Wm. Hurst. Presented to the Common Council, Monday Evening, December 19, 1859* (Albany, 1859).
32. *Ibid.*, pp. 62–63.
33. Albany Common Council, *Proceedings, 1858–59*, p. 659; *ibid.*, 1860, pp. 1, 3, 237.
34. Kings Co., N.Y., Superintendents of the Poor, "Annual Report for the Year Ending July 31, 1858," in Kings County Board of Supervisors, *Documents, 1858* (Brooklyn, 1858), pp. 12, 13.
35. *Ibid.*, p. 30.
36. *Ibid.*, p. 86.
37. New York State Assembly, *Documents* (81st sess. [Albany, 1858]), I, Doc. No. 10, pp. 9–11; *ibid.* (82d sess. [Albany, 1859]), III, Doc. No. 101, p. 7.
38. Frederick Phisterer, *New York in the War of the Rebellion, 1861–65* (3d ed.; Albany, 1909), I, 282, 284.
39. New York State Bureau of Military Record, *Third Annual Report, 1866*, in New York State Assembly, *Documents* (89th sess. [Albany, 1866]), Doc. No. 71, p. 29.
40. Union Defense Committee of the Citizens of New York, *Reports, Resolutions and Documents* (New York, 1862), p. 23.
41. *Ibid.*, pp. 64, 66.
42. N.Y.C. Bd. of Aldermen, *Proceedings, 1861*, LXXXIII, 5-6.
43. N.Y.C. Bd. of Councilmen, *Proceedings, 1861*, LXXXIII, 119-23.

44. *Ibid.*, *1861–62*, LXXXIV, 389–94.
45. N.Y.C. Bd. of Aldermen, *Proceedings*, *1862*, LXXXVI, 497–99.
46. Albany Common Council, *Proceedings*, *1861*, pp. 207–8.
47. *Ibid.*, pp. 209–10.
48. *Ibid.*, *1862*, pp. 241–42.
49. *Ibid.*, pp. 243–44.
50. *Ibid.*, *1861*, p. 267.
51. *Ibid.*, *1862*, p. 264.
52. *Ibid.*, p. 420.
53. *Ibid.*, *1863*, pp. 59, 84, 85.
54. New York State, *Laws of 1863*, chap. 514.
55. New York State Bureau of Military Statistics, "Fourth Annual Report, 1867," in New York State Assembly, *Documents* (90th sess. [Albany, 1867]), X, Doc. No. 235, pp. 23–24.
56. *Ibid.*, V, 757.
57. Charles J. Stillé, *History of the United States Sanitary Commission* (Philadelphia, 1866), pp. 39–67.
58. New York State, *Laws of 1862*, chap. 458.
59. Phisterer, *op. cit.*, p. 41.
60. New York State, *Laws of 1865*, chap. 15.
61. Albany Common Council, *Proceedings*, *1865–66* (Albany, 1866), chap. 15.
62. New York State, *Laws of 1866*, chap. 185; *Laws of 1867*, chap. 255; *Laws of 1868*, chap. 717; *Laws of 1869*, chap. 822.
63. Phisterer, *loc. cit.*
64. New York State, *Laws of 1876*, chap. 270.
65. ———, *Laws of 1878*, chap. 48.
66. *Ibid.*, chap. 252.

CHAPTER XVI

IMMIGRATION AS A RELIEF PROBLEM

The depression period of 1837–43 marked the rise of a strong, organized, antiforeign movement throughout America, and particularly in New York. There was a widespread tendency to place the onus of the economic crisis and its attendant suffering upon the influx of foreigners. Over 79,000 immigrants had entered the United States in 1837, breaking all previous records. Earlier, the cholera epidemic of 1832 had also brought about hostility against foreigners, who were blamed for bringing the plague over from Europe. Native American associations sprang up in New York City and elsewhere during the 1830's, and the movement attained considerable proportions in the 1850's, following the great waves of immigration between 1845 and 1854. Nativism expressed itself politically in efforts to restrict drastically the inflow of immigrants, to lengthen greatly the time required to obtain naturalization, and to prevent the foreign born from gaining public office. "America for the Americans" was the slogan raised. The movement had a strong Protestant tinge and was directed mainly against Irish Catholics.

By 1835 nativism was very much in evidence in New York. In that year Samuel F. B. Morse, the famous artist-inventor, was a candidate for mayor on the Native American party ticket, polling 1,500 votes.* Acting jointly with the Whigs in 1837, the Native Americans succeeded in electing their candidate for mayor, Aaron Clark.

* In 1834 and 1835 Morse wrote two series of articles for New York newspapers advancing the thesis that the rise in immigration from Ireland and other Catholic countries was attributable to a Roman Catholic plot to gain control over this country in the name of a "foreign despot and dictator," the pope. The first appeared in the *New York Observer* under the pseudonym "Brutus" and was later published in pamphlet form as *Foreign Conspiracy against the Liberties of the United States*. This pamphlet enjoyed a remarkably wide circulation over a long period of years. The second series, signed "An American," appeared in the *New York Journal of Commerce* and was afterward published as a book under the title, *Imminent Dangers to the Free Institutions of the United States through Foreign Immigration*.

In their antialien propaganda the nativists leaned heavily upon the "pauper statistics" of the period, which tended to show a far greater incidence of dependency among the foreign born than among the natives in the states and cities along the Atlantic seaboard. This phenomenon had attracted the attention of poor-law officials in New York long before the rise of the nativist movement and had occasioned frequently expressed alarm among these authorities. But it remained for the nativists to play up the foreign-pauper scare for all it was worth, greatly exaggerating the real situation and seldom troubling to seek an understanding of basic factors behind the bare statistics. That the conditions surrounding immigration during that period did result in an extraordinary amount of public dependency among newly arrived foreigners cannot be gainsaid. In fact the great inflow of immigrants beginning about 1837 threatened to throw out of gear the entire poor-relief machinery in New York State and led to the establishment in 1847 of a board known as the Commissioners of Emigration—the first permanent state body with supervisory and administrative power in the field of poor relief.

Some of the conditions leading to the relatively large incidence of dependency among immigrants have already been described.* It may be well to summarize some of the major causes here. The great majority of immigrants were very poor, barely able to pay for their passage. The transatlantic passage via steerage was a terrible ordeal, frequently beset by hunger, starvation, disease, and death. Of 90,000 persons carried in British ships in 1847, 15,000 died on the passage or soon after arrival.[1] Whole passenger lists were decimated by the dread typhus or ship fever, by cholera, and other diseases. Federal legislation requiring minimum rations per passenger was not enacted until 1854; before that time many poor emigrants actually died of starvation on the long voyage across. Large numbers who survived the ordeal reached the Promised Land weak from malnutrition or racked with disease. The hospitals of New York and other eastern ports were filled to overflowing with foreigners. Large families would often arrive homeless and helpless in a strange new world after the breadwinner had been buried at sea during the westward voyage. Other immigrants were stripped of what meager funds they

* See chapter vii.

possessed soon after their arrival by various types of swindlers, extortionists, boarding-house racketeers, and common thieves who regarded these unprotected bewildered people as easy prey. The almshouse frequently was the first residence the immigrant found in America. Others were forced to apply for admission within a short time after arrival, while still others wandered penniless about the streets begging alms from passers-by. Before 1847 no effective legislation existed in New York to protect the immigrant, and until the 1880's the federal government did little or nothing to aid the immigrant in his efforts to adjust himself to his new surroundings.

It took many years of unceasing work to stamp out even the most obvious forms of immigrant exploitation. Powerful interests— steamship companies, transportation brokers, real estate interests, employers of labor—were constantly trying to prevent any legislation tending to correct abuses.

ASSISTED IMMIGRATION

As many contemporary documents prove, it was a common practice for localities in Great Britain and elsewhere to rid themselves of the necessity to support public dependents by paying their passage to America. It is certain that many poor persons who came as "assisted immigrants" made satisfactory adjustment as honest, hardworking citizens of their adopted country.[2] Others became objects of support by public or private welfare agencies.

In 1836 the United States government had occasion to make an official protest to Great Britain against a peculiar practice obtaining in the British-owned island of Jamaica. A law on the statute books of Jamaica required each foreign vessel, upon the order of the authorities, to carry at least one pauper or other undesirable person on its return voyage from Jamaica, at the rate of $10 for each such passenger. A penalty of $300 was imposed for failure to comply. Many American shipmasters were victimized by this statute, and their repeated protests to the American authorities led to extended diplomatic correspondence on the subject between the United States and Great Britain.[3]

The American consul at Leipzig wrote on March 8, 1837: "It has of late also become a general practice in the towns and boroughs of Germany, to get rid of their paupers and vicious members, by collecting the means for effectuating their passage to the United States among the inhabitants, and by supporting them from the public funds."[4] In January, 1839, *Niles' Weekly Register* reported the arrival in New York City of a number of paupers whose passage had been paid by the overseers of the poor of Edinburgh. The majority of these passengers, it was reported, still wore the uniform of the Edinburgh almshouse upon their debarkation in New York.[5] A memorial from the authorities of New York City to Congress in 1847 declared that within the year past two ships—the "Sardinia" and the "Atlas"—had arrived from Liverpool, each bearing in her steerage about 300 paupers whose expenses had been paid by their native parish of Grosszimmern in Hesse Darmstadt, Germany. According to the memorial, 234 of these immigrants were supported at the New York City almshouse.

Protests against this form of publicly subsidized "pauper emigration" were loud and frequent. In 1837 the mayor of Boston communicated with the mayors of New York City and other ports on the Atlantic seaboard recommending a joint petition to Congress, "praying for its interference to prevent the great evils arising from the influx of paupers among us."[6]

As the main gateway to America, New York City naturally was hardest hit by the impact of mass immigration upon poor-relief resources. In his opening message to the Common Council in 1837, Mayor Clark, the Native American candidate, made a lengthy reference to the problem of foreign pauperism, and on June 5 of the same year he sent a special message to the council on this question. Referring to the danger of assisted emigration, Clark condemned the practice of debarking poor passengers at certain New Jersey landing places in order to avoid posting bond for them in New York as required by the laws of the latter state. Many of these foreigners left adrift in New Jersey arrived without funds in New York City where they joined the ranks of recipients of public relief. In his message Clark painted a gloomy picture of the resulting situation:

Our streets are filled with the wandering crowds of these passengers— clustering in our city—unaccustomed to our climate; without money; without employment; without friends; many not speaking our language, and without any dependence for food, or raiment, or fireside; certain of nothing but hardship and a grave. . . . . They necessarily drive our native workmen into exile, where they must war again with the savage of the wilderness. . . . . It is apprehended they will bring disease among us; and if they have it not with them on arrival, they may generate a plague by collecting in crowds within small tenements and foul hovels. What is to become of them is a question of serious import. Our whole Alm House Department is so full that no more can be received there without manifest hazard to the health of every inmate. Petitions signed by hundreds, asking for work, are presented in vain; private associations for relief are almost wholly without funds. Thousands must therefore wander to and fro on the face of the earth, filling every part of our once happy land with squalid poverty and profligacy.[7]

The mayor's message ended with a diatribe against foreigners, who were charged with taking employment from native workers, with stealing the bread of charity rightfully belonging to native paupers, and with stirring up discontent and discord. He recommended that immigration be restricted and placed under rigid control and that a high commutation tax be imposed on all aliens arriving at the port of New York. His sentiments were indorsed by the Common Council.

A report of the Commissioners of the Almshouse, Bridewell and Penitentiary, submitted to the Common Council in September, 1837, echoed the alarmist attitude expressed by the mayor, although the commissioners exhibited a keener insight into fundamentals than the mayor had shown. Declaring that more than two-thirds of the city charges were foreigners and that there were signs that this proportion would increase, the commissioners described the unhappy immigrants as victims of a vicious band of unscrupulous individuals:

Law is set at defiance, and this metropolis forced to be the recipient of the poor objects who have been deluded from home by "agents" who draw from them the remaining hard earnings of their life, for expenses of transportation, and then shamelessly leave them a prey to want, and subjects of a despondency, produced by the reverse of what these "agents" had informed them was the demand for labor in our country.[8]

While New York City felt the brunt of the influx of poor immigrants, the problem was by no means confined to the metropolis. Other areas throughout the state were affected, albeit in lesser degree. Many assisted emigrants from the British Isles were landed in Canada and immediately made their way into New York State, as documents of the time attest. The upstate counties, particularly those along the Canadian border, were continually dunning the state legislature for reimbursement of expenses incurred in maintaining large numbers of foreign-born dependents. Artemas Simonds, an agent appointed by the Boston authorities in 1835 to make a survey of "houses of industry, correction and reformation" in the northern and middle states of the Union, reported in 1835 that he had learned that only 35 of 187 paupers admitted in 1833 to the poorhouse of Clinton County, New York, were natives, the remainder being foreign born. The overseer of the poor of Rochester informed him that fully seven-eighths of the relief applicants came from Europe. The number of alien paupers in Niagara County had risen from 33 in 1830 to 111 in 1833.[9]

Congress was frequently petitioned by various state and local authorities, acting individually and in concert, to check the inflow of alien paupers through appropriate federal legislation. On the other hand, there were many liberal statesmen who exhibited a more tolerant view toward immigration and did all in their power to encourage it. Among these was Governor William Seward of New York, who, during his service as state executive (1839–43), vigorously defended the immigrants from their maligners, pointing out their already considerable contributions to the progress of industry and agriculture in the United States.[10] Friendly sentiments toward aliens were also frequently expressed on the floor of the state legislature by statesmen appreciative of the invaluable services of the immigrant in the building of America. It was pointed out by other defenders of a liberal immigration policy that the "menace of foreign pauperism" was greatly exaggerated by antialien zealots in New York State and elsewhere. Public provision for foreigners presented a serious problem only in the larger cities like New York, Albany, and Buffalo. They also pointed to the fact that the dependency of the newcomers was usually of a temporary nature, covering the period of adjustment to a strange environment. The percentage of permanent dependency among them was relatively small. Furthermore, those who required public relief at one time or another constituted a very small proportion of the total number of immigrants arriving annually in New York.

Whatever might be the mitigating circumstances, however, dependency among immigrants reached sizeable proportions, and its prevention or alleviation was one of the great public welfare problems of the day. The situation required protective legislation for the immigrant at three major points: protection against disease and sickness on the passage to America, against illness and destitution upon his arrival, and against physical and economic disablements after arrival. Legislative protection for the emigrant on the voyage to America could be provided only through federal channels. The federal law of 1819, intended to alleviate overcrowding and unsanitary conditions aboard immigrant ships, was hopelessly inadequate, and even the few feeble regulations it contained were poorly enforced. Beginning with the late 1830's Congress was continually petitioned by municipal and state authorities along the eastern seaboard and by immigrant aid societies for the enactment of laws affording greater protection to steerage passengers. This was particularly true during the decade 1845–54, a period marked by great tidal waves of immigration. More than 114,000 immigrants landed on our shores in 1845, and the annual influx rose until it reached 427,833 in 1854, a record which remained unsurpassed until 1873.[11] Immigration in this decade alone was three times greater than that of the preceding half-century. Ireland and the German states accounted for the preponderant part of the incoming tide. Famine, particularly that following the disastrous potato blight of 1846, was a major factor in the Irish migration, while the failure of the revolutionary movement of 1848 sent hundreds of thousands of Germans—representing in many instances the best blood of the old country—flocking to America. Over 1,512,000 Irish immigrants arrived here in the years 1845–54, while 1,226,392 Germans landed during the same period.[12]

Reference has already been made to the disease-breeding conditions aboard the ships which brought most of these Irish, German, and other immigrants to American ports. When the great influx began in 1845, a tremendous strain was placed on the hospital resources of New York by the numerous casualties of the transatlantic voyage. The constant threat of epidemics attributable to diseases contracted by steerage passengers en route to America was another very alarming factor. In 1847 both the New York State Legislature and the New York City Common Council sent urgent petitions to Congress recommending immediate enactment of a law effectively regulating health conditions aboard immigrant ships.[13] Referring to conditions on these ships as "shocking to our sense of humanity and disgraceful to any country," the memorial of the state legislature proposed the passage of a law that would limit and define the number of passengers for each vessel according to her tonnage, require a definite quantity of provisions and water for each person on the voyage, make mandatory the presence of a physician aboard each vessel, and, finally, include "such other regulations as may be thought necessary or proper to prevent the great and crying evils which at present so often occur." In response to these and other petitions, Congress enacted a law on February 22, 1847, superseding the act of 1819 and aimed primarily at alleviating overcrowded conditions. This law, like its predecessors, soon proved grossly inadequate as a remedial measure. A new federal statute was passed May 17, 1848, requiring a certain allotment of open-deck space per passenger in addition to limiting the number of passengers according to tonnage. On March 3, 1855, this act was supplemented by another which remained in force for almost thirty years. While the latter contained much broader provisions than previous statutes, it apparently did not gain the ends toward which it was directed.

Theoretically [says a report of the United States Immigration Commission in 1910] the law of 1855 provided for increased air space, better ventilation, and improved accommodations in the way of berths, cooking facilities, the serving of food, free open-deck space, and so forth. Although the evil of overcrowding, which had been attended with such disastrous results in former years, appears to have been especially aimed at by the makers of the law, the wording of the act was, unfortunately, such that the provisions relating to the number of passengers to be carried were inoperative, and there was practically no legal restraint in this regard, as far as the United States law was concerned, between 1855 and 1882.[14]

The legislation of the United States regulating conditions on immigrant ships, it should be noted, was supplemented by similar regulations in England and other countries during this period.

Meanwhile a serious health situation was developing because of the lack of adequate hospital facilities in New York and other ports for the many sick immigrants requiring treatment immediately upon landing or soon thereafter. Before 1847 the only special provisions for the care of immigrants were contained in the state and local laws governing quarantine and poor relief. The state maintained the Marine Hospital at Quarantine for passengers suffering from communicable diseases or otherwise so sick as to require immediate care. The hospital was supported by the Mariners' Fund built up by a head tax imposed on passengers and crews of seagoing vessels arriving in New York. By the terms of the original law of 1797 the head tax had been fixed at $1.00 for captains and cabin passengers, 50 cents for steerage passengers and mates, and 25 cents for common sailors. But the head tax was changed several times in subsequent years, and an act of 1845 set it at $1.50 for every captain, $2.00 for every cabin passenger, 50 cents for each steerage passenger, and $1.00 for each mate and sailor.[15] Although the original and exclusive purpose of the head tax was to provide hospitalization for sick passengers and sailors at the port of New York, large portions of the proceeds were diverted to other purposes. Part of it was annually applied toward the support of the House of Refuge and other charitable institutions in New York City through special acts of the legislature.

In 1843 the New York Common Council addressed a memorial to the legislature protesting against this diversion of money from the Mariners' Fund. It was charged that provision for sick immigrants at the Marine Hospital was seriously inadequate and that all the money received through the Fund should be utilized in expanding hospital facilities for the immigrants to whom it rightfully belonged. The memorialists pointed out that the surplus of the Mariners' Fund, after deducting $8,000 annually earmarked toward the support of the House of Refuge, had amounted to $117,000 during the last three years. Instead of being used for immigrant relief this surplus had been distributed by the state to various private charitable institutions and agencies. It was also recommended by the memorialists that immigrants be entitled to the services of the Marine Hospital for at least two years following their arrival, instead of the existing provision that medical aid be afforded only immediately upon arrival.[16] No concrete results were obtained by this memorial. It had evidently been the intention of the Common Council in seeking legislative action to relieve the pressure on city-supported hospitals created by the needs of foreigners who fell sick after arriving in New York and were barred from treatment at the Marine Hospital. It should be emphasized that no provision was made out of the Mariners' Fund for passengers who required types of assistance other than medical aid upon arrival or who fell sick or destitute afterward. The city was receiving at the time an annual state grant of $10,000 toward the support and care of foreign poor,* but this covered only a small fraction of the municipal expenditures for relieving this class of indigents.†

Besides the head tax the state required masters of vessels coming from a foreign country or a state other than New York to post a bond of $300 for each alien passenger to indemnify the authorities of the port of New York and of other localities within the state against such passenger becoming a public charge. The vague procedure used in bonding passengers proved irksome to honest shipowners and provided many loopholes for those who were unscrupulous. One very unfortunate effect of the bonding system was the rise of bond brokers who took over, for a consideration, the responsibility for indemnifying passengers. To avoid forfeiting bond money in cases where immigrants became destitute or sick, some of these brokers resorted to the practice of maintaining private poorhouses and hospitals on the outskirts of New York for indemnified persons who would otherwise have to become public charges. Accommodations afforded at these places were not fit for animals to live in, and the situation became so scandalous as to result in a great public demand for an investigation. In response to this demand the Common Council conducted several inquiries into the private almshouses and hospitals. Particularly shocking conditions of filth and overcrowding were revealed by a committee of the Board of Assistant

* This annual grant of $10,000, which had been voted in 1817 in lieu of the auction moneys previously assigned to New York City for the support of the foreign poor, was finally suspended in 1850.

† According to the poor-law statistics for 1843, 4,934 persons, of whom 3,077 were foreigners, received public relief in New York City at a total cost of $192,909 (New York State Senate, *Documents* [67th sess. (Albany, 1844)], Vol. II, Doc. No. 73).

Aldermen in February, 1846, following the investigation of one of these institutions known as "Tapscott's Poor House and Hospital" conducted by the brokerage firm of W. & J. T. Tapscott. Needy immigrants were herded in filthy rooms, the sick and the well together, and forced to eat tainted food. Children died at the institution for lack of proper attention. As a result of its investigation the committee recommended the abolition of poorhouses and hospitals managed by passenger brokers.

The proprietors are certainly not likely to provide liberally for the necessities, much less the comforts, of a household which is a constant source of individual trouble and expense. The same selfishness that would induce them to evade relieving the applicants, would dictate the reduction of their fare when admitted to the Work-house, to the lowest standard, both of quality and quantity.[17]

Ordinances were enacted from time to time by the New York City authorities with the aim of mitigating the more glaring abuses practiced upon the newcomers. These ordinances, however, emasculated through the machinations of powerful groups who were waxing fat at the expense of the immigrant, usually accomplished little or nothing in his behalf.

The plight of many poor immigrants after landing made a deep impression on contemporaries. A report of the almshouse commissioner of New York City in January, 1847, described the immigrants as exhibiting

so sickening a picture of human destitution and suffering as no pen, however eloquent in the sad gloom of misfortune's description, could well paint in illustration of the dark and solemn truth. . . . . Many of them had far better have been cast into the deep sea, than linger in the pangs of hunger, sickness and pain, to draw their last agonizing breath in the streets of New York.[18]

In his diary for January, 1837, Philip Hone drew an equally pessimistic picture of the condition of poor immigrants in New York. Pointing to the ever present contrast of luxury and squalid misery in the city, he emphasized the "sights of woe with which we are assailed in the streets" where newly arrived foreigners were begging for alms—"indigent and helpless, having expended the last shilling in paying their passage-money, deceived by the misrepresentations of unscrupulous agents, and left to starve amongst strangers, who,

finding it impossible to extend relief to all, are deterred from assisting any."[19]

The inhumanities and indignities, the frauds and extortions, that
were practiced on the immigrant finally led to the crystallization of
a considerable sentiment in favor of protective state legislation that
would not only benefit the stranger but would result in the savings
of public money which otherwise would have to be expended for his
relief. As stated by Friedrich Kapp, a contemporary authority on
immigration, the legislative problem was

to protect the newcomer, to prevent him from being robbed, to facilitate his
passage through the city to the interior, to aid him with good advice, and, in
cases of the most urgent necessity, to furnish him with a small amount of money;
in short, not to treat him as a pauper with the ultimate view of making him an
inmate of the Almshouse, but as an independent citizen, whose future career
would become interwoven with the best interests of the country.[20]

Finally, on May 5, 1847, the state legislature enacted a law "concerning passengers in vessels coming to the city of New York,"
which had a marked effect on the treatment of poor immigrants in
this state. Certain sections of the act were substantially reaffirma-
tions of the provisions of the passenger act of 1824. Masters of
vessels arriving at the port of New York from any other state or
country were required to present a detailed report to the mayor or
his deputy within twenty-four hours of arrival, stating the name,
place of birth, last legal residence, age, and occupation of every alien
passenger. The report was further to specify "whether any of said
passengers so reported are lunatic, idiot, deaf and dumb, blind or
infirm, and if so, whether they are accompanied by relatives likely
to be able to support them."[21] A forfeit of $75.00 was to be paid for
each passenger omitted in the report or falsely described therein.
A commutation tax of $1.00 was to be paid by the shipmaster to
the city chamberlain for each person or passenger reported.

The most important feature of the act was the creation of a
Board of Commissioners of Emigration, which may be regarded as
the first permanent state body authorized to administer some aspect
of poor relief. The Board consisted of six unpaid commissioners
serving rotating terms ranging from two to six years. The original
six commissioners were named in the act, with the provision that the

governor thenceforth should appoint individuals to fill vacancies as they occurred. In addition it was specified that the mayors of New York City and Brooklyn and the presidents of the Irish Emigrant Society and the German Society should serve on the board ex officio.*

If, upon inspection of the ship's passengers, there should be found among them persons who were likely to become public charges because of insanity, feeble-mindedness, or other causes, the master of the vessel was to be required to post a bond of $300 for each such person, in order to indemnify every city, town, and county within the state from any cost or charge incurred should he become a public charge within five years after entry.

The task of inspecting ships upon arrival for the purpose of seeing if there were potential public charges aboard was delegated to the commissioners, who were given charge of the commutation and bond money. Out of these funds they were required to pay for the support or maintenance of all foreigners becoming public charges in New York State within five years after commutation money had been paid for them or a bond posted in their behalf. They were to "prescribe such rules and regulations as they shall deem proper, for the purpose of ascertaining the right, and the amount of the claim of any city, town or county, to indemnity" under the provisions of the act. The Commissioners of Emigration were also given control over the money collected from passengers by the health commissioners of the port of New York for the Mariners' Fund. Besides being empowered to use the funds under their control for the relief of their charges, they were authorized to make expenditures for removing such persons from one part of the state to another part or to another state, or for "assisting them to procure employment, and thus prevent them from becoming a public charge." The commissioners were further empowered to apply any part of the funds to the purchase or lease of property or the erection of any building which they might deem necessary for their purposes. The Marine Hospital located on

* The original Commissioners of Emigration were Julian C. Verplanck, James Boorman, Jacob Harvey, Robert B. Minturn, William F. Havemeyer, David C. Colden, Mayor William V. Brady of New York, Mayor Francis B. Stryker of Brooklyn, Leopold Bierwirth, president of the German Society, and Gregory Dillon, president of the Irish Emigrant Society.

Staten Island for the use of sick immigrants was placed under their supervision.

The statute creating the Commissioners of Emigration and defining their duties was far from perfect. For example, it made no provision for immigrants coming into the state by way of Canada. Such persons who became destitute remained a charge upon the local communities as before. The counties along the Canadian border made vigorous protests against this situation and demanded an immediate remedy. The legislature responded to this demand in December, 1847, by enacting chapter 431, extending certain provisions applicable to the port of New York to ports and landing places in northern New York, including Lakes Erie and Ontario and the St. Lawrence and Niagara rivers. Masters of vessels landing passengers at such places were to report to the heads of the city or village or to an overseer of the poor of the town in which the port of landing was situated, in the same manner as in the port of New York, and were to pay one dollar in commutation money for every person or passenger reported. The funds so obtained were to be turned over to the county superintendents of the poor, who were to use the money for the maintenance and support of destitute or sick foreigners. Passengers who became public charges in any city, town, or village of the state within three years after entry at the ports along the aforementioned waterways were to be chargeable to the superintendents of the poor of the county where they had landed.

Chapter 483 of the *Laws of 1847* authorized the Commissioners of Emigration to take charge of the personal property of emigrants dying on the ocean passage or at the Marine Hospital and leaving minor children. Such property was to be managed solely for the benefit of the orphan minors. An amendment passed in 1849 gave the commissioners the same powers and authority in protecting the interests of illegitimate children of immigrant women under their charge as were held by the municipal poor-law authorities.[22] Chapter 523 of the *Laws of 1851* extended this authority to all poor children "actually chargeable upon or receiving support from" the Commissioners of Emigration.

Organized on May 8, 1847, the Commissioners of Emigration were immediately confronted with a host of difficulties. There was constant friction between the commissioners and the health officers of the port of New York concerning the divided authority over the Marine Hospital. Several years passed before additional legislation clarified the division of responsibility. In 1849 a decision of the United States Supreme Court invalidated the state law imposing head taxes on immigrants, on the ground that such state laws violated the right of Congress to regulate commerce, that they infringed on existing treaties, and that it was presumptuous of states to tax immigrants when Congress had intentionally permitted them free entry in order to encourage immigration. An additional factor cited in the Supreme Court decision was that a large portion of the head-tax money—the collection of which was being justified as a means of financing health measures—was diverted to the House of Refuge for Juvenile Delinquents, which had no relation to the health of immigrants who paid the tax.[23]

In April, 1849—within a few days after the Supreme Court decision was rendered—the New York legislature enacted a law requiring of each shipmaster a five-year bond of $300 for every passenger landing at the port of New York. This bond could be commuted for $1.50 within three days after the landing of such passenger.[24] Of course payment of the commutation fee was invariably preferred to the posting of bond. By this device, which served the same purpose as a head tax, while apparently avoiding constitutional difficulties, funds were once more made available to the Commissioners of Emigration for the maintenance of the Marine Hospital and for other purposes. The same act required, in addition to the commutation money, an indemnity bond of $500 covering a period of ten years for all "lunatic, idiot, deaf, dumb, blind or infirm persons not members of emigrating families or who from attending circumstances are likely to become permanently a public charge, or who have been paupers in any other country, or who from sickness or disease, existing at the time of departing from the foreign port are, or are likely soon to become a public charge."

An amendment enacted in 1851 extended the list of immigrants requiring special indemnity bonds to include the maimed, persons above the age of sixty years, widows with children, husbandless women with children, and "any person unable to take care of himself or herself without becoming a public charge."[25] As before, a bond of $500 in addition to the commutation money was required for those in the "undesirable" categories, but the period of indemnity was reduced from ten to five years. It was directed in the act of 1851 that all commutation and bond money be expended exclusively upon persons in whose behalf it was paid. Passengers leaving New York State and absenting themselves therefrom for more than a year were deprived of the right to be helped by the Commissioners of Emigration.

From the first the funds collected by the commissioners were never sufficient to satisfy the claims of local poor-law officials in New York State for reimbursement of expenditures for the support of foreigners within their jurisdictions. As a result the commissioners were constantly faced with the problem of how to distribute the available funds equally among the claimants. Authorities of upstate counties and towns were continually accusing the immigration officials of favoring New York City in making allocations. They demanded a greater share of the commutation funds. In 1853 the state legislature attempted a partial solution to this problem by raising the commutation money from $1.50 to $2.00 for each passenger, and provided that 50 cents of every such sum collected should be set aside as a separate fund "for the benefit of each and every county in this state except the county of New York."[26] This part of the commutation money was to be distributed among the several counties concerned every three months.*

The passage of this measure failed to solve the financial problems of the Commissioners of Emigration. The funds at their disposal still were not sufficient to take care of all the needy immigrants properly chargeable to them. Another financial difficulty arose from the fact that the amount of the funds in any given year was highly uncertain, since it depended upon the number of immigrants arriving at the port of New York, which varied greatly from year to year. Sources of funds would tend to contract at precisely the periods when the demands upon the commissioners were greatest, particu-

* The commutation money was again raised in 1869 from $2.00 to $2.50. In 1875 the United States Supreme Court rendered a decision again declaring the New York commutation system unconstitutional, putting an end to the practice.

larly in depression years. For example, the number of alien immigrants arriving at the port of New York fell from 319,223 in 1854 to 136,233 in 1855, owing to the existing economic crisis, which discouraged emigration from Europe to this country. Immigrants arriving in New York increased gradually through 1856 and 1857, totaling 183,773 during the latter year, but the number fell precipitately to less than 79,000 in 1858—when news of the new economic crisis had reached Europe. Immigration remained on a relatively low level during the Civil War years, rising above the 200,000 mark only after the termination of the conflict.[27] Income from commutation money declined correspondingly in these emergency periods when it was needed most.

A large part of the funds had to be applied by the commissioners to the treatment of sick immigrants, many of whom had to be placed in hospitals as soon as they debarked. As has been noted, the property of the Marine Hospital at Quarantine was transferred to the commissioners for this purpose. The hospital buildings soon became overcrowded, however. Persons afflicted with milder diseases were placed in the same rooms with those having contagious diseases. The situation became intolerable. Hundreds of the immigrants were sent to private hospitals, others to city hospitals, and still others to the almshouses. So rapidly did the number of sick immigrants increase that the commissioners had to apply to the federal government for permission to use the public stores at Staten Island and the public buildings at Bedloe Island for hospital purposes. These improvised hospitals proved wholly inadequate to receive the sick.

To provide sufficient accommodation for all the needy sick in their charge the commissioners then decided to erect new hospital buildings at Ward's Island, which was selected as a suitable location because of its accessibility during all the seasons of the year. An old five-story building on the island, originally planned as a factory, was leased by the commissioners in 1847 and remodeled for use as a hospital. Beside it a two-story shack was built, to serve as a "refuge" for immigrants who could not find employment or were unable to work. At a short distance from this building still another structure was erected and was occupied as a hospital on November 1, 1848, with accommodation for 250 patients. A nursery for immigrant children was also built about the same time. In subsequent years the Commissioners of Emigration purchased and leased many acres on Ward's Island and continually expanded the facilities for sick and destitute immigrants under their charge.[28] By the act of April 11, 1849, the Marine Hospital at Quarantine was restricted exclusively to the reception of cases of contagious and infectious disease.[29] All other cases were cared for at the Emigrant Refuge and Hospital on Ward's Island.

The annual report of the Commissioners of Emigration for 1852 affords us an insight into the scope of their activities and the difficulties encountered in carrying on their work. During that year 340,144 passengers landed in New York, of whom 300,992 were aliens. A severe epidemic of typhus or ship fever raged among these immigrants in the winter of 1852, and cholera and smallpox also made their appearance in the establishments at Quarantine and Ward's Island. A total of 8,887 persons were treated for various diseases at the Marine Hospital. More than 15,000 were cared for at the Emigrant Refuge and Hospital on Ward's Island. Several hundred sick immigrants under the charge of the commissioners were sent to private hospitals in New York City; 355 who were mentally ill were committed to the municipal Lunatic Asylum. Temporary relief, consisting in many cases only of a night's lodging and two meals, was provided for more than 117,000 individuals by the immigration commissioners. The cost of 763 interments of outdoor poor in the city of New York and the expense of forwarding over 4,000 immigrants to inland destinations were charged to the commissioners in whole or in part. The cost of supporting or removing 18,432 aliens in or from the several upstate counties was also charged to them.[30]

The total receipts of the Commissioners of Emigration from all sources in 1852 amounted to $572,529, including $455,236 in commutation money. Expenditures for the same year totaled $569,516. At the end of the year, however, an indebtedness of over $200,000 was charged against the Commissioners of Emigration, including unpaid reimbursements to county superintendents of the poor amounting to $55,104, a debt of $19,200 to the New York City almshouse officials, and a loan of $130,000 contracted that year under the authority of a state law.[31]

The extent of the financial reimbursements made by the Commissioners of Emigration is indicated by the fact that during the years 1847–60 total reimbursements of $658,280 were made by them to poor-law authorities in the several upstate counties and cities, and $97,882 was reimbursed to the New York City authorities, while nearly $100,000 was paid to various orphan asylums, hospitals, and other charitable institutions under private operation for the care and support of immigrants chargeable to the commissioners.[32]

Among other functions the Commissioners of Emigration were expected to give practical advice to newly arrived immigrants regarding problems of adjustment, to help them get to their destinations in the interior with as much dispatch as possible, to aid them in procuring lodgings and employment whenever possible, and above all to give them much-needed protection against the swarm of parasites—boarding-house runners, unscrupulous transportation agents, and others. These worthies would pounce upon the unsuspecting strangers as soon as they landed, or even while they were still aboard ship. Early in their labors the commissioners discovered that they could offer immigrants little or no protection against the various frauds practiced upon them as long as they had no effective supervision over their landing. At the time there was no central immigrant depot; newcomers landed at whatever pier their boat docked. The commissioners therefore petitioned the legislature to authorize them "to lease a dock or pier where all immigrants could be landed and which no outsiders would be allowed to enter without the permission of the Commissioners." Such authorization was granted by an act of the legislature on April 11, 1848.[33] Owing to various complications, however, the immigration commissioners were unable to establish a permanent landing-depot until 1855. On May 5 of that year they leased the old fort at the foot of Manhattan, known as Castle Garden,* and proceeded to convert it into a landing depot for all immigrants arriving at the port of New York. It was formally opened on August 1, 1855. The operation of this depot served to eliminate or mitigate many of the abuses to which the immigrant had been subjected and aided him immeasurably in getting a fair start in the New World. It continued in operation until 1891, when

* The old fort now serves as the municipal aquarium.

an act of Congress placed immigration at the port of New York under federal supervision. The Commissioners of Emigration of New York State ceased to function as a result of this statute. In 1892 Ellis Island was opened as the landing-place for immigrants under federal control, superseding Castle Garden.

SUMMARY

Mass immigration during this period brought in its wake grave problems in public health and poor relief. A widespread hostility toward immigrants found political expression in the Native American movement which sprang up in the 1830's and was particularly strong in the 1850's following the great Irish and German influx of the decade 1845–54. Poor-relief authorities were alarmed by the large proportion of dependency among foreigners in the port cities and the states along the Atlantic seaboard, especially in New York. Most of the immigrants were poverty-stricken and became destitute immediately upon arrival or soon thereafter. Many were stricken by disease on the long grueling voyage via steerage in overcrowded, unsanitary immigrant ships and needed public care and support upon landing. Others were stripped of their meager possessions by the various types of swindlers and thieves who lay in wait for the bewildered immigrant. Urgent demands arose for state and federal legislation regulating immigration that would remove from the local communities the mounting burden of public relief to destitute and sick immigrants. Finally, in 1847, the New York legislature created a Board of Commissioners of Emigration charged with the responsibility of reimbursing local communities in New York for relief granted to certain categories of foreigners. Funds for this and other purposes were to come out of the head taxes and indemnity bonds imposed on immigrants and crews of vessels arriving at the port of New York. The immigration commissioners were also given control of the Marine Hospital at Quarantine and other buildings designed for the care of sick and destitute immigrants. This Board may be considered as the first permanent state body vested with administrative power in a certain category of poor relief. The state head tax on immigrants was declared unconstitutional by the United States Supreme Court in 1849, but a commutation fee was immediately imposed as a substitute, serving as a source of funds for the immigration commissioners until 1875, when it too was declared unconstitutional. Shipmasters were required to post a $500 bond to indemnify localities in New York State against certain classes of passengers becoming public charges within a period which was at first set at ten years after arrival and later reduced to five years. The classes for whom indemnity bonds were required included mentally and physically handicapped persons and husbandless women with children.

As a means of more effectively protecting immigrants against unscrupulous boarding-house keepers, runners, transportation agents, and other parasitic types, a central landing-depot for all immigrants arriving in the port of New York was established in 1855 at Castle Garden, a remodeled fort located at the foot of Manhattan Island. Here the immigrants were given advice by the commissioners and their agents on matters of lodging, employment, transportation, and safety of baggage, and were also afforded material aid in cases where it was needed. The State Board of Commissioners of Emigration functioned until 1891, when it was superseded by federal immigration authorities under a Congressional act of that year. The following year Ellis Island was opened as the central immigrant depot under federal supervision.

BIBLIOGRAPHICAL REFERENCES

1. Samuel P. Orth, *Immigration and Labor*, "Chronicles of America Series" (New Haven, 1926), XIX, 112.
2. Examples illustrating this fact may be found in G. Poulett Scrope, *Extracts of Letters from Poor Persons Who Emigrated Last Year to Canada and the United States, Printed for the Information of the Labouring Poor, and Their Friends in This Country* (London, 1832).
3. U.S. President, *Foreign Paupers: Message Transmitting Information Required by the Resolution of the House of Representatives in Relation to the Introduction of Foreign Paupers into the United States*, in U.S. House, *Documents* (25th Cong., 2d sess., 1837-38), Vol. X, Doc. No. 370.
4. *Ibid.*
5. *Niles' Weekly Register*, January 19, 1839, p. 322.
6. New York City Corporation, *Paupers and Criminals: Memorial*, in U.S. House, *Documents* (29th Cong., 2d sess., 1846-47), Vol. III, Doc. No. 54; *ibid.* (25th Cong., 2d sess., 1837-38), Vol. X, Doc. No. 370.
7. N.Y.C. Bd. of Aldermen, *Documents, 1837-38*, IV, Doc. No. 10, p. 71.
8. *Ibid.*, Doc. No. 32, p. 221.

9. *Niles' Weekly Register*, October 3, 1835, p. 69.
10. See the annual messages of Governor Seward to the legislature, 1839, 1840, 1842, in *Messages from the Governors*, III, 728–29, 802–4, 1039.
11. Frederick C. Croxton, *Statistical Review of Immigration, 1820–1910*, in U.S. Immigration Commission, *Reports* (Washington, D.C., 1911), *Sen. Doc. No. 756* (61st Cong., 3d sess.), III, 4.
12. Friedrich Kapp, *Immigration, and the Commissioners of Emigration of the State of New York* (New York, 1870), pp. 13–14.
13. New York State Assembly, *Journal* (70th sess. [Albany, 1847]), I, 165, 280; U.S. House, *Documents* (29th Cong., 2d sess., 1846–47), Vol. III, Doc. No. 54.
14. U.S. Immigration Commission, *Abstract of Report on Steerage Legislation, 1819–1909* (Washington, D.C., 1910), p. 11.
15. New York State, *Laws of 1845*, chap. 227.
16. New York State Assembly, *Documents* (66th sess. [Albany, 1843]), Vol. VI, Doc. No. 139.
17. N.Y.C. Bd. of Assistant Aldermen, *Proceedings and Documents, 1845–46*, XXVII, Doc. No. 20, p. 120.
18. Moses G. Leonard, "Communication to the Committee on Laws of the New York City Common Council," in N.Y.C. Corporation, *Paupers and Criminals, Memorial*, pp. 8–9.
19. *Hone, Philip, Diary of, 1828–1851*, ed. Allan Nevins (New York, 1927), II, 785.
20. Kapp, *op. cit.*, p. 85.
21. New York State, *Laws of 1847*, chap. 195.
22. ———, *Laws of 1849*, chap. 350.
23. Passenger Cases: *Smith* v. *Turner, Health-Commissioner of the Port of New York*, and *Norris* v. *City of Boston (1849)*, 7 How. 283. Extracts from these decisions may be found in Abbott, *Historical Aspects of the Immigration Problem*, pp. 151–60.
24. New York State, *Laws of 1849*, Chap. 350.
25. ———, *Laws of 1851*, chap. 523.
26. ———, *Laws of 1853*, chap. 224.
27. Kapp, *op. cit.*, pp. 232–33.
28. *Ibid.*, pp. 125–51; New York State Commissioners of Emigration, *Third Annual Report for the Year 1849*, in their *Annual Reports from the Organization of the Commission, May 5, 1847, to 1860, Inclusive* (New York, 1861), pp. 48–52.
29. New York State, *Laws of 1849*, chap. 350.
30. New York State Commissioners of Emigration, *Sixth Annual Report for the Year 1852*, in their *Annual Reports*, pp. 111–32.
31. *Ibid.*
32. *Ibid.*, Appen., Table E, opp. p. 354.
33. New York State, *Laws of 1848*, chap. 219.

CHAPTER XVII

DELINQUENT, NEGLECTED, AND DEPENDENT CHILDREN

The first great event in child welfare during this period was the opening on January 1, 1825, of the House of Refuge for Juvenile Delinquents in New York City, the first institution of its kind in this country. The establishment of such a refuge in New York had been recommended as early as 1812 by the Rev. John Stanford. As the preacher assigned to the municipal penal and charitable institutions, Dr. Stanford had noticed the large numbers of children committed to jails and prisons, where they were exposed to the harmful influences of hardened adepts in crime.

In a long letter to the Common Council dated February 13, 1812, he urged the erection of a publicly controlled Asylum for Vagrant Youth as a means of rescuing "from indolence, vice and danger, the hundreds of vagrant children and youth, who, day and night, infest our streets; many of whom have, in the course of divine Providence, been cast upon the world as friendless orphans."[1] At the time, children convicted of crime were treated in much the same manner as their elders. When arrested they were sent to the common jail, tried in the common courts, and, if found guilty, were sentenced to the same penal institutions as adults, sharing common cells with the latter. Many children were sent to the jail or workhouse for no crime other than that of being vagrant or abandoned. Aware of the corrupting influences of these institutions on children, progressive-minded judges and juries at times refused to convict minors accused of crimes even when they were convinced of the defendants' guilt. In such instances the children were simply left to drift back to their old haunts and resume their delinquent careers. Stanford, in his letter, stressed the opinion that a juvenile reformatory would serve as a potent agency for the prevention of much pauperism and crime. His appeal was turned down by the Common Council on the ground that it would involve a financial burden too heavy for the city to assume at that time. The project was again

317

advanced by Stanford in 1821, but the Common Council once more rejected his petition.[2]

Meanwhile, as we have noted in chapter xii, the Society for the Prevention of Pauperism in New York City was constantly making inquiries into the causes of dependency. In pursuing these investigations the attention of the Society was increasingly drawn to the problem of juvenile delinquency as a factor in producing pauperism. In the *Second Annual Report* of the Society an item, "defects in the penitentiary system," appeared as one of the causes of dependency regularly listed. The city penitentiary at Bellevue was characterized as a "fruitful source of pauperism" and "one great school of vice and desperation" where unfortunate children were indiscriminately herded with "confirmed and unrepentant criminals." The *Report* suggested that "a building could be erected at a moderate expense, within the precincts of the penitentiary, and moral, religious and elementary instruction" be given the juvenile convicts.[3] The *Fourth Annual Report* of the Society (1821) likewise included juvenile delinquency in its list of causes.

In 1822 the Society appointed a committee to investigate penal systems in operation throughout the United States. The committee, which included Charles G. Haines, Thomas Eddy, Cadwallader D. Colden, Peter A. Jay, and Isaac Collins among its members, presented its *Report* in 1822. Published under the title, *The Penitentiary System of the United States*, the *Report* with its wealth of information on contemporary American prisons and penological theories of the time constitutes a valuable historical document. Of interest to our present study is the fact that the committee mentioned the lack of a separate juvenile reformatory as one of eight principal defects of the existing penal system and recommended "that prisons be erected in the different states, exclusively for juvenile convicts."[4] These institutions, the committee suggested, should be schools for instruction rather than places of punishment:

> The youth confined there should be placed under a course of discipline, severe and unchanging, but alike calculated to subdue and conciliate. A system should be adopted that would prove a mental and moral regimen. . . . . The wretchedness and misery of the offender should not be the object of the punishment inflicted; the end should be his reformation and future usefulness.[5]

JOHN GRISCOM, AN EARLY PHILANTHROPIST

Two courses should be pursued to attain these ends: (1) training in branches of industry that would enable the inmate to earn a livelihood in normal life; and (2) elementary education and careful inculcation of religious and moral principles.

The Society for the Prevention of Pauperism by this time was convinced that a real preventive program for dependency should be centered around the rehabilitation of delinquent and neglected children, and that the greatest contribution it could make toward solving this problem in New York would be the establishment of a reformatory for these children. A model for such an institution had been described by one of its leading members, John Griscom,[6] after a European journey in 1818. During his trip abroad Griscom had visited an institution for abandoned and delinquent children established by the Philanthropic Society in London. This institution maintained about one hundred and fifty boys and fifty girls, most of whom were sent from prisons, bridewells, and courts. Its facilities included schools as well as workshops, where they could learn such trades as bookbinding, shoemaking, tailoring, ropemaking, and twine-spinning. The most promising inmates were apprenticed to tradesmen under the supervision of the Philanthropic Society. Upon his return Griscom enthusiastically described the London institution to his fellow-members of the Society for the Prevention of Pauperism, and they were evidently deeply impressed by his account.[7]

The subject of juvenile delinquency and its reformation made up the greater part of the last *Annual Report* of the Society submitted by the board of managers on February 7, 1823. "The first subject of investigation the Board now wish to lay before the public," they stated, "is the one of the first importance . . . . we mean the subject of *juvenile offenders*."[8] Pointing to an alarming increase in the incidence of juvenile delinquency, to the lack of classification in the existing penal institutions, and to the need for saving children from the stigma of such terms as "prisoner" and "convict," the *Report* laid before the public a proposal for the establishment of a "house of refuge for young delinquents when discharged from prison." It is interesting to note that the Society was not yet prepared to suggest a complete substitute for the ordinary prison, but recommended only that the proposed house of refuge receive "those of a tender age who had already been in prison" as a sort of halfway house to normal life. The proposal was based on the Temporary Refuge established several years earlier by the London Society for the Improvement of Prison Discipline and the Reformation of Juvenile Offenders,* and an Appendix to the *Report* contained a series of case histories culled from the files of the London organization, illustrating its success in reclaiming wayward children.

In June, 1823, the Society for the Prevention of Pauperism appointed a committee headed by John Griscom to prepare an appeal to the public urging support for its proposed plan. The document drawn up by this committee went far beyond any of the previous recommendations made by the Society.

The design of the proposed institution [read the committee's report] is to furnish, in the *first place*, an asylum, in which boys under certain age, who become subject to the notice of our Police, either as vagrants, or houseless, or charged with petty crimes, may be received, judiciously classed according to their degrees of depravity or innocence, put to work at such employments as will tend to encourage industry and ingenuity, taught reading, writing and arithmetic, and most carefully instructed in the nature of their moral and religious obligations, while at the same time they are subjected to a course of treatment that will afford a prompt and energetic corrective of their vicious propensities, and hold out every possible inducement to reformation and good conduct. . . . . Such an institution would in time exhibit scarcely any other than the character of a decent school and manufactory. It need not be invested with the insignia of a prison.[9]

The committee also recommended that the institution receive neglected children and

youthful convicts, who, on their discharge from prison, at the expiration of their sentence, finding themselves without character, without subsistence, and ignorant of the means by which it is to be sought, have no alternative but to beg or steal, ... delinquent females who are either too young to have acquired habits of fixed depravity, or those whose lives have in general been virtuous, but who, having yielded to the seductive influence of corrupt associates, have suddenly to endure the bitterness of lost reputation.

Initiated by the Society, a public meeting was held at the City Hotel in New York on December 19, 1823, at which the aforemen-

---

* This organization should not be confused with the Philanthropic Society, which was founded much earlier and which had somewhat different aims, although maintaining an institution for juvenile delinquents similar to that of the Society for the Improvement of Prison Discipline.

tioned committee's report was read. It was resolved at this meeting to form a Society for the Reformation of Juvenile Delinquents. With the founding of the new organization the Society for the Prevention of Pauperism went out of existence, its members feeling that their major mission had been accomplished.

The new Society was incorporated by chapter 126, *Laws of 1824*, as the Managers of the Society for the Reformation of Juvenile Delinquents in the City of New York. The act authorized the Society to establish a House of Refuge to be governed by a self-perpetuating board of thirty managers who were empowered to receive in the institution children "taken up or committed as vagrants, or convicted of criminal offenses" in New York City. The managers were also given the power of binding out as apprentices or servants children under their care and were directed to report annually to the legislature. Private subscriptions collected by the Society netted $17,000, and a site for the institution was selected at the junction of Broadway and the Bowery. The grounds were donated by the city of New York, while buildings standing on the site formerly used as a federal arsenal were secured by the Society from the United States government for $6,000.*

Philip Klein, in his *Prison Methods in New York State*, tells us that the theory behind the House of Refuge constituted an entirely new system in American penological evolution. The essentials of this system according to Klein were:

First, a general paternal attitude towards the inmate. Secondly, an indefinite term of sentence, its actual duration depending entirely upon the judgment of the board of managers, and based not mainly upon the crime for which the child was committed, but upon plans for his future in education and industry. Thirdly, responsibility for the child continuing after his discharge from the institution and until his attainment of the twenty-first birthday in the case of boys, and of the eighteenth in the case of girls. It is not so much as a clear cut system that the House of Refuge represents an important type, but more in having introduced an entirely different general attitude towards the prisoner, one which slowly and imperceptibly entered the general public consciousness and affected fundamentally the future development of the prison system.[10]

---

* Only $2,000 was actually paid to the federal government. The Society petitioned the government from time to time to discharge the remainder of the debt. This action was finally taken by a special act of Congress in July, 1848.

THE NEW YORK HOUSE OF REFUGE, AS IT APPEARED IN 1835

The state began to act as a subsidizing agent through chapter 107, *Laws of 1825*, which authorized an appropriation of $2,000 annually to the Society for a period of five years.

The opening of the House of Refuge was hailed by social reformers as a historic occasion, and great expectations were held out for it. Within a year the district attorney of New York County declared that its existence had already resulted in a drastic reduction of juvenile delinquency. In his annual message to the legislature in 1826 Governor De Witt Clinton characterized it as "the best penitentiary institution which has ever been devised by the wit, and established by the beneficence of man."[11] Emphasizing the preventive role of the juvenile reformatory, the governor repeated the claim that its existence had already diminished juvenile criminality in New York City and recommended that delinquent children from all parts of the state should share in its benefits. Several weeks after hearing the governor's message the legislature enacted a bill providing that juvenile delinquents from all parts of the state should be received in the House of Refuge.* The same statute directed the health commissioners of the port of New York to turn over annually to the Society for the Reformation of Juvenile Delinquents the surplus remaining from the moneys raised by them for the maintenance of the Marine Hospital.[12] Three years later the legislature changed this variable appropriation to a fixed sum of $8,000 annually, to be taken out of the Marine Hospital funds. At the same time the legislature voted that certain license fees received from tavern-keepers, circuses, and theaters in New York City be turned over to the Society.[13] Chapter 186 of the *Laws of 1831* authorized the city of New York to appropriate $4,000 annually toward the maintenance of the House of Refuge, to be taken out of the municipal poor funds raised by excise duties and license fees. Further ap-

* The *Revised Statutes of 1827–28* provided: "Whenever any person, under the age of sixteen years, shall be convicted of any felony, the court, instead of sentencing such person to imprisonment in a state prison, may order that he be . . . . confined in the house of refuge, established by the society for the reformation of juvenile delinquents in the city of New York; unless notice shall have been received from such society, that there is not room in such house for the reception of further delinquents" (*Revised Statutes*, Part IV, chap. i, Title 7). Chapter 181, *Laws of 1830*, provided for the transfer of convicts under seventeen years of age from the state prisons to the House of Refuge, upon recommendation of the prison inspectors.

propriations to the Society were voted by the state and New York City in the succeeding decades, while private contributions constituted a small fraction of the Society's income.

A noteworthy effort at classification was introduced early in the history of the House of Refuge. The method, however, seems somewhat unscientific from the modern point of view. We learn from the rules and regulations adopted on January 2, 1827, that the inmates were divided into four classes, based on "moral conduct." The first class consisted of the best-behaved and most orderly boys and girls—"those who do not swear, lie, or use profane, obscene or indecent language or conversation, who attend to their work and studies, are not quarrelsome, and have not attempted to escape." The second class comprised "those who are next best, but who are not quite free from all of the foregoing vices and practices." The third class consisted of "those who are more immoral in conduct than Class No. 2," and the fourth included "those who are vicious, bad and wicked." Each inmate was to wear on the arm at all times a badge designating the class to which he or she belonged. Inmates could be promoted or demoted in accordance with changes of character, and rewards and punishments were held out as inducements to good behavior. Punishments permitted at the institution included deprivation of play, exercise, and certain meals, solitary confinement on a bread and water diet, whipping, and restraint with fetters and handcuffs.[14]

A picture of the daily routine practiced at the House of Refuge during the early years is provided in the *Tenth Annual Report* for 1835:

At sunrise, the children are warned, by the ringing of a bell, to rise from their beds. Each child makes his own bed, and steps forth, on a signal, into the Hall. They then proceed, in perfect order, to the Wash Room. Thence they are marched to parade in the yard, and undergo an examination as to their dress and cleanliness; after which, they attend morning prayer. The morning school then commences, where they are occupied in summer, until 7 o'clock. A short intermission is allowed, when the bell rings for breakfast; after which, they proceed to their respective workshops, where they labor until 12 o'clock, when they are called from work, and one hour allowed them for washing and eating their dinner.

At one they again commence work, and continue at it until five in the after-

THE WESTERN HOUSE OF REFUGE, AS IT APPEARED IN 1855

noon, when the labors of the day terminate. Half an hour is allowed for washing and eating their supper, and at half-past five, they are conducted to the school room, where they continue at their studies until 8 o'clock. Evening Prayer is performed by the Superintendent; after which, the children are conducted to their dormitories, which they enter, and are locked up for the night, when perfect silence reigns throughout the establishment. The foregoing is a history of a single day, and will answer for every day in the year, except Sundays, with slight variations during stormy weather and the short days in winter.[15]

During the first ten years 1,120 boys and 360 girls were admitted into the institution; of the total, 1,148 were bound out as apprentices. It is interesting to note that many of the boys were indentured to masters of sailing ships, especially whaling vessels.

In 1839 the House of Refuge was removed to Twenty-third Street and First Avenue in New York City where a large group of municipal charitable institutions was clustered. Owing to the encroachments resulting from the city's expansion northward and the need for larger quarters, the institution again moved on October 31, 1854, this time to Randall's Island in the East River, where it remained for eighty years. In 1935 the House of Refuge was abandoned, its inmates having been transferred according to their ages to the new New York State Training School for Boys at Warwick, and the New York State Vocational Institution at West Coxsackie.

WESTERN HOUSE OF REFUGE ESTABLISHED

The legislative act of 1826 authorizing the House of Refuge to receive children from all parts of the state failed to fulfil the expectation of the authorities that this institution would suffice for the entire state. The expense and difficulty involved in the transportation of children from remote counties proved an effective deterrent to sentencing delinquents from these areas to the New York institution. Juvenile delinquents were generally sent to local penal institutions or the more accessible state prisons rather than to the distant refuge, or else were left at large for want of a suitable institution.

Beginning with 1838 the state legislature began to receive petitions from officials and inhabitants of the western counties urging the establishment of another institution for juvenile delinquents in that part of the state. In his annual message to the legislature in

1840 Governor William H. Seward urged favorable action on these petitions.[16] The assembly committee to which this part of the governor's message was referred agreed that the erection of a western house of refuge was desirable, but recommended that action be deferred until the state, which was then slowly recovering from the great depression of 1837, should be in better financial condition.[17] Finally, in 1846, the assembly received a favorable report from a committee appointed to inquire into the need for a western house of refuge. The committee observed that juvenile delinquency was increasing in western New York, particularly in the districts along the canals. It was estimated that about five thousand boys were employed on the canals. Of these, about half were orphans and nearly half were under twelve years of age. Without guardianship or wholesome guidance, they were often "grievously imposed upon" by their employers and thrown out of work without means of support at the close of navigation in winter. Thus set adrift, many homeless boys

by their destitution and want of moral culture are compelled (as they suppose) to commit petty thefts at first, in order to obtain their bread, and from the habit and a loss of the dread of jails, are led to greater acts of criminality. It is a fact perhaps noteworthy of remark that a large portion of the inmates of the State prison at Auburn have been canal boys.[18]

Acting on recommendation of this committee, the legislature passed a law on May 8, 1846, establishing the Western House of Refuge for Juvenile Delinquents.[19] The act authorized the governor to appoint three commissioners to select a suitable site for the institution. A sum not exceeding $22,000 was to be paid out of state funds for the purchase of the site and the erection of the building, and the state controller was authorized to grant further sums to the commissioners not exceeding $5,000 at a time. Provision was made for a revolving board of managers for the institution to consist of "15 discreet men" serving three-year terms without compensation. The members of the first board were to be appointed by the governor, lieutenant-governor, and controller; thereafter vacancies were to be filled by the governor with the consent of the senate. The managers in turn were empowered to appoint a superintendent and other necessary officers of the institution.

The Western House of Refuge was to receive all male children under eighteen years of age and females under seventeen who should be legally committed to the institution as vagrants or on a conviction for any criminal offense by any court having authority to make such commitments. It was provided that upon completion of the institution the governor should issue an order designating the counties authorized to commit their juvenile delinquents to the Western House of Refuge.* Courts of criminal jurisdiction in these counties were ordered to send to that institution all children under the prescribed ages who might be convicted of a felony. Children convicted of petty larceny could be committed to the institution at the discretion of the court, while magistrates of the county wherein the institution was located might also commit juvenile vagrants. Each designated county was to pay fifty cents per week for each child maintained in the House of Refuge under conviction from the county, a provision that was repealed by chapter 387 of the *Laws of 1852*. A site was selected at Rochester, and the Western House of Refuge was opened there on August 11, 1849.

As in the case of the New York House of Refuge, the managers of the western institution were empowered to bind out or place at employment any child put under their charge, each child remaining under their supervision during his or her minority. The Western House of Refuge differed from its New York prototype in one very important respect, however: it was the first institution of its kind in America† financed and controlled by the state from the beginning, while the New York House of Refuge, though maintained mainly by state funds, remained technically a private institution. It was originally intended to receive into the institution male offenders under eighteen years of age and females under seventeen. The amendment of 1850, however, limited the institution to receiving boys

---

* Chapter 24, *Laws of 1850*, directed that juvenile delinquents from the first three judicial districts of the state should be committed to the House of Refuge in the city of New York, and that those sentenced in the remaining five judicial districts (comprising the western and northern counties) should be committed to the Western House of Refuge.

† The Lyman School in Massachusetts was the first to be opened (1848), but it was established in 1847, while the Western House of Refuge was established a year earlier.

under sixteen years of age.[20] The New York House of Refuge served as the only reformatory for delinquent girls until 1875, when a girls' department was opened at the Rochester institution.* The Western House of Refuge was enlarged several times during the first few years of existence, and by 1856 it had a capacity of four hundred inmates. The name of the institution was changed to the State Industrial School in 1886 and to the State Agricultural and Industrial School in 1902. The institution is now located at Industry, about eighteen miles from Rochester.

The scaling-down of the maximum age limit from eighteen to sixteen had come about after repeated protests on the part of the managers of the Western House of Refuge to the effect that the presence of the older offenders, some of whom were "hardened criminals," was producing evil effects on the younger, more impressionable inmates. When the maximum age limit for the juvenile reformatory was reduced, however, the problem arose of applying the principle of reformation to youths who were first offenders but who were too old to be admitted to the institutions for juveniles. The agitation over this question was a major factor in the establishment of the New York State Reformatory at Elmira in 1870, the first reformatory for adults in this country, receiving first offenders between the ages of sixteen and thirty convicted of felonies.

ORGANIZATIONS FOR NEGLECTED AND VAGRANT CHILDREN

Meanwhile, efforts to cope with the problem of vagrant and neglected children led to the founding of two significant organizations in New York City, subsidized in part by public funds. The establishment of the New York Juvenile Asylum may be traced to the activities of the New York Association for Improving the Condition of the Poor, organized in 1843. In the course of its ministrations the Association had been confronted with the problem of dealing adequately with the neglected children of some of its charges. It appears that in 1848 Robert M. Hartley, secretary and founder

* A law passed by the state legislature in 1853 required both reformatories to receive all offenders under sixteen years of age sentenced by any federal court sitting within New York State for an offense against the United States, the federal government to pay for the maintenance of such offenders (*Laws of 1853*, chap. 608).

of the organization, advanced the idea of establishing a separate institution for such children somewhat along the lines suggested by John Stanford thirty-six years before. His proposal resulted in further discussion, and in October, 1849, a group of citizens including Hartley, Benjamin F. Butler, Luther Bradish, and Apollos R. Wetmore participated in a meeting called by the A.I.C.P. to consider the expediency of founding an institution for neglected and vagrant children.[21] The movement thus begun was stimulated by a report of Chief of Police George W. Matsell of New York in January, 1850, in which he described at some length a "deplorable and growing evil" requiring immediate remedy:

I allude [Matsell wrote] to the constantly increasing numbers of vagrant, idle and vicious children of both sexes, who infest our public thoroughfares, hotels, docks, &c. Children are growing up in ignorance and profligacy, only destined to a life of misery, shame and crime, and ultimately to a felon's doom. Their numbers are almost incredible, and to those whose business and habits do not permit them a searching scrutiny, the degrading and disgusting practices of these almost infants in the schools of vice, prostitution and rowdyism, would certainly be beyond belief. The offspring of always careless, generally intemperate, and oftentimes immoral and dishonest parents, they never see the inside of a schoolroom. . . . .[22]

Chief Matsell estimated that in eleven of the twenty wards of the city there were nearly three thousand such neglected and vagrant children from six to sixteen years of age wandering about the streets and dives, stealing, fighting, or engaging in prostitution. Most of these children, he added, were of immigrant parentage, products of the great waves of German and Irish emigration during the 1840's. He concluded his report with the opinion:

Some method by which these children could be compelled to attend our schools regularly, or be apprenticed to some suitable occupation, would tend in time more to improve the morals of the community, prevent crime and relieve the city from its onerous burden of expenses for the Alms-House and Penitentiary, than any other conservative or philanthropic movement with which I am at present acquainted.

Later in the same month a committee met in the mayor's office to draft an act of incorporation. Largely as a result of their efforts, the New York Juvenile Asylum was incorporated by chapter 332, *Laws of 1851.*

This act authorized the asylum to receive children between the ages of five and fourteen years who might be sent there by their parents or guardians. Also any child found in any street, highway, or public place in New York City "in the circumstances of want and suffering, or abandonment, exposure or neglect, or of beggary" could be committed to the asylum by a magistrate. Formerly such neglected and abandoned children had been committed to the almshouse or the House of Refuge. The affairs of the organization were to be conducted by a board of directors upon which the mayor and several other New York City officials were to serve as ex officio members. The directors were empowered to bind out any child placed under their charge.

The articles of incorporation authorized the board of supervisors of the city and county of New York to appropriate $50,000, raised by tax, toward the building and maintenance of the institution as soon as a like amount had been raised by private subscription. It was further authorized to pay to the asylum a sum not exceeding $40 per annum for each child committed there from that city. This sum was raised to $75 per capita annually in 1858, and again to $90 in 1863.

The New York Juvenile Asylum was opened in 1853 in a house on Bank Street, with fifty-seven neglected and homeless children admitted the first day. Later in the year it removed to Fifty-fifth Street, with two hundred charges on its register. More than one thousand children were admitted to the asylum during its first year of operation. They were received first at a "house of reception," where they usually remained for two or three weeks before admittance to the asylum proper. Here they were accorded "moral, intellectual and industrial" instruction, and, whenever possible, they were indentured or placed out at employment. The institution was removed in 1904 to a site near Dobbs Ferry, New York, which it still occupies as the well-known Children's Village, this name having been assumed in 1920 by order of the Supreme Court.

THE CHILDREN'S AID SOCIETY

A second and very significant organization to emerge in the mid-nineteenth century as a result of the problem of neglected and vagrant children in New York City was the Children's Aid Society. This organization was founded in 1853 by Charles Loring Brace, for "the training and the general improvement of the conditions of the homeless and friendless children roaming the streets of New York."

Born at Litchfield, Connecticut, in 1826, Brace had come to New York in 1848 after studying at the theological seminary at Yale. As a Sunday preacher at the almshouse chapel on Blackwell's Island, he came into close contact with the prisoners and paupers sent there and arrived at the conclusion that the great city which produced these outcasts was an "immense vat of misery and crime and filth." In 1850 he journeyed to England and the Continent, where he visited many of the humanitarian institutions, including the "ragged schools" established for children of the streets in Edinburgh and London and the "workshops" of Paris, set up by the French Socialists during the Revolution of 1848.

Returning to New York Brace joined the Five Points Mission, organized in 1850 to bring the gospel to the inhabitants of the worst quarter of New York's slums. He soon was convinced of the futility of this type of missionary work among adults. The sight of the homeless children thronging the streets and wharves of the city, begging, stealing, blacking boots, and selling papers for a pittance, attracted his attention more and more.

In January, 1853, a group of influential citizens, including William C. Russell, B. J. Howland, William L. King, and John L. Mason, held a meeting with Brace, as a result of which the latter was invited to organize and head a "mission to the children." According to Brace his duties were "to organize a system of boys' meetings, vagrant schools, etc., which shall reach the whole city; to communicate with press and clergy; to draw in boys, find them homes in the country, get them to schools, help them to help themselves, to write and preach, etc., etc."[23] The following month the Children's Aid Society was formally organized with Charles Loring Brace as its secretary. Its first circular, issued in March, 1853, apprised the public of the aims of the new Society and the proposed methods for achieving these aims. The Society based its claim for public support not only on humanitarian grounds but on the self-protective instinct

of the more opulent citizenry. In the circular it pointed with alarm
to the increasing hordes of lawless children, comprising mainly the
offspring of newly arrived immigrants, spawned in the poorer sections of the city:

They grow up passionate, ungoverned; with no love or kindness ever to soften
the heart. We all know their short, wild life, and the sad end. These boys and
girls, it should be remembered, will soon form the great lower class of our city.
They will influence elections; they may shape the policy of the city; they will,
assuredly, if unreclaimed, poison society all around them. They will help to
form the great multitude of robbers, thieves and vagrants who are now such a
burden upon the law-respecting community.[24]

The organization disclaimed any intention of conflicting with
existing institutions for children; its emphasis was placed on non-
institutional work. It proposed to district the city so that every
ward might have an agent of the Society to act as a friend of the
vagrant children. These workers were to arrange street and indoor
Sunday meetings for boys, with every district having its place of
preaching. The Society was also to conduct "industrial schools"
where the children could be taught trades. The circular stated that
arrangements had already been made with manufacturers to supply
five hundred boys with paying work throughout the city as soon as
funds necessary to carry out the Society's plans were obtained. The
circular continued:

We hope, too, especially to be the means of draining the city of these children, by communicating with farmers, manufacturers or families in the country,
who may have need of such for employment. When homeless boys are found
by our agents, we mean to get them homes in the families of respectable persons
in the city, and to put them in the way of an honest living.[25]

These methods were not new. They were already in use by various
organizations at the time the Children's Aid Society was established.
The religious meetings had been held before. The Five Points Mission of New York City, as well as the American Female Guardian
Society, used the workshop as a means for the rehabilitation of
youth. Placing out or binding out children had been practiced for
centuries. The method of the Society was the old practice applied
with more discrimination and with the object of settling the children
in remote rural areas.

Many orphan asylums had placed children in family homes before, but the work had not been systematized and there were no societies engaged especially in this work. Charles Loring Brace was the first to make organized use of the family home as a substitute for institutional care for dependent and neglected children. He was against keeping children in institutions for long periods, claiming that healthy, normal children had no need of institutional care. He became the pioneer of the organized child-placing movement.

The children were usually sent out in groups or "companies." The first company, consisting of forty-six boys and girls between seven and fifteen years of age, was sent to Michigan on September 24, 1854, in charge of a minister.[26] Soon other groups of children were sent in a steady stream to various parts of the Union, reaching as far west as Michigan, Iowa, and Wisconsin. The number of children placed in family homes during the first decade (1854–64) totaled 4,614, averaging 384 placements annually.

At first the only form of contact between the Society and its charges consisted of correspondence with the families where these children had been placed, inquiring into their progress. But many persons with whom children had been bound out either could not write or showed no disposition to do so, and correspondence in general soon proved a very unsatisfactory method for checking up on placed-out children. A better form of supervision was obviously required; complaints were being made of the ill treatment of many children placed out without effective follow-up. Brace formulated a plan for employing permanent agents for the work. It was not until 1869, however, that the first permanent agent was appointed, with Chicago as his headquarters. Agents for other districts were gradually employed, improving the situation somewhat, but leaving the basic problem of effective organized supervision unsolved. Constant abuses under this system, or rather lack of it, finally led to the passage of a law prohibiting the placing of children beyond the borders of New York State.

Brace was also responsible for the establishment in 1854 of the first Newsboys' Lodging House (now known as the Brace Memorial Newsboys' Home) in the old *Sun* building in New York. The boys who lodged at the house were treated as independent "dealers," paying for their lodging, meals, and supplies, but receiving more for their money than they could obtain elsewhere. They were encouraged to take up some trade and to develop a "sense of property" by putting their earnings in savings banks. A girls' lodging-house was also established soon afterward, and by 1867 the Society was operating sixteen industrial schools and four lodging-houses for children of both sexes.

In its early years the Society financed its work wholly out of private contributions, but in 1865 the legislature enacted a bill providing that the supervisors of New York County should pay to the Children's Aid Society the sum of $10,000 annually out of tax moneys.[27]

The influence of the Children's Aid Society on child-saving practice in America was immediate and widespread. Similar organizations sprang up in various cities throughout the country; a number of existing philanthropic societies dropped their traditional work to participate in child-placing activities along the lines established by Brace.

A Children's Aid and Reform Society was established in Buffalo in January, 1856, but this organization was merged into the Buffalo Juvenile Asylum several months later. The latter institution was incorporated through chapter 123 of the *Laws of 1856*, which authorized the city of Buffalo to issue bonds for $45,000 in aid of the Juvenile Asylum and also to pay from tax levies $60 per annum for each child sent to the asylum from that city. The Buffalo institution was patterned after the New York Juvenile Asylum established five years earlier. A Children's Aid Society was organized in Buffalo in 1872, being preceded by an identically named society in Brooklyn, founded in 1866, along the lines set down by the New York original.

Meanwhile, many existing agencies and institutions for dependent, neglected, and delinquent children in New York State had adopted the idea of placing out children, particularly in western states. This movement led to an interesting and significant development in the field of Catholic charities.

THE CATHOLIC PROTECTORY

While the Children's Aid Society was professedly nonsectarian, it was peculiarly Protestant in conception and method. Many of its charges from the slum districts were of Roman Catholic parentage, and these were invariably sent into Protestant homes. This situation soon developed an antagonism between the Society and Catholic leaders in New York. The charge was made that the Society was interested mainly in proselyting Catholic children. Furthermore, the theory of the Children's Aid Society was constitutionally at odds with the Catholic idea of child care, the prime object of which was to insure that the Catholic child should be brought up in the faith of its fathers. Catholic care tended to be mainly institutional in character, administered by religious orders. Institutional care was abhorred by Brace, while family care outside the precincts of the Catholic faith was anathema to the church. Hence it was that the work of the Children's Aid Society gave rise to a countermovement aimed toward placing dependent, neglected, and delinquent children of Catholic parentage in Catholic homes or institutions.

This Catholic countermovement led to the establishment in 1863 of the Society for the Protection of Destitute Roman Catholic Children in the City of New York, with the avowed intention of checking what it called the proselyting objects of the placing-out societies organized under Protestant auspices. The Society received children between the ages of seven and fourteen intrusted to it by parents, committed by the courts, or transferred to its care by the municipal Commissioners of Public Charity and Correction. Its first home, consisting of two small buildings, was opened on Thirty-sixth and Thirty-seventh streets. The Christian Brothers were placed in charge of the boys, while the Sisters of Charity cared for the girls. The name of the organization was changed to the New York Catholic Protectory by chapter 83, *Laws of 1871*. As Lane puts it, "the Protectory insisted on, first, the proper religious training of the children; secondly, the preservation of family ties as much as possible; and finally, a period of discipline and training before the child's release into the world."[28]

The society received a lump-sum grant of $2,000 from the state treasury in 1864, along with other institutions for destitute and homeless children. In the same year the legislature authorized the supervisors of New York County to raise $15,000 by taxation to be paid to the society on condition that the latter would raise an additional $20,000 for the current expenses of the institution.[29] When the removal of the Protectory to Westchester County was undertaken, the state legislature, through chapter 647, *Laws of 1866*, authorized the New York County supervisors to raise $50,000 toward the erection of the new buildings and to pay $50 per capita annually toward the support of children maintained in the institution.

In 1864, the year following the establishment of the Catholic Protectory, the Society for the Protection of Destitute Roman Catholic Children in the City of Buffalo was incorporated, with objectives identical with those of its New York prototype.

THE THOMAS INDIAN SCHOOL

During the last decade of the eighteenth century a group of Quakers, whose friendly endeavors in behalf of the Indians were already a tradition in America, began missionary work among the Seneca Indians located on the Cattaraugus Reservation in western New York. For many years subsequently they carried on intermittent instruction among the children with varying degrees of success. One of their major objectives was to persuade the Indians to engage in agricultural pursuits in place of hunting. Another object was to bring about a division of labor between the sexes, whereby the males would take up farming, while the women would confine themselves to household tasks. In pursuance of the latter aim a delegation of Quakers at a conference with Seneca Indians held in July, 1845, offered to open a school on the reservation for the instruction of girls in domestic employment.[30] This plan was accepted and a Female Manual Labor School was opened that year at Cattaraugus with between twenty and thirty pupils in attendance. There the children were taught the various branches of housework. Most active among the Quakers working with the Senecas was Philip E. Thomas of Baltimore, a founder and first president of the Baltimore and Ohio Railroad, who had retired from business some years earlier. In recognition of his work he was adopted an honorary member of the Seneca Nation and given the name *Sagaoh*, "The Benevolent." Several years later the Senecas appointed him as their representative in Washington, changing his name to *Hai-wa-noh*, meaning "Ambassador."[31] Soon the attention of the Quakers was drawn to the problem of instructing destitute orphan children on the reservation. The death of an Indian in 1854 who left behind a large family in destitute circumstances precipitated an inquiry into the total number of dependent orphans on the reservation, and it was found that there were fifty such children. The treasury of the Indian government was empty, and these children could be aided only through private benefaction. The case was presented to Mr. Thomas who directed that a few children be maintained for the winter at his own expense. The idea of a permanent asylum was next broached, and the Council of the Seneca Nation passed resolutions indorsing the plan and setting aside land for the purpose.[32]

The following year ten persons, five of them white and five Indian, associated themselves as trustees and petitioned the legislature for a charter. As a result the Thomas Asylum for Orphan and Destitute Indian Children, named after the Quaker philanthropist, was incorporated on April 10, 1855.[33] It had been the intention of the founders to confine the work of the asylum to the children on the Cattaraugus Reservation, but the articles of incorporation directed the institution to receive orphan children from all other reservations within the state.* An appropriation of $2,000 toward the erection of the asylum buildings to accommodate at least fifty children was authorized by the legislature in addition to an annual grant of $500 for two years, whenever it should be ascertained that at least fifty children were being maintained in the institution. The United States Commission of Indian Affairs also contributed $1,000 out of a general fund for Indian aid toward the erection and support of the asylum. Other funds were received through private contributions. The objects of the institution as stated by the trustees in a circular issued in 1857 were: "First, to relieve the sufferings of orphan and destitute Indian children throughout the State. Second, to prevent these children from growing up idle and vicious vagabonds and beggars. Third, to train them to industry, intelligence and virtue." This was to be effected through "an effectual manual labor boarding school."[34]

---

* There were at the time about 4,000 Indians inhabiting reservations in New York State, including some 900 children under sixteen years of age.

The institution continued to be supported by state and private contributions until 1875, when a situation resulting from revision of the state constitution made it necessary for the state to take over the institution entirely, and it thenceforth functioned as a state institution.*

PRIVATE INSTITUTIONS FOR DESTITUTE CHILDREN

Private institutions for orphan and destitute children continued to increase steadily throughout this period. Many of these were subsidized by local public funds, several by both state and local appropriations.† In 1847 the legislature enacted a bill providing for an annual appropriation of $3,000 for "public instruction in orphan asylums." This sum was to be apportioned among the several incorporated orphanages in the state on a per capita basis according to the number of inmates between the ages of three and twelve years in each asylum.[35] Institutions receiving funds under this act were to provide an elementary education for these charges by qualified teachers, at least four months during the year, and were to be subject to the visitation and inspection of local educational officers. Three years later an act was passed "for the better education of the children in the several orphan asylums in this State other than in the city of New York," providing that these institutions should henceforth participate in the distribution of the common-school funds of the state in proportion to the number of inmates receiving instruction, on the same basis as the common schools in their respective districts.‡ The institutional schools were to be subject to the rules and regulations of the public common schools but were to remain under the immediate management and direction of the institutional officers.[36] Chapter 386 of the *Laws of 1851* extended the privilege of sharing in the common-school fund to the principal child-caring institutions of New York City.

Beginning with 1855 the state began to appropriate a general

---

* This development will be described in a subsequent chapter. In 1905 the name of the institution was changed to the Thomas Indian School.

† See chap. x, pp. 188–92.

‡ The common-school fund was established by the state of New York in 1805, when certain public lands were set aside, the proceeds of which were to be placed in a permanent school fund. Additional lands were added to the original allotment in later years.

grant of money in aid of private orphan asylums to be distributed through county officials among the various institutions on a per capita basis. Chapter 538 of the *Laws of 1855* appropriated $35,000 to be distributed among the "incorporated orphan asylums of the State." The same amount was appropriated in 1856 and 1857. In the latter year it was estimated that there were twenty-six orphan asylums maintaining a total of 2,816 children, which were receiving state support. The general state grant for orphan asylums was reduced to $30,000 for 1858 and 1859, but in 1861 it rose to $40,000. The heavy toll of lives taken by the long-drawn-out Civil War was reflected in the rapid increase of orphanages as well as in a tremendous rise in the number of children maintained in public almshouses. By 1866 there were sixty-three private child-caring institutions sharing a general state appropriation of $80,000.[37]

In addition to this annual appropriation to be divided among incorporated child-caring institutions on a per capita basis, the state was also making lump-sum grants to individual child-caring institutions under private auspices, in keeping with the precedent set in the early years of the century in the case of the New York Orphan Asylum, the Roman Catholic Orphan Asylum, and others. During the Civil War the number of such institutions receiving lump-sum grants increased notably, as did the amount of the individual appropriations. Special state grants of this nature to private institutions caring for destitute children (excluding institutions for delinquents) amounted to nearly $60,000 in 1863. The next year the total fell to $40,000, followed by a rise to about $45,000 in 1865, and a decline to $26,000 in 1866.[38] A report of the state controller presented to the Constitutional Convention of 1867 showed that from 1847 to 1867 a total of $617,120 had been appropriated by the legislature to more than sixty private institutions for dependent children. During the same period the New York Society for the Reformation of Juvenile Delinquents alone had received $647,691 in state grants.[39]

CHILDREN IN ALMSHOUSES

Despite the growth of special child-caring institutions, almshouses throughout the state continued to receive children in increasing numbers. While sporadic efforts were made to improve the condition of children in poorhouses, their situation continued to be highly unsatisfactory, and by the end of the period under discussion there was a marked movement to remove all children from almshouses.

In 1831 a statute was enacted providing that all children in county poorhouses between the ages of five and sixteen should "be taught and educated, in the same manner as children are now taught in the common schools of this State, at least one fourth of the time the said paupers shall remain in said poor-houses."[40] The same year witnessed a notable effort in New York City to remove dependent children from the almshouse proper. Since 1816 pauper children of the city had been maintained at the Bellevue almshouse at Twenty-sixth Street and the East River. While the children were lodged in separate buildings, they were hemmed in on all sides by the state prison for women, the county penitentiary, the city bridewell, and other almshouse structures occupied by adults, besides additional groups of buildings comprising the "Bellevue establishment." Ophthalmia and other diseases were of common occurrence among the almshouse children, reaching serious proportions for several years following 1829.[41]

In the spring of 1831 a particularly severe outbreak of ophthalmia occurred among the six hundred children maintained at the almshouse. There was no means of segregating the infected children at the institution which was already overcrowded. An investigation by the Common Council resulted in a recommendation that a special building or buildings should be erected on Blackwell's Island in the East River, which had just been purchased by the city, for the reception of the afflicted children.[42] During the same year buildings for almshouse children were erected on grounds (also recently purchased by the city) located in Queens County facing Blackwell's Island and known as the Long Island Farms. The condition of the children sent to the Long Island Farms proved so satisfactory that in 1832 the almshouse commissioners recommended that all the remaining children at the Bellevue establishment (the temporary building at Blackwell's Island had by this time been abandoned) be removed thereto. The Common Council acted favorably upon this proposal, and all the children were subsequently removed to the Long Island Farms. In September, 1834, six hundred and eighty children were being maintained in the Department for Children at the Long Island Farms.[43]

In 1848 the city abandoned the children's institution on the Long Island Farms and removed the inmates, who now numbered over one thousand, to the newly built "nurseries" on Randall's Island.[44]

Similar efforts to separate pauper children from the common almshouse were made in other parts of the state, although the degree of segregation accomplished in New York City was not reached elsewhere. The general treatment of children in almshouses throughout the state remained shocking during this entire period. The "Letters of Franklin," which were published in 1853 in the *Columbia Republican* as open letters to New York's secretary of state, and which had a noticeable influence on public welfare legislation of the time, include biting criticism of the condition of pauper children.* The letters show unmistakable evidence of a very careful study of contemporary poor-relief practice in this state, and the author evidently made a personal investigation of many poorhouses. The writer charged that in spite of the state's encouragement of education in poorhouses, only a few of the children in such institutions were obtaining an education that would be useful to them in making a living. "In many cases," he charged, "the teacher is a pauper, generally an old drunkard whose temper is soured and whose intellect is debased and who spends the school hours in tormenting rather than teaching his pupils."[45] No textbooks, slates, pen, or paper were to be found in many of the almshouse schools, he charged; some counties had not expended a single dollar on such supplies for years.

The enlightened Senate Committee which investigated the charitable institutions of the state in 1856, went even farther than "Franklin" in condemnation of the condition of almshouse children. After declaring that the general picture of poorhouses, if revealed in detail, "would disgrace the State and shock humanity," the Committee continued:

But with respect to *children*, the case is far worse; and the committee are forced to say that it is a great public reproach that they should ever be suffered to enter or remain in the poor houses as they are now mismanaged. They are for the young, notwithstanding the legal provisions for their education, the worst

* The "Letters of Franklin" have already been alluded to in chapter xiii.

possible nurseries; contributing an annual accession to our population of three hundred infants, whose present destiny is to pass their most impressible years in the midst of such vicious associations as will stamp them for a life of future infamy and crime.[46]

The Committee recommended that the children should be removed from the almshouses and placed in public asylums "devoted to their special use," or else in private orphanages, to be maintained there at the expense of the counties and towns properly chargeable for their support, or even by the state itself.* Here was a radical proposal, not only foreshadowing the legislation enacted two decades later prohibiting the retention of children in almshouses, but actually suggesting state care for dependent children.

Although the legislature turned down the major proposal of the Senate Committee relating to the establishment of a state supervisory body over charitable institutions, it did enact a law encouraging the removal of children from poorhouses. Chapter 61, *Laws of 1857*, authorized superintendents of the poor in counties where no orphan asylum was located and also the town overseers of the poor in such counties to place children chargeable to these districts in any incorporated orphan asylum in any part of the state, at the expense of such county or town. The same act, incidentally, made it mandatory for each child-caring institution authorized to bind out children to keep a book, open to inspection at all times, in which should be registered "the names, age and parentage, as near as the same can be ascertained, of all children committed to their care or received into such institution," and also "the time such child left the institution, and if bound out or otherwise placed out at service, or on trial, the name and occupation of the person with whom it is so placed and his or her place of residence." This provision was evidently enacted in response to a growing protest against abuses in unsupervised private child-caring agencies. Steps were taken by several counties in subsequent years to effect the removal of children from the common almshouse.

Declaring that special institutional treatment was far superior to almshouse care, the supervisors of Cayuga County in 1861 au-

---

* This suggestion was embodied in one of the seven recommendations formulated by the Senate Committee on the basis of its investigation.

thorized the superintendents of the poor to send all county-supported children of proper age to the privately managed Cayuga Asylum for Destitute Children.[47] The supervisors, who had been paying $1,000 annually to the asylum, the maximum fixed by the articles of incorporation passed in 1852, petitioned the legislature to amend the incorporating act so that they could thenceforth make appropriations to the asylum on a per capita basis for county-supported inmates at the rate of eighty cents per week for each child. The legislature responded favorably by enacting chapter 69 of the *Laws of 1862*, removing the fixed limit of the annual appropriation made by the county to the Cayuga asylum. An agreement was then entered into whereby all county-supported children were sent to the asylum instead of the county poorhouse. The proposal to make payments on a per capita basis was abandoned, however, the annual appropriation merely being raised to $1,500 annually and later to $2,500.[48]

Similarly, in 1863, the supervisors of Jefferson County adopted the following resolution:

WHEREAS, An association of charitably disposed persons in Watertown,* have for a series of years, provided for the support and education of such destitute, friendless and orphan children as have been committed to their care; and,

WHEREAS, By the aid of an appropriation by the last Legislature, of the sum of $5,000, the Trustees of said association have been enabled to provide more ample accommodations for the maintenance of the class of children; therefore,

Resolved, That the Superintendent of the Poor and Supervisors of the several towns of the county be authorized to send such children, under twelve years of age, as now are, or may become, a public charge and as the officers of the Home may decide to receive to the Orphan Asylum at Watertown instead of the Poor House, at an expense to the county of a sum not exceeding $1 per week for every child thus received and maintained. And that for this purpose, the Superintendent of the Poor of the county be, and is, hereby authorized and required to make, out of the temporary relief fund, such advances, from time to time, as may be necessary for their support, upon order of the officers of such association, approved by the Chairman of the Board of Supervisors.

Notwithstanding these efforts made by certain counties, the number of children in almshouses continued to increase. In 1847 there

* This was the Watertown Home for Destitute, Friendless and Orphan Children, the name of which was changed to Jefferson County Orphan Asylum in 1864 and to the Children's Home of Jefferson County in 1930.

had been about 3,000 children under sixteen years of age in the poorhouses throughout the state. By 1857 there were 5,403. The outbreak of the Civil War, which orphaned and impoverished tens of thousands of children in New York, occasioned a sudden and tremendous rise in the numbers of children in almshouses. In 1861 there were 7,962 such children; the following year there were 24,961 minors under sixteen in poorhouses; by 1866 there were over 26,251.[49] The intensification of the problem of child dependency resulting from the Civil War must be considered as one of the contributing factors leading to the organization of the Board of State Commissioners of Public Charities in 1867.

SUMMARY

This period saw very important developments in the field of child welfare. In harmony with the general trend in poor relief, institutionalization was one of its principal features. Its most significant characteristic was the rise of special institutions for dependent, delinquent, and neglected children. The opening of the House of Refuge in New York City, the first juvenile reformatory in America, marked a great forward stride in the evolution of our public welfare, advancing the concept that juvenile delinquency was a special problem to be treated apart from adult criminality. From the beginning, the state of New York contributed generously to its support. The Western House of Refuge (now the State Agricultural and Industrial School), established in 1846, was the first juvenile reformatory to be operated and controlled completely by the state.

The existence of large numbers of homeless and neglected children in New York City resulted in the organization of two important societies: the New York Juvenile Asylum (now the Children's Village) and the Children's Aid Society. Similar agencies sprang up throughout the state during the third quarter of the century. The founding of the Children's Aid Society by Charles Loring Brace marked the beginning of the organized child-placing movement in the United States, which was eventually to turn back the tide of the institutionalization of dependent children. Dissatisfaction on the part of Catholics with the predominantly Protestant character of the early child-placing activities led to the establishment of Catholic protectories in New York City and Buffalo.

Many orphanages were founded during these four decades. There were but two orphan asylums in New York State in 1825; by 1866 there were over sixty. A number of institutions for neglected and truant children also were established. Organized and operating under private auspices, these institutions received funds from state and local sources. The state contributed to the building and maintenance of many of these institutions through general annual appropriations to be distributed by the several counties on a per capita basis and through direct lump-sum grants to specified institutions.

The financial participation of the state in the upkeep of these organizations increased steadily and was one of the main factors leading to the establishment of a central supervisory body by the state in 1867. Institutions for physically and mentally handicapped children founded during this period will be described in the following chapter.

Meanwhile, in spite of the growth of special child-caring institutions, the number of children in almshouses continued to increase. By 1866 there were more than 26,000 children under sixteen years of age being supported in poorhouses throughout the state, under conditions so shocking as to result finally in the passage of the Children's Act of 1875, forbidding the retention of children between the ages of three and sixteen years in almshouses.

BIBLIOGRAPHICAL REFERENCES

1. Sommers, *Memoir of the Rev. John Stanford*, pp. 271–77.
2. *N.Y.C., M.C.C., 1784–1831*, XI, 722–23.
3. Society for the Prevention of Pauperism in the City of New York, *Second Annual Report of the Managers* (New York, 1819), pp. 31, 35.
4. ———, *Report on the Penitentiary System in the United States, Prepared under a Resolution of the Society* (New York, 1822), pp. 19, 60.
5. *Ibid.*, pp. 60–61.
6. John Griscom, *A Year in Europe* (New York, 1823), I, 121–23.
7. John H. Griscom, *Memoir of John Griscom* (New York, 1859), p. 166.

8. Society for the Prevention of Pauperism in the City of New York, *Sixth Annual Report of the Managers* (New York, 1823), p. 4.

9. ———, *Report of a Committee on the Expediency of Erecting an Institution for the Reformation of Juvenile Delinquents* (New York, 1823), pp. 24–25.

10. Klein, *Prison Methods in New York State*, p. 393.

11. *Messages from the Governors*, III, 130.

12. New York State, *Laws of 1826*, chap. 24.

13. ———, *Laws of 1829*, chap. 302.

14. Society for the Reformation of Juvenile Delinquents in the City of New York, *Documents Relative to the House of Refuge Instituted by the Society in 1824* (New York, 1832), pp. 107, 110.

15. Society for the Reformation of Juvenile Delinquents in the City and State of New York, *Tenth Annual Report of the Managers* (New York, 1835), pp. 6–7.

16. *Messages from the Governors*, III, 765–76.

17. New York State Assembly, *Documents* (63d sess. [Albany, 1840]), Vol. VIII, Doc. No. 360.

18. *Ibid.* (69th sess. [Albany, 1846]), Vol. IV, Doc. No. 93.

19. New York State, *Laws of 1846*, chap. 143.

20. ———, *Laws of 1850*, chap. 304.

21. Isaac S. Hartley (ed.), *Memorial of Robert M. Hartley* (Utica, 1882), pp. 210–11.

22. Published as an Appendix to Thomas L. Harris, *Juvenile Depravity and Crime in Our City* (a sermon) (New York, 1850), pp. 14–15.

23. Emma Brace (ed.), *Life of Charles Loring Brace* (New York, 1894), pp. 156–57.

24. *Ibid.*, pp. 489–90.

25. *Ibid.*, p. 491.

26. *Ibid.*, pp. 492–501.

27. New York State, *Laws of 1865*, chap. 70.

28. Francis E. Lane, *American Charities and the Child of the Immigrant, 1845–1880* (Washington, D.C., 1932), p. 122.

29. New York State, *Laws of 1864*, chaps. 401, 405.

30. Society of Friends, *Proceedings of the Joint Committee Appointed by the Society of Friends, Constituting the Yearly Meetings of Genesee, New York, Philadelphia and Baltimore, for Promoting the Civilization and Improving the Condition, of the Seneca Nation of Indians* (Baltimore, 1847), pp. 135–40, 169–71.

31. Rayner W. Kelsey, *The Friends and the Indians, 1655–1917* (Philadelphia, 1917), pp. 124–25.

32. Thomas Asylum for Orphan and Destitute Indian Children, *Circular of the Trustees, 1857*.

33. New York State, *Laws of 1855*, chap. 233.

34. Thomas Asylum, *op. cit.*

35. New York State, *Laws of 1847*, chap. 485.

36. ———, *Laws of 1850*, chap. 261.

37. ———, *Laws of 1866*, chap. 774.

38. ———, *Laws of 1863*, chap. 210; *Laws of 1864*, chap. 401; *Laws of 1865*, chap. 641; *Laws of 1866*, chap. 774.

39. New York State Constitutional Convention, 1867–68, *Documents* (Albany, 1868), Vol. I, Doc. No. 55.

40. New York State, *Laws of 1831*, chap. 277.

41. N.Y.C. Bd. of Aldermen, *Documents*, *1831*, Vol. I, Doc. No. 14 (submitted January, 1832).

42. ———, *Proceedings*, *1831* (New York, 1835), I, 39.

43. ———, *Documents*, *1834–35*, Vol. I, Doc. No. 20.

44. N.Y.C. Commissioner of the Almshouse, *Annual Report*, *1848*, in *ibid.*, *1848–49*, Vol. XV, Doc. No. 44.

45. New York State Senate, *Documents* (78th sess. [Albany, 1855]), Vol. III, Doc. No. 72.

46. *Ibid.* (80th sess. [Albany, 1857]), I, Doc. No. 8, p. 7.

47. Cayuga Co., N.Y., Board of Supervisors, *Proceedings*, *1861* (Auburn, 1861), pp. 43–44.

48. *Ibid.*, *1862* (Auburn, 1862), pp. 61–63; *ibid.*, *1863* (Auburn, 1864), pp. 57–59; *ibid.*, *1872* (Auburn, 1873), pp. 38–39.

49. New York State Constitutional Convention, 1867–68, "Statistics of Pauperism," *New York Convention Manual* (Albany, 1867), Part II: *Statistics*, p. 27.

CHAPTER XVIII

INSTITUTIONS FOR THE MENTALLY AND PHYSICALLY HANDICAPPED

The trend toward the establishment of special institutions for the dependent classes was quite as marked in the care and treatment of the mentally and physically handicapped as it was in the care of destitute and delinquent children.

STATE ASYLUMS FOR THE MENTALLY ILL

As has been noted in chapter xi, the only hospital for the insane at the opening of this period was the Bloomingdale Asylum in New York City, a corporate institution which until 1857 received an annual state grant of $12,500 toward its maintenance. County officials were authorized to send pauper patients to Bloomingdale, the cost of their support to be charged to their respective counties. The capacity of the asylum, however, was very limited, and its managers were vested with the authority to refuse admission to public charges at their discretion. Comparatively few pauper patients were maintained there. Poorhouses and jails were the only public institutions for the reception of the insane at the time.

The *Revised Statutes of 1827* intrusted to the overseers of the poor the care and safe-keeping of "lunatics" deemed too dangerous to be at large and unprovided for by their relatives or guardians. Upon warrant of any two justices of the peace, such persons were to be apprehended and "safely locked up and confined in such secure place as may be provided by the overseers of the poor," or else sent to the county poorhouse or to the Bloomingdale Asylum. An important section of the *Revised Statutes* forbade the commitment *as a disorderly person* of any dangerous or "furiously mad" lunatic to any prison, jail, or house of correction, except with the consent of the jail-keepers. Such a person, however, could be detained in jail for a maximum of four weeks and "if he continue furiously mad or dangerous, he shall be sent to the asylum in New York (Blooming-

dale) or to the county poor-house or almshouse, or other place provided for the reception of lunatics by the county superintendents."
No insane person was to be confined in the same room with any
person charged with or convicted of any crime.[1]

Relatives able to pay for the care of insane persons were to be
charged with the costs of maintenance by the overseers of the poor.
An insane person could be placed in the custody of friends or relatives if they were able to furnish a suitable place for his confinement and to keep him there in a manner approved by the local
overseers. Many instances were revealed in later years where insane
persons were locked up in filthy pens and cages by relatives who
found this less expensive than the cost of maintenance at the
Bloomingdale Asylum or even at the county almshouse.

The great majority of the mentally ill under public charge continued to be kept in almshouses. In most of these institutions they
were herded indiscriminately with other pauper groups, receiving
no special treatment for their illness. The legislative investigation
of the Genesee County poorhouse in 1838, described in chapter xiii,
brought to light a shocking instance of this indiscriminate mingling.
In some places, however, efforts were made to segregate the mentally
ill in buildings apart from those housing the sane inmates. For example, in 1828 the state legislature authorized the supervisors of
Washington County to raise $1,500 for the purpose of erecting addi-
tional buildings at the poorhouse for "idiot and lunatic paupers."[2]

FOUNDING OF NEW YORK CITY ASYLUM

The New York County authorities early adopted the policy of
sending insane paupers who were deemed curable to the Bloomingdale Asylum as county charges, while chronic cases went to the
poorhouse. When Bellevue Hospital was opened in 1826 under the
supervision of the almshouse commissioners, the two lower stories
of the four-story structure were fitted out for the reception of
the insane poor, and the patients belonging to New York City and
County were removed thereto from Bloomingdale and from the
general almshouse. We are told that the wards for the insane at
Bellevue consisted of "twenty-four rooms and thirty-two cells." On
June 1, 1826, there were 107 insane patients at the hospital.[3]

Hardly had the hospital been opened than overcrowding set in. The close association of the insane with other groups of patients, and the impossibility of carrying out an appropriate system of classification led to a serious state of demoralization. In 1830 the Commissioners of the Almshouse urgently requested the Common Council to remedy the situation by removing the insane from Bellevue. "If a separate and distant place could be provided for the lunatics," they suggested, "the present hospital might be sufficient for the ordinary cases of sickness; and the commissioners would respectfully suggest the propriety of making an establishment on Blackwell's Island, especially for the accommodation of this most unfortunate class of our fellow-creatures."[4]

No immediate action followed the recommendation of the almshouse commissioners that a special institution for the insane be erected on Blackwell's Island, which had been purchased by the city in 1828. On February 25, 1833, the commissioners again placed their proposal before the Common Council, declaring that the continuation of the existing situation at Bellevue was having a very harmful effect on all the patients, sane and insane, crowded together in the institution.[5] Their request was given due consideration this time, and in 1834 the Common Council voted an initial appropriation of $3,000 toward the building of a separate insane asylum on Blackwell's Island.[6] Dr. James Macdonald, who was then superintendent of the Bloomingdale Asylum, was asked to draw up plans for the new institution, and building was commenced that year. But for various reasons construction was delayed, and it was not until June 10, 1839, that the New York City Lunatic Asylum was finally opened at Blackwell's Island with a capacity of over two hundred patients.[7] At its opening, 197 mental patients were received from Bellevue Hospital and the city almshouses.

This was the first publicly owned mental hospital in New York State, and also the first local institution of its kind to be opened in this country.* Let it be noted that it did not become a distinct institution until many years later, being operated as a component part of the almshouse department.

* The Boston Lunatic Hospital established in 1837 was opened December 11, 1839, several months after its New York prototype.

UTICA STATE HOSPITAL

Meanwhile there had been a strong movement toward the establishment of a mental hospital by the state. Virginia had opened the first state hospital as early as 1773. Kentucky had followed suit in 1824 and South Carolina in 1828. In the latter year a second state hospital was opened in Virginia. The Massachusetts State Hospital at Worcester was organized in 1832.

In his annual message to the legislature in January, 1830, Governor Enos T. Throop called the attention of that body to the privations and neglect suffered by the insane poor in almshouses and jails. He referred to the state census of 1825 which had indicated that there were then 819 insane persons in the state, of whom 263 were able to pay for their own support, 208 were in penal or pauper institutions, leaving 348 insane paupers at large.* Contrasting the horrible treatment of the mentally ill in poorhouses and jails with the humane, intelligent treatment accorded them at the Bloomingdale Asylum, Throop pointed out that the latter institution admitted very few poor patients and recommended the establishment of a public asylum "for the gratuitous care and recovery of that most destitute class of the human family, who are suffering from a darkened understanding and the evils of poverty at the same time."[8]

Responding to the governor's suggestion the legislature appointed a Committee of Inquiry on the condition of the insane. The Committee's report, submitted in 1831, included extensive material on contemporary theory and practice in the treatment of mental disease. It was a model report of its kind, exhibiting a rare degree of discernment and social consciousness on the part of its framers. Estimating that there were about 2,695 mentally handicapped persons in the state—including "lunatics" and "idiots"—the Committee noted that there were but two special institutions for their care and treatment, namely, the Bloomingdale Asylum, with accommodations for about two hundred patients, and a private asylum which had been established in 1830 by Dr. Samuel White at Hudson, with

* It should be kept in mind that census-taking at that time did not produce very accurate results, particularly with reference to the enumeration of the mentally handicapped.

a capacity of fifty patients. Both institutions were intended primarily for private patients, with only a few indigent patients being maintained at the cost of their respective towns or counties. The Committee asserted that there were practically no public facilities for the comfortable care and proper treatment of the insane poor:

> The whole system as to pauper lunatics and idiots, is radically defective. It makes no provision for their recovery. It does not effect the best mode of confinement. It does not sufficiently guard the public from the consequences of furious madness. And it is the most expensive mode of providing for them.[9]

Condemning the practice of confining the insane poor in county poorhouses, bidding them off to the lowest bidder, or simply neglecting them, the Committee firmly advocated the principle of state care for all the insane.

> The most powerful considerations of humanity address themselves to the State, to provide asylums for the gratuitous reception and treatment of those who are unable to bear the expense, and also for those who possess the ability of sustaining such expense, upon receiving from them a fair compensation for their support, and medical and moral treatment. The poor are a public charge. The State is bound to provide for their bodily wants; and if afflicted with mental disorder, the obligation is equally great to administer to their intellectual wants.

It is interesting to note that the Committee in its report subscribed to the fallacious belief of the period, that nearly all recent cases of mental disease could be cured *with the knowledge then available*.* This supposition was used by the Committee as an important argument in favor of building state hospitals. It was argued that prompt treatment in such institutions would insure prompt cure in most cases and save the expense of public support over long periods of time.

Recommending the erection of at least one state hospital, the Committee submitted a plan for such an institution based on a comprehensive study of existing systems here and abroad. In spite of the strong case presented by the Committee and the support of its stand by another committee reporting on the same subject later that year, the legislature for some reason failed to take action on its

---

* Deutsch has characterized this widespread fallacy, which was evolved from a curious combination of unsound statistics and institutional rivalries, as "the cult of curability."

proposal. Governor Throop again urged upon the legislature the need for a state hospital in his annual messages of 1831 and 1832, a recommendation repeated by his successor, Governor William L. Marcy, in his messages of 1834 and 1836.[10] In February, 1836, the legislature also received a memorial from the State Medical Society requesting state care for the insane. Estimating that there were about three thousand mentally handicapped persons in New York State, the memorialists declared that only one-third of this number had sufficient means for their support, the remaining two-thirds being dependent upon the public bounty. To provide curative treatment for the insane poor would be less expensive than to continue the existing methods of confining them in poorhouses, and the memorialists therefore recommended the erection by the state of a "proper asylum."[11]

As a result of this mounting pressure, the legislature finally enacted chapter 82, *Laws of 1836*, authorizing the establishment of the New York State Lunatic Asylum. By the terms of this act the governor was empowered to appoint three commissioners to select a suitable location. In 1837 a 130-acre site located in the city of Utica was purchased, and building operations were begun. But more than five years passed before the institution was ready for occupancy. An act was passed in 1841 calling for the appointment by the senate, upon the nomination of the governor, of five trustees of the State Lunatic Asylum for three-year terms. These trustees were authorized to visit existing mental hospitals in this and other states, to study the different types of management, and to report to the next session of the legislature on a practicable system of management for the institution at Utica.[12] In compliance with these directions a committee of the trustees visited fourteen of the twenty existing American institutions for the insane, and a report based on their survey was drawn up and submitted to the legislature in January, 1842.

This report, containing a fund of information on the contemporary care and treatment of the mentally ill in America, together with sound advice on institutional management, constitutes a highly valuable document.[13] Most of the recommendations of the trustees were embodied in chapter 135 of the *Laws of 1842:* "An act to organize the State Lunatic Asylum, and more effectually to provide for the care, maintenance and recovery of the insane." Control was vested in a nonsalaried board of managers consisting of nine men appointed by the senate upon the nomination of the governor for three-year terms. These managers were empowered to employ a superintendent who should be a well-educated physician, to frame rules and regulations, and to maintain an effective inspection of the asylum by frequent visits. The managers were directed to notify all county superintendents of the poor, through the county clerks, as soon as the institution should be ready for the reception of patients. Pauper patients were to be given preference over private pay patients in the selection of applicants. Furthermore, recent cases were to receive priority over chronic cases. As it happened, the admission to the institution was restricted almost exclusively to recent cases.* Persons could be committed by order of county or town poor-law officials, by court order, or through a certificate of insanity signed by two reputable physicians. Each county was entitled to send to the asylum at least one indigent insane patient whose disease was of recent origin, and as many additional patients—either recent or chronic cases—as the institution could accommodate, in proportion to the total insane population of that county. A person in indigent circumstances who was not a pauper but whose estate was insufficient to support him or his family while mentally ill could be admitted to the asylum upon court certification of both his insanity and his indigence, and maintained there at the expense of the county, city, or town of residence. A patient maintained at the asylum for one year or more could be removed to the county poorhouse upon the superintendent's certificate to the effect that he was harmless and likely to continue so and that his condition probably could not be improved by further treatment in the asylum or that he was apparently incurable. As an alternative to removal to the poorhouse, a patient could be discharged into the custody of friends or relatives who would give proper surety for "his peaceable behavior, safe custody and comfortable maintenance, without public charge." Rates to be charged to the localities for the dependent in-

---

* The definition of "recent case" varied from time to time. Usually it referred to persons who had been mentally ill less than six months or one year.

NEW YORK STATE LUNATIC ASYLUM, UTICA, IN 1843

sane were temporarily fixed at $2.50 per week for each patient, until April 1, 1843; thereafter rates not exceeding the actual cost of support and attendance, exclusive of officers' salaries, were to be fixed annually by the managers.

Bills were to be paid by the county treasurer. The county authorities, in turn, were given the right to require "any individual, town, city or county that is legally liable for the support of such patient, to reimburse the amount of said bills, with interest from the day of paying the same." In areas where the system of county responsibility for the poor prevailed, the county of course assumed the burden of paying for poor patients at the asylum; in cases where each town or city was charged with the support of its own poor, the county could require reimbursement for its payments to the institution.

The State Lunatic Asylum was opened on January 16, 1843, although it was still in an unfinished condition.* This was an event of great historic importance in the development of public welfare in New York, marking the establishment of the first charitable institution owned, operated, and controlled by the state. From the date of its opening until November 30, 1843, 276 patients were admitted into the asylum. Of these, 164 were supported at county or town expense, the remainder being paid for by friends or relatives.[14] Of the publicly supported patients, 76 had been committed by court order and 88 by poor-law officials.

Dr. Amariah Brigham, one of the foremost American psychiatrists of his day, served as the first superintendent of the institution, remaining in that capacity until his death in 1849. A man of broad humanity and progressive ideas, Dr. Brigham tried to conduct the asylum along the most advanced principles of the time. He was an enthusiastic proponent of the system of "moral treatment," intro-

---

* "Many of the necessary arrangements had not been completed; only a small part of the furniture had been procured; the furnaces intended for warming the apartments to be occupied by the patients were unfinished, the verandas uninclosed, and no means then in readiness for furnishing an adequate supply of water. But so strong was the desire expressed in applications from different parts of the State, to have the institution opened at the earliest day practicable, that we fixed on the 16th of January . . . ." (New York State Lunatic Asylum, *First Annual Report, 1844*, p. 5).

The institution was finally completed in 1847, at a total cost of $448,980.

duced into the care and treatment of the mentally sick by Philippe Pinel of France and William Tuke of England toward the close of the eighteenth century. This system included the use of a minimum amount of mechanical restraints such as strait-jackets, chains, and handcuffs; kind and considerate treatment of patients; occupational therapy, and adequate provision for amusements. Unfortunately, in spite of good intentions, the restrictions and difficulties under which Dr. Brigham and his contemporaries labored made inevitable certain institutional conditions that appear shockingly brutal to our generation.

The expectation that the centrally located Utica asylum would provide ample accommodations for all or most of the insane poor was soon shattered. The United States Census of the mentally handicapped in 1840—the first national census of its kind—had listed 2,340 "lunatics and idiots" in New York State.* A survey made by the trustees of the Utica State Asylum in 1841 revealed that there were 263 insane paupers confined in jails and poorhouses of 34 counties, besides 305 patients in the New York City Lunatic Asylum on Blackwell's Island.[15] The poor-relief statistics for 1843, gathered by the secretary of state, showed that there were 449 lunatics in the county poorhouses at the end of that year, exclusive of New York City.[16]

In their first annual *Report*, submitted to the legislature in January, 1844, the managers of the Utica State Asylum announced that the institution, which could accommodate only 225 patients, was already nearly filled to capacity and urgently recommended increased facilities.

The condition of the mentally ill in the county poorhouses of New York was brought to public attention in a masterly *Memorial* submitted to the state legislature in January, 1844, by the great reformer, Dorothea Dix. Several years before, Miss Dix had embarked on her epoch-making crusade in behalf of the mentally ill in America, and she had already won signal success in Massachusetts, Rhode Island, and New Jersey. The plan she invariably

---

* The census of the insane and the feeble-minded in 1840 was very inaccurate, and this figure should be regarded as merely approximate. The census enumerated the two groups together, without distinction.

followed was to make a personal tour of inspection of poorhouses, jails, and other institutions housing the insane in a particular state, and then to draw up a petition to the legislature giving an account of her observations together with recommendations for improving conditions. Her memorials usually contained a plea to remove the insane from poorhouses and jails to special institutions for their care and treatment. In her *Memorial* to the New York legislature, Miss Dix advanced the principle that the insane were the wards of the state—a principle finally adopted nearly a half-century later.

Your attention [she wrote] is solicited to the condition of many indigent and pauper insane persons in the county-houses of this State. . . . . Your petitioner asks to present their wants and their claims, regarding this unfortunate class not as being properly the charge of those towns and counties where their lot may have fallen, but as Wards of the State, made so by the most terrible calamity that can assail human nature. . . . .[17]

In spite of the recent opening of the Utica asylum, Miss Dix found that even the acute insane were inadequately provided for. Both curable and chronic patients were confined in large numbers in the county poorhouses, where the former were permitted to sink into "irrecoverable insanity" for lack of therapeutic treatment, while the latter fell "into states of the most shocking and brutalizing degradation—pitiable objects, at once sources of greatest discomfort to all brought within their vicinity, and exposed to exciting irritation from the reckless sports of the idle and vicious." The *Memorial* constituted a biting indictment of the county poorhouses of the time, supported by irrefutable facts obtained at firsthand. Here and there Miss Dix found insane persons relatively well treated at the poorhouse, but for the most part her *Memorial* was a long recital of men and women chained in "crazy dungeons" and outhouses, left stark naked in cold, clammy, dark cells and unventilated rooms, fettered with manacles, iron balls, and chains and collars, and whipped and beaten at the slightest provocation.

What was the proper remedy for this state of affairs? "There is but one remedy," she declared. "Prevent the possibility of such monstrous abuses by providing hospitals and asylums where vigilant inspection, and faithful care, shall protect and minister to those who, in losing reason, can no longer protect themselves."[18] Miss Dix urged the removal of all the insane from county poorhouses, suggesting that the curable cases might be sent to the Utica and Bloomingdale asylums. Between four and six separate state asylums should be established for the incurable insane, she said. These could be built and maintained at a lesser cost than the curative institutions for, while providing the inmates with comfort and careful attendance, they could dispense with certain features absolutely essential to hospitals for the curable insane. This policy of separate state institutions for the curable and incurable insane was adopted in New York two decades later. The eminent reformer insisted that the state was the only administrative unit able to provide adequately for the mentally ill.

Miss Dix's splendid *Memorial* bore no immediate fruit, but within a few years the problem of public care of the insane became so acute as to lead to a widespread movement toward the establishment of additional state hospitals. Noting the overcrowded condition of Utica State Asylum, Governor Horatio Seymour, in his annual message to the legislature in 1853, urged the erection of another state hospital in the western part of New York and repeated his recommendation the following year. His successor, Myron H. Clark, also advocated this course in his annual messages of 1855 and 1856.[19] At the time Governor Seymour's message of 1854 was delivered, there were 446 patients in the Utica State Asylum and 556 in the New York City Lunatic Asylum on Blackwell's Island. Together, these public asylums accounted for less than half the 2,506 insane persons in New York State enumerated by the United States Census of 1850.[20]

Agitation for the erection of additional state hospitals for the insane came from an unexpected source at this critical stage. County authorities often had been censured for a tendency to confine insane paupers in the poorhouse, where the cost of their care seldom amounted to more than a dollar a week, instead of sending them to the state asylum at Utica, where the charge for maintaining pauper patients was two dollars a week. But strangely enough these officials played a leading part during the 1850's in the strong movement toward state care for the insane. In August, 1855, a convention of county superintendents of the poor of New York State was held at

Utica to consider the subject of provision for the insane poor.* At this convention the following preamble and resolutions were unanimously adopted:

WHEREAS, It is already conceded, and has been adopted as the policy of this State, that insanity is a disease requiring, in all its forms and stages, special means for treatment and care; therefore,

Resolved, That the State should make ample and suitable provisions for all its insane, not in a condition to reside in private families.

Resolved, No insane person should be treated, or in any way taken care of in any county-poor or alms-house, or other receptacle provided for, and in which paupers are maintained or supported.

Resolved, That a proper classification is an indispensable element in the treatment of the insane which can only be secured in establishments constructed with a special view to their treatment.

Resolved, Insane persons considered curable, and those considered incurable, should not be provided for in separate establishments.[21]

The last resolution stood in sharp contrast to Miss Dix's recommendation that the curable and incurable insane should be provided for in separate establishments.

Another meeting of the county superintendents was held in Syracuse in September, 1855, at which a committee of five was appointed to memorialize the state legislature for speedy action in providing for the insane poor.[22] A memorial "on Lunacy and its relation to Pauperism and for relief of Insane Poor" was drawn up and presented to the legislature in January, 1856. It was estimated by the memorialists that on December 1, 1854, there were 2,419 pauper lunatics in New York State. Of this number, 296 were in the state asylum at Utica, 1,352 were confined in county almshouses, and 771 were residing in private families or were otherwise provided for.[23] Replies to a questionnaire sent out to poor-law officials indicated that a large majority of the insane who were public charges had been self-supporting before the onset of their disease, a fact which led the memorialists to conclude that insanity was a frequent cause of pauperism. The cure of the insane, therefore, was not only a matter of humanity but of public economy. But even the incurable

* This convention was the forerunner of the annual conventions of the county superintendents of the poor, beginning with 1871. Organized on a permanent basis as the Association of County Superintendents of the Poor in New York State, the body is now known as the Association of Public Welfare Officials of New York State.

insane, according to the county superintendents, were entitled to care in special institutions for the mentally ill. The memorial ended with the recommendation that the legislature "at once cause the immediate erection of two state lunatic hospitals, so located that they may accommodate the largest number of insane at present unprovided for, and so relinquish the undersigned the pain of longer continuing a system fraught with injustice and inhumanity." This appeal was eloquently supported in a report of a select committee appointed by the senate to consider the memorial.[24] It seemed at this time that the establishment of at least one additional state hospital could no longer be delayed, particularly in view of the fact that the Utica State Asylum was rejecting scores of applications for admission each year because of overcrowded conditions. A bill calling for the founding of two state hospitals was actually introduced and failed of passage only by a narrow margin. When, in 1857, the famous senate inquiry of conditions in almshouses and jails (described at length in chap. xiii) revealed the terrible treatment of the insane in these institutions, the investigating committee recommended the immediate construction of at least two more state asylums. It again appeared that concrete action was at last inevitable. Nevertheless, nearly a decade was to pass before another state hospital was founded.

RISE OF COUNTY ASYLUMS

In the meantime a number of counties were establishing county insane asylums usually consisting of a separate building on the poor farm presided over by the almshouse authorities. These county asylums varied considerably, representing at times little more than names. For example, Dorothea Dix relates in her *Memorial* of 1844 that "at a recent meeting of the supervisors and superintendents of Erie County, these gentlemen voted that the series of cells at the county alms-house should be called the *County Hospital for the Insane!* It will require a great many votes to convert that little building, with its few cell-rooms, into a hospital or even an asylum."[25] On the other hand, Westchester County maintained a department for the insane at the poorhouse grounds, which Miss Dix praised very highly in her survey, comparing its accommodations with those

provided at Bloomingdale and Utica. She also visited the Kings
County Insane Asylum which had been established at the Flatbush
poor farm in 1838. It was rated by Miss Dix as greatly inferior to
the insane department at the Westchester County poorhouse, although well ordered in comparison with other county "receptacles."
Influenced perhaps by the Dix report, the Kings County supervisors
in 1844 applied to the state legislature for permission to borrow
$6,000 for the erection of a new lunatic asylum on the almshouse
grounds. This authorization was granted by chapter 203, *Laws of
1844*, and the building was completed the following year.[26] This
structure failing to meet the need, the county supervisors in 1853
were authorized by the legislature to raise $50,000 for the erection
of still another county asylum at Flatbush. It was completed in
1855 at a cost far exceeding the original estimate and was placed
under the management of the county superintendents of the poor.[27]

In the latter year the supervisors of Monroe County voted to build
an asylum for the indigent insane as part of the poorhouse system.
The building was opened in 1857 with accommodations for about
forty patients; within a few months the supervisors' committee on
lunacy revealed serious overcrowding and other unfavorable conditions at the new asylum.[28] In 1863 the legislature passed an act
separating the Monroe County Insane Asylum at Rochester as an
institution distinct from the poorhouse and vesting full control and
management of the asylum in the county supervisors. The latter
were empowered to appoint a warden to have full charge of the institution under their supervision.[29]

In 1853 the Almshouse Committee of the Albany Common Council submitted a plan for the reorganization of that institution, a
prominent feature of which was a proposal for the erection of a
separate building for the insane.[30] Four years later the state legislature appropriated $2,000 to both the Albany Lunatic Asylum and the
Marshall Infirmary (a corporate hospital for the destitute insane established in the city of Troy in 1851), "provided that said institutions
shall each arrange for the reception and treatment of twelve pauper
lunatics, other than [from] the counties of Rensselaer and Albany,
upon the same terms upon which such patients are received at the
state lunatic asylum at Utica."[31] The provision relating to the Al-

bany institution apparently marked the first state appropriation for a county asylum. Evidently the Albany authorities were unable to comply with the condition that the institution should receive twelve pauper lunatics from other counties on the same terms as those in effect at Utica, for the state grant went unclaimed for at least two years.[32]

Counties having no special accommodation for their insane poor sometimes sent them to local asylums in other counties, where they were maintained at specified rates which were in most instances cheaper than those charged at the Utica State Asylum. Ordinarily the feeble-minded as well as the insane poor were maintained in these county asylums.

THE WILLARD STATE ASYLUM FOR THE CHRONIC INSANE

The rise of the county asylums did little to alleviate the condition of the insane poor in this state. They were usually lacking in the most elementary facilities for special treatment of the mentally ill; in most cases their virtue lay primarily in the separation of the sane and insane paupers. The agitation for additional state provision for the insane finally became so intense that the legislature in 1864 enacted a bill directing Dr. Sylvester D. Willard, secretary of the State Medical Society, to conduct a comprehensive survey of the condition of the insane in poorhouses, asylums, and other institutions where the mentally ill were kept, and to submit a report on his findings.[33] With the co-operation of physicians and poor-law officials, Dr. Willard was able to gather a great deal of information on the subject, which he incorporated in an important *Report* submitted to the legislature in January, 1865.[34] His investigation revealed the state of the insane in poorhouses to be as desperate as that found by Miss Dix in 1845 and the senate investigating committee in 1857. The *Report* constituted a strong indictment of the existing system and was supported by many specific examples of the cruelty and neglect suffered by the insane poor. Dr. Willard pointed out that there were then 1,345 insane persons confined in the almshouses of fifty-five counties, exclusive of New York and Kings. Although most of these seemed to be incurable cases, there was a number of hopeful cases among them. All, curable and incurable, should be cared for in special state institutions, Dr. Willard declared. Like Miss Dix, he was of the opinion that the best means of solving the problem would be to set aside the asylum at Utica for acute cases and to provide for the chronic cases in a separate institution. "Let an institution for incurables be established," he said. "Let the incurables be there colonized. Take the insane from the counties where they are ill provided for first, and change the law relative to the insane poor, so that counties shall not have the management of them, nor any authority over them."[35]

The recommendation of Dr. Willard, ably seconded by Governor Reuben Fenton, was promptly acted upon by the legislature through the passage of chapter 342, *Laws of 1865*, authorizing the establishment of a state asylum for the chronic insane. As accommodations were made available at the new institution, the county superintendents of the poor were to remove thereto all the chronic insane from the almshouses. Thereafter, instead of transferring unrecovered pauper patients to the county poorhouse, the authorities of the Utica State Asylum were to remove such persons to the new asylum for chronics. With the exception of those counties authorized by law to maintain their own insane asylums, county judges and superintendents of the poor were to commit the indigent and pauper insane classified as recent or acute cases to the Utica institution and chronics to the newly established asylum. As originally drawn up, the bill had designated the new institution as the Beck Asylum for the Chronic Insane, named after Dr. T. Romeyn Beck, who had been a prominent leader of medicine in this state. But through an eleventh-hour amendment the name was changed to the Willard Asylum in honor of the man whose report had inspired the legislation and who had died suddenly a few days before enactment of the law.

The governor was authorized to appoint six trustees, with the consent of the senate, to serve for terms varying from two to six years. All the indigent and pauper insane received into the institution were to be charges upon the county from which they were sent. The trustees were directed to fix the rate of maintenance, not to exceed two dollars a week for each patient.* This low maximum, which

* Chapter 541 of the *Laws of 1872* repealed the provision fixing the maximum rate at $2.00 per week, merely requiring that the weekly rate should not exceed the actual

covered less than two-thirds the cost of supporting a patient at the asylum, was a concession to the county authorities, whose ardor for a state-care system had cooled by this time and who were now protesting against the "expensiveness" of maintenance in state institutions.

The establishment of the Willard Asylum marked several distinct departures in the care and treatment of the mentally ill in New York State. Previously state care had been confined to recent cases received at the Utica asylum, while the county poorhouse remained the common receptacle for the chronic insane. Now it was intended to remove all the insane from county poorhouses and to place them in state institutions designed for their special care. The Willard Asylum also represented the first application in the United States of the principle of operating two distinct types of state institutions for the insane—hospitals for acute cases and asylums for chronics. A site for the new institution was selected near the village of Ovid, in Seneca County. Work was begun in 1866, and in 1869 the asylum was opened under the superintendency of Dr. John B. Chapin. The founders of the Willard Asylum intended it to accommodate fifteen hundred patients, making it by far the largest institution of its kind in the United States up to that time. This plan, which differed radically from contemporary psychiatric opinion on the proper size of mental hospitals, grew out of the desire to provide for all the chronic insane then confined in county poorhouses. But when the institution was opened in October, 1869, it had accommodations for only two hundred and fifty patients. Not until 1880 did the capacity reach the goal of fifteen hundred set by the founders.[36]

HUDSON RIVER STATE HOSPITAL

Hardly had the Willard Act of 1865 been passed than it was realized that even should the proposed asylum absorb all the chronic insane poor then in county poorhouses, greater institutional facilities would be required to take care of acute cases that could not gain admission into the already overcrowded state hospital at Utica. In

---

cost of support and attendance, exclusive of officers' salaries. The rate was thereupon raised to $3.00 weekly, but by 1876 it was lowered to $2.78, owing to the pressure of county poor-law officials.

1866 the state legislature authorized Governor Fenton to appoint five commissioners to secure a suitable site "on or near the Hudson river, below the city of Albany, upon which to erect the Hudson river asylum for the insane."[37] A site was duly selected at Poughkeepsie, comprising a 206-acre farm presented to the state by the city of Poughkeepsie and the county of Dutchess. On March 16, 1867, the legislature established the Hudson River State Hospital for the Insane, to be built on the site chosen by the commissioners, and appropriated $100,000 toward its erection.[38] It should be noted that this was the first institution of its kind in New York to be officially designated "State Hospital." The statute authorized the governor to appoint the first board of nine managers for the new hospital to serve for terms varying from four to six years. They were vested with the government of the hospital, including the power to appoint a medical superintendent. It was specified in the act that the capacity of the institution should be limited to five hundred patients.* Building proceeded at a snail's pace, and the new state hospital was not opened until October, 1871, a total of seven patients being received up to the end of November that year.[39] So slow was the process of construction that by 1886 accommodations for only four hundred patients had been provided, although over $1,500,000 had been expended on the institution. The cost of building this hospital became a public scandal, and a legislative investigation was conducted in 1872.

The original act of establishment and organization not having specified the class of insane persons to be admitted into the Hudson River State Hospital, the managers voted to admit only acute or recent cases. Chapter 337, *Laws of 1870*, limited admission to patients from the eastern counties. A Hudson River State Hospital district was constituted, consisting of the counties of Albany, Clinton, Columbia, Dutchess, Essex, Franklin, Greene, Kings, New York, Orange, Putnam, Queens, Rensselaer, Richmond, Rockland, Saratoga, Suffolk, Sullivan, Ulster, Warren, Washington, and Westchester.

* This limit was a concession to the Association of Medical Superintendents of American Institutions for the Insane (now known as the American Psychiatric Association), which had severely condemned the massive scale on which the Willard Asylum was planned and had issued a dictum fixing the maximum capacity for a state hospital at six hundred patients.

This was the first creation of a state-hospital district in New York, anticipating the time when the entire state was divided into such districts. Dr. Joseph M. Cleaveland was appointed the first medical superintendent, serving in that capacity until 1893.

A significant development during this period was the assumption by the state of the expense for maintaining an insane Indian at the Utica State Asylum for nearly thirty years. In 1853 the legislature appropriated $150 to that institution for the maintenance of one Mark Jack, the Indian in question. Thereafter until 1881 the state annually appropriated sums varying from $175 to $300 for his care at the asylum.[40] As far as can be ascertained this represented the first concrete instance involving the principle that the Indian poor were properly a state charge; it was also the first instance where the state assumed complete financial responsibility for the care of an insane person.*

FIRST STATE INSTITUTION FOR MENTAL DEFECTIVES

In his annual report for 1845, Dr. Amariah Brigham, superintendent of the Utica State Asylum, included a long discussion on the condition of the feeble-minded in New York State. He pointed out that the state census of 1845 had enumerated more than sixteen hundred idiots† and that most of these were either confined in county poorhouses or left to wander about in total neglect. In contrast to this situation he went on to report the successful European experiments then being carried on, especially by Dr. Edward Seguin of Paris, in teaching and training feeble-minded children, an achievement popularly considered impossible at that time. His enthusiasm aroused by the results obtained in the pioneer European schools, Dr. Brigham expressed the hope that a similar experiment might soon be undertaken here under the auspices of the state of New York.[41]

On January 13, 1846, Dr. F. F. Backus, a member of the New York State Senate, successfully introduced a resolution to appoint a

* In 1871 and for several years afterward the state legislature voted appropriations for the maintenance of Susan Green, an insane Indian woman, at the Willard State Asylum (*Laws of 1872*, chap. 541; *Laws of 1878*, chap. 29).

† It should be remembered that the term "idiot," was then used in a generic sense, synonymous with "feeble-minded" and "mentally defective," as currently used.

committee to consider that part of the state census of 1845 relating to idiots. Ten days later Dr. Backus, as chairman of the committee, submitted a report calling for the establishment of a state institution for the education of idiot children.[42] This constituted the first legislative effort toward separate provision for the feeble-minded in America. A bill embodying this measure was drawn up by Dr. Backus and passed the senate, but failed of passage in the assembly by a narrow margin. A similar bill brought before the legislature in 1847 likewise met with defeat.

Nothing concrete was accomplished in this direction until 1851. In that year progressive individuals conducted an intensive campaign to get favorable legislative action in behalf of the feeble-minded. During the campaign Dr. Samuel Gridley Howe, director of the Massachusetts School for Feeble-minded and Idiotic Youth which had been opened at Boston in 1848 as the first public institution of its kind in this country, brought some of his pupils before the legislators at Albany and gave a demonstration of the teachability of this group. So impressed were the legislators with this demonstration that they enacted a bill establishing an Asylum for Idiots, on an experimental basis. A suitable building was to be procured by a board of trustees appointed by the governor, and the trustees were to select as state pupils not more than twenty children —some from each judicial district in the state—"whose parents or guardians were unable to provide for their support." In addition to these state-supported pupils the trustees could admit pay pupils at their discretion. The sum of $6,000 for each of two years was appropriated to the institution, with the provision that the trustees should report annually to the legislature.[43] A building in Albany was rented for the purpose, and it was opened as the New York State Asylum for Idiots in October, 1851. Dr. Hervey B. Wilbur, who had been conducting a private school for the feeble-minded at Barre, Massachusetts, since 1848, was selected as superintendent and served in that capacity until his death in 1883. Twenty-five pupils—eighteen of them supported by the state and seven paid for by parents or friends—were admitted to the school during the first year. All were very young children, since the educational character of the institution as opposed to the purely custodial was stressed from the first, and selections were made from those applicants who seemed most teachable.[44] So successful did the experimental school at Albany prove that the legislature in 1853 decided to place it on a permanent basis, appropriating $20,000 toward the erection of new buildings on a site to be selected by the trustees.[45] A site was chosen at Syracuse, and in August, 1855, the first institution in America built expressly for the reception of the feeble-minded was opened there. Fifty pupils were transferred to Syracuse from the temporary asylum at Albany, and by the end of the year the pupils in the new school numbered between eighty and ninety, most of whom were state supported.[46]

The State Asylum for Idiots was reorganized in 1862 by chapter 220 of the laws of that year. The act provided for a board of trustees consisting of eight specified persons, with the governor, lieutenant-governor, secretary of state, controller, and superintendent of public instruction serving ex officio. Trustees were thereafter to be appointed by the senate upon nomination of the governor for terms of eight years. A significant feature of the statute was its detailed directions for the keeping of careful records by the institutional authorities. According to the law the asylum was to maintain 120 pupils at state expense, to be designated as "state pupils," and in addition as many pay pupils as could be conveniently accommodated. County supervisors were required to pay twenty dollars annually for the clothing of state pupils received from their districts. State pupils discharged from the asylum were to be sent to the keeper of the county poorhouse, the cost of such removal to be charged to the county.

By 1866 the number of feeble-minded children at the asylum rose to 141, of whom 125 were state supported, the remainder being pay pupils.[47] In his report for that year Dr. Wilbur emphasized the fact that the school could accommodate but a fraction of the mental defectives in the state and urged the expansion of state facilities for the education of those who were teachable and trainable.

In the same year the city of New York established a School for the Mental and Physical Improvement of Idiot Children on Randall's Island, under the supervision of its Department of Public Charities and Correction. The school was opened in October, 1866, with twenty pupils, ranging from eight to fourteen years of age, in charge of a teacher who had studied under Dr. Wilbur.[48] By the end of 1867 there were forty children at the city school, some of whom were graded as unteachables and kept in a ward apart from the others.[49]

PUBLIC PROVISION FOR DEAF-MUTES

As has been noted in chapter xi, the New York Institution for the Instruction of the Deaf and Dumb was established at New York City in 1817 and five years later was authorized by the legislature to maintain, at state expense, thirty-two indigent pupils at the annual rate of $150 each. Counties were authorized to send to the institution at their own expense any deaf-mute not provided for under the terms of the act. In 1823 a similar institution was established at Canajoharie in Montgomery County, but it proved unsuccessful and was dissolved in 1836. Its pupils were transferred to the New York school, which, for many years thereafter, remained the only place of its kind in the state. The number of state-supported pupils was gradually increased by legislative action, and in 1854 the legislature removed the limit entirely. A statute of that year directed the institution to admit every indigent deaf-mute between the ages of twelve and twenty-five years whose parents (or nearest friend, if an orphan) should have been residents of the state for three years, upon application made in his or her behalf and approved by the state superintendent of public instruction. The state undertook to pay for the board, lodging, and tuition of such pupils at the prevailing rate of $150 per annum for a maximum of five years, which could be extended, upon recommendation of the superintendent of public instruction, for an additional three years in individual cases.[50]

At the end of 1854 there were at the institution 279 pupils, of whom 203 were state-supported. The remainder included pupils sent and supported by New York City and New Jersey, and private pupils.[51]

A series of events in 1857 almost brought the institution under state operation and control. Its removal from Fiftieth Street to Washington Heights in New York City took place during that year, occasioning a debt of several hundred thousand dollars. Deciding that the financial situation was too difficult for a private body to cope with, the directors offered to turn over the institution to the state if it would agree to continue to operate the school. This was accepted, and an act was passed appropriating $29,000 toward the completion of the new buildings, to be paid when the directors should convey all the institutional property to the state. Upon fulfilment of this condition, the governor was to appoint three commissioners to examine the accounts and affairs of the school and to recommend "the best method to be adopted by the state for government thereof."[52]

The property conveyance was duly executed, and three commissioners appointed by Governor King submitted their report to the legislature in 1858. Finding the institution to be in excellent condition, the commissioners recommended that it be taken over immediately and "governed in like manner with other charities of the State."[53]

A bill reorganizing the institution on the basis of state ownership and operation was drawn up by the commissioners and placed before the legislature. But for some reason the legislature failed to act on the report. Furthermore, because of the poor condition of the state treasury resulting from the depression of 1857, the $29,000 appropriation was not paid out, in spite of the fact that the directors of the New York institution had met the requirements of the act. In 1859 the superintendent of public instruction brought this situation to the attention of the legislature,[54] but again no action was taken, and the whole matter of bringing the institution under state control was dropped. As the New York School for the Deaf it is operated to this day as a corporate institution, although still receiving most of its funds from the state.

The statute of 1854 had authorized the institution to receive an indefinite number of state pupils between the ages of twelve and twenty-five years, permitting the counties to send (at their own expense) deaf-mutes who did not come within the age group set by the act or who were otherwise ineligible for state support. In 1863 the legislature enacted a bill making it mandatory for county supervisors or town overseers of the poor to send to the institution all indigent deaf-mute children between six and twelve years of age, upon application of the parents, guardians, or friends of such children, who were to be maintained there at town or county expense

From a contemporary wood engraving, "A Place in the Country"

NEW YORK INSTITUTION FOR THE BLIND, 1860

until reaching the age of twelve years.[55] If still retained at the institution upon passing this age, it was inferred that the state would thereafter undertake the responsibility of supporting the child there.

The second permanent school for the deaf in New York State dates from 1839, when Louis Le Couteulx of Buffalo bequeathed a one-acre plot in that city to be used as the site of such an institution. As a consequence the Le Couteulx St. Mary's Institution for the Improved Instruction of Deaf-Mutes was started there in 1859 under the direction of the Roman Catholic Order of Sisters of St. Joseph, with four deaf-mute children in attendance. Owing to lack of support the institution was forced to suspend within a few months, but in 1862 it was reopened on a permanent basis with six pupils. In 1865 it received an appropriation of $500 from the state, and lump-sum state grants were made regularly for several years thereafter.[56] Legislative enactments of 1871 and 1872 authorized the Le Couteulx St. Mary's Institution to admit indigent deaf-mutes at the expense of towns, counties, or the state, on the same basis operative with reference to the New York institution.[57] Incorporated in 1853 as Le Couteulx St. Mary's Benevolent Society for the Deaf and Dumb, it is now known as St. Mary's School for the Deaf.

INSTITUTIONS FOR THE BLIND

The New York Institution for the Blind, founded in 1831, was the second of its kind to be established in the United States, and the first to go into operation. It was organized through the efforts of Dr. Samuel Akerly, Dr. John D. Russ, Samuel Wood, and other philanthropists, whose interest in the project was awakened by the pioneer work in educating the blind then going on in Scotland, England, and other countries, and by the organization of a like institution at Boston in 1829. The national census of 1830, which enumerated eight hundred blind persons in New York State, including many children, served as a stimulating factor to the movement.

Incorporated through chapter 214, *Laws of 1831*, the New York Institution for the Blind was opened March 15, 1832, under the direction of Dr. Russ. Its first pupils were three pauper children who had been blinded during one of the frequent outbreaks of ophthal-

mia at the city almshouse.* Two months later three more boys from
the same place were added to the list of pupils.[58] At first the school
was supported entirely by private contributions and the proceeds of
fairs, but in 1833 it received a grant of $500 from the city of New
York. During that year the need for expansion brought about the
removal of the institution from its original location on Mercer
Street to Ninth Avenue, between Thirty-third and Thirty-fourth
streets, which was then regarded as a suburban district. It is now
known as the New York Institute for the Education of the Blind.

Acting favorably upon a petition for aid, the state legislature in
1834 authorized the school to receive four indigent blind persons between the ages of eight and twenty-five years from each of the eight
senate districts, to be maintained and taught as state pupils at the
rate of $150 each per annum. An act of 1836 appropriated $12,000
toward the erection of a new building and raised the number of state
pupils to eight from each senate district.[59] This number was again
doubled by chapter 200, Laws of 1839, which also directed the state
superintendent of common schools to visit and inspect the institution and to submit an annual report on its condition. Thereafter the
school received frequent lump-sum grants from the state in addition
to the per capita payments for state pupils. From 1834 to 1866 it
received a total of $647,621 from the state. During this period more
than 90 per cent of its pupils were supported at state expense.[60]

In 1862 the state assembly appointed a committee "to investigate
the charges of mismanagement and malappropriation of funds"
made against the officials of the New York Institution for the Blind.
Although it found no evidence to substantiate the charges, the investigating committee urged the passage of a law requiring all
scientific and eleemosynary organizations receiving state funds to
submit an annual financial report to the state controller.[61] Acting
on this recommendation the legislature enacted chapter 419, Laws
of 1864, providing:

No moneys shall be paid from the treasury of this State pursuant to any act
of the legislature making appropriation to any hospital, orphan asylum, benevo-

* A large proportion of the inmates of charitable institutions were stricken with
blindness in those days, as a result of the unbelievably insanitary conditions then prevailing in such establishments.

lent association, educational, scientific, charitable or other similar institution not under control of the State, until the president and secretary, or the managers of such institution, shall have made a report to the comptroller of the operations, purposes, financial condition, expenditures and management of such institution.

This law marked a significant step in the development of state supervision over private welfare organizations in New York.

NEW YORK STATE SCHOOL FOR THE BLIND, BATAVIA

Another investigation into the affairs of the New York Institution for the Blind was conducted early in 1864 by the Senate Committee on Charitable and Religious Societies, upon the petition of a group of pupils who complained of "improper treatment, neglect and inefficiency of their teachers." After holding hearings and inspecting the institution, the Committee dismissed some of the charges as baseless, but felt compelled "most reluctantly to say that the general condition and management of the institution is far below the proper standard. A complete reformation seems to be necessary, from the kitchen to the school room."[62]

In January of the following year another petition from the pupils of the New York Institution was referred to the same Committee. The contents of the memorial have not been ascertained, but the Committee which considered it evidently came to the conclusion that an additional school for the blind was needed, so they submitted a bill embodying this object three weeks after receiving the memorial.[63] This bill was enacted as chapter 587, *Laws of 1865*, authorizing the establishment of the New York State Institution for the Blind. It directed the governor to appoint one group of commissioners to select a site for the school and, acting together with the controller and secretary of state, another group to supervise its erection. As soon as the school was ready for occupancy the governor was to appoint a board of nine managers to take charge of it. Application for admission to the institution was to be made to a justice of the supreme court or the common pleas court, or to a county judge. If satisfied, after inquiry, that such person or his parents or guardians were unable to pay for his support and that the county of residence was entitled to send him to the school, the justice or judge could make out an admission order for a term not exceeding seven years.

Blind children whose parents had died in the service of the Union Army, or from wounds or injuries received during the Civil War, were to receive preference over other applicants. Counties were permitted to send indigent applicants to the institution in proportion to the ratio of their blind population to the total number in the state and were to pay fifty dollars per annum toward the support of such persons.[64]

It was at first decided to locate the school at Binghamton, but a fifty-acre plot at Batavia, Genesee County, presented by that village for the purpose, was finally selected as a suitable site. In 1867 a statute was passed defining the objects of the newly established school and making some important changes in the act of 1865. The qualification of indigence as a requisite for admission was removed, it being provided that "all blind persons of suitable age and capacity for instruction, who are legal residents of the State, shall be entitled to the privileges of the New York State institution for the blind, without charge, and for such a period of time in each individual case as may be deemed expedient by the board of trustees of said institution." Under the previous act the counties were required to pay fifty dollars a year for each pupil belonging to them, but the state now undertook the financial support of all those sent to the school. Expenses for clothing and for travel to and from the institution were to be defrayed by friends or relatives of the pupil; upon their failure to do so, such cost was to be charged to the county. Pupils from upstate counties were to be transferred from the New York Institution for the Blind as accommodations were made available at the new school. The former institution was to retain and to continue to receive all blind pupils sent from the counties of New York and Kings.[65] The New York State Institution for the Blind (now New York State School for the Blind) was opened September 2, 1868, receiving forty pupils during its first month of operation. Twenty-nine of these were transferred from the New York Institution.[66]

NEW YORK STATE INEBRIATE ASYLUM, BINGHAMTON

The temperance movement in America reached tremendous proportions during the 1830's and 1850's. As has already been indicated in previous pages, there was a common tendency throughout this entire period to attribute the greater part of pauperism and crime to inebriety. A great deal of interest was displayed in the relationship between drink and the social ills, as exemplified in the personal survey of the poorhouses and jails of New York State conducted by Samuel Chipman in 1833 to formulate a statistical measurement of this relationship. At the end of his survey Mr. Chipman concluded that "more than three-fourths of the pauperism is occasioned by intemperance, and more than five-sixths of those committed on criminal charges are intemperate."[67] A necessary corollary of the emphasis on intemperance as an etiological factor in crime and pauperism was the idea that its cure would bring about a great diminution of the two social ills and also of mental disease, in the causation of which inebriety was given an exaggerated role. By the beginning of the fifties a definite movement was forming in various parts of the country in favor of special public hospitals for the treatment of inebriates. This movement was very articulate in New York State, where a group of citizens led by Dr. J. Edward Turner petitioned the legislature in 1852 for a charter enabling them to establish an inebriate asylum. Their request was rejected that year and the next, but in 1854 they succeeded in obtaining a charter through the passage of an act "to incorporate the United States Inebriate Asylum for the reformation of the poor and destitute inebriate." A board of twenty directors was set up with authorization to build an institution in New York City where poor and destitute inebriates would be received for treatment.[68] Apparently this was the first institution of its kind to be established in America; its founders claimed it was the first in the world.[69] An amendment enacted the following year removed the specification that the asylum be built in New York City and empowered it to retain all committed persons for a period of from three to six months.[70] Indicative of the strength of the temperance movement at this time was the passage in 1855 of a drastic statewide prohibition act—the first in New York—forbidding the sale or use of intoxicating liquors except for medicinal or sacramental purposes and significantly entitled: "An act for the prevention of Intemperance, Pauperism and Crime."[71] This statute was declared unconstitutional in 1856.

Notwithstanding the popularity of the temperance movement, a four-year subscription campaign instituted by the directors of the United States Inebriate Asylum to raise $50,000 fell far short of its goal, owing partly to the economic crises of 1854 and 1857. In the latter year an amendment to the charter was made changing the name to the New York State Inebriate Asylum and raising the number of trustees to forty. It empowered the institution to "receive and retain all inebriates who enter said asylum either voluntarily or by order of the committee of any habitual drunkard."* All poor and destitute inebriates admitted to the asylum were to be employed at useful labor on the premises. Earnings accruing from their labor, after deducting the expense of their support, were to be sent to their families monthly or were to be paid to them upon their discharge.[72] In 1858 a 252-acre grant of land donated by the citizens of Binghamton was accepted as the site for the asylum, and building was started there the same year. Meanwhile urgent requests for state aid on the part of the trustees were repeatedly rejected, but in 1859 the legislature voted that each county in the state should annually pay to the institution 10 per cent of the excise moneys.[73] The payments made to the asylum by the counties under this law amounted to $13,345 in 1863 and $17,130 in 1865, being used toward defraying the cost of building.[74] Although still far from complete, the institution was opened for the reception of patients on July 3, 1864, under the superintendency of its principal founder, Dr. J. Edward Turner. Only fifteen patients were received during its first seven months of operation.[75] The asylum was closed temporarily in October, 1866, with its affairs, financial and otherwise, in a chaotic state. A sharp disagreement had arisen between the trustees and the superintendent over matters of authority, which culminated with the resignation of Dr. Turner. Charges and countercharges disclosed astonishing instances of financial juggling and general mismanagement. Reopened in May, 1867, the asylum's condition continued in a poor state, and in 1871 it was reorganized by the legislature, which empowered the governor to appoint the board of trustees. In 1873 the state took over full control, ownership, and operation of the institution.[76] But the experiment proved such an utter failure that the

---

* The term of commitment was extended to one year in 1865.

asylum was abolished by legislative enactment in 1879, and the buildings were converted into the Binghamton Asylum for the Chronic Insane.[77]

SUMMARY

A distinguishing feature of public welfare developments during this period was the rise of state institutions for the mentally and physically handicapped. The State Lunatic Asylum at Utica, opened in 1843, was the first charitable institution under state ownership, operation, and control. The cost of supporting indigent patients, however, was charged to the counties whence they came. The hope of the founders of the Utica institution, that it would make possible the removal of all mentally ill persons from county poorhouses, proved illusory; it could accommodate only a small proportion of even the recent or curable cases. Although the need for additional hospital facilities for the indigent insane soon became apparent and public agitation toward that end was strong and continuous, more than a score of years passed following the opening of the Utica asylum before another state asylum was established. Meanwhile the more populous counties established county asylums usually consisting merely of a separate building on the poor farm maintained as an integral part of the poorhouse system, but in a few instances operated as distinct institutions. The New York City Lunatic Asylum on Blackwell's Island was the first municipal mental hospital to be established in this country. The founding of the Willard State Asylum in 1865 marked the inauguration of a new policy entailing the operation of separate state institutions for the acute and the chronic insane. This policy was to continue in force for a quarter-century. By 1866 three state hospitals for the insane had been established, although but one was actually in operation.

When the experiments of Edward Seguin and other pioneers proved that the higher grades of feeble-minded children were teachable and that many could be trained to a point where they could find satisfactory adjustment to normal society, a demand for proper institutions for their education arose. As a result of this demand and of the general trend toward removing various dependent groups from almshouses to special institutions, the State Asylum for Idiots (now the Syracuse State School) was established in 1851. It was the first of its kind to be opened under state ownership and control.

The New York Institution for the Instruction of the Deaf and Dumb, which had been established in 1817, was dependent on the state for most of its financial support throughout this period. It almost became a state institution as a result of developments starting in 1857, when its property was formally conveyed to the state, but for some inexplicable cause the legislature failed to place the school under state control, and it retained its corporate character. Except for the short-lived Central Asylum for the Instruction of the Deaf and Dumb at Canajoharie, this remained the only institution of its kind until the opening of the Le Couteulx St. Mary's Institution for the Improved Instruction of Deaf-Mutes at Buffalo in 1859.

Soon after the opening of the New York Institution for the Blind in 1832 it began to receive state aid, which was continued throughout the history of the school. Its enrolment consisted chiefly of state pupils, and the state was its main source of funds. In 1865 a state school for the blind was established by the legislature and was located at Batavia. Arrangements were later made whereby the New York Institution for the Blind was authorized to receive state pupils from the counties of Kings and New York, while the New York State School at Batavia received pupils from the upstate counties.

The New York State Inebriate Asylum, established in 1854 as a corporate institution and later taken over by the state, arose as a result of the strong temperance movement of the time and the widespread belief that inebriety was a major, if not the principal, cause of crime, pauperism, and insanity. The enterprise was ill fated, and after a long-drawn-out series of mishaps it was finally abandoned in 1879, and its buildings were converted into a state asylum for the chronic insane.

The rise of these state-owned and state-aided institutions for the mentally and physically handicapped made increasingly evident the need for a central state body that could serve to integrate the expanding scope of state supervision and control in public welfare enterprises. Together with other factors it led to the establishment in 1867 of the Board of State Commissioners of Public Charities, now the State Board of Social Welfare. The creation and development of this board will be described in the second volume.

BIBLIOGRAPHICAL REFERENCES

1. New York State, "Of Safe Keeping and Care of Lunatics," *Revised Statutes of 1827*, chap. 20, Title 3.
2. ———, *Laws of 1828*, chap. 84.
3. James Hardie, *Description of the City of New York* (New York, 1827), p. 269.
4. New York State Assembly, *Documents* (54th sess. [Albany, 1831]), I, Doc. No. 66, p. 34.
5. N.Y.C.Bd. of Asst. Aldermen, *Documents, 1832–33*, Vol. II, Doc. No. 52.
6. ———, *Proceedings, 1833–34*, III, 381.
7. J. F. Richmond, *New York and Its Institutions, 1609–1871* (New York, 1871), p. 545.
8. *Messages from the Governors*, III, 293–94.
9. New York State Assembly, *Documents* (54th sess. [Albany, 1831]), III, Doc. No. 263, p. 29.
10. *Messages from the Governors*, III, 345, 378, 451, 543.
11. New York State Senate, *Documents* (59th sess. [Albany, 1836]), Vol. I, Doc. No. 38.
12. New York State, *Laws of 1841*, chap. 278.
13. New York State Senate, *Documents* (65th sess. [Albany, 1842]), Vol. I, Doc. No. 20.
14. New York State Lunatic Asylum, *First Annual Report, 1844*, in Assembly *Documents* (67th sess. [Albany, 1844]), I, Doc. No. 21, pp. 18–20.
15. ———, *Report of the Trustees*, in Senate *Documents* (65th sess. [Albany, 1842]), I, Doc. No. 20, pp. 12–13.
16. *Ibid.* (67th sess. [Albany, 1844]), II, Doc. No. 73, p. 23.
17. Dorothea L. Dix, *Memorial to the Legislature of the State of New York*, in New York State Assembly, *Documents* (67th sess. [Albany, 1844]), I, Doc. No. 21, p. 67.
18. *Ibid.*, p. 78.
19. *Messages from the Governors*, IV, 642, 718, 791, 848.
20. *Ibid.*, pp. 642–718.
21. New York State Senate, *Documents* (79th sess. [Albany, 1856]), I, Doc. No. 17, pp. 1–2.
22. *Ibid.*, p. 2.
23. *Ibid.*, p. 5.
24. New York State Senate, *Documents* (79th sess. [Albany, 1856]), Vol. II, Doc. No. 71.
25. New York State Assembly, *Documents* (67th sess. [Albany, 1844]), I, Doc. No. 21, p. 88.

26. Stiles, *Civil History and Commercial Record*, I, 470–71.

27. *Ibid.*, p. 480.

28. Monroe Co., N.Y., Board of Supervisors, *Proceedings, 1855* (Rochester, 1856), pp. 54–55; *ibid., 1857* (Rochester, 1858), pp. 118–19.

29. New York State, *Laws of 1863*, chap. 82.

30. Albany Co., N.Y., *Report of the Alms-House Committee on the Subject of a Reorganization of That Institution, Together with a Plan for the Same* (Albany, 1853).

31. New York State, *Laws of 1857*, chap. 787.

32. Albany Common Council, *Minutes, 1859*, pp. 220–21.

33. New York State, *Laws of 1864*, chap. 418.

34. Sylvester D. Willard, *Report on the Condition of the Insane Poor in the County Poor Houses of New York*, in New York State Assembly, *Documents* (88th sess. [Albany, 1865]), Vol. II, Doc. No. 19.

35. *Ibid.*, p. 15.

36. *Plans and Elevations and a Historical Sketch of the Willard Asylum for the Insane* (Willard, N.Y., 1887), pp. 6–7.

37. New York State, *Laws of 1866*, chap. 666.

38. ———, *Laws of 1867*, chap. 93.

39. Hudson River State Hospital, *Sixth Annual Report, 1872*, in New York State Senate, *Documents* (96th sess. [Albany, 1873]), III, Doc. No. 54, p. 5.

40. New York State, *Laws of 1853*, chap. 615; *Laws of 1854*, chap. 397; *Laws of 1881*, chap. 185.

41. New York State Lunatic Asylum, Utica, *Third Annual Report, 1845*, in New York State Senate, *Documents* (69th sess. [Albany, 1846]), I, Doc. No. 25, pp. 57–59.

42. New York State Senate, *Documents* (69th sess. [Albany, 1846]), Vol. I, Doc. No. 23.

43. New York State, *Laws of 1851*, chap. 502.

44. New York State Asylum for Idiots, *First Annual Report, for 1851*, in New York State Senate, *Documents* (75th sess. [Albany, 1852]), Vol. I, Doc. No. 30, *passim*.

45. New York State, *Laws of 1853*, chap. 159.

46. New York State Asylum for Idiots, *Fifth Annual Report, for 1855*, in New York State Assembly, *Documents* (79th sess. [Albany, 1856]), III, Doc. No. 99, pp. 9, 11.

47. ———, *Sixteenth Annual Report, for 1866*, in New York State Senate, *Documents* (90th sess. [Albany, 1867]), I, Doc. No. 14, p. 10.

48. New York City Department of Public Charities and Corrections, *Seventh Annual Report, 1866* (New York, 1867), pp. 353–55.

49. ———, *Eighth Annual Report, 1867* (Albany, 1868), pp. 396, 410.

50. New York State, *Laws of 1854*, chap. 272.

51. New York Institution for the Instruction of the Deaf and Dumb, *Thirty-*

sixth Annual Report, 1854, in New York State Assembly, *Documents* (78th sess. [Albany, 1855]), III, Doc. No. 80, p. 6.

52. New York State, *Laws of 1857,* chap. 787.

53. New York State Senate, *Documents* (81st sess. [Albany, 1858]), Vol. II, Doc. No. 107.

54. ———, *Documents* (82d sess. [Albany, 1859]), Vol. II, Doc. No. 89.

55. New York State, *Laws of 1863,* chap. 325.

56. ———, *Laws of 1865,* chap. 641; *Laws of 1866,* chap. 774.

57. ———, *Laws of 1871,* chap. 548; *Laws of 1872,* chap. 670.

58. New York Institution for the Blind, *First Annual Report, 1836–37,* in New York State Assembly, *Documents* (60th sess. [Albany, 1837]), III, Doc. No. 199, pp. 3, 44.

59. New York State, *Laws of 1834,* chap. 316; *Laws of 1836,* chap. 226.

60. New York Institution for the Blind, *Statement Submitted to the Legislature, March, 1867,* p. 6.

61. New York State Assembly, *Documents* (85th sess. [Albany, 1862]), Vol. VIII, Doc. No. 241.

62. New York State Senate, *Documents* (87th sess. [Albany, 1864]), IV, Doc. No. 89, p. 220.

63. ———, *Journal* (88th sess. [Albany, 1865]), pp. 24, 100, 954.

64. New York State, *Laws of 1865,* chap. 587.

65. ———, *Laws of 1867,* chap. 744.

66. New York State Institution for the Blind, Batavia, *Third Annual Report, 1869,* in New York State Senate, *Documents* (92d sess. [Albany, 1869]), III, Doc. No. 28, p. 4.

67. Samuel Chipman, *Report of an Examination of Poor-Houses, Jails, &c., in the State of New-York* (Albany, 1834), p. 76.

68. New York State, *Laws of 1854,* chap. 243.

69. J. Edward Turner, *The History of the First Inebriate Asylum in the World* (New York, 1888).

70. New York State, *Laws of 1855,* chap. 576.

71. ———, *ibid.,* chap. 231.

72. ———, *Laws of 1857,* chap. 184.

73. ———, *Laws of 1859,* chap. 381.

74. New York State Inebriate Asylum, *Second Annual Report, 1863,* in New York State Senate, *Documents* (87th sess. [Albany, 1864]), III, Doc. No. 45, p. 32; *Fourth Annual Report, 1865,* in New York State Senate, *Documents* (89th sess. [Albany, 1866]), II, Doc. No. 100, p. 9.

75. ———, *Third Annual Report, 1864,* p. 2, in New York State Senate, *Documents* (88th sess. [Albany, 1865]), Vol. III, Doc. No. 64.

76. New York State, *Laws of 1871,* chap. 935; *Laws of 1873,* chap. 625.

77. ———, *Laws of 1879,* chap. 280.

INDEX

INDEX

Chipman, Samuel, survey of poorhouses and jails, 375

Cholera. *See* Public health

Cholera Bulletin, 256

Civil War. *See* War relief

Clark, Aaron, mayor of N.Y.C.: on foreign pauperism, 298; "Native American," 295; on relief needs, 260 f.

Clark, Myron H., governor, on care of insane, 358

Clarkson, Matthew, philanthropist and abolitionist, 143, 207, 211, 212

Cleaveland, Joseph M., Dr., work with insane, 366

Clinton, De Witt, mayor and governor: on House of Refuge, 323; on poor laws, 216; on work for unemployed, 172

Clinton, George, governor, supports state school system, 182

Clinton, Sir Henry, petition to, 109

Colden, Cadwallader, governor, on quarantine facilities, 58 f.

Colored Orphan Asylum, 191

Columbia County, dependency problem in, 220

Comforters of the sick, first social workers, 10

Committees of safety: functions of, 94, 101 f.; organized, 93

Committees of superintendence of poor, 101 f.

Congregational relief. *See* New Netherland

Connecticut State Asylum for the Deaf and Dumb, 201, 202, 202 n.

Contract system of relief, 221, 222

Cornbury, Governor Lord: and education, 78; in epidemic, 84

Corporal punishment. *See* Whipping

Cortland County, town responsibility restored in, 245 f.

County: care of insane (*see* Insane); poorhouses, rise of, 235–45; responsibility for poor, 34, 35, 235–38, 242, 243, 245, 246; superintendents of the poor, 358 ff. *See also* Settlement and removal

Crime, inebriety as cause, 375

Croton Aqueduct, built after epidemic, 256

Crowell, Stephen, secretary, Brooklyn A.I.C.P., 267

Deacons. *See* New Netherland

Deacons' houses. *See* Almshouses

Deaf-mutes: census of, follows public meeting, 202; first instruction of, 201; pupils cared for by state, 369, 370. *See also* Central Asylum for the Instruction of the Deaf and Dumb; Connecticut State Asylum for the Deaf and Dumb; New York School for the Deaf; St. Mary's School for the Deaf

De Beauvois, Carel, Dutch schoolmaster, 21

Debtors, imprisoned, relief of, 143, 145, 146, 147

Delaware County, settlement and removal in, 225

Depressions: discontent of laboring classes during, 259 f., 262; distress during, 157 f., 258, 269, 272 f., 278 ff.; embargo causes, 129; increasing severity of, 234; public and private relief measures in, 158 f., 166, 167, 168–76, 263, 264, 265, 270 ff., 276 ff.; rise of antiforeign movement during, 295; share-the-work plan in, 170, 261. *See also* Work relief

Deutsch, Albert, quoted on insane, 352 n.

Diseases, contagious and infectious. *See* Public health

Dispensaries. *See* New York Dispensary

District meetings, for poor relief, 111

District-union plan of relief, 34. *See also* Town unions

Dix, Dorothea, campaign on behalf of the mentally ill, 356 ff., 361

Dodge, Samuel, N.Y.C. almshouse keeper, relief of refugees, 103

Dongan, Thomas, governor: order of, against runaway servants, 48; on relief administration, 61, 65

Duane, James, mayor of N.Y.C., on almshouse management, 148 f.

Duke's Laws: amendment as to care of insane, 34, 81; provisions of, 33, 35, 61 n.

Dutch period. *See* New Netherland

Dutch West India Company, 4, 5

Dutchess County: apprenticeship in, 76; care of war refugees in, 100, 103; relief of poor in, 34, 35, 63; town responsibility for poor relief in, 245

Eddy, James, Dr., work of, with insane, 201

Eddy, Thomas: leads in humanitarian reforms, 145, 146, 183, 200, 201, 207, 211, 212; report of, on causes of dependency, 318–19